Fixing Broken Cities

Sarah L. Coffin, Ph.D.

Through the insightful lens of an experienced practitioner, this book describes the origin, execution, and impact of urban repopulation strategies—initiatives designed to attract residents, businesses, jobs, shoppers, and visitors to places that had undergone decades of decline and abandonment. The central question throughout the strategies explored in the book is *who should benefit*? Who should benefit from the allocation of scarce public capital? Who should enjoy the social benefits of urban development? And who will populate redeveloped areas? Kromer provides realistic guidance about how to move forward with strategic choices that have to be made in pursuing the best opportunities available within highly disadvantaged, resource-starved urban areas. Each of the cases presents strategies that are strongly influenced by geography, economics, politics, and individual leadership, but they address key issues that are major concerns everywhere: enlivening downtowns, stabilizing and strengthening neighborhoods, eliminating industrial-age blight, and providing quality public education options.

John Kromer is a nationally recognized expert on urban policymaking and neighborhood reinvestment strategies. As the City of Philadelphia's Director of Housing from 1992 to 2001, he supervised the expenditure of more than a billion dollars in public investment. Currently, Kromer is a Senior Consultant at the Fels Institute of Government at the University of Pennsylvania.

D1188548

Fixing Broken Cities

The Implementation of Urban
Development Strategies

John Kromer

University of Pennsylvania

Routledge
Taylor & Francis Group

NEW YORK AND LONDON

First published 2010
by Routledge
270 Madison Ave, New York, NY 10016

Simultaneously published in the UK
by Routledge
2 Park Square, Milton Park, Abingdon, Oxon OX14 4RN

Routledge is an imprint of the Taylor & Francis Group, an informa business

© 2010 Taylor & Francis

Typeset in Bembo by
Florence Production Ltd, Stoodleigh, Devon
Printed and bound in the United States of America on acid-free paper by
Edwards Brothers, Inc.

All rights reserved. No part of this book may be reprinted or
reproduced or utilized in any form or by any electronic, mechanical,
or other means, now known or hereafter invented, including
photocopying and recording, or in any information storage or
retrieval system, without permission in writing from the publishers.

Trademark Notice: Product or corporate names may be trademarks
or registered trademarks, and are used only for identification and
explanation without intent to infringe.

Library of Congress Cataloging in Publication Data
Kromer, John, 1948–.
　Fixing broken cities: the implementation of urban development
strategies/John Kromer.
　　　p. cm.
　　Includes bibliographical references and index.
　1. City planning—Pennsylvania—Case studies.　2. Urbanization—
Pennsylvania—Case studies.　3. City planning—New Jersey—
Case studies.　4. Urbanization—New Jersey—Case studies.　I. Title.
　HT167.5.P4K76 2009
　307.1'21609748—dc22　　　　　　　　　　　　　　　　2009019293

ISBN10: 0–415–80098–6 (hbk)
ISBN10: 0–415–80099–4 (pbk)
ISBN10: 0–203–87860–4 (ebk)

ISBN13: 978–0–415–80098–3 (hbk)
ISBN13: 978–0–415–80099–0 (pbk)
ISBN13: 978–0–203–87860–6 (ebk)

Sarah Coffin

**now is the time
to invent.**

> Sleater-Kinney
> "#1 Must-Have"
> from *All Hands on the Bad One*

Sand Coffin

Contents

Illustrations

Figures

Tables

Acknowledgments

Fixing Broken Cities could not have been written without the support of my friend Joanne Barnes Jackson, who patiently taught me some basic rules of organization and structure and helped me find the best ways to present my views systematically and coherently. In addition to reading, correcting, and commenting on the entire manuscript, Joanne contributed many valuable insights that improved every chapter.

I am grateful to Kathleen and Andrew for their love and support during the challenging period in which this book was conceived and written.

Several chapters draw on experience that I gained over the course of nearly a decade at the University of Pennsylvania's Fels Institute of Government. The experience of teaching, conducting research, and participating in consulting projects while at the Fels Institute has been exciting and inspiring. Thanks are due to the current Executive Director of the Fels Institute, David Thornburgh, as well as to his predecessors, Donald Kettl and Lawrence Sherman, for supporting my work. In addition, much of the activity described in *Fixing Broken Cities* was supported directly or indirectly by members of the Fels Institute staff, including Christopher Patusky, Danielle Costo, Anthony Banks, Leigh Botwinik, Allison Brummel, Michelle Garcia-Navarro, Karen Kille, Catherine Lamb, Jillian Marcussen, Rebecca Perry, and Alyson Ricketts.

I am grateful for comments and advice provided by a number of people who read portions of the manuscript, including Amanda Frazier, Rose Gray, Maxine Griffith, Michael Groman, Lucy Kerman, Daniel Kildee, Catherine Lamb, Paul Levy, Monica Lesmerises, Victoria Mason-Ailey, Hallie Mittleman, Karen Beck Pooley, and Eric Weiss. Thanks also to Marlie Wasserman and her reviewers for a constructive and helpful early critique.

Most of the photos and maps in *Fixing Broken Cities* were produced by Jane Whitehouse Thouron of Tiger Productions, who worked tirelessly to respond to my requests and deliver spectacular results. Jessica Bloomfield contributed excellent photographs and completed a variety of support tasks over the course of several months. The University of Pennsylvania Cartographic Modeling Lab (Vicky Tam), Karen Beck Pooley, and Kenneth Steif completed maps that help provide a frame of reference for the issues discussed in several chapters.

Sleater-Kinney granted permission for the use of their lyrics in the epigraph. The assistance of Tony Kiewel and Lacey Swain at Sub Pop Records is much appreciated.

The research conducted by the Fels Institute on the City of Philadelphia's ten-year tax abatement, described in Chapter One, was funded by a grant from the William Penn Foundation.

The Central Philadelphia Development Corporation/Center City District made available two photographic images for inclusion in Chapter Two. Paul Levy provided a wealth of information about the creation of the Center City District and reviewed and commented extensively on draft text.

The Philadelphia City Planning Commission provided the base for the Eastern North Philadelphia map that appears in Chapter Three.

Information, comments, and advice were also provided by Joanne Aitken, John Claypool, Michael Dean, Councilman Frank DiCicco, Robert Fina, Carl Greene, Barry Grossbach, William Hankowsky, Jim Hartling, Liz Hersh, David Hornbeck, Feather Houstoun, Lindsay Johnston, Jerry Jordan, Debra Kahn, Barbara Kaplan, Michael Koonce, Melani Lamond, Mark Frazier Lloyd, Alan Mallach, Jeremey Newberg, Liza Nolan, Richard Redding, Emilymarie Romin, Lance Rothstein, Ronald Rubin, Patricia Smith, and Fred Tarlino.

I very much appreciate the help of Stan Wakefield in finding the right publisher for *Fixing Broken Cities*. The interest, assistance, and support of Michael Kerns and Felisa Salvago-Keyes at Taylor & Francis to date have been invaluable, and I look forward to continuing an enjoyable and fruitful working relationship with them.

Photo and Map Credits

Jane Whitehouse Thouron/Tiger Productions: Cover photo; Figures 1.3, 3.1, 3.2, 3.3, 3.4, 5.1a, 5.1b, 6.1, 7.2, 9.1, 9.2, 9.3, 9.4, 9.5, 9.6, 10.1, 10.3.

Jessica Bloomfield: Figures 1.2, 2.2, 2.3, 6.2, 6.3, 6.4, 7.1.

Central Philadelphia Development Corporation/Center City District: Figures 2.1, 2.4.

Kenneth Steif: Figures I.1, 8.1

Karen Beck Pooley: Figure 10.2.

University of Pennsylvania Cartographic Modeling Lab (Vicky Tam): Figures 1.1, 1.4.

The source for Figure 4.1 is City of Philadelphia, Office of the Mayor, Neighborhood Transformation Initiative, 2001. The map was adapted for this book by Jane Whitehouse Thouron, Tiger Productions.

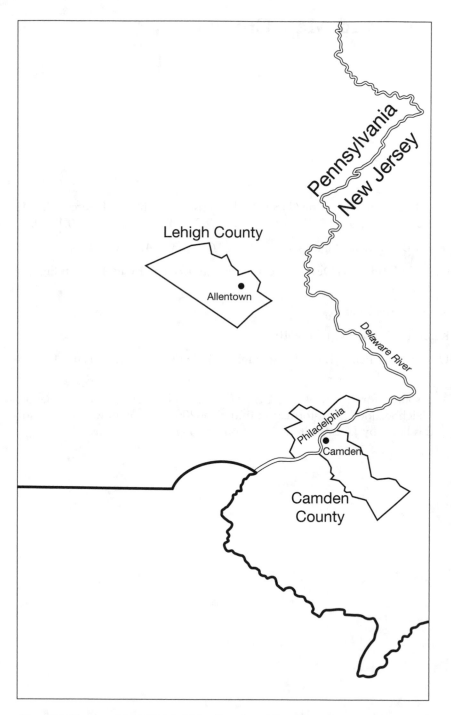

Figure I.1 Context Map: Philadelphia, Camden, Allentown

Introduction

This book was completed shortly after the inauguration of Barack Obama, the first U.S. President in half a century to come from an older city with an industrial past. Among the high priorities identified at the start of the new administration were better public education for a new-economy workforce and the repair and replacement of aging infrastructure, two vitally important issues for postindustrial cities. Although a fresh, informed federal perspective on the needs of older cities is welcome, new federal initiatives, by themselves, will not be sufficient to reverse the trend of economic disinvestment that has persisted in these places for more than half a century. Urban government, business, and civic leaders need to make more effective use of available local resources to promote their economic self-interest and reposition their cities for future success. Nowhere is this need for local self-help more evident than with respect to the issues of investment and development in urban downtowns and neighborhoods.

Fixing Broken Cities is about the planning, execution, and impact of investment strategies designed to improve postindustrial urban downtowns and residential communities. The central focus of this book is how to implement and operationalize proposals for transformative change. Many good ideas for remaking and redefining older cities have been proposed over the years. However, even the best of these ideas will not make a difference without an awareness of where to begin and what to do.

An Implementer's Worldview

I do not have a degree in city planning, economics, or public administration; I have no political credentials to speak of, and have little name recognition outside of a relatively small number of researchers and practitioners specializing in urban policymaking. However, unlike many writers on urban affairs who possess more of these credentials, I have devoted most of my career to implementing downtown and neighborhood reinvestment strategies in cities that are disinvested, depopulated, and cash-starved. Based on what I have learned through my own successes and failures, I have gained firsthand knowledge of how some of the complex problems confronting these places can be addressed effectively.

Most of *Fixing Broken Cities* derives from my personal experience, so some biographical detail will help place the chapters that follow in context. I grew up in a middle-class household in two suburban cities (Meriden, Connecticut, and Waltham, Massachusetts), had an opportunity to take Russian language courses during high school, and became interested in the study of Soviet politics during my undergraduate years at Haverford College. To me, one appeal of the Sovietology of the time was the challenge of deciphering news coverage in *Pravda* and speeches from Communist Party congresses in order to gain insights into the current power structure and political climate in Moscow and elsewhere in the Soviet empire. Embedded within government-approved news articles and tedium-inducing oratory were nuanced messages, conveying information about the political standing of a party official or constituency, or about policies that were to be launched, expanded, cut back, or scrapped. Soviet Union experts had found this embedded information to have been particularly useful in tracking Nikita Khrushchev's rise to power, his success in prevailing over political rivals, and his subsequent downfall.

I entered graduate school at Indiana University with the intention of continuing to pursue my interest in Soviet studies, but left after one unhappy semester. At the time, the Political Science department was dominated by members of a group who had convinced themselves that, if they just worked hard enough, social scientists could achieve a status comparable to that of practitioners of natural science; through a more intensive use of statistical analysis and information technology, they could test hypotheses, formulate theories, and ultimately predict human behavior. I moved to Philadelphia to live with my girlfriend (who became my wife a few years later), who subsequently helped me get a job with a nonprofit organization in the China-town community.

Although I had lived most of my life in the suburbs, I had learned a lot about cities by this time, based on a series of personal experiences. During my middle- and high-school years, I had explored New York and Boston on my own, and I knew my way around the downtown areas of both cities. I had lived and worked in Chicago, loading airplanes at O'Hare, for half of a one-year leave of absence from Haverford, and I had lived for a summer in a Philadelphia row house. I enjoyed city street life, architecture, nighttime entertainment, and the experience of going to sleep and waking up in an urban neighborhood.

In Chinatown, I participated in a community campaign to block the state Department of Transportation's plans to expand the nearby Vine Street Expressway, an action that, if implemented, would have had dire conse-quences for a community anchor, the Holy Redeemer Church and School. Community advocates ultimately prevailed, and the expressway plans were scaled back. Through this experience, I learned about the structure, responsi-bilities, leadership, and management of the city's Planning Commission,

Redevelopment Authority, Department of Streets, and Department of Licenses and Inspections (a Soviet-sounding name), and about the political dynamics of community interaction with municipal government.

A few years later, I was hired as staff director of another nonprofit organization, a community group in the Washington Square West area, a mostly residential neighborhood located just south of Philadelphia's central business district. Washington Square West had been designated as a redevelopment area during the urban renewal era, and about 20 percent of the neighborhood's real estate was owned by the Philadelphia Redevelopment Authority. This government-owned inventory consisted of vacant and occupied buildings—some of them historically certified—including abandoned factories, apartment buildings, row homes, and rooming houses, as well as large and small vacant lots. At that time, the community organization, known as the Washington Square West Project Area Committee (PAC), was dominated by young professionals whose liberal outlook was diametrically opposed to that of then-Mayor Frank L. Rizzo, the former police commissioner who was elected mayor in 1971 and re-elected in 1975. The PAC successfully lobbied for the preservation of historic buildings from demolition and for the development of subsidized housing for tenants who were to be displaced from properties scheduled for redevelopment. The PAC survived a bitter, community-wide conflict over the question of whether certain vacant lots in the area should be developed for new housing (as specified in the approved redevelopment plan) or as surface parking lots to accommodate current residents' cars. The PAC gave me experience in managing a relationship with a community board and in working on a day-to-day basis with real estate developers and development agency staff, including the Redevelopment Authority's project manager for Washington Square West, William J. Way.

In the late 1970s, shortly after the City formed a new Office of Housing and Community Development (OHCD) to lead and coordinate the activities of Philadelphia's development agencies, Way was hired to supervise the new office's neighborhood projects division, and he offered me a job as a project manager for the Kensington area. I accepted and moved to an office in City Hall Annex. After two years, I became supervisor of OHCD's South Philadelphia project managers.

The experience of working with Bill Way was challenging, sometimes exhilarating, and occasionally overwhelming. Way was a highly skilled manager of information and people. He constructed elaborate budget and fund-allocation matrices nearly two decades before computers loaded with electronic spreadsheet technology could be found on city employees' desks. He managed ongoing communications with a variety of municipal agencies, from the Philadelphia Industrial Development Corporation to the Fairmount Park Commission, in order to keep program activities on track. He engaged community organizations in extensive dialogue about neighborhood development priorities and how they should be addressed through city resource allocation. He was candid and open in discussions with neighborhood residents and business owners about the manner in which city funding and services could be used to support reinvestment goals. He shared information that other city agency staff routinely withheld. He engaged in dialogue with community members, including those who were suspicious of the City and hostile towards him. He had faith in the possibility of consensus or compromise, and he worked to achieve one or the other. Believing that public service was an honor and a high responsibility, he spent many evenings and weekends participating in community meetings without compensation. After a typical event of this kind, Way would often return to the office to prepare a detailed memorandum documenting the results of the discussion, to be mailed to all participants on the following morning. He rarely expressed anger or frustration. Although he didn't try to impose all his standards on the employees he supervised, most of his staff, myself included, were inspired by his enthusiasm and commitment, and we tried to follow his example, although with somewhat less intensity and singleness of purpose.

After four years, Way resigned, following a change in mayoral administrations, and, months later, I was pink-slipped in an initial round of cost-cutting layoffs at OHCD. For most of the next decade, I worked on development consulting projects as an employee of Urban Partners. The co-founders and three principals of this small consulting firm had previously been the first generation of senior administrators at OHCD; John Andrew Gallery had been the first OHCD director. While in city government, Gallery and his partners, James E. Hartling and Peter Lapham (who had served as OHCD deputy directors for economic development and administration/operations, respectively), had become aware of many potentially promising development opportunities which, to their disappointment, were not being pursued by conventional real estate developers or by the handful of nonprofit organizations with development capability. Gallery, Hartling, and Lapham formed Urban Partners in order to move some of the best of these opportunities to an implementation stage by providing advice to others and, in some cases, by pursuing these opportunities directly.

During my years of employment there, Urban Partners supervised the rehabilitation of a vacant building in Pittsburgh's East Liberty neighborhood for mixed retail/office reuse, explored the feasibility of chartering a community bank in Philadelphia's East Germantown neighborhood, and financed the conversion of a vacant South Philadelphia public school building into subsidized apartments for elderly people. As consultants to others, Urban Partners completed strategic development plans for downtown and neighborhood sites and obtained financing for many development ventures, often working on behalf of entrepreneurial neighborhood-based organizations. During this period, the firm also packaged many proposals for financing through the federal Urban Development Action Grant program (one of the programs described in Chapter One), assisted a community organization in strategic planning for the Ludlow neighborhood in Lower North Philadelphia (one of the centers of new housing construction activity described in Chapter Three), and, as a favor to me, acted in the role of fee developer for the West Philadelphia Fire House venture (the subject of Chapter Seven). This experience provided me with a wealth of knowledge about development financing strategies, many of which involved a leveraging of government and private funds, as well an understanding of the best ways to move high risk/high opportunity projects to implementation.

All of these activities made me conscious of the critical role that municipal government could play in stimulating development in urban downtowns and neighborhoods, and of the benefits that cities could achieve if government resources were used creatively and responsibly. In pursuit of this interest, I worked as a volunteer on housing issues for the mayoral campaign of Edward G. Rendell in 1991 and drafted the campaign's housing position paper. Rendell was elected that November and took office in January, 1992. His plans to recruit a person whom he had viewed as a promising candidate for the position of Housing Director fell through, and I was asked to manage OHCD for what he and I both thought would be a few days.

The Mayor and I barely knew each other. At the time, neither of us regarded me as a suitable candidate for the permanent appointment. During subsequent months, however, in a period when Rendell and his staff were hauling the city back from the brink of bankruptcy, I had the opportunity to convince both the Mayor and myself that I could do the job. I formed good working relationships with elected officials and neighborhood organizations. I cleared a federal audit finding for which the previous administration was responsible, enabling the City to avoid a $14 million payback of U.S. Department of Housing and Urban Development (HUD) funds. I spent eight continuous hours in a City Council budget hearing, delivering testimony, responding to questions, and dodging Whack-A-Mole-style attacks launched by a couple of Council members who were angered that development ventures they had endorsed had not been proposed to receive City financing. My staff, all hired during prior administrations, did most of the hard work that made these accomplishments possible and enabled me to succeed.

After I had managed the OHCD for nearly six months on an interim basis, Mayor Rendell offered me the job as a permanent appointment on June 14, 1992, a day known to some as Flag Day. We met at the Lombard Street Swim Club at lunchtime. Sitting at a picnic table in our business suits, eating cheeseburgers and potato chips off paper plates, we discussed the job and his plans. That year was the last in which Flag Day would remain on the list of paid city holidays. In upcoming contract negotiations with the municipal labor unions, Rendell would succeed in getting June 14 removed from the list.

Five months earlier, during the January days following Mayor Rendell's inauguration, I had felt totally unqualified to lead the city's $100 million housing and community development program. By Flag Day, I had convinced myself that no one else could possibly do the job as well as I. My half-year's experience had given me new insights while reaffirming what I had learned a decade earlier as an OHCD project manager. The City's approach to investing public funding was too piecemeal and scattershot. Decisions about funding development ventures and service programs were too often politically driven. Underperforming programs and organizations were grandfathered into the budget process and funded year after year. Every new OHCD director (there had been five of them during the 1980s) came into office convinced that he or she would manage the City's resources strategically and systematically, as though the idea had never occurred to the previous director. But each director's attempts had proven unsustainable, undermined by politics, constrained by underachieving development agency managers, and hampered by bureaucratic squabbling. Some worthwhile development ventures were completed and some valued services were delivered; but, looking at the city's neighborhoods, the impact of a $100 million dollar annual budget seemed negligible. You could drive through the city and ask, where did all the money go?

During those months, I recognized and appreciated the advantage I had over most of my predecessors: the unwavering support and political cover provided by Mayor Rendell. The principles guiding the working relationship I had formed with the Mayor were straightforward. He wouldn't undercut me or make commitments of housing resources behind my back. I would manage the program professionally and deliver results. I would defuse crises and solve problems on my own; but if I ran into an impasse that couldn't be overcome, he and his staff would step in—and I might not like their version of a solution. Because other department heads had similar understandings with the Mayor, the latter principle provided a powerful incentive for the city's development agencies—which could not be characterized as a happy family under the best of circumstances—to deal with problems behind the scenes, to experiment cautiously with teamwork and collaboration, and to avoid badmouthing one another.

Following my appointment in June, I remained at OHCD for nine years, then resigned in mid-2001 to take a position as a consultant on the staff of the University of Pennsylvania's Fels Institute of Government.[1] This position brought me more experience in organizing development strategies in other disinvested cities. I supervised the completion of vacant-house inventories and housing investment strategies in Reading and York, Pennsylvania. With two nonprofit partners (10,000 Friends of Pennsylvania and the Housing Alliance of Pennsylvania), I organized three well-attended, annual statewide conferences on "Vacant Property in Pennsylvania Cities and Towns." Under a contract arranged by the administration of New Jersey Governor Jon S. Corzine, I spent thirteen months in Camden, New Jersey as interim director of the city's redevelopment authority, during a period in which Camden's municipal government had been placed under state control. These activities gave me more experience in organizing development strategies for cities characterized by disinvestment and depopulation trends similar to Philadelphia's.

Learning Experiences

Through these experiences, I gained knowledge and insights into how to fix broken capital assets—the deteriorated, underused or abandoned real estate of the industrial age—in postindustrial cities. Individual chapters of *Fixing Broken Cities* describe the most important elements of this learning.

Each of the first seven chapters describes the origin, execution, and consequences of a particular strategy undertaken in Philadelphia: the City's ten-year tax abatement; the formation of a business-led downtown management organization; the build-out of largely abandoned sections of Eastern North Philadelphia; Mayor John F. Street's citywide neighborhood revitalization policy, the Neighborhood Transformation Initiative (covered in two chapters); the creation of a high-quality new public school as part of a University of Pennsylvania neighborhood reinvestment program; and an attempt to convert a vacated fire station into a neighborhood retail center.*

Chapters Eight and Nine describe my experience in managing the Camden Redevelopment Agency, as part of a state-mandated municipal reform and economic recovery plan for the city. The first of these two chapters describes the state takeover and its short-term results, as well as the emerging conflicts that arose in Camden and elsewhere regarding the circumstances under which government should use eminent domain powers to acquire real estate in support of development activities. The second describes the approach designed for the revitalization of Lanning Square, a downtown-area neighborhood, which involved community dialogue leading to the drafting of a redevelopment plan. This activity was accompanied by a broader civic engagement process that resulted in the publication of a human capital development plan: a strategy for addressing the neighborhood's education, public safety, and employment needs.

Chapter Ten is about Allentown, Pennsylvania—a place that is contrarian among postindustrial cities: unlike Philadelphia, Camden, and many other older urban areas, this northeastern Pennsylvania city did not experience severe population loss during the late twentieth century. For Allentown, a more pressing concern is the quality and condition of rental housing, a concern which for reasons described in this chapter and the one that follows, will become more widespread during the coming years.

The final chapter, "The Future of Reinvestment," describes how the experiences described in the preceding chapters can be used to inform the

---

*   I was not personally involved in the formation of the downtown management organization or the development of the new public school. However, both of these activities took shape in places where I was working at the time, giving me an opportunity to witness their impact on the environment and to recognize their relationship to my work in or near these areas.

design of new federal, state, and local policies for urban revitalization and about how business, institutional, and community interests can play more effective roles in ensuring that these policies have the best prospects for success.

Although *Fixing Broken Cities* is not an autobiography or memoir, many of my own biases, predispositions, and prejudices become evident in the chapters that follow. I have tried to balance these personal perspectives with detailed descriptions of other points of view, particularly those in opposition to my own. In addition, the descriptive passages in each chapter draw on or refer to other published works that readers may consult in order to consider views other than mine. The value of this personal perspective element of *Fixing Broken Cities* is that—in a different way than many works of academic or popular literature—it can better acquaint readers with the realities and consequences of decision-making in a politically charged urban environment.

The activities described in the chapters that follow are not best practices that can be replicated as-is in other settings, because they were strongly influenced by geography, economics, politics, and the personalities of the individuals who managed them. However, all of these interventions are relevant to other urban areas because they address key issues that are major concerns everywhere: enlivening downtowns, stabilizing and strengthening neighborhoods, eliminating industrial-age blight, and providing quality public education options. Knowledge gained through an understanding of these experiences can help guide the planning and execution of strategies for addressing these issues in other cities.

These interventions cannot be regarded as urban revitalization success stories either. None of them can be characterized as an unqualified success or an unmitigated failure; each is noteworthy in terms of both achievements and shortcomings. For example, although the Penn Alexander School (described in Chapter Six) gained national recognition as a model for institutional engagement in neighborhood revitalization, the designers of this venture were not able to anticipate and address a serious related outcome: the influence of a successful school on the surrounding neighborhood housing market and on future student body diversity. Although serious flaws in the organization of the West Philadelphia Fire House venture (described in Chapter Seven) became apparent during the first stages of implementation, a second-generation use of the restored fire house building more than a decade later demonstrated promising results during its start-up years. With attention devoted to both achievements and shortcomings, *Fixing Broken Cities* is intended to provide a combination of information, inspiration, and cautionary advice.

In order to enable readers to apply the knowledge gained through these experiences elsewhere and to make their own judgments about what can be learned from each of them, every chapter includes background information that provides a broader context for the narrative and my comments. Chapters Six and Seven, for example, begin with a discussion of strategic problems confronting city-based academic and health care institutions and an overview of the economic history of the Baltimore Avenue commercial corridor, respectively.

The common goal of all of the strategies described in this book is the transformation of a postindustrial urban setting. With respect to these strategies, "transformation" can be defined in terms of three activities:

- Removing or remaking Industrial Age infrastructure through actions such as demolishing obsolete buildings, clearing environmental hazards from construction sites, and repairing or replacing streets and utility services.
- Improving an area's competitive position by developing or upgrading housing, stores, schools, and service facilities to a level of quality approaching that of the metropolitan region's most desirable communities.
- Building wealth by attracting and sustaining jobs and creating opportunities for business development and expansion.

All postindustrial cities face a similar challenge: how to implement transformative change under circumstances in which the key elements of urban transformation as practiced successfully a half-century earlier—powerful political leadership, access to public and private capital, the ability to use government powers to acquire real estate without risk of significant legal or political challenges, and the ability to readily gain community buy-in or ignore community opposition—are significantly reduced or no longer exist.

Repopulation for Whom?

Why, during much of the twentieth century, did people leave cities that had previously enjoyed success as vital centers of the national economy? They left because their jobs were being relocated to the suburbs or to other regions of the country. They left because local factories were shutting down as manufacturing became globalized. They left because attractive, government-insured housing options were emerging in older suburbs and developer-designed new communities. They left because the quality and reliability of public education and municipal services were steadily declining as the municipal tax base shrank. They left because they hated, feared, or didn't trust nonwhites. They left because more streets and public spaces were becoming less attractive. They left because crime was increasing. They left because blight—in the form of litter, graffiti, and abandoned real estate—was proliferating.

Why, during the years before and after the turn of the twenty-first century, were people induced to come to certain previously disinvested urban downtowns and neighborhoods? They came because these places had become less blighted and more attractive, cleaner and safer. They came because they enjoyed urban diversity and did not feel threatened by racial and ethnic differences. They came because many cities offered a variety of education options, including more magnet schools and charter schools, along with previously established, well-regarded private and parochial schools. They came because these places offered desirable eating, drinking, entertainment, and shopping choices, day and night. They came because new townhouses, lofts, and condominiums were being developed through new construction on vacant land and through creative adaptive reuses of architecturally noteworthy former office and industrial buildings. They came because their children had moved on, to college or jobs, and their suburban homes were now too large and too empty. They came because they were bored with the suburbs where they had spent their childhoods and found the urban environment exciting and stimulating. They came because these places were populated by many young people passionately engaged in music, art, food, fashion, and politics. They came because the suburbs were becoming older, less attractive, and, in some instances, less safe and more beset by social problems. They came because city living was not incompatible with their work: their jobs were located in the city, were located within a reasonable commuting distance, or were internet-facilitated, enabling them to work almost anywhere they chose.

Population loss had a devastating effect on many cities that had been America's largest urban centers during the industrial age, as shown in Table I.1 (as already described, Allentown is an exception to this trend).

As central cities shrank, the predominantly suburban counties to which they were adjacent grew rapidly. As shown in Table I.2, Philadelphia's suburban counties added more than twice as many people as the city lost between 1990 and 2007. Modest growth in Allentown during this period was dwarfed by an order-of-magnitude population increase in Lehigh County.

More significant was these cities' loss of wealth. During the 1990s, median household income growth in suburban counties adjacent to Philadelphia was nearly three times that in the city. In 1999, Allentown's median household income reached a level slightly below that which Lehigh County had achieved ten years earlier. In 1999, Camden County was more than twice as wealthy as Camden city.

Organized efforts to reverse population decline and revitalize cities began well before the reality of disinvestment was documented in post-World War Two statistics on population decline and job loss.[2] Revitalization initiatives that were designed, in part, to repopulate urban areas, can be categorized broadly in terms of two types of remedies for disinvested cities: promoting economic development by attracting and sustaining commerce, generating new jobs, and increasing tax ratables; or promoting human capital development by improving or expanding education, health care, and employment opportunities, as well as producing or preserving affordable housing.

Supporters of economic development include the real estate and banking industries, local and regional business leaders, building-trades unions (in recent decades), and the government officials that these constituencies help

Table I.1 Population Change in Sixteen U.S. Cities, 1950–2000

	1950	1960	1970	1980	1990	2000
Chicago, IL	3,620,962	3,550,404	3,369,357	3,005,072	2,783,726	2,896,016
Philadelphia, PA	2,071,605	2,002,512	1,949,996	1,688,210	1,585,577	1,517,550
Detroit, MI	1,849,568	1,670,144	1,514,063	1,203,339	1,027,974	951,270
Baltimore, MD	949,708	939,024	905,787	786,775	736,014	651,154
Cleveland, OH	914,808	876,050	750,879	573,822	505,616	478,403
St. Louis, MO	856,796	750,026	622,236	453,085	396,685	348,189
Washington, DC	802,178	763,956	756,668	638,333	606,900	572,059
Boston, MA	801,444	697,197	641,071	562,994	574,283	589,141
Pittsburgh, PA	676,806	604,332	520,089	423,938	369,879	334,563
Buffalo, NY	580,132	532,759	462,768	357,870	328,123	292,648
Minneapolis, MN	521,718	482,872	434,400	370,951	368,383	382,618
Cincinnati, OH	503,998	502,550	453,514	385,457	364,040	331,285
Newark, NJ	438,776	405,220	381,930	329,248	275,221	273,546
Rochester, NY	332,488	318,611	295,011	241,741	231,636	219,773
Camden, NJ	124,555	117,159	102,551	84,910	87,492	79,904
Allentown, PA	106,756	108,347	109,871	103,758	105,090	106,632

Source: U.S. Census

Table I.2 Changes in Population and Median Household Income: Three Cities and Their Suburbs

	Population				Median Household Income		
	1990	2000	2007 est.	Change, 1990 –2007	1989	1999	Change, 1989 –1999
Philadelphia	1,585,577	1,517,550	1,449,634	-135,943	$24,603	$30,746	$6,143
Suburban Counties★	2,143,332	23,32,097	2,438,060	294,728	$42,332★★	$58,841★★	$16,509
Camden City	87,492	79,904	78,675	-8,817	$17,386	$23,421	$6,035
Camden County	502,824	508,932	513,769	10,945	$36,190	$48,097	$11,907
Allentown	105,090	106,632	107,117	2,027	$25,983	$32,016	$6,033
Lehigh County	291,130	312,090	337,343	46,213	$32,455	$43,449	$10,994

★ Bucks, Chester, Delaware, and Montgomery Counties
★★ Weighted average

Source: U.S. Census

elect. Supporters of economic development advocate for government-administered policies that stimulate real estate development downtown and in the strongest real estate markets and that lower the costs of doing business.

The public investment priorities of economic development advocates include high-profile public works projects such as expressways, bridges, and tunnels; the development or expansion of major recreational or civic facilities such as stadiums, marinas, convention centers, and performing arts centers; and the construction of privately-owned hotels, office buildings, apartments, condominiums, and townhouses that have an amenity level and a price structure comparable to that associated with suburban housing. To support the financing of these development ventures, they favor the use of government grants, low-interest loans, tax exemptions, and tax credits. On a national level, their strongest political supporters are Presidents, members of Congress, Cabinet members, and federal agency directors. During the past half-century the most influential individuals who held these positions in federal administrations came from the Sunbelt or from suburban or rural regions rather than postindustrial cities. At the end of the administration of President George W. Bush, for example, the President was a Texan, the Vice President was from Wyoming, the House Majority Leader was from southern Maryland, and the Senate Majority Leader was from Nevada.

Supporters of human capital development include health care, education, and human services institutions and agencies, congregations of faith, service-employee unions, charitable foundations, civic groups, neighborhood-based organizations, and the government officials that these constituencies help elect. Supporters of human capital development advocate for government-administered policies that stimulate affordable housing construction, and rehabilitation (as well as some neighborhood retail commercial development), primarily in neighborhoods with weaker real estate markets; that lower the cost or increase the quality of neighborhood-based education, health care, and human service programs; and that provide job training and placement for neighborhood residents.

The public investment priorities of human capital development advocates include affordable sales and rental housing construction and the rehabilitation of existing vacant and occupied housing; the development of neighborhood stores and the implementation of improvement programs for neighborhood commercial corridors; the development and improvement of public schools and charter schools, as well as the funding of early childhood education programs, after-school programs, and a variety of other education programs; the construction or improvement of health clinics, service agencies, parks, and recreation facilities; and funding for job-training programs that lead to full-time employment for trainees that graduate. To support the financing of these development activities, they favor the use of government grants, low-interest loans, and deferred loans, as well as incentive programs or government mandates that encourage or require investing in economically distressed target areas, contracting with or purchasing from neighborhood-based or minority businesses, or employing neighborhood residents. On a national level, their supporters are members of Congress who represent urban districts, as well as some Cabinet members or federal agency heads—in most administrations, relatively few in number—from older cities, along with a small number of older city mayors who have gained national name recognition.

Economic development and human capital development remedies have never been mutually exclusive, nor were the actions of the individuals and groups associated with them. Philanthropy by industrial-age captains of industry provided substantial social benefit to a broad cross section of urban residents. James Rouse, developer of Boston's Faneuil Hall Marketplace and Baltimore's Harborplace, also spearheaded the development of the racially and economically integrated new community of Columbia, Maryland and co-founded The Enterprise Foundation as a resource for supporting affordable housing and community development ventures. Many other for-profit developers have participated in affordable housing and neighborhood retail ventures. By the same token, community development corporations have engaged in profit-making housing and commercial development ventures, often in partnership with private developers or corporations.

The most effective urban reinvestment strategies are those that achieve the best blend of both economic development and human capital development. In order to implement the best of these strategies, three volatile political issues have to be resolved, all related in different ways to a single question: Who should benefit?

> *1. Allocation of public capital.* Who should benefit most from decisions made about the allocation of scarce government funding to support a reinvestment strategy? Should more public money be allocated to downtown development ventures, in order to strengthen the city's urban core and create jobs (including many retail and service-sector jobs for neighborhood residents)? Or, alternatively, should the rebuilding of one of the most devastated communities in the city, through the construction of new housing, community facilities, and neighborhood stores, become an equally high or greater priority? Or should the top priority be the repair and preservation of older neighborhoods populated by moderate- and middle-income working families, those people who had remained in the city while others fled?

> *2. Social benefits.* Who should benefit from real estate development associated with a reinvestment strategy, wherever it occurs? Who will have best access to the construction and permanent jobs associated with the development? In support of the ideal of equitable investment, should a public commitment to a major real estate development venture (such as the construction of a performing arts center, a hospital, or a shopping center) necessitate a corresponding commitment to human capital development in the affected community, through the funding of education, community services, and affordable housing?

3. New population. Who is going to populate the area as a result of the implementation of the reinvestment strategy? If wealthier residents move in and property values rise, how can longtime residents avoid being priced out of their homes as a result of property tax increases? Are new residents being attracted through the promotion of financial incentives (such as property tax abatements) that are not available to current residents? Will some of the new residents be former public housing residents or formerly homeless people? Will the influx of new residents change the community's economic or demographic profile in ways that will create new disadvantages for current community members?

In order to illustrate the differences in political dynamics associated with attempts to resolve these issues and achieve a balanced approach to reinvestment, *Fixing Broken Cities* focuses on strategies undertaken in three postindustrial cities, each possessing different repopulation characteristics. In Philadelphia, continued population decline in the city as a whole has been somewhat offset by population growth downtown and in some resurgent neighborhoods. In Camden, leaders faced a dual challenge: reforming a dysfunctional city government and making the best use of a $175 million state capital fund to finance development ventures that would generate jobs and expand the tax base. In Allentown, population stability is linked to an unwelcome new trend: the conversion of many formerly single-family homes to overcrowded, unsafe rental housing. Each chapter describes different ways in which the economic development/human capital development balance was attempted in these places, with varying degrees of success.

Fixing Broken Cities is intended to interest and inform readers who support the revitalization of older cities, especially those who are or will be pursuing economic development and human capital development in urban downtowns and neighborhoods. With knowledge gained through an awareness of the successes and shortcomings of the strategies described in this book, I hope that others will be inspired and challenged to think and act creatively in addressing the problems and opportunities that pervade these places.

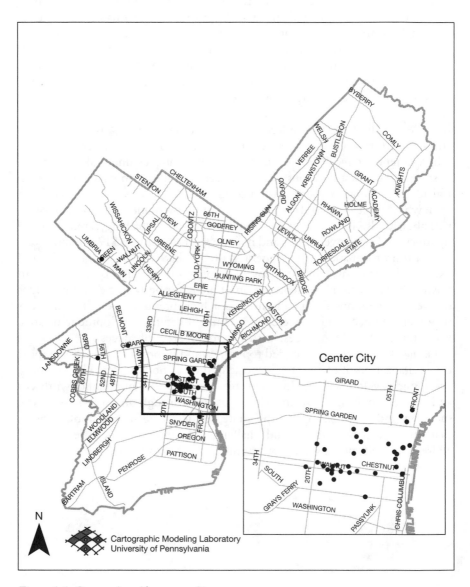

Figure 1.1 Conversion Abatement Sites

1 Financing Without Cash

The Ten-Year Tax Abatement

The City of Philadelphia's ten-year property tax abatement was one of the most important of several contributors to the revival of downtown Philadelphia during the 1990s. Without this generous financial incentive, the downtown area's turn-of-the-century success would have been severely limited.

The tax abatement was a purely economic development remedy—the use of a property tax exemption to leverage bricks-and-mortar real estate development. At the time when the abatement was launched in 1997, there was no substantive debate over the appropriateness of this financial incentive and no significant controversy over the question of who would benefit most from it. When eligibility for the abatement was expanded in 2000, however, the policy generated increasing opposition on the part of many taxpayers, based on the fact that the abatement provided the greatest direct benefit to the wealthiest investors, developers, and property owners—those with the most capital to spend in the city's hottest real estate markets.

An important issue underlying this controversy is the question of how a distressed city can attract new investment without creating disadvantages for long-term residents, as well as the question of whether unfairness to these community members is an unfortunate but unavoidable by-product of a successful economic development initiative.

Time Travel

On the sidewalk outside City Hall, they were preparing a scene for "Twelve Monkeys," a production by the British filmmaker Terry Gilliam that would later achieve cult-film renown. They sprayed the granite walls to make them look deteriorated and frost-blasted. They wreathed the arched portal with dessicated vines that spread down to the sidewalk. They dusted the area with fake snow that clung to the walls and accumulated in little piles where the building and sidewalk met. They parked wrecked, scorched cars across the street. In the movie, a time-traveling Bruce Willis, entering a deserted, devastated city, wanders toward the portal and encounters a snarling bear.

Although the site could be viewed clearly from my corner office a half-block away, I never saw the work in progress. My job as Philadelphia's

Director of Housing kept me elsewhere, in windowless conference rooms by day and in churches and community centers on many nights. One day I glanced out my office window, and there it was: frost-scarred walls, snow-dusted sidewalks, tangled vines and all.

Back then, in mid-1990s Philadelphia, you could imagine that scene of abandonment and devastation as a not-too-distant reality. A pandemic of the type portrayed in "Twelve Monkeys" would not be needed to set the stage; the stage was already set. You could find torched cars and weed-choked buildings within a five-minute drive of City Hall in three directions, in neighborhoods like Francisville to the north, Point Breeze to the south, and Mantua to the west. To the east, across the Delaware River, lay an even more wrecked Camden, New Jersey. Many blocks in Lower North Philadelphia, where residences for newly wealthy families had been developed a century earlier, were now haunted places. Along a section of Diamond Street once designated a National Register Historic District (thanks to the initiative of Christine Washington and the Advocate Community Development Corporation), you could see Rittenhouse Square-quality cornices, lintels, brickwork and stonework in houses that were deteriorating, emptying out, and falling apart.[1]

The signs of Philadelphia's disintegration could be found much closer than North Philly however; they could be found right across from City Hall. The John Wanamaker department store building, once a major regional shopping attraction, had closed and reopened several times, with an inventory that became smaller and less interesting with each reopening. The office building at One East Penn Square: empty. City Hall Annex: empty. The park at JFK Plaza: a way station for homeless people. Meridian Plaza, where three fire-fighters had lost their lives in a dreadful 1991 blaze: an empty shell. The white marble Girard Trust Company building, occupied for decades by Girard Bank, then by Mellon Bank: empty. The ground-floor banking center and upstairs offices of CoreStates Bank: empty. City Hall was encircled by many thousands of square feet of vacant space.

Late twentieth-century Philadelphia no longer seemed to make sense. So when had it made sense? Philadelphia had made lots of sense a hundred years earlier, when factories in or near rowhouse neighborhoods produced all kinds of goods—textiles, chemicals, clothing, hand tools, motor cars, electrical products, and more—that were transported worldwide from a busy port. Philadelphia had made sense when a network of railroads had been the quickest and most cost effective way to move raw materials, finished goods, mail, and people up and down the Atlantic Seaboard and into the Midwest. And Philadelphia had made sense when, as the state's biggest population center, the city had more legislators in the General Assembly than any other region of Pennsylvania, more representatives in Congress than most other cities, and a correspondingly greater degree of political clout. The combination of manufacturing strength, accessibility via water and rail, and political muscle had worked well in the industrial-age economy of a century ago.

In that economy, the houses on Diamond Street, the John Wanamaker store, and the white marble Girard Bank building were valued assets. In the economy of the mid-1990s, they were worn-out museum pieces.

To characterize this deterioration and abandonment, wartime adjectives and metaphors abounded: "bombed-out"; "like a war zone"; "like Beirut"; "like Berlin"; "in need of a Marshall Plan." Mayor Rendell had another wartime comparison in mind. "Other cities have recovered from bigger crises," he told a group of city department heads meeting in his conference room one afternoon. "Look at London during World War Two. They were dropping bombs on the place!" No one was dropping bombs on 1990s Philadelphia, but no one was airlifting aid either. Bill Clinton's proposed economic stimulus program, which would have provided postindustrial cities with needed public investment capital, had been sandbagged in Congress.

The Economic Development Cabinet, consisting of a group of city development agency administrators, met periodically on an upper floor of the old CIGNA building at 16th and Arch, across the street from JFK Plaza. An early twentieth-century high-rise, the CIGNA building had been the headquarters of the Insurance Company of North America for decades until INA merged with Connecticut General. Now the place was one of an increasing number of vacant or nearly vacant older office buildings that contributed to an oversupply of office space in the downtown area. Some of the vacant square footage had been leased by the City and was being used as temporary offices by a handful of municipal agencies. A security guard monitored an amber-lit, high-ceilinged lobby where Victorian-era firefighting artifacts sat unnoticed in glass display cases.

After one Economic Development Cabinet meeting, William Hankowsky, head of the Philadelphia Industrial Development Corporation, brought up an interesting question: which of our agencies should be responsible for handling a few inquiries he had recently received from real estate developers about financing the construction of unsubsidized, "market-rate" housing in the downtown area? Should these developers be assisted by his agency, because PIDC provided financing for most for-profit development, downtown and elsewhere? By the Redevelopment Authority, because the RDA was the City's housing finance agency? Or by OHCD, because that agency set the standards for public investment in housing development?

The question hadn't come up previously because the development of market-rate housing (which could be defined as housing priced for middle- and upper-income homebuyers and renters) had been almost non-existent in Philadelphia during the past two decades. Most new housing produced during those years had been financed with federal subsidies and had been subject to federally-imposed restrictions on sales prices and rent levels. Little evidence existed of a demand for higher-priced housing by buyers and renters with incomes at or above the median.

In contrast, housing prices were substantially higher in all four of the adjacent suburban Pennsylvania counties, where the number of people and jobs had grown in each decade while population and employment declined in the city. In Philadelphia, the 1995 median sales price for a single-family house was $42,900, compared with $139,900, $155,000, $117,000, and $140,000 in Bucks, Chester, Delaware, and Montgomery counties, respectively.[2] The quality of public schools was much better and the crime rate was much lower in most suburban neighborhoods. Although the members of the Economic Development Cabinet wanted to do as much as possible to attract private investment, most for-profit developers were working exclusively in the suburbs during the 1980s and the early-to-mid-1990s. Most Philadelphia neighborhood markets weren't strong enough to generate the level of sales proceeds or rental income needed to repay development financing from a private lender and turn a profit. So, although Hankowsky's comments about the possibility of market-rate housing down-town were noteworthy, the news did not seem to require a major change in policy or practice. The Cabinet members agreed to share information about developer inquiries as they came in, then to decide as a group about the appropriate assignment of responsibility for follow-up. In light of past experience, this activity did not appear to represent a major new opportunity for any of us.

Then everything downtown began to change.

Scenes for another movie—Kevin Smith's ill-fated "Jersey Girl"—were filmed in Philadelphia in 2001. A *Philadelphia Inquirer* columnist reported that two of the stars, Ben Affleck and Jennifer Lopez, were sharing a sixteenth-floor penthouse suite at The Phoenix in Center City. The Phoenix, a "ritzily renovated" apartment building with "marble-manteled fireplaces, hardwood floors, high ceilings, and doormen with amnesia"[3] was the former CIGNA building, the location where our Economic Development Cabinet meetings had been held less than six years earlier.

Other changes followed. Between 2000 and 2008, City Hall Annex was fully renovated and became a Marriott Courtyard Suites hotel. The Girard Bank building was tastefully converted into a Ritz Carlton hotel. Across Broad Street from the Ritz, the ground-floor space in the building that had been occupied by CoreStates became a Borders book store and a McCormick and Schmick's seafood house; office tenants moved into the upper floors. The formerly vacant One East Penn Square became a Marriott Residence Inn. Construction of the first of two expensive high-rise condos was under way on the Meridian Plaza site. The retail space in the John Wanamaker store had been taken over by Macy's. JFK Plaza, cleaned up with new planters, paving, and benches, was now a spot where one could stop, sit, play with a laptop, read a paper, or eat lunch.

The owner of the made-over CIGNA building had benefited from a financial incentive launched by the City of Philadelphia in 1997: a ten-year real estate tax abatement designed to encourage developers to convert vacant or deteriorated factory and office buildings to residential use (tax abatements were subsequently made available for commercial and industrial development

Figure 1.2 CIGNA Building

ventures, including the new hotels). Thanks to this incentive, the "ritzy" improvements, which, by 2006, had a market value of about $29.7 million, were designated property tax-free for a decade. During the ten-year abatement term, taxes would be payable only on the assessed value of the building in its "pre-improvement" condition—the dismal state that had been evident during the time of our Economic Development Cabinet meetings—and on the assessed value of the underlying land. Thanks to the abatement, the owner's 2006 property tax bill amounted to about $212,000; without it, the bill would have been more than four times as much, about $996,000. Over the ten-year abatement term, the total property tax savings would be likely to exceed $10 million.

The ten-year tax abatement offered developers a generous financial incentive which could be particularly effective in attracting prospective townhouse and condo buyers, to whom the decade-long tax break could be transferred at sale. The phrase "TEN YEAR TAX ABATEMENT" made a frequent appearance in many post-2000 real estate display ads promoting newly-developed housing in Philadelphia. In the mid-1990s and earlier, there had been no comparable real estate ads for Philadelphia properties—there had been nothing to promote.

Remedy for the Cash-Starved

A tax abatement is an especially desirable economic development remedy because it does not involve an outlay of government cash and because the benefit is contingent on the completion of development. Until a real estate venture is finished and ready for occupancy, the tax exemption does not exist, except in spreadsheets, budget projections, and financing-proposal documents. Until development is completed and a new asset is created, the exemption is, in effect, imagined money. For a financially distressed city, the benefits of a tax abatement approach are clear. Why make available publicly-funded grants or loans to stimulate investment and development when you can use imagined money? Why hand over cash to developers when you can achieve results by leveraging projected tax revenues and forgiving projected property tax obligations that have no current impact on the city's finances?

Although in older cities, federal money has traditionally been the primary source of funding for reinvestment, federal funding was in short supply during the late twentieth century because the economic well-being of postindustrial cities was not a high federal government priority at that time, and had not been for decades. Presidential candidates and those members of Congress whose districts fell within the nation's metropolitan areas could be counted on to speak about the need to revitalize urban centers; but these expressions of concern did not, for the most part, generate major new federal funding commitments to help finance the adaptation of formerly industrial cities to an economy that was no longer manufacturing-centered. In part, this lack of commitment was related to the fact that the number and influence of voters living in suburban and exurban areas had increased greatly during that time, making the prospects for congressional action supporting reinvestment in older, depopulating postindustrial cities increasingly remote.

Even the highest-profile urban crises did not generate substantive federal funding commitments and associated follow-through. The Bush Administration's response to the U.S. city most in need of reinvestment is a case in point; as of late 2006, the level of federal funding available for post-Katrina rebuilding had fallen to a fraction of the $60 billion-plus that President Bush had committed in his September 2005 speech in Jackson Square.[4] And once the federal funding began to flow, inept state and local government administration contributed to further delays in rebuilding.

Most state governments are unlikely to be providing cities with substantial new investment capital either. According to a 2004 report by The Century Foundation, thirty-three states had projected budget shortfalls for the 2005 fiscal year. The report indicated that budget problems were likely to persist in many states, due to several factors: the after-effects of short-sighted state tax cuts that had been enacted during the 1990s; the need to increase funding for Medicaid and education; the Bush Administration's tax-cut policy (including the elimination of taxes on dividend payments); and new unfunded mandates.[5] An Associated Press survey of the fifty states conducted four years later found that "Financially strapped states are looking to take away government health insurance and benefits from millions of Americans already struggling with a sour economy," with nearly half the states "grappling with deep [budget] cuts and tax proposals to close shortfalls totaling more than $34 billion."[6]

In light of these circumstances, older cities continue to be starved for public investment capital, as they have been for decades. Some mayors have been able to obtain special funding allocations for trophy projects backed by public- and private-sector leaders with political juice: loans and grants for stadiums, convention centers, hotels, performing arts facilities, and waterfront development ventures. But special funding allocations are rarely provided to implement large-scale revitalization plans for disinvested downtowns and neighborhoods.

In desperate attempts to stimulate development or generate quick cash, some cities have given away and sold assets or have made commitments of support for questionable schemes. During the 1980s, Philadelphia launched a plan to acquire a thousand vacant houses and convey them to prospective homeowners for a dollar apiece; the plan proved costly, time-consuming, and counterproductive.[7] Later, the cities of Philadelphia and Camden each sold property tax liens (in effect, the right to collect back taxes on a tax-delinquent property or acquire it through foreclosure) to private third parties at a discount, giving up their opportunity to plan systematically for the disposition of thousands of houses and lots in many neighborhoods. During Mayor Rendell's tenure, I reviewed separate proposals from a football star and a media mogul, each of whom expressed a desire to "give something back to the city" by constructing new homes on vacant land, working in coordination with their own teams of architects and contractors. It was fortunate that Rendell chose not to support these proposals, because, in each case, the precondition for this form of giving back was a commitment from the city to spend millions acquiring and clearing multiple city blocks, which would then be conveyed to the prospective developers for free.

To stimulate reinvestment in this unfavorable environment, cash-starved cities search for new development financing approaches. Understandably, the most popular are those that do not require cash outlays.

A New "But-For"

Philadelphia's ten-year tax abatement can be viewed as a turn-of-the-century application of what is known as the "but-for" argument. The but-for argument, a mainstay of several public sector financing programs, is a presentation of evidence of the need for subsidized financing. Philadelphia's ten-year tax abatement could be seen as a legislatively authorized but-for argument used to justify a non-cash incentive (rather than direct funding), that was to be made available on a citywide (rather than project-specific) basis.

During the first quarter-century after the approval of the 1949 Housing Act (the authorizing legislation for major post-World War Two urban renewal financing programs), the flow of government funding was based on an established pattern: in response to proposals from private developers, municipal governments, or quasi-public housing and redevelopment authorities, government money was loaned, granted, invested, or reserved as a guarantee, and a specified real estate activity was completed; a civic center was constructed, a public housing high-rise was built, a federally-insured suburban split-level was sold. This pattern began to change in the later decades of the twentieth century, as underwriters for some public sector programs began to impose a greater burden of proof on development project sponsors, requiring more evidence that proposed ventures could not be financed conventionally and would not be feasible without—but for—the requested public financing.

Three programs that precede the ten-year tax abatement illustrate varying uses of the but-for argument and different uses of cash and non-cash incentives to stimulate development.

Urban Development Action Grant

A developer's ability to obtain financing through the Urban Development Action Grant (UDAG) program during the 1970s and 1980s depended in large part on the quality and credibility of an extensive but-for justification, including income and expense projections and a detailed narrative explanation, submitted for review by HUD underwriters. Authorized in 1977, UDAG provided federal financing for real estate development ventures that generated new jobs and new tax revenues. Funding was awarded in cutthroat national competitions conducted by HUD headquarters staff. Local governments submitted proposals on behalf of developers, and the available funding was awarded to the highest-scoring proposals. In Philadelphia and other cities, UDAG funds were used to finance projects such as hotels, office buildings, health care facilities, and shopping centers.

UDAG transactions involved real money. When a proposal scored well enough to win an award, the sponsoring city received federal grant funds that a local public or quasi-public agency then made available to the developer under the loan repayment or dividend payment terms set forth in the proposal. Although UDAG was terminated in 1989, the but-for concept remained a key element of other government financing programs. The latter included a state-enabled financing-without-cash program that gained widespread popularity during the 1970s and afterward: tax increment financing, or TIF.

Tax Increment Financing

In a tax increment financing deal, a developer borrows money from a private lender or public agency to finance the development venture. Development activity starts and is completed. Based on the added real estate value associated with the completed development venture, property values within the TIF target area increase; as a result, tax assessments go up and property taxes go up. For an extended period (often twenty years or more), property tax revenue generated within the TIF target area is divided into two categories: the property tax revenue associated with the value of target-area property in its condition prior to development goes into the treasury of the city and other taxing authorities, as it always had. However, the property tax revenue associated with the increased value of target-area property (the value generated as a result of the completed development) is used to pay off principal and interest on the debt financing. From the perspective of the city government that authorizes a TIF, the latter category of revenue, the "tax increment," is new money, available only because the development venture was completed and caused an increase in property values.

Following enactment of state legislation authorizing TIF in Pennsylvania, the City of Philadelphia used TIF to finance several major downtown ventures, including the construction of new infrastructure to link the historic Reading Terminal Headhouse with a subway station and the Pennsylvania Convention Center; the development of new office facilities for SmithKline Beecham and for PNC Bank; the construction of parking garages for the convention center and the Kimmel Center, a new performing arts facility, as well as the redevelopment of the former Philadelphia Navy Yard for office and light-industrial reuse.

TIF is particularly appealing because the public sector does not need to give away cash in order to make development happen. Even in cities where a public agency provides the debt financing, the loan principal and interest are fully repaid. Nor does TIF involve a diversion of tax revenues; the taxes on the pre-existing value of the TIF target area continue to be paid to taxing authorities. The increased taxes—the tax increment that pays back the debt financing—did not exist before the development plan was implemented, and, if the developer's but-for argument is believed, would not have existed if the plan had not been implemented. The public sector is using an imagined future tax revenue stream to catalyze real development activity in the present.

By the turn of the century, more than two thirds of the states had granted authorization to their counties to use TIF. In addition, the National Association of Counties reported that by 2000:

> Some states . . . removed "blighted" and "substandard" from their TIF designation criteria. As a result, local governments . . . have greater latitude to pursue a broader range of eligible projects, including public improvements such as golf courses and parks, and private improvements such as hotels and skywalks.[8]

TIF can be problematic in several respects. If the development venture does not generate the level of operating revenue projected or if property values do not grow as anticipated, the lender may not be repaid and the expected taxes will not be generated. On the other hand, if TIF target area real estate development potential turns out to be stronger than had been represented in the TIF proposal—in which case, the development plan could have been implemented without the TIF—twenty-plus years of tax revenue may have been foregone unnecessarily (TIF agreements often include "clawback" provisions that call for accelerated repayment in the event that operating results prove to be more successful than projected).

TIF critics have complained that TIF-supported ventures generate no taxes to pay for the city service needs associated with the new development, such as the cleaning and maintenance of new streets, sidewalks, and other public spaces in TIF-financed districts. In response, TIF advocates have maintained that the occupants or users of TIF ventures pay lots of other taxes—on personal income, business income, parking, and entertainment, for example—and that these tax payments, in the aggregate, generate more than enough revenue to offset the cost of additional municipal services in the vicinity of TIF-financed properties.

Keystone Opportunity Zones

UDAG and TIF are incentives for developers that are seeking financing to improve disadvantaged properties. Pennsylvania's Keystone Opportunity Zone (KOZ) program, launched in 1999, is an incentive for disadvantaged properties seeking both developers and financing. UDAG and TIF provided or facilitated financing based on repayment plans that varied from proposal to proposal. The KOZ program provides across-the-board tax breaks only—nothing to be paid out, nothing to be repaid.[9]

To get a KOZ designation in Pennsylvania, a local government or government-related agency submits a request to the state. A KOZ can be one or more city blocks, a collection of dispersed properties, or a single building. The key to designation is demonstrating that the proposed KOZ site is generating little or no economic benefit—no jobs, little or no tax revenue—but could produce substantial benefit if sufficient incentives were available to stimulate investment and development. State designation criteria for the first KOZs specified that prospective KOZ sites must have "evidence of adverse economic and socioeconomic conditions . . . such as high poverty rates, high unemployment rates, percentage of abandoned or underutilized property, and/or population loss."[10] Following designation, the local agency markets KOZ sites to prospective developers and reviews any development proposals that are subsequently received. New development within the KOZ is eligible to receive partial or full exemption from a variety of state and local taxes for a decade or longer. A company that locates in a KOZ will not have to pay state corporate net income taxes or local gross receipts taxes during the exemption term. Employees of firms that have moved into developed KOZ properties will not have to pay state income taxes.

TIF and KOZ have a guiding principle in common: an argument that, because a particular property has been unproductive for an extended period, the public really has nothing to lose by offering major tax incentives. The properties at stake are proven underachievers and non-achievers, with no prospect of improved performance in the foreseeable future. What is the risk in offering tax breaks on real estate that is not generating taxes?

One early KOZ success was the acquisition of KOZ-designated land for the construction of a one million square foot warehouse distribution facility for the clothing retailer TJ Maxx, a development venture that generated 1,100 jobs. The KOZ incentive was a key factor in influencing the company to locate in Philadelphia, in preference to suburban and New Jersey sites that had previously been under consideration.

The threat that a Philadelphia-based business would leave the city for a location elsewhere or that an out-of-town business would not consider a Philadelphia site without special financing is a theme that recurs in several proposals for UDAG and TIF financing and KOZ designation. In making the case for the authorization of TIF to support the expansion of SmithKline Beecham's headquarters at a downtown Philadelphia site, William Hankowsky of the Philadelphia Industrial Development Corporation (the agency that administered TIF in Philadelphia) informed a City Council member that:

> There was an internal struggle at SmithKline in which a number of people preferred to locate in the Philadelphia suburbs, believing the increased development and operating costs of the City imposed a 10%

to 20% premium over costs in a suburban location . . . In terms of negotiations, the TIF was critical to obtaining internal support from SmithKline
. . . Only with the prodding of Liberty Property [the developer] and the
proposed TIF package were individuals within SmithKline who wanted
to stay in the city able to prevail.[11]

The reality underlying this recurring theme was more compelling than the
substance of any but-for presentation: Philadelphia as a city was not competitive with the surrounding region. The city had higher business taxes, a city
wage tax that had no equivalent in most Philadelphia suburbs, and a property
tax assessment system that was inconsistent and archaic. Consider the wage
tax, for example, which in 2000 was 4.6 percent for Philadelphia residents
and 4.0 percent for non-residents employed at Philadelphia-based businesses.
The act of moving a business from the city to a suburban site would have
the effect of giving employees a 4 to 4.6 percent raise at no expense to the
owner. Alternatively, for the employees of a firm moving into Philadelphia
from another region, the wage tax would be an equivalent pay cut.

Viewed from this perspective, every property in the city could be
considered disadvantaged and in need of special assistance. One might also
conclude that the best-located properties—sites that were downtown, near
existing centers of investment such as academic and health care institutions,
or in stable or strong neighborhood real estate markets—would produce the
greatest economic benefit (that is, new tax ratables and jobs) if they received
public subsidies or tax breaks. Consistent with this thinking, many UDAG,
TIF, and KOZ sites were located in areas with these favorable characteristics.
But this approach can produce unintended consequences. The Cira Center,
a new office building developed on a KOZ site across the street from the
Amtrak 30th Street Station in West Philadelphia, had a successful initial lease-
up; but more than half the tenants that were the first to lease space in the
completed building turned out to be firms that moved there from other
locations in the city, where they had been paying taxes prior to relocating
to this KOZ-assisted site.[12]

Just as TIF-designation criteria had been broadened in many states by the
deletion of "blighted" and "substandard" defining characteristics, the scope
of KOZ was broadened as well. An expansion of the program in 2002 permitted the Governor to designate an unlimited number of "Sub-zones" for
fifteen-year tax breaks. In 2004, Governor Rendell proposed a KOZ
designation for a site at 17th and Arch Streets, two blocks west of City
Hall, where Philadelphia-based Comcast Corporation planned to build a
fifty-seven-story office tower as a headquarters location. The president of
the local Building Owners and Managers Association complained that this
action would, in effect, be "subsidizing handpicked new office building
construction" and would "create an unfair balance of competition against
existing buildings in Center City."[13] Among the real estate industry leaders
who lobbied against this action were the owners of office buildings that had

received UDAG and TIF funding years earlier. The KOZ-designation proposal for this site failed when the Pennsylvania House of Representatives voted to oppose it; however, the Comcast development venture received $43 million in state financing.

While the battle over the proposed Comcast KOZ designation was being waged, *Inquirer* columnist Andrew Cassel wrote that,

> desperation can be costly. With Rendell opining publicly that Philadelphia faces a job crisis if employers don't receive big incentives to stay, it's hard to imagine any local business not asking for a subsidy to stay in Philadelphia.
>
> The sad part is that little of this would be necessary if the pols had stayed focused on their "core business": running an efficient government, keeping taxes reasonable, and making the region attractive to development.[14]

Some time after the issue had been resolved, Liz Hersh, Executive Director of the Housing Alliance of Pennsylvania, ran into a Comcast executive at a social event. Like everyone else, Hersh knew that Comcast had persisted in its efforts to obtain public subsidies although the firm did not appear to be seriously considering moving out of town and despite the evidence that the 17th and Arch Streets site couldn't be characterized as a blighted or distressed property. So why did you do it? she asked. "Because we could," the executive replied. "It's business."

Your Tax-Exempt Decade

UDAG, TIF, and KOZ have all been criticized as programs that provide special favors to well-off developers. A December 2000 *Philadelphia Daily News* editorial entitled "TIFs: Totally Inappropriate Financing? Why Build the Cow Unless You Can Milk the City for Free?" published in early December 2000 began by describing a hypothetical situation:

> You want to move your family into the city, and build them a nice big house. You go to City Hall and say, "Hey, the city benefits if I'm here, since I'll be paying property taxes and wage taxes, plus taxes every time I park, shop, drink, or go to a game. Since I'm going to need to borrow money to build my dream house, why don't you lend it to me, and forgo charging me property taxes so I can use that money to pay the loan back. Then I'll agree to move here."
>
> How fast do you think it'll take before you get fitted for handcuffs?[15]

"Unless you're a developer," the editorial continued, "Then, it's not the cuffs that would come out, but the kid gloves."

The editorial writer was apparently unaware that City Council had already passed legislation enabling any owner of a newly-built house in Philadelphia to obtain a tax break almost identical to that described in the editorial and that a government agency was to begin accepting applications for this tax break later that month.

Many cities offer tax abatements—temporary tax-free status associated with the development or improvement of real estate—as a way of attracting developers. The amount of tax abated, the term of the abatement, and the portions of the property made eligible for abatement all may vary from city to city. The ten-year tax abatements that were instituted in Philadelphia starting in 1997 brought a new generation of housing developers and housing products to Philadelphia and sparked a debate about equitability in city development policy.

A provision of the Commonwealth of Pennsylvania's General County Assessment Law gives cities the power to create their own programs for the abatement of taxes as an incentive for development in blighted or deteriorating areas. The wording of the state legislation presents an immediate problem for local elected officials: which parts of the city should be declared "blighted" in order to establish eligibility for tax abatement? By the mid-1990s, many sections of Philadelphia had been designated redevelopment areas, through a process that included a "certification of blight" by the Philadelphia City Planning Commission and the approval of a redevelopment plan. These two actions enabled the city's Redevelopment Authority to use eminent domain powers to acquire property and assemble sites for new development. As a result, many areas of the city, some of which contained a large number of vacant and deteriorated properties, had already been designated as blighted. Should eligibility for the abatement be limited to these places?

On the other hand, vacant and run-down properties could also be found on otherwise stable, fully-occupied city blocks downtown and within neighborhoods where the real estate market was functioning and property values were holding steady or increasing. Designating some of these places as blighted for the purpose of establishing eligibility would give prospective developers an incentive to build, fix up, and strengthen the local real estate market. But what broader impact would the label "blighted" have on the neighborhood's market potential? If you learned that the home that you were considering buying, located on a fully-occupied, attractive residential block, was located in an area that had been designated "blighted," would you decide to look elsewhere? There were a lot of vacant and neglected buildings in Philadelphia's downtown; should the downtown area then be designated as blighted—and, if so, what kind of image of Philadelphia would that present to the world?

Philadelphia finessed the "blight" issue by designating the entire city as blighted for the purposes of establishing eligibility for tax abatement programs. The fallout was imperceptible. Downtown and neighborhood real estate markets were not adversely affected, and the image that Philadelphia presented to the outside world was unchanged. The difference between blight designation to qualify for a financial benefit and blight designation to establish a redevelopment plan, the implementation of which might involve subsequent property taking, relocation, and demolition was apparently recognized and accepted by anyone who might have been interested.

After resolving the geography question, the City had to make other decisions: what properties would be eligible, how much investment would trigger the abatement, and how long would the abatement term last? The manner in which these questions were resolved was strongly influenced by City Councilman Frank DiCicco, whose district encompassed roughly half of the downtown as well as many neighborhoods characterized by varying degrees of stability or deterioration. DiCicco had been concerned about the increasing number of vacant multi-story office and industrial buildings in and near the downtown area. The location was good enough. Thanks to the accomplishments of the Center City District, the downtown-area special services district created in 1990, conditions in the central business district had been steadily improving (as described in the next chapter, the Center City District also played a key role in setting the stage for legislative approval of the abatement). So why couldn't these buildings be rehabilitated for lofts, apartments, or condominiums? Developers told DiCicco that the numbers didn't add up; the combination of rehab costs plus the tax increase that would take effect after the completed venture was reassessed at a higher value made development infeasible—in effect, the City was penalizing development. So what if we got rid of the higher taxes? DiCicco asked.

The Rendell Administration and City Council supported the enactment of Ordinance 97 0274, which offered a decade-long real estate tax abatement on improvements associated with the conversion of deteriorated industrial, commercial, and other business properties to "commercial residential use," meaning apartments. Hotels, new construction ventures, and improvements to owner-occupied homes did not qualify for this abatement (they were granted eligibility a few years later). The first ten-year terms for development ventures that received this "conversion abatement" began in 1999.

The conversion abatement and subsequent ten-year tax abatements instituted in Philadelphia have several characteristics in common:

- The abatement term begins after the completion of improvements. In the case of for-sale properties, the abatement term begins at the date of sale.
- Geographic eligibility is citywide. Unlike targeted tax incentive programs such as the Keystone Opportunity Zone, any property in the city is potentially eligible.
- The abatement amount is the property tax associated with the market value of the improvements, as determined by staff of the City's Board of Revision of Taxes (BRT), Philadelphia's tax assessment agency. Land value and the value of any pre-existing building are not subject to abatement and remain taxable.

- The total abatement amount is unlimited; there is no "cap" on the value of improvements subject to abatement.
- The right to the abatement is transferable in the event that a property is sold during the ten-year abatement period; the new owner gets the benefit of the abatement for the balance of time remaining in the abatement term.

This initial ordinance generated abatement approvals associated with the completion of conversion projects in fifty-three buildings by the end of 2004. The aggregate market value of the development and improvement activities completed at these sites was $110.6 million, and the aggregate total of taxes abated in connection with these ventures was an estimated $29.2 million. In effect, the City had foregone nearly $30 million in hypothetical property taxes in order to attract new real estate investment totaling more than three times that amount.

Was the City giving away too much? At the end of 1999 when these ventures were ready for occupancy, not many people appeared to think so. Most of the converted properties were buildings that had been vacant or marginally occupied for years, with no development plans in the works. Some were older office buildings constructed nearly a century ago. At that time, a number of them had been suitable locations for corporate headquarters, as the CIGNA building at 1600 Arch Street had been. By the turn of the twentieth century, however, major corporations and other large office-space users were not scouting aging office towers as prospective headquarters sites. As a result, the owners of most of these buildings had three options: divide up the building and try to find a lot of smaller tenants; rent the ground floor as retail space, leaving the upstairs partially or entirely vacant; or close the property down entirely. Industrial buildings were problematic for similar reasons; modern industries were not interested in multi-story urban sites, and carving up the space for smaller office or residential re-use was rarely a feasible option.

The largest abatements approved under the conversion ordinance were for buildings with back stories similar to the above: the old Bell Telephone Company Building on Arch Street, the mid-rise at 15th and Chestnut Streets that had once housed an elegant Brooks Brothers store; the American Patriot Insurance Company Building on South 16th Street; a former American Society for Testing and Materials lab near Benjamin Franklin Parkway, and others. Nearly all of these buildings were located within central business district boundaries, with many close to City Hall or in Central Philadelphia neighborhoods adjacent to the downtown area.

The history of one of these properties, the American Patriot Building on South 16th Street, illustrates the potential profitability of tax-abated conversion ventures. According to a *New York Times* article, this twelve-story, 80,000 square foot building had become mostly vacant in December 1990; at the time, the only remaining tenants had been "a cigar store, a café, and the offices of a smoke-shop owner." A bank that acquired the building through federal bankruptcy liquidation had tried to auction it off without success; a local speculator's bid of $1.325 million was rejected, and the auction ended.[16] Eleven years later, following the conversion of the American Patriot Building to apartments, the property sold for $17.5 million. The 2002 market value of the improvements associated with the conversion was $14 million, with more than $370,000 in property taxes exempted in 2002, just one year of the decade-long abatement term.

Encouraged by these successes, the City of Philadelphia broadened the abatement program in 2000 to include almost every kind of real estate development or improvement activity that generated increased market value. Three abatement-authorization ordinances were enacted that year: one for new housing construction, one for the rehabilitation or upgrading of residential investment properties (not limited to former commercial or industrial properties, as the conversion abatement had been), and one for the improvement of homeowner-occupied housing. A suburban-style subdivision on cleared land would be eligible for abatement; so would the construction of a new apartment building or the upgrading of an older one; so would some home improvement projects, such as the installation of dormer windows or the addition of a sun porch.

In addition to being a potentially big money-saver, the abatement was relatively easy to obtain; the application and approval process was uncomplicated and straightforward. First, a property owner would apply to the City's code enforcement agency for a building permit. Once the permit was approved, the owner would fill out a one-page "Application for the Exemption of Real Estate Taxes due to Improvements" and submit it to BRT, along with a copy of the approved permit. BRT would then notify the City's Revenue Department, which would check its files to ensure that the owner was up to date with respect to all tax filings (if not, the application would not be processed until the owner paid any overdue taxes). Then a BRT assessor would determine the market value of the proposed improvements, and a report would be submitted to the Board of Revision of Taxes, which would approve the application.

This process compares favorably to that which a developer would have to undergo in order to obtain development financing through a City-administered real-money program such as the Community Development Block Grant (CDBG) program. To obtain CDBG subsidy funding in Philadelphia in 2000, a developer would have to submit a detailed proposal to the City, including a line-item construction budget, evidence of financing (in addition to the requested CDBG financing) being obtained to complete the activities proposed, detailed information about the developer's experience and qualifications, and evidence that the developer had been responsive to community questions and concerns. The proposal would be reviewed by development agency staff and would be subject to scrutiny by the Mayor and City Council as part of their review of the annual CDBG budget. If the City Council member in whose district the development site was located found fault with the venture for some reason, further action might be delayed until the issue was resolved. And even if all these hurdles were cleared, the proposal might have to wait, because CDBG funding is always in short supply.

Under the best of circumstances, the public sector process for reviewing and approving real-money transactions takes time and requires lots of documentation, because responsible government agencies want to show that any commitments of money they make have a sound basis and will produce the intended results. The latter is a particularly important consideration if public subsidy money is paid out during the construction period, before the venture is completed and occupied, during which time the City's investment is at risk. In contrast, with imagined-money transactions, no developer benefit is realized until all the construction work is done and the building is ready for occupancy. BRT rules specify that the abatement term begins after proof of completion is provided. Without a completed project, BRT approval of a tax abatement application has no value.

Of the three abatement incentives launched in 2000, the one that had the most dramatic impact on Philadelphia's landscape was the residential new construction abatement authorized by Ordinance 1456-A. This abatement category included most single-family sales housing developments, including condominiums and townhouses, with the ten-year abatement term beginning after the conveyance of title from developer to buyer. Because most of this development takes place on cleared land, there is usually no "pre-existing building," as there had been in every conversion-abatement project. The only tax obligation during the ten-year abatement term is that associated with the market value of the land underneath the newly constructed housing.

Two housing ventures completed after 2000 illustrate the substantial benefit associated with this abatement category. The Watermill at Manayunk is a condominium venture located on the north bank of the Manayunk Canal, near the city boundary that divides lower Northwest Philadelphia from suburban Montgomery County. The condominium building is entirely new; nothing but riverbank had existed previously on the site. Because a property developed for condominiums is subdivided for sale to individual condo buyers, the developer obtains a separate tax abatement approval for each condominium unit. As part of the approval process, the BRT assessor has to allocate to each unit a portion of the value of the land on which the venture is built. For a Watermill penthouse condominium purchased in 2003, BRT established a market value of $99,000, with $10,000 attributable to the land on which the Watermill was constructed and $89,000 attributable to the newly-constructed unit itself. The 2005 real estate tax for the owner of this penthouse condo was $264, the owner's share of the taxes owed on the land. Without the abatement, the condo owner's 2005 tax bill would have been $2,618—nearly ten times as much.

The Reserve at Packer Park, a new for-sale townhouse development, was built on a South Philadelphia site that used to be part of the Philadelphia

Figure 1.3 Reserve at Packer Park

Naval Base. The site, developed long ago by the Navy as housing for military personnel, was turned over to the City during the 1990s after the Navy downsized its operations in Philadelphia. The empty houses on the site, none of them architecturally noteworthy or feasible for rehabilitation, were demolished and the area was cleared for new development. A subdivision plan was created and new streets were constructed. The site plans and townhouse designs were of a type that can be found in many subdivisions, and the development was advertised as a place that offered up-to-date amenities in a "Center City" location (City Hall was actually about three miles away). Because the single-family townhouses, like the Watermill condos, were built on a cleared site, there was no pre-existing building value to tax; for their first ten years of residency, the buyers would pay taxes on the value of the land only. In 2005, the total market value of a typical house in this development, including both land and building, was $308,000, with a 2005 tax obligation of $1,402. Without the tax abatement on the newly-constructed house, the owner's 2005 tax bill would have been $8,145, nearly six times as much.

A total of 1,038 single-family units approved by BRT for the new-construction abatement were completed between 2001 and mid-2005. The aggregate amount of 2005 real estate taxes abated for these properties was about $4.6 million, or (to again use an oversimplified calculation) about $46 million in potential City tax revenue over a ten-year period. Is $46 million, or $44,000-plus per home, too much to pay for more than a thousand new condos and townhouses? In 2005, $44,000 was less than half the amount of CDBG subsidy needed to finance the construction of one house in a typical City-financed low- and moderate-income sales housing venture. And, to be honest, was the City really forgoing $46 million in tax revenue? Developers would insist, predictably, that the ventures they completed during this period would not have been feasible without the tax abatement incentive. The fact that the shorter-term or less generous abatement incentives that had been offered prior to 1997 had not attracted much interest would support the developers' contention. If this interpretation is accurate, then the 1,038 units did not cost the City anything; without the tax abatement, the foregone tax revenues did not really exist.

The Jumping Woman

The BRT staff had never seen anything like it; the woman from Boston who had stopped into their office for a copy of the BRT handout on the tax abatement program was literally jumping up and down with excitement. What made her so overjoyed? She was about to buy a new condominium, fully accessorized with swimming pool, fitness club, spa, concierge, and trendy street-level restaurant in an attractive downtown location at a price that was an order of magnitude lower than the cost of a comparable property in Boston; and she had just learned that her property tax bill would be small change—a few hundred dollars a year.

Lower prices and lower taxes—wouldn't you jump up and down too? In order to really understand what was going on, you had to view the jumping lady in a broader economic context.

First, the lower prices. For most of the late-twentieth century, Philadelphia home prices had been consistently lower than prices in other cities. As a row-house town with a declining population, Philadelphia had an oversupply of older houses, and because many middle- and upper-income households had been moving from the city to new homes in the suburbs, the prospects for marketing higher-priced new housing products in the city had not been good. However, these circumstances changed noticeably after the turn of the century. As the national housing market grew stronger, more developers and investors found that they could make big profits by developing undervalued properties and marketing them at prices that would be high but still competitive with comparable housing products in other cities. Philadelphia's housing market strengthened rapidly as a result. Between 2003 and 2004, the number of local listings of single-family housing units priced at more than a million dollars rose by 43 percent.[17]

Then the taxes. With the benefit of the tax abatement, you could buy a condo unit in a newly restored, historically noteworthy building in the Rittenhouse Square area and, for ten years, pay a fraction of the real estate taxes that you would have paid for an identical condo in a newly restored, historically noteworthy building on Commonwealth Avenue in Boston. Or you could buy a house with a big yard and a garage in a subdivision in Northeast Philadelphia or at The Reserve at Packer Park and pay a fraction of the taxes due on the same house in King of Prussia or Blue Bell.

The sub-par quality of most Philadelphia public schools remained a significant marketing obstacle, although the system was making steady, incremental improvements under the energetic leadership of Superintendent Paul Vallas. But public school quality was not a make-or-break issue for everyone. Many of the buyers in the market for high-end housing products didn't have school-age children, and many that did had more than enough money to pay for tuition at one of the privately-managed alternatives: an established private school such as Friends Select, on the Parkway near Logan Square; or a newer school such as the Philadelphia School on Lombard Street a few blocks south of Rittenhouse Square. For parents, the tax savings could be viewed as the equivalent of a substantial contribution toward the tuition expense for a child entering one of these well-regarded schools.

By mid-2005, the total market value of tax-abated townhouses and condo development completed since the enactment of the new ordinances was $168.5 million, and the total market value of tax-abated apartment development was $164.6 million.[18] Philadelphia's real estate market had changed greatly since 1997. By 2006, downtown condominiums priced at multimillion dollar levels were no longer a rarity. New high-end apartments were being developed downtown, in Philadelphia's inner-core neighborhoods, and in West Philadelphia. New subdivisions with suburban characteristics were emerging in Northeast, Northwest, and South Philadelphia. Single houses with neatly landscaped yards lined newly constructed streets. Some of the new streets were even given suburban-sounding names: Lantern Lane, Cherry Blossom Lane, Peach Tree Lane.

Given the momentum that had been growing for years, was this incentive too generous? A 2006 report commissioned by the Building Industry Association of Philadelphia found that additional tax revenues generated by abatement-related construction and other activity would more than compensate for the short-term taxes foregone and concluded that "if the current abatement program were reduced or eliminated . . . the City would generate less tax revenues[and] would have to choose between reduced expenditures and higher tax rates in order to balance future budgets."[19]

Developers that had been active in the city before and after 2000 agreed that the abatement needed to be continued. One of them put it simply: until Philadelphia cures some of its chronic disadvantages relative to the suburbs— namely, the quality of the public schools, the disproportionately high labor costs (influenced by the political power of the city's building trades), the city's wage tax (which had been reduced to 4.3 percent for residents and 3.77 percent for non-residents by Fiscal 2006 but was still a major disincentive), and the length of time required to obtain a building permit or zoning variance—then a significant financial incentive would be needed to offset them and make development feasible.

The value of the abatement in a competitive regional real estate market was particularly evident with respect to sales housing; the buyer of a new house in Philadelphia would always pay far less in property taxes than the buyer of a comparable new house in the suburbs. In an apples-to-apples city-versus-suburbs comparison of property taxes associated with new sales housing, Philadelphia would win every time.

Legislating Fairness

No, the woman was not jumping up and down with joy; not this woman. "The wealthy owners of new construction (who could obviously pay high real estate taxes)," she wrote in an email message to the Director of the Fels Institute, "are given a ten-year abatement while their older neighbors' taxes are quadrupled!!"

Her message continued,

> As the owner of an older home in the city, am I and all my neighbors supposed to sit back and pay higher and higher taxes so that the wealthy and the poor can pay none?????
>
> The across the board acceptance of this policy is the main reason I will be moving from the city at my first opportunity.[20]

She was not alone. Residents in many areas of the city were not happy with the tax abatement programs, including residents of neighborhoods where no tax abatements had been approved, as well as residents of blocks that had changed fundamentally as a result of tax-abated development. A *Philadelphia Daily News* article headlined "Street mulling end to tax abatements" reported that the Philadelphia Mayor John F. Street (who took office in 2000) had asked his Secretary of Housing and Neighborhood Preservation to study the abatement issue and recommend possible changes in policy.[21]

What was not to like about this economic development incentive that had proven to be more effective than many others in so many ways? One answer could be found in a December 2005 report that I co-authored, which verified what many people already knew or could have surmised on their own. During the period between 1997 and mid-2005, the abatements were most often used within downtown and neighborhood real estate markets that are already strong or that are showing signs of growing development potential. In weaker real estate markets that have a need for reinvestment, the abatement is rarely used, except in connection with housing development ventures that are receiving financing through government subsidy programs.[22]

A series of accompanying maps illustrated this finding. The conversion abatement had been used almost exclusively in and near downtown; so had the biggest abatements for other investor-owned residential properties.

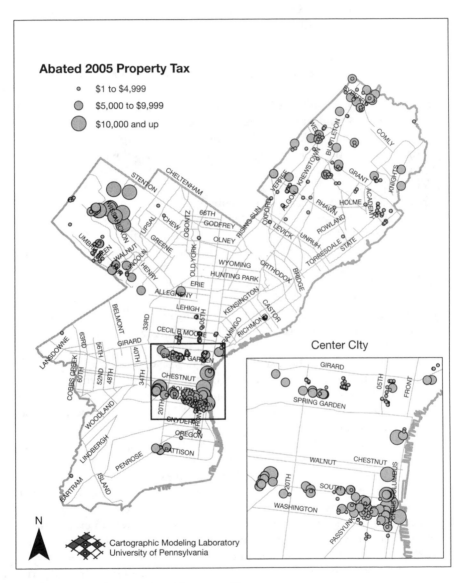

Figure 1.4 New Construction Abatement Sites

The subsequently-enacted new construction abatement had supported a lot of condo and townhouse development in neighborhoods adjacent to the downtown business district, where infill new construction, almost unheard of a decade earlier, had now become commonplace. The new-house abatement had also stimulated growth in up-and-coming neighborhoods such as Manayunk and East Falls, as well as in city-suburb boundary areas of Northwest and Northeast Philadelphia, in those well-landscaped enclaves where the streets had been given suburban-sounding names. But little tax-abated activity, and none of the big-ticket tax-abated activity, was occurring anywhere else.

The tax abatement followed the money. Developers and investors with enough capital to fund high-end real estate ventures downtown and in the hottest Philadelphia neighborhoods qualified for the largest abatements, in light of the substantially increased market value associated with projects such as the conversion of the American Patriot Building. Smaller developers who undertook projects such as the rehabilitation of abandoned row houses in less desirable neighborhoods got far less benefit from this incentive. A vacant house rehab project on North 41st Street in the Belmont neighborhood of West Philadelphia, for example, generated about $800 in abated 2005 taxes, compared with the approximately $6,700 in abated 2005 taxes associated with a newly constructed townhouse in The Reserve at Packer Park.

Individual buyers of the most expensive condominiums or new homes, like the buyers of the penthouse units at the Watermill or the Packer Park townhouses, had benefited disproportionately from the tax abatement for the same reason: a brand new house in a well-regarded neighborhood generates a higher level of added market value, which means a higher tax abatement. So the biggest benefits of the abatement programs went to those people with the most wealth to invest or spend. The tax abatement might be Philadelphia's most effective economic development incentive; but it was also one of the most inequitable, surpassed only by KOZs such as the one proposed for the Comcast site.

But what's so bad about attracting more private capital investment to support housing development to a city plagued by a half-century of past disinvestment—of capital fleeing to suburban and exurban communities? The tax abatement stimulated the reclamation and restoration of buildings that had been in limbo for years and catalyzed new construction on cleared lots that had remained vacant for decades. The tax abatement was an embodiment of wealth-building, a new-millennium buzzword among both economic development professionals and human capital development advocates. Having witnessed the economic setbacks experienced by Philadelphia during the last half of the twentieth century, how could anyone have misgivings about wealth-building during the first years of the twenty-first?

The controversy was multi-faceted. One facet was the issue of geography, the fact that, although the tax abatements were offered citywide, most of them ended up in or near downtown and upscale neighborhoods. Residents who bought new homes in these areas would pay lower taxes than most residents of the rest of Philadelphia—often order-of-magnitude lower taxes. The 2005 tax bill at the Watermill penthouse was $264; in the same year, the tax bill for a rowhouse on Mitchell Street a few blocks away, was $4,400.

Another facet was property condition. Most of the tax-abated housing products were homes with brand new major systems, finishes, and amenities. Many residences in weaker Philadelphia neighborhood real estate markets were century-old homes in need of upgrading: reroofing, repointing, rewiring, repainting, or the repair or replacement of heaters, sewer laterals, and water lines. Most owners of these residences had little access to capital to finance such improvements, which, when completed, would generate little or no added market value eligible for abatement. And the completion of this work would not reduce their existing, unexempted property taxes; the pre-existing $4,400 tax bill for the Mitchell Street house would not decrease, no matter how much upgrading the owner might be able to afford to complete.

The contrast between owners of tax-abated properties and everyone else was most evident in those instances in which new housing was built on a vacant lot within an otherwise occupied block. Many would regard a change of this kind as encouraging: the elimination of a longstanding nuisance and the emergence of occupied housing, producing a more attractive block. However, this increased attractiveness would probably also produce higher property values—which would also mean higher assessments and higher taxes. When such a change occurred, the long-term residents' added tax exposure would be much higher than that of their new neighbors, because their tax increase would be associated with the total assessed value of their properties. On blocks such as these, where the tax abatements had produced some of the most dramatic improvements in the neighborhood environment, the inequitable nature of the abatements generated some of the most animosity. Because the abatements had been so widely promoted in the for-sale housing market, everyone knew that the buyers of the new homes on the block were getting major tax breaks.

For some people, the "fairness" issue was overriding. You could produce documentation that would prove how valuable the new development and new residents were to the Philadelphia economy. Real estate transactions generated tax revenue for the City. New residents who moved in from the suburbs and were employed in Philadelphia paid more city wage tax. More households in Philadelphia's downtown and neighborhoods meant more spending on food, clothing, recreation, and entertainment—and some of these households had lots of discretionary income to spend—creating opportunities for retail business development and expansion. The new households generated little or no additional demand on the resources of public-service agencies such as the Department of Public Health and the Department of Public Welfare. Many of them paid for health club memberships rather than using Department of Recreation facilities. Many of them did not have school-age children or sent their kids to private school. Most important, the newly developed and improved real estate and the influx of new residents into underpopulated areas gave the city more curb appeal and, yes, higher property values—meaning more net gain for longtime residents if and when they decided to sell their homes. The economic benefits to the city as a whole were extraordinary and documentable. But no amount of documentation would change the perspective of many residents who shared the view of the angry woman: "Am I and all my neighbors supposed to sit back and pay higher and higher taxes so that the wealthy and poor can pay none?"

In this highly-charged political environment, what should be done about the ten-year tax abatements? Several proposals for addressing the "fairness" issue were advanced during the months leading up to the 2007 mayoral election:

- Un-blight Center City, so that the state's abatement-authorizing legislation would restrict eligibility to the areas with most need for reinvestment. This approach would probably have gained more support if the central business district were nearly blight-free—but the downtown area still was not; despite the high level of investment and development that had occurred during the preceding decade. Vacant and deteriorated upstairs space could be found in many properties with occupied ground-floor retail. Many smaller older buildings downtown were vacant or needed substantial upgrading. Un-blighting better-off neighborhoods would have been problematic as well, because vacancy and deterioration was so widely dispersed. Only totally made-over neighborhood subareas in places such as Packer Park could be declared unconditionally suitable for un-blighting—and such an action would have no effect because no abatable properties existed there.

- Use post-abatement term tax revenue to support affordable housing, through the allocation of a portion of the new tax revenue that the City would gain starting in the year after the expiration of each ten-year tax abatement term. The first ten-year abatements terms, those associated with the conversion ordinance, would end on December 31, 2008. By 2013, these expired abatements would generate nearly $3 million in new property tax revenues. The other three abatement categories would produce an estimated $12 million in new property tax revenue by 2015, bringing the total to roughly $15 million in annual revenues (based on 2005 tax levels, unadjusted for inflation and other factors).

  In response to this proposal, for which I expressed support in the publication I had co-authored, some critics pointed out that the post-abatement-term revenues are not "new" and are not separable from the rest of the city budget; these anticipated revenues had already been programmed into Philadelphia's general fund as part of the City's five-year financial plan, along with revenue from other sources, and would be needed to support the cost of government operations. But, through its administration of TIF loan repayments, the City had already demonstrated that it had the ability to reallocate a portion of the tax revenue associated with a specific property to a destination other than the general fund; and five-year plans can always be revised.

- Allocate a portion of revenue received through the City's real estate transfer tax to affordable housing. The transfer tax is a charge on each real estate sales transaction, with the City's share of the tax amounting to 3 percent of the sales price. In Fiscal Year 2001, transfer tax revenues totaled $77 million. By Fiscal 2006, thanks in large part to the influence of the expanded abatements instituted at the start of the decade, transfer tax revenues reached $236 million.

If the latter two measures were to be adopted, supporters pointed out, then affordable housing could be financed through two sources: one that could be predicted reasonably well in advance, and one that varied with changes in the real estate market. However, even if both measures were to be instituted, the additional funding would not be nearly enough to compensate for the inequity between tax-abated new owners and fully-taxed longtime residents.

Interestingly, some of the discussion of tax abatement policy alternatives took place at Kate's Place, an older apartment building that had been acquired and rehabilitated for affordable rental housing by Project H.O.M.E. Project H.O.M.E. is a nonprofit organization that initially devoted itself exclusively to developing housing and providing services for homeless people. During the 1990s, the organization broadened its capability to take on a range of real estate development and service-program activities without departing from its primary focus on homelessness. Kate's Place, located just a block and a half away from Rittenhouse Square, in one of Philadelphia's priciest neighborhoods, was not a homeless shelter; the building provided apartments both for formerly homeless people as well for others who were simply seeking a safe and comfortable place to live. Thanks to the availability of the ten-year tax abatement, the 2005 real estate tax obligation of the Project H.O.M.E.-controlled limited partnership that owned the building was about $20,000; without the abatement, the 2005 tax bill would have been more than ten times that amount.

In 2006, State Representative Dwight Evans, who would become an unsuccessful candidate for Mayor in 2007, introduced two bills designed to protect homeowners from the risks associated with rapidly rising property values. One would authorize cities to grant "homestead exemptions"—property tax reductions—to certain classes of homeowners. Another would permit cities to assist low-income homeowners by gradually phasing in any real estate tax increases over a six-year period. Councilman DiCicco had introduced bills with similar goals into City Council. However, none of these bills were acted on.

The debate over the issue of property tax abatements, like past debates about UDAGs, TIFs, and KOZs, would not have been necessary if the city had been able to do more to address the chronic problems that weakened its competitive standing: school quality, high taxes, inflated construction labor costs, and a burdensome permitting and zoning process. If these problems could have been addressed, no special financial incentives would need to be offered to anyone. Over each of their eight-year administrations, Philadelphia Mayors Edward G. Rendell and John F. Street had both taken action to begin substantively addressing some of these problems; but no one would maintain that they had been solved or were about to be solved. You could blame the mayors and City Council for lacking the political will to deal with these critical issues. But business, civic, and community constituencies were not mobilizing effectively to press for fundamental reform during most of these years.[23]

At the public gatherings that he attended in his district every week, Councilman DiCicco listened to many complaints about the fairness issue. He told me that he responded to these complaints by systematically describing the benefits of the abatement—new investment and development on previously vacant or run-down property, an increase in overall neighborhood real estate values, the financial benefits to the city other than tax revenue— and said that his constituents responded favorably to this explanation "90 percent of the time."

Like the other sixteen members of Philadelphia's City Council, DiCicco was up for re-election in 2007. Before the campaign season began in earnest, a prospective opponent charged that a recent home purchase by DiCicco amounted to an unfair use of the tax abatement for personal gain. The charge was unfounded and failed to gain traction; DiCicco was re-elected by a substantial margin.

If 1997, the year of the conversion ordinance, could be replayed, I asked DiCicco, what would he have done differently, based on what had happened since then? How would he advise elected officials in other cities who might be considering similar strategies?

"I wouldn't change anything," he said. "My advice would be, 'Just do it. Go for it.'"

Scorecard for a Strategy

With reference to the three defining characteristics of "transformative" activity described in the Introduction, the ten-year tax abatement can be said to have had a transformative impact on downtown Philadelphia and in some of the city's stronger real estate markets. The tax abatement strongly influenced investment in the adaptive reuses of older buildings and in infill development on vacant land, made more Philadelphia housing options competitive with those in the suburbs, and promoted wealth-building by attracting wealthier people who paid property and wage taxes and whose purchasing power stimulated retail business development.

With respect to the tax abatement, transformative activity had a price: the direct benefits associated with this initiative were almost exclusively skewed in favor of higher-than-median income people. With reference to the three criteria described in the "Repopulation for Whom?" section of the Introduction, the tax abatement favors wealthier geographies (that is, stronger real estate markets), provides no direct social benefits (except in terms of the somewhat limited use of the abatement to support affordable housing development), and creates disadvantages for longtime residents, in the form of higher property taxes resulting from the rising property values associated with tax-abated development occurring near their homes.

The dual policy described in the preceding section—funding affordable housing through an allocation of post-abatement property tax revenue and transfer tax proceeds—would somewhat offset the skewed impact of the tax abatement. But these actions would not generate nearly enough funding to resolve the equitability issue. The cost of a measure such as providing tax breaks to homeowners in areas experiencing rapidly rising property values would far exceed the funding generated through these two actions; and, in any case, such a measure would probably be unconstitutional in Pennsylvania due to tax-uniformity provisions of the Commonwealth Constitution.

Does a rising urban real estate market always have to produce disadvantages —higher property taxes, in this instance—for longtime neighborhood residents, the people who are most deserving of a reward for enduring past years of disinvestment? Under ideal circumstances, there are two ways in which the property tax disadvantage could be offset or overcome, and these circumstances did not exist in Philadelphia during the years following the introduction of the ten-year tax abatement.

One way is through the enactment of legislation similar to the measures proposed by Evans and DiCicco, establishing a cap on the rate of property tax increases. If such legislation had been enacted at that time, however, it would have been seriously flawed, because at that time properties in Philadelphia were not being assessed uniformly. Although mandated by state law to do so, Philadelphia had not implemented a uniform assessment plan for all properties in the city; as a result, significant variations between BRT-established assessed value and true market values were evident throughout the city. Without uniform assessment, some property owners would unfairly gain more than others.

The best time to have addressed the issue of equitable treatment would have been during the years prior to the approval of the additional abatements (especially the new-construction abatement) that occurred in 2000. Ideally, a citywide property revaluation would have been completed and a rate cap on property tax increases legislated before the expansion of the abatement policy. These actions would not have prevented the post-2000 controversy from happening, but they would have placed some of the most adversely affected homeowners in a better position. However, a citywide revaluation takes time to complete, and the uncertainty associated with revaluation is a political powder keg. In 2000, nearly every District Councilperson's legis-lative district included a neighborhood that was experiencing rapidly rising property values. In these neighborhoods, homeowners' post-revaluation property assessments would be likely to increase by orders of magnitude. Higher tax assessments could be offset by City Council action to lower the tax rate in order to try to achieve an outcome that would be revenue-neutral for many property owners. However, such an action would be one of the most controversial legislative challenges that the incumbent Council members would have to address. Regardless of the outcome, a substantial number of people would feel convinced that they had been treated unfairly, and they would make their feelings known at the polls (all Council members' seats were up for election in 1999). As a result of these factors, the revaluation and the associated rate cap legislation could not have taken place during or before 2000. Nearly a decade later, in July, 2008, the BRT finally approved the launching of an "Actual Value Initiative," through which all properties in the city would be assessed uniformly at 100 percent of market value.

The only other way to counter the property tax imbalance is through the creation of more new, higher-paying jobs in Philadelphia. In an ideal urban-transformation scenario, resident access to more higher-wage employment opportunities would accompany an upswing in the real estate market and provide more homeowners with increased income, some of which could be used to pay higher property taxes. However, this scenario was not characteristic of Philadelphia during the turn-of-the-century years. According to the Bureau of Labor Statistics, Philadelphia employment was at 577,782 in 2007, down from 606,566 in 1998.[24] According to the U.S. Census, Philadelphia median household income declined from an estimated $32,362 in 2000 to an estimated $30,631 in 2004; the latter was significantly below the 2004 U.S. median of $44,684.[25]

Based on these considerations, the ten-year tax abatement could be viewed as a success in economic development terms and a failure in terms of human capital development. But in mid-1990s downtown Philadelphia, economic development was desperately needed. Thanks in large part to the abatement; the former "war zone" had become a highly desirable urban center. The tax abatement may have been over-generous to some extent, but it was essential; the early twenty-first century surge in real estate values across the nation would not, by itself, have generated the investment and development activity that occurred after the abatement was launched. The Philadelphia-specific disadvantages cited by developers—the city wage tax, the quality of most public schools, the higher labor costs associated with the political power of the building trades, and the cumbersome zoning and permitting process—had not been overcome, and the real estate market, at its strongest, did not offset these disadvantages.

Michael A. Nutter, a former City Councilperson, was elected Mayor in 2007 and took office in January 2008. Nutter's former West/Northwest Philadelphia district had included neighborhoods that had been untouched by the tax abatement as well as neighborhoods such as Manayunk, where the abatement had helped to fuel new development. "The Nutter Plan for Better Housing Now," issued during the campaign, called for two actions related to the tax-abatement debate:

> Reform the Property Tax Abatement program to more effectively generate housing development throughout the City that would otherwise not occur and to more fairly spread the burden of taxation between longtime and new homeowners.

> Reform the Property Tax itself by supporting responsible reassessments that increase fairness and protect residents from large tax increases each year.[26]

During Nutter's first year in office, a significant decline in the city's real estate market was reported, although this decline was not as precipitous as that which had been occurring in the previously hyperactive real estate markets of the West and South. According to Wharton economist Kevin Gillen, a downturn in Philadelphia home sales in the nine-month period following spring 2007 "effectively resets citywide home values to mid-2006."[27] By mid-2008, real estate sales in the city were reported to have been about 28 percent lower during the first six months of 2008 than in the first half of the previous year.[28] Under the circumstances, 2008 did not appear to be the best year in which to propose reducing or doing away with an incentive with proven effectiveness in stimulating Philadelphia's strongest real estate markets.

In August 2008, Alan Domb, Philadelphia's most experienced condominium developer, told a reporter that half the condos in some recently completed downtown buildings were unsold. As further evidence of the downturn in the real estate market, the developer of a newly-built Center City condo high-rise had launched a sales promotion that month, offering Smart Cars and parking spaces worth $75,000 each to buyers of units available in his new building, located down the street from the TIF-enabled Kimmel Center parking garage.

At the same time, Domb stated, other condominium projects were experiencing much higher occupancy levels, with vacancy rates of less than 2 percent. Which projects were the most successful in attracting and keeping residents in a changing real estate market? According to Domb, the most marketable buildings were the adaptive reuse projects, the formerly non-residential buildings for which the initial 1997 "conversion abatement" had originally been designed.[29]

Properties that had been among the downtown area's biggest problems a decade earlier had now become competitive in a challenging real estate market.

Figure 2.1 CCD "Attack" Advertisement

2 A Managed Downtown

The Center City District

Over the past four decades, special services districts (also known as business improvement districts or district management organizations) have been established for the purpose of maintaining and improving downtowns and other areas within many cities. The histories of these organizations have been well documented, and the impact of their activities has been researched and assessed.[1] However, the circumstances under which Philadelphia's Center City District (CCD) was created and the major achievements of this organization are worth recounting for several reasons. The formation of the CCD and the staging of its activities over two decades illustrate how such an organization can have a transformative effect in revitalizing a downtown that had previously been in a condition of deep distress. Philadelphia's experience also demonstrates the need for urban planning, so that opportunities that emerge in a constantly changing environment can be identified and pursued. A review of CCD milestones and performance measures also suggests ways in which an effective downtown management organization can be distinguished from others that have limited or negligible impact.

The most successful downtowns are populated by residents, workers, shoppers, diners, tourists, and business visitors, who occupy buildings and enliven streets and public spaces during different days and hours. In the aggregate, the activities of these groups give the downtown area daytime and nighttime vitality on work days, weekends, and holidays. A large and diverse downtown population generates real estate market demand, broadens opportunities for business and retail commerce, supplies ridership for the local public transit system, and produces the sensations of energy, motion, and constant activity that make the downtown environment attractive and engaging.

Downtowns succeed or fail based on the performance of three real estate markets—residential, office, and retail—that connect and overlap with one another. Proximity to lunchtime and after-work dining and shopping attractions will make an office building more marketable. Downtown-area neighborhoods with desirable housing options will become homes for business-district office workers who will rent or buy places to live there. Strong downtown office and residential markets will increase the demand for retail services that are open more hours of the day and days of the week, and these retail establishments will generate more activity on the downtown streets and sidewalks.

The hospitality market, consisting of tourists, participants in conferences and business meetings, and other visitors, also has a critical influence on the downtown economy. However, the potential of this market can vary widely from one city to another, depending on the number, location, quality, and level of popularity of tourist and visitor attractions. Although all cities pursue available hospitality-market opportunities as a high economic development priority, the other three markets are more important because of the added value associated with their relationship to one another and because more of the key participants in these markets are people who belong to the city—residents, workers, and year-round shoppers—and who define the city's identity.

Existing conditions—such as the presence or absence of a well-designed street grid, historic attractions, or a waterfront—can significantly influence the prospects for a successful downtown revitalization strategy. So can the contribution of past public investment in supporting or undermining the downtown economy through the financing and construction of expressways, street infrastructure, convention centers and performing arts centers, subsidized housing, pedestrian promenades, and prisons.

The Planners' Legacies

Public investment designed to strengthen Philadelphia's residential, office, and retail markets during the latter half of the twentieth century produced mixed results.

Residential

Philadelphia was more fortunate than many other cities in having strong neighborhood real estate markets adjacent to three of the four quadrants of the city's rectangular downtown core: Rittenhouse Square, where wealthy residents had occupied elegant homes for many decades; Society Hill, where an ambitious redevelopment plan launched during the late 1950s resulted in the restoration of historic houses, complemented by well-designed infill new construction on residential blocks interwoven with a system of walkways and small parks; and the row house and brownstone blocks of the Logan Square, Spring Garden, and Fairmount neighborhoods in the Benjamin Franklin Parkway museum district. The adjacency of these neighborhoods created a critical mass of downtown users, many of whom, as homeowners, were, in effect, co-investors in the downtown's future.

Other downtowns, particularly those located in fast-growing Sunbelt regions, did not possess as strong a residential base by the end of the twentieth century. Of forty-four U.S. cities included in an analysis of downtown population, household, and income trends by Eugenie L. Birch of the University of Pennsylvania, five of the ten cities with the largest downtown populations were located in the Northeast and mid-Atlantic regions: New York, Boston, Philadelphia, Baltimore, and Washington, D.C.[2] By contrast, Houston, the fourth largest city in terms of overall 2000 population, was not included in Birch's study, "due to the large percentage of prisoners comprising its downtown population." Without the contribution of this group to its downtown, "Houston actually lost downtown population in the 1990s."[3]

A more relevant indicator of the contribution of downtown neighborhoods to a city's economy is the median income of the residents. Birch found that each of the six Northeastern and mid-Atlantic cities included in her study (New York, Philadelphia, Baltimore, Washington, Boston, and Pittsburgh) had at least one downtown census tract in which median household income was higher than median household income in the region (that is, the metropolitan statistical area, or MSA) as a whole. For example, 2000 median household income in Philadelphia's wealthiest downtown census tract was 183.1 percent of the MSA median. In cities with this characteristic, it could be said that the downtown real estate market included consumers who were wealthy enough to afford other housing options in the region but had chosen downtown living as the most desirable option. In contrast to Birch's findings with respect to Northeastern and mid-Atlantic cities, only one of twelve Western cities (San Francisco) had a census tract with median household income higher than MSA median.[4]

Office

Post-World War Two suburban development, linked to a new regional highway system, produced attractive alternatives to the downtown as a location for offices and retailers. According to Carolyn Adams and her co-authors, "by 1980, the office and industrial parks, shopping malls, and other suburban employers [in the eight-county Philadelphia metropolitan region] were providing close to two thirds of the region's jobs." Philadelphia's share of regional employment shrank from 67.5 percent in 1951 to 38.6 percent in 1980, while the four adjacent suburban counties' share grew from 22.5 percent to 44.9 percent during the same period.[5]

During the 1950s, an ambitious construction program undertaken in the area west of Philadelphia's City Hall repopulated this area of Center City with thousands of office workers. A twenty-two-acre site that emerged after the demolition of a massive and unsightly railroad viaduct was developed as Penn Center, a series of office buildings surrounded by surface-level and sunken plazas and parks and connected by outdoor stairways to an underground pedestrian concourse with retail stores and access to train and subway stations.[6] This development was the outcome of plans originated by Philadelphia City Planning Commission Executive Director Edmund N.

Bacon. The significance of Penn Center and Bacon's contribution are described in a history of the project posted on the Ed Bacon Foundation website:

> By the end of 1953, Penn Center was bustling with construction activity and the first tower was fully occupied. In 1956, while Penn Center was under construction *Time* magazine published a rendering of the completed project —a stunning vista from the air looking through the building corridor with City Hall rising up prominently in the background. *Time* proclaimed that Penn Center was a "gleaming triumph." The project was written about widely as one of the nation's most significant downtown developments, and as a successful example of how good planning can guide private development.
>
> The Penn Center story is emblematic of Bacon's career. Relying on the power of his design concepts to inspire others and attract investment, he raised public consciousness in projects that were previously unimaginable. Without Bacon, it is likely that Penn Center would have been developed piecemeal instead of as a coordinated set of public and private spaces that contribute to the civic landscape. Before Bacon's involvement in the future of what would become Penn Center, there was much talk of building department stores and other commercial structures on the site. Bacon ensured that Penn Center became a mixed-use, office and retail complex, with significant amounts of public space, views of City Hall, and an intrinsic connection to mass transportation.[7]

By the end of the century, however, the shortcomings of this development plan had become clear. During the decades after 1950, the construction of a double corridor of Penn Center office buildings north of Market Street was complemented by additional office development on Market Street's south side, producing a series of office blocks with little other activity. The largest concentrations of street-level retail space could be found inside buildings— in the atrium-style lobby of Centre Square at 15th and Market, for example, or in the food court and mall at Liberty Place at 17th and Market—with no adjacency to the street. Other ground-floor retail uses, almost exclusively dependent on the office-worker customer base, closed during evenings and weekends, leaving the sidewalks, parks, and plazas silent. By the turn of the century, retail activity on the subsurface concourse level was anemic. Much of the concourse space was occupied by discount stores and fast food restaurants, with many square feet of unoccupied and unappealing space throughout.

In *The Death and Life of Great American Cities*, Jane Jacobs wrote that: "Most big-city downtowns . . . have become . . . too predominately devoted to work and contain too few people after working hours . . . A Central Business District that lives up to its name and is truly described by it is a dud."[8] Although this outcome had not been intended, the planning and

Figure 2.2 Penn Center

design principles underlying Penn Center produced an office corridor possessing less vitality than a downtown center deserved, while nullifying residential market potential and minimizing retail market potential in the area west of City Hall.

Retail

During the early decades of the twentieth century, the region's largest companies and the business-service firms that supported them were based downtown, as were the region's largest department stores and a variety of other retail establishments. In 1935, Philadelphia's downtown accounted for major proportions of the city's total retail sales, including 71.1 percent of citywide general merchandise sales, 58.4 percent of apparel sales, and 25.2 percent of household furniture sales.[9]

A half-century later, retail development had spread across the region, with suburban retailers capturing a disproportionate share of regional sales. Between 1974 and 1980, for example, retail sales rose only 1.2 percent in the city while increasing 90 percent in the remainder of the region (standard metropolitan statistical area). Total retail sales in the city amounted to only $4 billion, compared with $13.7 billion in the region outside Philadelphia.[10]

During this period, the most ambitious initiative to bring more shoppers to Philadelphia's downtown was the construction of the Gallery, a glass-enclosed multi-level mall at 9th and Market Streets east of City Hall, with 125 stores, a food court, and a subway and commuter rail connection, linked to two adjacent department stores. Completed in 1976–1977 through a partnership between the City and the Rouse Company, the Gallery was based on a concept introduced by Edmund Bacon in the 1960 plan for Center City, which called for the development of a "multi-use complex of transportation . . . shopping, and office space covering several blocks of Market Street East."[11]

In his *Design of Cities* (published in 1967, with a revised edition published in 1974, prior to the completion of The Gallery), Bacon described his vision of this complex and the broader development of which it was a part:

> The [Market East] courts on each side, open to the sky, bring fresh air down to the subway level and give abundant light to the glass-enclosed pedestrian mall to the north. The architecture of the buildings which penetrate this space rises clear from the pedestrian level to the level above the street with no expression of the street plane . . .
>
> [The pedestrian mall is] a new kind of people street, paralleling and reinforcing vehicle-laden Market Street, providing a new kind of experiential continuity in Center City.[12]

Although The Gallery was a commercial success, the encapsulated design of the complex created an interior "people street" that not only lacked "expression of the street plans" but also had little real connection to the adjacent outdoor space along Market Street. The Gallery's Market Street frontage consisted primarily of display windows, with most pedestrian access limited to corner entrances. In addition, the complex was attached to a multi-story parking garage, providing shoppers with the ability to drive in, enter and leave the mall, and drive away without setting foot on the city's streets.

William H. Whyte's criticisms of the design of "megastructures" seem applicable to the Gallery. In his 1988 work, *City: Rediscovering the Center*, Whyte states that:

> There is something about the internal world of the megastructures that inhibits people from venturing out of them. The idea was that their retail shops would stimulate the provision of more in the downtown around. It has rarely worked out that way. They have more often deadened competition than stimulated it.[13]

The opening of The Gallery took place during the period in which an outdoor pedestrian-mall plan, the Chestnut Street Transitway, was being implemented. The plan, encompassing ten blocks of Chestnut Street, one of the city's strongest retail corridors, called for brick-paving and widening

Figure 2.3 The Gallery

sidewalks, decorating the streetscape with new lighting, trees, and benches, and closing the street to all traffic except shuttle buses that had been specially designed for the project. Merchants' fears about the loss of customers due to traffic and parking problems proved to be well-founded; *Philadelphia Magazine* reported an 83 percent turnover among Chestnut Street retailers between 1975 and 1987.[14] The opening of the Gallery a block away from one end of the Transitway may also have helped bring about, to use Whyte's term, the "deadening" of Chestnut Street and the redefinition of this corridor as a poorly-maintained, lower-end shopping district.

Late twentieth-century Center City development ventures produced valued new assets for the downtown area but did not solve existing or emerging problems. The positive and negative characteristics of the downtown area were described in a late 1989 *Philadelphia Inquirer* editorial:

> In many ways Center City is a vibrant commercial and residential district—a growing job market, a retail destination with everything shoppers might want along with diverse cultural attractions ranging from the Philadelphia Orchestra to nightclubs offering female wrestlers. But in many ways Center City is being despoiled—by litterers tossing candy wrappers, panhandlers shaking plastic cups, muggers snatching shoulder bags, shoplifters fingering the merchandise and street people doing their personal business in the public stairwells.[15]

Before and after the turn of the century, downtown planners and advocates in many cities proposed and launched strategies designed to rebrand business districts and attract residents, workers, shoppers, and visitors. Some of these strategies are summarized in two publications by the Brookings Institution's Center on Urban and Metropolitan Policy: "Ten Steps to a Living Downtown" (1999) and "Turning Around Downtown: Twelve Steps to Revitalization" (2005).[16]

The authors of the Brookings publications do not claim that adherence to the "steps" will guarantee success in every city's downtown. However, a number of the most important "steps" are irrelevant or infeasible in older city downtowns because they require substantial investments of public and private capital. The 1999 paper describes how bond financing was used to improve roads and bridges leading to Denver's downtown, a project that would have been far beyond the City of Philadelphia's bond-financing capability at the time.[17] Characterized as a critical "step to revitalization" in the 2005 paper is the creation of a "catalytic development company" that will undertake actions such as land assembly, development site preparation, the administration of development-subsidy financing, and the implementation of development activities to compensate for the reluctance of risk-averse conventional developers to venture downtown. During this period, the catalytic development firm must be prepared to accept little return on equity, in order to support projects "that will take far longer to develop and lease up than conventional development," to finance ventures that may not appear to be worth the market risk, and to be prepared to experience some project failures.[18] Through this risk-taking, the firm is expected to set the stage for private investment in the future. Not addressed is the identification of a funding source to pay this firm's capital and operating expenses. In a city with a weak downtown real estate market, the likelihood of assembling enough funding from government, private, or charitable sources to support an organization such as this one seems remote.

In many older cities, activists who want to launch revitalization strategies for aging downtowns encounter a significant problem: the absence of strong business leadership associated with large companies that employ many people in the downtown area. During the early twentieth century, at a time when Philadelphia's population had reached its peak, the city's planning boards had been populated by "downtown merchants, utility, transit, and bank directors, real estate men, [and] railroad and ocean carriers" who primarily supported downtown-oriented projects designed "to bring traffic to the downtown, to beautify it, and to raise or maintain downtown business property values."[19]

After the middle of the century, however, business leadership had become far less concentrated and less downtown-oriented. Between 1956 and 1974, the number of Fortune 500 companies headquartered in Philadelphia dropped from fourteen to eight.[20] At the same time, business leadership organizations became more regionalized. The Greater Philadelphia First Corporation (GPFC), created in 1982 to serve as the region's premier business leadership organization, was governed by a twenty-seven member board consisting of CEOs of companies located throughout Greater Philadelphia.

Commenting on the dispersion of leadership as a characteristic affecting many cities, Paul R. Levy (President and CEO of the Center City District, who has headed the organization since its founding) wrote:

> As more companies are publicly traded, or directed from headquarters outside the region, fewer captains of industry are willing or able to play the old-style civic role. Leadership thus devolves to a more diverse group, power becomes more diffuse, and strategic alliances with other civic groups must become the norm.[21]

In cities where political, business, and civic leaders have grown accustomed to viewing the downtown as an environment that is stagnant or in a state of gradual decline, the creation of a downtown management organization may not make much of a difference. However, in cities where the downtown is perceived as being in a state of economic and social crisis, the prospects for a successful management organization are much improved. If local leaders perceive themselves as confronting a do-or-die situation, the organization they create is more likely to be a catalyst for transformative change.[22]

Lowering the Bar

April, 1985: "I saw hundreds or thousands of people kicking in store windows and yelling and screaming," said the owner of Chestnut Street store. "There were girls and guys grabbing as much as they could and just running."

It was "like mad looting in the streets," said an office worker who witnessed the scene from a third-floor window.

"This is crazy. This is insane," said a police officer, one of the first of scores who rushed to the scene, shut down the street, arrested about a dozen people, and ended the disruption, which extended along four blocks, west from Broad Street to Rittenhouse Square.

By the time order was restored, about four hours later, Chestnut Street retailers had experienced tens of thousands of dollars worth of losses due to theft and vandalism. Predictably, the most window-breaking and looting had occurred at stores that sold sporting goods, clothing, shoes, specialty eyewear, and tobacco. As evening fell, broken windows were being boarded, and broken glass was being swept up. The street reopened. The events of the day were covered by the news media nationwide. One retailer estimated that he would have to remain closed until midweek.

The melee was attributed to two incidents that happened to occur on Easter Sunday, a day of the year when more people than usual were drawn to the west-of-Broad area: shoving matches among youths who had just exited a kung fu film, and the outburst of a large, angry group of young people who had been turned away from a sold-out showing of *Friday the 13th Part V*. "There were so many people out there that there wasn't anything anybody could do," said a cashier at one of the theatres.[23]

Within seventy-two hours, Philadelphia Mayor W. Wilson Goode had organized a task force of city officials and business representatives "to look at all the issues dealing with the Chestnut Street Transitway," had ordered an increased police presence on Chestnut Street, and had assigned city youth workers to the area. While acknowledging the seriousness of the incident, businesspeople expressed support for the mayor's actions. "When something like this occurs and it gets national publicity, it doesn't help," said Chamber of Commerce President G. Fred DiBona. "I don't think there is any question about that, but I don't think it will hurt to any great degree as long as it is an isolated incident." A representative of the Chestnut Street Association, a group representing businesses on the corridor, said that publicity about the disturbance "has to have an ill effect for the time being. The important thing to do is to see it doesn't happen again."[24]

April, 1987: "Close the doors!" shouted the security guard to his fellow employees at Foot Locker, on the third level of the Gallery, the Market Street East shopping mall, as he saw a crowd of about seventy-five teenagers running up the stairs from the lower level. The teenagers charged down the corridor leading to the store, and moments later Foot Locker employees were struggling to close the heavy sliding glass entrance doors while some of the youths tried to jam them open.[25]

Other retailers were not as well prepared. According to witnesses, four waves of young people raced through the J.C. Penney store, snatching merchandise and knocking over display racks as they ran. "There was nothing we could do, we were caught off guard," said one of the store managers. "We were conducting business normally, and all of a sudden it was like a herd of elephants came trampling through the store." The manager of a nearby shoe store saw "a mob coming from J.C. Penney" and rushed to close his store entrance. According to a newspaper account, "As he slammed the gate down, the youths pressed against the window and pushed it off the track. He warded them off with a wooden pole."[26]

Incidents of looting and vandalism occurred up and down Market Street that afternoon, on a day when Center City was filled with people who had come to see a parade honoring Philadelphia 76ers basketball star Julius Erving. A jeweler reported that $60,000 worth of merchandise had been stolen after the display window of his store was smashed. "I'll open again," the owner said. "But after my lease ends this year I'm going to move. It's too dangerous downtown."[27]

"We shop owners knew this was going to happen," said the owner of a sportswear store at 13th and Market, where vandals had broken a window and stolen sneakers. "Why didn't the police know?"

However, the City's Managing Director termed the police response to the disruption "more than outstanding" and told *The Philadelphia Inquirer*: "I have not found anything to indicate that the department did anything that it should not have done, or failed to do something that it should have done."

A Deputy City Representative reported that a group of city agency managers would meet to evaluate the events of that afternoon and said: "An awareness of this experience will obviously be part of everything that we do in the future." The Police Commissioner said that he planned to meet with school administrators to explore ways to prevent a recurrence of such an event and added that, "The overwhelming majority of young people there Monday did not participate in any criminal behavior."[28]

"I just think these things happen sometimes," said the general manager of the Gallery. "It's unfortunate, but it's a fact of life in the city . . ."[29]

The subtext of the response by Philadelphia's city government to these incidents, as well as to related complaints about the poor maintenance of public spaces downtown, was consistent: we're doing the best we can under the circumstances; but we may not be able to do a better job.

Three Campaigns

A series of events that were initiated by an organization known as the Central Philadelphia Development Corporation (CPDC) in the mid-1980s and led to the creation of the Center City District in 1990 gave the CCD its defining characteristics and influenced the CCD's activities from the date of its founding to the present. The core of the CCD's approach to downtown revitalization can be summarized in three words:

- *Focus*. Real estate developer Ronald Rubin agreed to serve as the first Chairman of the CCD on condition that the organization focus on achieving two key goals—making Center City clean and safe—before broadening its scope to include activities that other cities' district organizations were undertaking, such as area promotion and infrastructure development. Based on this directive, the CCD focused exclusively on the cleaning and patrolling of streets and public spaces during its first eighteen months. Although the CCD has engaged in a variety of other activities since that first phase of operation, each year the organization has devoted priority to one or a small number of initiatives, for which the associated purpose, goals, approach, resource allocation, and anticipated impacts are clearly defined.

- *Planning*. Before they began attempting to convince business leaders of the value of a district management organization and to ask some of them to serve on the organization's board, district management organization proponents studied existing improvement-district business models, visited the Grand Central Partnership district in New York City, and met with the organization's founder, leaders, and managers. Before launching two related campaigns to gain support for the improvement-district concept, they designed a detailed operating plan and budget that was sufficiently comprehensive to ensure that the organization's activities would be adequately funded and managed (these actions are also a requirement of the state enabling legislation that authorizes the formation of such organizations). Before seeking support for the district from downtown-area property owners, they decided that billing and collection associated with the property assessment that would finance district management organization operations would be handled exclusively by CCD staff, so that city government, mistrusted by many, would have no access to these funds. Before entering the political arena to seek legislative authorization of the district from Philadelphia's City Council, they decided that the uniformed sidewalk cleaners who would constitute most of the district's workforce would be unionized but not represented by the municipal employees' union to which City of Philadelphia street cleaning personnel belonged. Before opening the CCD organization for business, they decided that both street-cleaning services and public safety functions would be outsourced (through a competitive bidding process) to reliable private contractors, so that the new organization would not have to start from scratch in building in-house capacity to perform these core functions. All of this advance planning enabled CCD supporters to benefit from others' experience, to anticipate and address potential problems beforehand, and to design a well-informed, coherent presentation of the district organization concept and implementation plan.

- *Quality*. The earliest advocates of the concept that became the CCD knew that a district management organization would not succeed unless it was directed by high-quality leadership—by some of the city's best-recognized and most influential business executives—and they pursued their leadership recruitment strategy accordingly. The business plan and budget for the CCD provided sufficient resources to ensure that the organization's performance in cleaning and providing supplementary security in Center City would improve the public environment to a level of quality that was beyond the capacity of municipal government (in part due to an insufficient allocation of government funding for this purpose). The professional staff that were recruited to manage the CCD organization had substantial executive-level experience and, as the organization expanded its activities, the credentials of additional program staff and professional service providers were consistently equal to or better than those of their counterparts in government or elsewhere in the private sector.

These defining characteristics were the major contributors to CCD's success and are the factors that distinguish the CCD from many other district organizations across the country that have not achieved comparable success.

Three campaigns undertaken between 1985 and 1990—one corporate, one civic, one political—resulted in the formation of the CCD. The Central Philadelphia Development Corporation was the original organizational base for these campaigns prior to the CCD's creation in 1990. CPDC was a rebranding of an older organization, the Old Philadelphia Development Corporation, which had played a leading role in the redevelopment of Society Hill but had a less prominent leadership role in the 1970s and 1980s. As part of a plan to reduce the number of business-related organizations active in the region, the Greater Philadelphia First Corporation had proposed to end OPDC's existence. However, several downtown business leaders insisted on the need for an organization that represented the business community's interests in Center City. A compromise was reached: OPDC changed its name to the Central Philadelphia Development Corporation and broadened its focus to represent all of Center City.

The first campaign associated with the creation of the Center City District had its roots in a June, 1985 presentation by Richard C.D. Fleming, then President of the Denver Partnership, at a special meeting of the CPDC board. Fleming described his role in organizing and managing Denver's 16th Street Mall Management District, and his presentation was reported to have "stimulated much interest in downtown management for Philadelphia."[30] A series of CPDC-sponsored meetings and forums was organized to consider how the opportunity to create a similar district in Philadelphia might be pursued.

CPDC Executive Director Peter Wiley was particularly enthusiastic about the Denver model, as well as about the successful performance of a district management organization in New Orleans. Wiley engaged the interest of Center City attorney Michael Dean in a more ambitious pursuit of the idea, and when Dean became chair of CPDC, the two of them began working together to promote it. Dean had been interested in the concept of a district management organization from the start. He was convinced that Center City needed far better management than city government could provide and had concluded that the City lacked both sufficient resources to do the job properly as well as the desire to make downtown maintenance a priority. Dean and Wiley visited New York City and met with representatives of the Grand Central Partnership, including its founder, Daniel Biederman. A key to the Partnership's success had been the recruitment of CEOs and COOs from the biggest corporations in the business district to serve on the organization's governing board. The two Philadelphians were convinced that CPDC had to do the same thing in order to succeed.

Business leaders shared Dean's view of the shortcomings of municipal government as a downtown manager. During the late 1980s, they were anticipating the forthcoming opening of the Pennsylvania Convention Center at a new location in the heart of downtown (to replace an outmoded convention hall located in West Philadelphia), and they were concerned about the city's ability to present itself effectively as a visitor attraction. In most instances, however, this concern did not translate into commitments of support for a private district management organization. In presenting the concept to corporate executives, Dean and Wiley were frequently met with two responses: nice idea, but no thanks; and, we're already doing the best we can.[31]

In addition, Dean and Wiley encountered resistance from proponents of competing target-area improvement strategies, who were not enthusiastic about the idea of a broader, downtown-wide organization. Stockton Strawbridge, head of the family-owned Strawbridge & Clothier department store, had already organized a voluntary, merchant-funded sidewalk-cleaning program for a segment of Market Street East in the vicinity of his store and did not support an expanded program (over which his influence would be more limited). Willard Rouse, developer of the Liberty Place office towers on Market Street West, had been discussing with Chamber of Commerce representatives the possibility of creating an improvement program limited to Chestnut Street. These targeted plans would have produced some improvements, but the associated benefits would have been outweighed by the significant problems that existed on nearby streets that intersected Market and Chestnut.

Other business leaders supported the larger concept and were prepared to serve on the governing board of a Center Citywide district management organization, but none of them were willing to chair it. After a series of unsuccessful recruitment attempts, Dean and Wiley were surprised when an ideal candidate made his interest known.

Ronald Rubin was a real estate developer and entrepreneur, not a corporate leader. Head of the family-owned Richard I. Rubin and Company, Rubin was characterized in a 1990 *Philadelphia Inquirer* article as "the city's most visible can-do developer," who was advancing ambitious Center City office development projects at a time when "other developers are retrenching in today's real estate downturn." With the opening of the fifty-four-story Mellon Bank Center in 1990, Rubin's firm was to become Philadelphia's largest office landlord, managing more than five million square feet of office space.[32]

For Rubin, a defining moment had occurred a few years earlier, at the time when he was supervising the renovation of the former Bellevue-Stratford Hotel, which had been vacated following the outbreak of Legionnaire's Disease in 1976. The Rubin Company was making a major investment in the rehabilitation of the property for reuse as a high-quality retail, office, and hotel building. Rubin had invited representatives from Tiffany & Company to come to Center City from New York to look over available retail space. However, the appearance of the surrounding downtown area was dreadful. The sidewalks were littered, and the curbsides were lined with uncollected trash bags. The Tiffany representatives would be meeting Rubin at his office five blocks away, and they would see it all.

Rubin called the Mayor to ask if the City could do something to improve the appearance of the area. "What route are you going to take?" the Mayor responded, implying that the City could not guarantee to maintain reasonable standards of cleanliness except when notified in advance, in preparation for special occasions.

Years later, in explaining his decision to take on the leadership of the district management organization, Rubin said, "I come from a family of activists. Someone had to take the first step." As a businessperson who was very active in the downtown area, he was well aware that problems such as litter, uncollected trash, and the growing incidence of aggressive panhandling created an environment that kept people away from Center City and that made it particularly hard to promote the city to suburbanites.[33]

In coordination with Dean, Rubin assembled a who's-who business board to govern the district management organization. In 1994, Stockton Strawbridge's maintenance organization was dissolved and his Market Street East target area—which had initially been left out of the Center City District —was made part of the district. The plan for a separate Chestnut Street maintenance program never materialized, and the area was incorporated into the boundaries of the CCD.

Rubin's board was reinforced by corporate and institutional leaders who had previously signed on to the proposal and had been working actively to advance it. One key institutional participant in planning for the CCD was Thomas Jefferson University, Center City's largest private employer, whose president, Lewis Bluemle, Jr. told the *Inquirer* that his institution "would survive only if patients perceive the area 'as a safe, secure place.' Bluemle . . . was prepared to pay the extra tax, despite [Jefferson's] having its own 100-member security force. 'It's not enough,' he said."[34]

Rubin joined Dean and Wiley in completing the second campaign; the effort to win buy-in for the district management proposal from members of the Center City business and residential communities. During the period between September 1989 and October 1990 alone, meetings were held with a total of thirty-four business and civic associations. By this time, a great deal of information had been assembled and organized for public presentation. The design of a business model for a Philadelphia special services district had been under study since 1986. A "Preliminary SSD [Special Services District] Feasibility Report," funded through a grant from Greater Philadelphia First Corporation, had been released in December 1987, and a final report was published in 1989. In a related action, the Philadelphia City Planning Commission had published a "Retail Strategy for Center City" in 1987, which had recommended the formation of a downtown management organization and had included a projection that more effective management and promotion of the downtown area could result in a 30 percent increase in retail sales.[35]

Rubin's leadership of the campaign was particularly valuable for two reasons. Since Rubin's company was a dominant property owner in Center City, his firm's property assessment payment would be larger than anyone else's, giving his commitment to the plan increased credibility. In addition, Rubin's friendships and business relationships with many of the other major property owners in Center City made it easier for him to persuade them to commit to the plan. As a result, Rubin and the others were soon able to report to participants in civic or business association meetings that the commitments already in hand amounted to a major portion of the property assessment revenue needed to support the district.

A decision made during the period leading up to City Council authorization of the district—to have the district management organization bill property owners directly rather than having the City's Revenue Department perform this function—also proved advantageous to presenters of the plan. The district organizers had initially asked the City to mail an invoice for the property assessment charge along with each owner's real estate tax bill, consistent with the practice used to collect special district assessment charges in most other district sites around the country. However, the City's antiquated computer system could not accommodate this additional task; the District would have no alternative but to handle billing and collections on its own. To address this unanticipated challenge, bank executive Rosemarie Greco, a board member, donated staff to help set up a CCD billing and collection operation. District organizers were subsequently pleased to discover that this approach was welcomed by many property owners. According to Paul Levy, the line most likely to generate applause during a typical presentation to a civic or business group was the statement that "The CCD will bill and collect directly, and the money will never pass through the hands of the City of Philadelphia." In the years that followed, this approach proved to be far more advantageous from a business operations standpoint as well. Levy later described his unsuccessful attempt to have the City bill the property owners on behalf of the district organization as "my most successful failure."[36]

The campaign was not an easy one. The prevailing level of confidence in city government was low, despite the fact that the district plan was not City-sponsored. The level of confidence in the downtown real estate market was also low, and the level of skepticism regarding new ideas was high. The reaction from many members of the audiences that heard the presentations was negative. "To me, it's an additional tax, and I can't afford to pay it," said one rental property owner. "It's a tremendous burden for a resident for city services the city should already be providing."[37]

"A more blatant swindle I have never seen in my life," said another rental property owner, speaking at a City Council hearing in early 1990. The board of the Washington Square West Civic Association, a group that represented the residential community adjacent to Society Hill south of Walnut Street, voted two-to-one to oppose the district proposal, fearing "that City Hall will cut back the already inadequate services it provides downtown once the private effort gets rolling."[38]

The presenters of the plan portrayed their proposal as a return-on-investment proposition: If you put people and equipment on the street, you can reduce litter and graffiti; if you have uniformed staff walking the sidewalks, crime will decline. The proposal began to draw positive reactions. The influential Center City Residents Association, representing the Rittenhouse Square area, supported the plan as an approach that, in the words of one board member, could "creat[e] a sense of order and progress."[39] William Boone, head of the neighborhood association in Logan Square, a residential area north of the Penn Center office district, was more blunt: "The basic question is: Will we be here, or will we leave?" he asked. "Frankly, you're looking at people desperate for solutions. Will I pay $75 more? The answer is a resounding yes."[40] When discussion at one meeting got sidetracked by a debate about whether the proposed property assessment amounted to a "confiscatory tax," Boone had declared, "This is not a confiscatory tax. A confiscatory tax is the smashed car window that I see when I walk out my front door in the morning." The conclusion that Boone and many other property owners reached: I don't want to pay more, but I have to.

Meanwhile, Rubin was forcefully advocating for the proposal in presentations before many business organization audiences. He told a meeting of Rotarians that too many businesspeople "yell and scream about the city's problems, but it's not going to change unless we change it."[41]

In late June and early July 1990, as required by state law, district organizers mailed information about the district plan, budget, and estimated charges to 2,732 property owners and more than 6,000 commercial tenants. Public hearings were held on August 1 and 2 to air the plan and respond to comments. Of the seventy-two persons who testified at the August hearings, only eighteen expressed opposition. However, a growing number of townhouse and condominium owners whose properties lay within the proposed district boundaries were voicing strong objections to the proposal. Some of the loudest expressions of opposition came from residents of Academy House, a high-end condominium and apartment building; ironically, these residents would benefit most from the district designation because of the building's central location in the downtown area. To counter these objections, which were reaching the ears of City Council members from whom the district proponents would be seeking approval of an ordinance that fall, the district proposal was altered in August to include a provision allowing town-house and condo owner occupants to apply to the district organization for an exemption from the property assessment; this loss of revenue would be offset by voluntary contributions that were being made to the district by nonprofit organizations and institutions.

At the time, this concession did not amount to a major sacrifice on the CCD's part. In 1990, it was estimated that these residential properties accounted for only about 3 percent of the district's proposed budget for the coming year.[42] However, after the turn of the century, following years of residential development in Center City (influenced in part by the accomplishments of the CCD), the district plan was amended to make owner-occupied properties subject to the assessment as had originally been proposed.

The Pennsylvania Municipal Authorities Act, the state enabling legislation for district management organizations such as the CCD, requires that district proponents provide an opportunity for affected property owners to file objections to a district proposal. If objections are filed by one third or more of the property owners, or by property owners who control one third or more of the proposed district's total assessed value, the proposal is defeated. In mid-September, at the end of the public comment period for the CCD, objections had been received from 316 property owners (12.2 percent of all property owners), who owned 11.7 percent of the taxable assessed value in the district.[43]

The goals of the third campaign were to win City Council support for the district through the approval of two ordinances: enabling legislation authorizing the creation of a downtown district (approved by Council in March 1990) and an ordinance authorizing the district boundaries and budget (approved in September 1990, after the public comment period described above had ended).

Philadelphia's seventeen City Council members were divided in their views of the district proposal, and many were initially opposed to or unenthusiastic about it. James Tayoun, whose district included that portion of Center City east of Broad Street, supported the authorization. John Street, whose district included much of Center City west of Broad, opposed it. Rules Committee Chair David Cohen, a political adversary of Street's, supported the measure. Joan Krajewski, whose district included blue-collar neighborhoods along the Delaware River, said that she supported the idea but would have to vote against the authorization because her constituents would interpret the measure as a benefit for downtown that was not being provided to the neighborhoods. Some of the Council opposition seemed to be based on turf considerations:

if citizens started relying on a nongovernmental entity for services that had previously been managed by the public sector, however inadequately, would Council members' influence and power be diminished?

CPDC engaged the services of an influential South Philadelphia ward leader, attorney and former State Representative, Nicholas Maiale, as a consultant, and Rubin and Maiale met individually with each of the seventeen Council members. Maiale's longstanding personal relationships with many Council members, such as fellow South Philadelphian Anna Verna, facilitated access and communication, but Maiale's influence was not the only factor that swayed Council members, More than a few, after hearing a presentation by Rubin and Maiale, supported the proposal on its merits. They were already convinced that the City did not have the capability to maintain the downtown area to high-quality standards, and the fact that the district would be funded by private property owners made the initiative far less politically risky than a taxpayer-funded plan would have been. In addition, Council's authorizing legislation was to contain a "sunset" provision, ending the plan unless Council voted to reauthorize it after the end of five years of operation. The sunset provision had been proposed by the CCD organizers in advance, in order to address concerns that had been raised by some owners that the CCD might evolve into a runaway authority that would end up producing more disadvantages than benefits over the long term. The Philadelphia Parking Authority's powers had been expanded in 1981, a decision that some had come to regret by the end of the decade as the Authority gained a reputation for political-patronage hiring and investments in questionable ventures.

Communication with Council members, designed to set the stage for formal Council buy-in to the district proposal, was extremely time consuming, and the experience was a new one for Ronald Rubin, who, during the course of his career, had done his best to avoid having to deal with elected officials. However, the effort paid off, with substantial majority votes in favor of both ordinances. The support of Mayor Goode for the district proposal may have influenced some Council members to vote for the measures, but the strong community sentiment in favor of the district proposal was likely to have been the most significant factor for Council members who had previously been undecided.

In October 1989, Peter Wiley, the person whose enthusiasm for the district concept had been the catalyst for the organizing activities that began four years previously, died in a plane crash. Without his involvement, the three campaigns of 1985–1990 would not have been launched. Given the proliferation of district management organizations that were created in cities across the country during the late twentieth century, the concept would eventually have emerged in Philadelphia at some other time, and would have been authorized and implemented in some form. However, the period in which Wiley was helping to advance the proposal was a time when—based on the condition of downtown, the political environment in Philadelphia, and the state of business leadership—the prospects for success were highly promising, a time when a sense of crisis and the perception of opportunity converged, with results that benefitted everyone.

Ronald Rubin had previously been introduced to Paul Levy, who was employed as a senior administrator at a University of Pennsylvania-affiliated real estate development organization, and Rubin subsequently interviewed Levy with the intent of hiring him to head the district. In March 1990, following City Council approval of the district concept, Levy was offered the job of Executive Director of CPDC, the position that had been held by Peter Wiley; he accepted, and began work that month. Rubin was especially pleased with Levy's ability to use his entrepreneurial skills to advance the district's key objectives. "He's just like Dan Biederman in New York City," a fellow board member recalls Rubin saying. Levy took charge of CCD operations in January, 1991. By that time, Levy had drafted the district plan and budget and had managed community meetings and the public hearings leading up to the City Council actions in the fall of 1990. The CCD street cleaning program was launched in March, 1991, followed by the introduction of its public safety program during the next month.

Milestones and Metrics

You don't start a business with ten different product lines, Ronald Rubin had said. So, for the first eighteen months of its existence, the Center City District focused almost entirely on cleaning and public safety. At its beginning, CCD operations were supported by a budget of $6.3 million and managed by an administrative staff of three people. Through contracts executed with a private firm, the CCD retained the services of one hundred uniformed maintenance personnel, who vacuumed the sidewalks daily and power-washed them monthly, as well as forty uniformed "community service representatives," who served as "eyes on the street," working in coordination with the Police Department. Following the receipt of competitive bid proposals for the operation of the community service representative program, the firm selected to contract with CCD was an organization that had previously operated the Philadelphia Park Ranger program. A year later, the CCD decided to operate this program element in-house rather than as a contracted service.

After the task of cleaning and providing security within the area had been mastered, the CCD launched its first promotional campaign in 1992, in collaboration with area businesses. "Make It a Night," designed to attract people to Center City shopping and dining destinations on selected Wednesday evenings, combined extended store hours, discounted parking rates and public transit fares, and live music and other entertainment on the sidewalks and streets. The first "Make It a Night" event in September generated significantly higher sales in some stores, and everyone was pleased with the turnout. By 8pm, according to a count conducted by CCD staff at key

Figure 2.4 CCD-Financed Streetscape Improvements

locations, pedestrian traffic was 144 percent higher than it had been during the same week night and time in June.[44]

In 1994, the year before the mandated "sunset" provision included in the City Council legislation approving the CCD was to take effect, Council approved a reauthorization of the district through 2015 without controversy. Prior to the reauthorization, the CCD had funded the design and implementation of a Center City streetscape plan; the project was known as "Investing in a Walkable City." The length of the new term that City Council had authorized, and the fact that the CCD collected its own property assessment revenue, enabled the organization to issue bonds to finance additional Center City streetscape improvements. The completion of the streetscape projects gave CCD staff valuable experience in project management and in leveraging funding from sources other than the property assessment. A decade later, the CCD was organizing and managing projects that were financed entirely by non-CCD sources.

A second reauthorization of the district, approved by City Council in 2004 and extending through 2025, enabled the CCD to refinance the 1995 streetscape improvement bonds at a lower interest rate.[45] In 1995, officers of the Central Philadelphia Development Corporation began exploring the possibility of reconnecting CPDC and the CCD. A merger of the two organizations had been proposed years earlier, but CPDC had rejected this proposal in light of the organization's desire to preserve the distinction between CPDC's role as an independent advocacy organization and CCD's status as a municipal authority. However, in light of the subsequent "greater visibility of the District, its similar geographic scope, and the continuing challenge of fundraising," CPDC's officers decided to revisit this issue. Subsequent dialogue and planning concluded in 1997, at which time the two organizations entered into an agreement to have the CCD manage the day-to-day operations of CPDC. The organizations did not merge, but retained their status as two distinct legal entities.[46]

In 1997, City Council instituted the first of the ten-year tax abatements by approving a bill drafted by an attorney who had been retained by CCD leadership. The CCD leaders had initially begun working on this project by themselves (influenced by the success of a similar abatement in Manhattan), but, after learning of Councilman Frank DiCicco's communication with real estate developers about the value of such a measure, subsequently collaborated with him in drafting the bill.

The ten-year tax abatement and the CCD's successful performance in managing downtown stimulated a high volume of new residential development in Center City, particularly after the turn of the century. According to CCD data, 3,273 new housing units had appeared within the CCD's service area boundaries between 2000 and mid-2008 alone.[47]

In 2008, The CCD opened a café on a formerly under-developed public plaza on the Benjamin Franklin Parkway, the boulevard that extends diagonally from the vicinity of City Hall to the Philadelphia Museum of Art. For this business venture, the CCD took on the role of designer, developer, owner, and landlord, a role similar to that of the "catalytic downtown company" recommended in the 2005 Brookings Institution "Turning Around Downtown" publication but with few of the risks associated with the model that had been proposed by the author of the Brookings report.

Two decades after its formation, the Center City District experience provides insight into how the performance and impact of a special services district can be evaluated, by examining performance metrics, observing characteristics of the physical environment, and obtaining anecdotal information and insights.

The Center City District's annual "State of Center City" publication highlights performance measures associated with key CCD goals. For example, consistent with the goal of "ensur[ing] that downtown opens clean each morning and remains that way throughout the day," the 2008 "State of Center City" publication reports that CCD employees bagged three million gallons of trash on sidewalks and removed more than 400 graffiti tags and stickers from the downtown streetscape during the report year.[48] Although the CCD community service representatives who circulate on the downtown streets seven days a week are not police officers, it would be difficult to argue that their presence did not contribute to reduced crime and increased perceptions of safety in the area. The 2008 State of Center City publication reported that major crime in Center City decreased by almost 39 percent since 1997, and nuisance crimes, such as theft from auto, declined by nearly 79 percent during this period.[49]

As important as actual performance is the perception of the downtown environment by the people whom the district wants to attract and keep. In order to monitor perceptions of the downtown consumer populations, the CCD engages a market research firm to conduct an annual customer satisfaction survey. In 2007, the firm surveyed 2,004 consumers, including residential and commercial property owners, apartment and office tenants, and retailers. Included in the survey were random "intercepts" of 937 individuals who were approached at eight different downtown locations. The 2007 survey results included the following findings:

- 80 percent of the respondents reported seeing uniformed CCD personnel on the streets "every time" or "nearly every time" they are in Center City.
- 63 percent indicated that Center City is much cleaner than other areas of the city.
- 73 percent stated that they feel safe in the downtown area all of the time or most of the time.
- 59 percent reported that the general atmosphere of the downtown was somewhat better or much better than in the prior year.[50]

The survey also provides an opportunity for consumers to report additional improvements that are needed, and emerging or persistent problems that should be addressed—in effect, identifying the issues that should become high priorities on CCD's agenda. In the 2007 survey, more than half of the respondents identified as "Priorities for Improving Center City" the following: "Reduce number of people sleeping or lying in public places" (70 percent of respondents) and "Provide more accessible and affordable parking" (54 percent). Between a third and half of the respondents identified as priorities "Better enforce municipal codes for deteriorated and neglected public properties" (45 percent), "Fix deteriorated sidewalks" (42 percent), and "Reduce the amount of traffic congestion" (38 percent).

The survey is detailed enough to make it useful to CCD management in identifying operational needs for improvement. In the 1993 survey, for example, one performance-related variable is "Proportion of respondents who believe the sidewalk cleaning staff seems to be standing around talking a lot."

Since, as of 2009, the CCD had been an investor in the downtown area for nearly two decades, CCD's impact can be assessed by measuring the organization's receipt, allocation, and expenditure of funds to develop and improve the area. For example, the CCD "capital program summary" for 2007 includes eight lighting, signage, and streetscape installation and improvement projects that were supported with $2.3 million in financing. A CCD funding commitment of $358,000 leveraged nearly $2 million in other funding, most of it from charitable foundations ($829,000) and other nongovernmental sources ($521,000).[51]

A district organization's impact can also be assessed by examining its role in creating an identity for the downtown area and in promoting opportunities for investors, developers, and consumers. For most of its existence, the CCD has demonstrated leadership in this role through planning and promotion initiatives.

The CCD has published a variety of planning studies, completed in-house as well as through the engagement of consultants, that have influenced subsequent government and private-sector investment decisions and have informed CCD's own work. In 1996, CCD published "Turning on the Lights Upstairs," a guide for converting upstairs space in older commercial buildings to residential use. To complete a 2007 publication, "Center City: Design for Growth 2007–2012," CCD engaged seven design firms to examine existing conditions and opportunities for improvement in four downtown subareas.[52]

The CCD promotes downtown attractions to consumers in many ways. Events such as Make It a Night and Restaurant Week achieved major success in bringing more shoppers and diners to Center City. In 1998, CCD launched a promotional campaign designed to contrast the appeal of downtown attractions with a negative portrayal of the suburban experience. One visual from this campaign, entitled "Culture," displayed a container of plain yogurt (suburbs) juxtaposed with a dramatic image of the Philadelphia

Orchestra (Center City). In another, entitled "Night Light," a photo of a plug-in night light (suburbs) was displayed next to a photo of Center City's vibrant nighttime skyline.

CCD has also achieved a high level of sophistication in publishing and disseminating direct marketing products. For example, CCD's Retail Attraction Kit includes market statistics and information on retail, restaurant, and visitor attractions in five Center City subareas, along with a Retail Occupancy Survey summary and a listing of major real estate development ventures, completed and under way.[53] A "Welcome to our Neighborhood" packet, distributed to each newly-occupied condominium and townhouse unit, contains brochures and flyers describing Center City events and attractions. The packet also includes a detailed regional transit map that is superior to comparable products available through the region's public transit agencies.

Although all of these factors can be useful in assessing a district organization's performance and impact, the best way to do so is to observe conditions in the downtown area firsthand. Look for the presence or absence of negatives: litter, graffiti, panhandling. Observe the characteristics of the "street culture": the appearance and activities of those who populate the sidewalks and public spaces. When downtown revitalization is successful, Paul Levy told me, "the public environment takes on a different character. 13th Street used to be a center for prostitution, vagrancy, and drug sales; now it's filled with restaurants and shops, as a result of private investment and consumer demand."[54] 13th Street is one of many Center City streets where outdoor "sidewalk cafés"—people dining at tables and chairs set up outside restaurants during the warmer months—has proliferated. In 1995, there were no sidewalk cafés in Center City; in 2008, there were 215.[55]

Other ways to assess performance and impact are to look for district organization staff, for evidence that streetscapes and stores are being improved. Look at the extent to which the area conveys a sensation of density and energy—of things going on—but also conveys a sense that downtown surroundings are managed and cared for. One of the best-known illustrations of such an environment is Michigan Avenue in downtown Chicago, where the streets are clean, attractively-landscaped, well-maintained, lined with retail attractions, and filled with people. Ironically, Chicago does not have a district management organization and has no need for one because, from Levy's perspective, the city has "a totally dedicated mayor, a dedicated [that is, downtown-specific] government workforce, a huge public investment in landscaping and parks, and a visible police presence."[56]

One of the best ways to gain insights into the impact of initiatives to improve a downtown area is by listening to stories and anecdotes about the nature of visiting, living in, or doing business in the area. Ronald Rubin's anecdote about his call to the Mayor in preparation for the Tiffany visit characterized the state of Center City in the late 1980s. By 1991, there would have been no need for a phone call to the mayor. By 2009, the idea that such a conversation would need to take place seems beyond belief.

The Future

Today, decades after the implementation of the Market Street West and East development plans, public recognition of the contribution of ventures such as Penn Center and the Gallery to the vastly improved downtown environment that now exists has faded, while awareness of the shortcomings of these plans has become more evident. In a similar way, the substantially higher standards of performance in downtown management that the CCD achieved, by using available resources skillfully in order to overcome extremely difficult challenges, are now taken for granted as the norm for Center City. A substantial number of the residents, shoppers, businesspeople, and visitors who now populate Philadelphia's downtown never saw the area during the 1980s. Many people's expectations of what Center City should look like were shaped entirely during the twenty-first century.

Downtown Philadelphia provides a good illustration of the need for planning and related strategic investment to be ongoing. Although the CCD is a model of success in postindustrial downtown management in many respects, significant problems remain to be addressed. Petty crime is a persistent problem on Market Street East, in and near the Gallery. Many upstairs spaces in retail-corridor properties remain vacant, even on blocks near Rittenhouse Square and Independence Hall. Homelessness—"a problem we thought had been solved," as one CCD board member put it—has re-emerged, and Center City's homeless population has grown. City officials and business leaders have yet to reach agreement on the best balance between the right of access to public spaces and the maintenance of appropriate standards of behavior in the public environment.

Two decades of high-quality downtown management has not stimulated enough of the real estate development that Philadelphia needs. In 1993, 41 percent of the region's office space had been located in Philadelphia's central business district; in 2007, Center City's market share had dropped to 28 percent, below the national average of 33 percent and lower than the regional market-share percentage of eight other cities.[57] Although "Ritten-house Row," extending along Walnut Street west of Broad, is the location for many upscale retail establishments, Center City needs much more higher-quality retail development in order to compete successfully for convention visitors and tourists, and to favorably influence return-visit decisions. In the early years of the twenty-first century, plans for a major new retail venture anchored by a Nordstrom's fell through when the prospective developer and the Board of City Trusts (a City-related entity, which owned the develop-ment site) were unable to reach agreement on the property acquisition transaction.

A late-2008 proposal to build a casino on top of the Gallery would seem to be the antithesis of the planning principles articulated by Jacobs and White, as described earlier in this chapter. The Gallery plan was being proposed by the casino developer as an alternative to building a gaming facility at a

Delaware River waterfront location that had previously been authorized by the state, but had drawn strong opposition from neighborhood and civic groups, and was opposed by Philadelphia Mayor Michael Nutter, who took office after the state approval. A casino atop the Gallery could drain the vitality out of the Market Street East area, increase traffic congestion, and generate new social problems. Alternatively, a casino atop the Gallery could leverage the development of a new hotel on a vacant lot across the street, could serve as the first demonstration of a major casino development directly linked to public transit (the rail lines at the Gallery's subsurface level), and would free the Delaware River site for better reuses. Which choice would be in the best interests of Center City and the citizens of Philadelphia?

No district management organizations existed in any city until well after the mid-twentieth century. In the twenty-first-century postindustrial city, should these district management organizations be regarded as a necessity? In a city led by a mayor with a Daley-like commitment to downtown, comparable political power, longevity unfettered by term limits, and comparable access to money, municipal government could take over downtown-management responsibilities. But how many cities possess these characteristics or are likely to have them in the foreseeable future?

The CCD is a good example of the alternative: the engagement of business leadership and funding (in the form of commitments to pay the property assessment) to buy an enhanced downtown environment. However, because many business leaders, and many citizens as well, did not regard the creation of a district management organization as a necessity for Philadelphia's downtown during 1985–1990, the success of the CCD plan as it had been proposed during these years was far from assured. Had the late-1980s version of the plan failed, Philadelphia's experience probably would have been comparable to that of other cities with less successful district management organizations: the responsibility for downtown revitalization would have been shared by a district organization with limited capability, working in coordination with municipal planning, development, and public service agencies—an approach that would make it difficult to both manage routine activities as well as to address new challenges.

The question of whether the primary responsibility for a particular downtown falls to municipal government, to a district management organization, or to some combination of both, though very important, is secondary. What is fundamental is the reality that, in the years ahead, older cities will have to be more effective in repositioning their downtowns to compete more successfully in the metropolitan region than they had been during the late twentieth century. To do so, real estate development and improvement activities designed to create a better physical plan for the downtown area need to be accompanied by an operating plan for downtown, one that will raise the quality of the social environment to the level needed to repopulate the city's center with more consumers in today's residential, office, retail, and visitor markets.

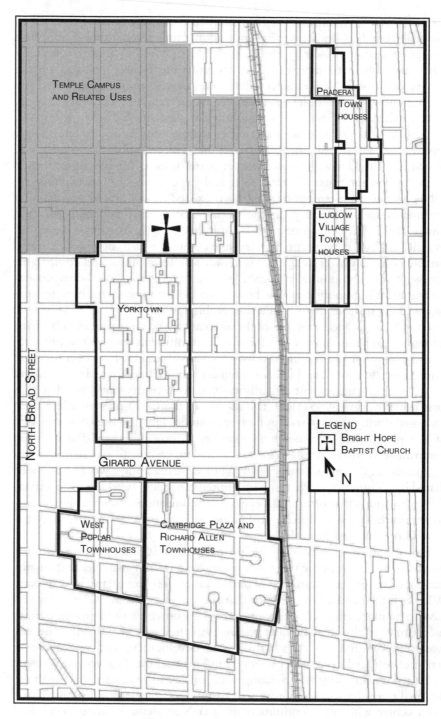

TEMPLE CAMPUS
AND RELATED USES

PRADERA
TOWN
HOUSES

LUDLOW
VILLAGE
TOWN
HOUSES

YORKTOWN

NORTH BROAD STREET

GIRARD AVENUE

LEGEND

BRIGHT HOPE
BAPTIST CHURCH

N

WEST
POPLAR
TOWNHOUSES

CAMBRIDGE PLAZA AND
RICHARD ALLEN
TOWNHOUSES

Figure 3.1 Eastern North Philadelphia

3   The Transition Zone

Rebuilding Eastern North Philadelphia

Depopulation Centers

A transition zone geographically links two urban areas, possessing characteristics of each but belonging to neither. In an older city, as you travel into a transition zone from a place that is defined by a consistent pattern of land use and development, the pattern is disrupted; the size, scale, design, use, and occupancy of land and buildings become more diverse and less organized. Development in many transition zones predated zoning laws. In these places, houses may share blocks with factories, garages, warehouses, stables, or scrap yards.

For postindustrial cities, the most important transition zones are those that lie between the central business district and the settled residential areas that can be found some distance away from the downtown edge. These central city transition zones, many of which had been developed as factories and high-density worker housing during the nineteenth and early twentieth centuries, later experienced high levels of property abandonment and population loss. By the end of the twentieth century, as some downtowns were achieving modest gains in population, adjacent transition zones were still losing residents.

Transition zone development can reinforce investment in the central business district and attract additional housing, business, and job opportunities on the downtown margin. Without a plan for reinvestment in the central city transition zone, the economic stability of both the downtown area and the neighborhoods that lie on the other side of the zone is weakened and economic opportunity is unnecessarily limited.

Some transition zones fix themselves; the private real estate market adapts to changing circumstances without the need for direct government intervention. Blocks of factories in Boston's Fort Point area, separated from the city's financial center by a narrow harbor channel, became part of a high-value housing market by the turn of the century, with many conversions of older multi-story industrial buildings into high-priced condominiums and apartments. Other transition zones experience a prolonged decline in property values and economic activity and appear to offer no prospects for improvement in the absence of government action. In Baton Rouge, a deteriorated, high-vacancy, mixed-use corridor that extends from downtown to the LSU campus is being considered for designation as a redevelopment area. The proximity of this corridor to the central business district on one end of the zone and the university campus on the other has not been sufficient to stimulate real estate market activity leading to a significant improvement of the physical environment.

At the turn of the century, Philadelphia had a large, unevenly proportioned transition zone bordering the northern edge of Center City. The most de-populated, least organized blocks in the zone could be found east of Broad Street. The lower segment of this east-of-Broad area, between Vine and Spring Garden Streets, began to fix itself starting in the late 1990s, as the city's ten-year tax abatement, downtown revitalization, and the resurgent national real estate market influenced the completion of many residential develop-ment projects (including infill townhouse construction on vacant land and industrial-to-residential factory building conversions) that gave this area a much stronger residential character.

The east-of-Broad area north of Spring Garden did not fix itself, and the redefinition of this area was achieved in large part as the result of three major interventions supported by public sector funding. These interventions illus-trate the ways in which planning, goal-setting, and the execution of develop-ment activity can resolve some key questions about the future of the transition zone and the city while leaving others unaddressed.

The Hollow Core

Older industrial cities originated as transportation nodes and centers of commerce. Cities expanded as new settlements were developed on former farmlands and forests. Urban expansion patterns were concentric but uneven rather than uniform, like misshapen tree-trunk rings or onion layers. Growth opportunities in one direction or another were enhanced or constrained by topography, by the location of natural resources such as rivers, mountains, and valleys, by pre-existing political boundaries, and by the extent of oppor-tunities to annex adjacent areas. However, a basic spreading-out pattern recurred in most cities; as one section was built up and filled in, development activity moved further outward.

Cities did not depopulate in the same way as they grew.[1] Population growth had been relatively systematic, a movement outward from existing boundaries or along transportation corridors. Population loss was unsystematic and disorderly. People did not leave cities in the same manner as they had entered them, with outer-edge population fading first as the city demographic shrank. Disinvestment occurred in dispersed pockets and clusters: a family moved away, a factory complex closed, an apartment building burned to the ground, a small business failed, an elderly homeowner died. The disinvested city did not resemble a peeled onion; it resembled a moth-eaten fabric, a woven surface disrupted by holes and frayed edges.

As citywide population decline became a chronic condition, some cities experienced a contradictory pattern, in which significant growth occurred in certain residential areas while population declined nearly everywhere else. Between 1950 and 1960, for example, the population of Philadelphia's Far Northeast, near the city's border with Bucks County, increased from 26,000 to 66,000 (152 percent), as the area was developed with single-family subdivisions, while the city's overall population shrank from 2,071,605 to 2,002,512 (−3 percent).[2]

By the turn of the century, this combination of growth and decline was still evident, but the geography had changed. In an analysis published by the Brookings Institution's Center on Urban and Metropolitan Policy, Alan Berube and Benjamin Forman reported that, while population in Philadelphia's central business district grew by 8.8 percent between 1990 and 2000, citywide population shrank by 4 percent during the same period. In their analysis, an examination of population change in one hundred U.S. cities, Berube and Forman focused on each city's central business district and three other groups of aggregated census tracts, which they defined in terms of their distance from the CBD: an "inner core," "middle ring," and "outer ring" (the "inner core" includes both the CBD and nearby census tracts).

For Philadelphia between 1990 and 2000, Berube and Forman reported the results shown in Table 3.1. As shown, the most depopulated area of Philadelphia—the non-CBD inner core—was immediately adjacent to the area experiencing the most growth during the 1990s. The rate of population loss in the non-CBD inner core tracts was high enough to offset the 8.8 percent rate of CBD population gain, producing a net inner core population loss of 7.2 percent. At the same time, the outer ring of census tracts, including those in the Far Northeast and elsewhere in the vicinity of Philadelphia's city-suburban boundaries, experienced the lowest rate of population decline of the three "rings." This "hollowing out" pattern, in which inner core tracts were found to experience the highest rate of population decline, was found in a number of other disinvested cities, including Buffalo, Dayton, Detroit, Indianapolis, and Kansas City.[3]

North Philadelphia, the northern tier of Philadelphia's "inner core" was Philadelphia's center of population loss and property abandonment. The Philadelphia City Planning Commission's "North Philadelphia Plan," published in 1978, characterized North Philadelphia as a place where:

> There is far more vacant land . . . than in any other area of the City
> . . .
>
> The inventory of unused land has steadily increased with the demolition of abandoned structures and the absence of marketable or locally acceptable alternative uses. Trash accumulates and weeds grow

Table 3.1 Philadelphia Population Change by Subarea, 1990–2000

Population Change	%
City	−4.0
Central Business District	8.8
Inner Core (including CBD)	−7.2
Middle Ring	−4.9
Outer Ring	−1.1

Source: Alan Berube and Benjamin Forman, "Living on the Edge: Decentralization Within Cities in the 1990s" (Washington, D.C.: The Brookings Institution Center on Urban and Metropolitan Policy, October 2002), p. 10.

on much of the vacant land . . . The presence of vacant lots and the lack of maintenance depress property values and discourage investment . . .

Ownership of these parcels is divided between an array of public agencies . . . and private owners. Most of the privately-held parcels are tax delinquent; many receive little or no ongoing maintenance by their owners.[4]

Re-emphasizing that "the market for development is relatively weak and parcels often have little prospect for new development," the Plan reported that, "The most successful land reclamation program in North Philadelphia has involved self-help gardening."[5]

North Philadelphia's vacant land was the result of government demolition of abandoned buildings, conducted over several decades. Lower North Philadelphia, the area between Spring Garden Street and Lehigh Avenue, "had the dubious distinction of being chosen as the first site for slum clearance under the 1949 federal redevelopment legislation. Between 1950 and 1962 more than 10,000 housing units were demolished . . . "[6] During the early 1970s, continuation of a slum clearance approach was supported by the chair of the Philadelphia City Planning Commission, based on the expectation that "many 'nonviable' neighborhoods would at some future time be able to attract private investment if the land were vacant and available at a low price."[7]

The effects of these policies were particularly evident in the West Poplar neighborhood where, according to the City Planning Commission's 1978 "Eastern North Philadelphia Plan," population had declined by 39 percent between 1960 and 1970, during which time the number of housing units decreased from 4,427 to 2,962. In 1977, 30.6 percent of the structures in the neighborhood were characterized as "abandoned."[8]

The eastern half of Lower North Philadelphia had experienced the most demolition, a substantial amount of which was associated with new construction plans that called for the assemblage of large cleared sites. Temple University, chartered as Temple College in 1888, expanded its campus during the post–World War Two decades, when, in the words of two historians, Temple, "with the aid of federal and state funds transformed what was formerly one of the worst slum areas of Philadelphia into a great university center."[9] Much of Temple's expansion took place within a rectangular area consisting of five pairs of blocks extending north and south along the east side of Broad Street.

During the late 1950s and early 1960s, nearly a dozen blocks south of the Temple main campus were cleared and developed as the Yorktown community, a new neighborhood of 635 sales townhouses built in a postwar suburban style, with front yards, driveways, and adjacent surface parking areas. The Yorktown plan was organized by a coalition of African-American church, civic, and neighborhood groups, with Bright Hope Baptist Church, centrally located between the southern edge of the Temple campus and the northern edge of the new community, playing a key role. Built by a suburban developer on blocks acquired and cleared by the city's Redevelopment Authority, Yorktown was marketed to African-American working families during a time when nonwhites were being denied access to suburban subdivisions elsewhere in the region. Yorktown succeeded in attracting homebuyers who represented a variety of blue- and white-collar professions. In the words of one resident, the community "had what was built for other races."[10]

During the late twentieth century, depopulated areas with large amounts of vacant land were selected as locations for the construction of public housing, based on then-prevailing federal regulations that influenced the development of high-rise buildings and densely populated blocks. Two post–World War Two public housing ventures, Cambridge Plaza and Richard Allen Homes, by the mid-1970s accounted for 40 percent of West Poplar's housing stock and occupied nearly one quarter of the neighborhood's land area.[11] Cambridge Plaza's 371 units were located in two high-rise towers surrounded by low-rise rowhouses, while the 1,324-unit Richard Allen Homes consisted of disconnected, barracks-style rows interspersed with parking areas and undeveloped or poorly maintained open space.

Notwithstanding the expansion of Temple University, the development of Yorktown, and the construction of the two public housing sites, the eastern half of Lower North Philadelphia remained a high-vacancy area until nearly the end of the twentieth century. Community anger over the residential displacement associated with Temple University's expansion during the urban renewal era resulted in the execution of a "covenant" by University administrators and community representatives, documenting Temple's commitment to limit further expansion of its campus to parcels within a restricted geography specified in the agreement. Redevelopment Authority-owned cleared-land parcels in West Poplar remained vacant, due to lack of marketability and to federally-imposed moratoriums (in effect during the 1970s and 1980s) prohibiting the use of HUD funding to finance new housing construction. In the "Eastern North Philadelphia Plan" and the "North

Philadelphia Plan," no major new development was proposed for West Poplar, for the Ludlow community east of Yorktown, or for the "Temple Area," immediately east of the Temple main campus.

In a city that has experienced a half-century of depopulation and property abandonment, why would it make sense to plan for any new development in inner-core areas such as Eastern North Philadelphia? Given the fact that, in a disinvested city, many of the homes that people leave will not be occupied by new residents, the city will accumulate an oversupply of existing houses. Why not focus on just upgrading those houses that are still standing and, consistent with the Planning Commission policy described above, wait for the private market to eventually take care of the rest?

Government investment in a depopulated urban "inner core" makes sense because of the area's proximity to valued assets: the downtown district, nearby academic and health care institutions, and, in many cities, adjacent waterfronts or parklands. A strategic approach to government investment in these areas can reinforce existing assets, such as Temple University, and make use of them as anchors for new development, as the Temple campus anchored the development of the adjacent Yorktown community. The alternative—years of inactivity, spent waiting for a private market fix for these areas—will lead to further degradation and, when development arrives, the result may be poorly organized and low quality.

On the other hand, not all depopulated centers should be considered priorities for development. Some should be given lower-priority status because of their poor location, because the cost of new development outweighs anticipated benefits, or because of severe social problems that need to be addressed before development can succeed. Plans to develop large vacant tracts in order to address a social goal or to conduct an experiment often prove to be risky, expensive, and far less successful than anticipated. Developer James Rouse committed the resources of the Enterprise Foundation (and leveraged substantial commitments of city government and charitable foundation resources) in support of the rebuilding of Baltimore's Sandtown-Winchester neighborhood because he "saw an opportunity to demonstrate that any inner city neighborhood, no matter how distressed, could be transformed." The results of an associated commitment to rehabilitate 600 vacant houses in the neighborhood "ignored the reality of the city's depopulation. While hundreds of these homes have been fixed up and sold . . . many other homes in the community had become vacant, with the pace of degradation exceeding that of rehabilitation."[12] In Philadelphia during the 1990s, OHCD rejected two ambitious proposals for rebuilding the Logan neighborhood, where more than 800 families had been displaced from "sinking homes" made structurally unviable due to soil-subsidence conditions (the neighborhood had been developed during the nineteenth and early twentieth centuries on a former cinder and ash landfill, which began to erode decades later due to inadequate stormwater drainage). Both Logan reconstruction proposals had significant political backing, and OHCD's rejection of them generated anger and controversy. But any large-scale new development would have necessitated a public investment, estimated at $40 million or more in site preparation costs, to install new infrastructure, acquire privately-owned properties, and complete intensive soil compaction throughout the area.

Beginning in the 1990s, real opportunities emerged to build out the eastern half of Lower North Philadelphia. The federal moratorium on the use of HUD funds to finance new housing construction had ended. Federal policies calling for the replacement of high-density public housing sites with mixed income communities were instituted, and financing became available to implement them. The City provided more funding for vacant property acquisition, and more non-government funding was available to be leveraged to support development by community-based organizations. Three different initiatives to develop large sections of this area were launched during the 1990s, producing similar results: the replacement of rowhouse or high-rise housing with new single-family homes on large lots. The appearance of these three development ventures was so similar that they might have been mistaken for a single project. However, these initiatives differed significantly in terms of purpose, execution, and impact, and the reasons for choosing the lower tier of Eastern North Philadelphia as a site for large-scale construction.

Robert Moses, Jr.

Following the Flag Day meeting at which Mayor Rendell offered to appoint me Housing Director on a permanent basis (described in the Introduction), I had to decide how I would do what my predecessors had been criticized for not doing: invest public funds strategically in a way that would produce positive results on a large scale. Twelve months later, I proposed a new approach for residential development in the core of Lower North Philadelphia, the area south of the Temple main campus and half a dozen blocks on either side of Broad Street. The concept was described in a publication issued by my office, entitled "Home in North Philadelphia." The first page summarized the reasons why "Lower North Philadelphia Needs a Better Housing Strategy":

- To protect the interests of current residents . . . who have chosen to live in Lower North Philadelphia neighborhoods [and] need to feel that their commitment is justified and that the area will be worth living in during the coming years . . .
- To balance nearby private development and stabilize neighborhood development patterns. [Corporate and institutional development in the area] needs to be complemented by reinvestment in housing . . . so that non-residential development will not become the dominant feature of the area.

- To offset development pressure . . . from nearby Center City neighborhoods . . . to protect the area as an affordable housing resource at a time when housing costs in adjacent Center City neighborhoods continue to increase.
- To protect past public and private investment [in neighborhoods that] have received substantial public funding through urban renewal and community development programs.[13]

The publication was critical of past development efforts in the area. "The lack of a coherent area-wide housing strategy," I wrote, "has generated some serious problems which need to be resolved to make Lower North Philadelphia a strong residential area for the 1990s and the 21st century." Publicly-subsidized sales housing development ventures were competing against each other in a weak homebuyer market. Proposed housing plans were calling for high-density rowhouse development, despite the fact that "Philadelphia in the 1990s does not need the same high level of housing density as it did a century before, when North Philadelphia was a manufacturing center with worker housing clustered around factories." Government funding was being spread around the area, with the most funding restricted to relatively small target areas, leaving the rest of the remainder "with far less funding than the amount needed to support a broad residential reinvestment program leading to permanent improvement." And the high level of vacancy and abandonment in Lower North Philadelphia (where an estimated 1,230 vacant houses and 1,711 vacant lots were located) made it particularly difficult to market the area for large-scale new development.[14]

To address these problems, "Home in North Philadelphia" called for a unified, area-wide housing strategy. The strategy should be supported by a consolidated pool of public funding, in order to produce higher-impact development and take advantage of economies of scale, and should be implemented on a long-term basis, over a period of five years or more. City interventions should build off prior investment, reinforcing "centers of strength" such as the Yorktown community. New housing development should be lower-density, in order to spread the impact of investment over a broader area, to make use of more of the area's substantial vacant acreage, and to provide residents with amenities such as side and rear yards.[15] Lower-density development pursued over a multi-year period would result in a build-out of the area, shrinking the vacant property inventory and linking previously disconnected target areas to create a broad zone of reinvestment.

Based on the principles set forth in the "Home in North Philadelphia" publication, a Lower North Philadelphia strategy was organized in late 1993, and this approach remained in effect through the end of the Rendell Administration in 1999. A "Home in North Philadelphia" category was created in the housing budget to fund acquisition and development in the neighborhoods on both sides of Broad Street. Federal Nehemiah funds were used to build 176 new houses in the West Poplar neighborhood, where the

Figure 3.2 West Poplar Townhouses

Redevelopment Authority employed eminent domain powers to acquire vacant buildings and lots. Some occupied housing was acquired and some residents were relocated, but large-scale displacement did not occur because so much of the area was already vacant. A beer distributor located in the center of the development area was moved out at great expense. Vacant buildings were demolished and toxic soil was removed or cleaned up. Based on recommendations that grew out of a community planning process, the vacant land was subdivided into larger lots to accommodate bigger new houses with yards and driveways. Narrow streets and alleys were closed and made part of the rear yards of adjacent homes. Two cul de sacs were created to shelter residential blocks from the heavily trafficked Broad Street on the west and the deteriorating Richard Allen Homes public housing site on the east.

The policy generated development in other Lower North Philadelphia neighborhoods as well. The City successfully competed for federal Home-ownership Zone funding to implement a plan for the Cecil B. Moore neighborhood west of Broad that involved new housing construction on vacant land accompanied by the rehabilitation of existing nineteenth-century rowhouses and brownstones. A design competition cosponsored by my office and the Foundation for Architecture produced creative solutions for a collection of blocks in the Francisville community. An apartment building was developed in Yorktown to provide another housing option for elderly residents who, having remained in homes they had purchased in the 1960s, might now be ready to move to rental housing. Each year, another new block of mostly vacant and abandoned properties in the Ludlow community was acquired and developed with new sales housing. Acquisition and development started across the street from an existing neighborhood asset—Ascension Manor, an apartment complex developed in two phases during the 1960s and 1970s—and moved eastward, block by block, year by year. All in all, the Home in North Philadelphia policy produced the first large-scale housing development in Lower North Philadelphia in nearly half a century: 176 new single-family homes in West Poplar, 52 new homes in Ludlow, 85 sales and rental housing units in Francisville, and 126 sales and rental housing units in the Cecil B. Moore Homeownership Zone (part of a 296-unit housing production plan that was completed during the subsequent mayoral adminis-tration of John F. Street). Additional houses were built in Ludlow and the Homeownership Zone after I left OHCD in 2001.

The development activity drew attention. An article headlined, "Hope for the city's core: In a once-dead area, houses are being built and dreams rebuilt" appeared on the front page of *The Philadelphia Inquirer* in early 1998.[16] Later that month, the implementation of the Home in North Philadelphia policy was described in a *New York Times* article entitled "Philadelphia Neighborhood Reborn: Housing and Business Programs Create Stability and Optimism," which referred to my role in instituting a new reinvestment approach.[17] Speaking at a social event later that year, Rendell feigned dis-pleasure that the *Times* coverage had not included him. "They said a lot of good things about my administration," he said, "but unfortunately, they spelled my name K-r-o-m-e-r."

Just a few years later, the story of Lower North Philadelphia was told and interpreted in a different way—as a major mistake. Another front-page article about Lower North Philadelphia appeared in the *Inquirer* in April 2001. In place of "Hope for the city's core" was a different headline: "Rethinking revitalization: City officials thought investment in North Phila construc-tion would revive the area; it didn't." I wasn't quoted in the article, but Ed Schwartz, whom I had replaced as housing director in 1992, was. Schwartz said that, during his tenure, spending public money on new housing construction in blighted areas was "the dumbest mistake I made." The *Inquirer* reporter characterized the Lower North Philadelphia policy as a practice of "building new homes in blighted areas where hundreds of properties are abandoned," while the revitalization needs of more stable neighbor-hoods were given lower priority. Newly elected City Council member Darrell Clarke was quoted as saying, "You can ride through North Philadelphia and say nothing is going on."[18] Clarke, a former aide to then–Council President John Street (who had been elected Philadelphia's Mayor in 1999) repre-sented the Fifth Council District, the area that had benefited most from the Home in North Philadelphia policy; now he appeared to be one of the policy's leading critics.

But the criticism of the policy was bigger than one *Inquirer* article. Smart growth advocates disliked the low-density sites in the West Poplar and Ludlow subdivisions, as well as the "suburban-style" housing that had been constructed there, based on the community-endorsed plan. Advocates of new-urbanist principles agreed, and they disliked the cul de sacs too. Supporters of transit-oriented development—the policy of promoting real estate development in close proximity to transportation assets such as the Broad Street and Girard Avenue transit lines a block away from West Poplar—thought that higher-density development should have been the obvious choice for this development area. The *New Urban News* suggested that the plan for the Cecil B. Moore Homeownership Zone, which emphasized the preservation of existing neighborhood fabric along with infill construction on vacant lots, was the least innovative of the Homeownership Zone awardees because it did not involve a major redesign of the area. In response to a presentation I made to the trustees of a charitable foundation, Mayor Street's wife—who happened to be one of the trustees—questioned the decision to build out West Poplar exclusively with new homes, without including any retail, service, or recreational facilities in the overall plan.

So how do you respond to criticism from the Mayor's wife? Was she really convinced that the production of 176 new houses in West Poplar, requiring a massive commitment of funding and a greater level of housing-agency coordination than had occurred in decades, should be deemed unsatisfactory because food stores, human services facilities, and recreation centers were not provided as well? Who did she think I was, Robert Moses, Jr.?

If it had been possible to debate the issue at that trustees' meeting—and it hadn't been possible, nor would I have welcomed the opportunity—a number of responses could have been considered. Most urban neighborhoods of fewer than two hundred households don't have their own shopping, human service, or recreational facilities. The city was already overbuilt with playgrounds and recreation centers that had been developed in the 1960s and 1970s, based on the expectation that Philadelphia's population would grow past two million by the twenty-first century rather than shrink to 1.4 million. West Poplar is close to the downtown area, where some of the region's largest and most accessible stores, academic and health care institutions, and recreational facilities are located. Per HUD regulations, the Nehemiah funding obtained for West Poplar could only be used to finance housing, not other types of development. Neither the Commerce Department nor the City Planning Commission had the funding or staff resources to work with us in organizing a broader, more ambitious mixed-use development plan for the area.

But these arguments would have missed the point. The West Poplar development had a limited number of goals, all of which were consistent with the overall Home in North Philadelphia development plan: to build new housing at a larger scale; to reinforce and build out from the adjacent York-town community; to spread development out over a larger area; and to create a housing product that would be more attractive than standard government-subsidized housing and therefore more likely to sell in the weak mid-1990s real estate market within a neighborhood that had not experienced a high volume of real estate transactions since Eisenhower's time. The West Poplar experience was an excellent illustration of the principle that, although well-executed urban real estate development projects generate tangible benefits, their impact is limited. After the ribbons are cut, after the balloons are released, after the grand opening event ends, after the well-designed buildings are fully occupied, many important issues inevitably remain unresolved. How many schoolchildren would occupy the 176 West Poplar homes, and what was the quality and capacity of the schools they would attend? Where would these children spend their after-school and weekend hours? Where would the new West Poplar families shop for food, and how would their food-shopping choices influence current planning for two new supermarkets in Eastern North Philadelphia? How would the vacant land on Girard Avenue, a highly active neighborhood commercial corridor decades earlier, be developed in a manner that would support both the West Poplar and Yorktown neighborhoods for which the avenue served as a common boundary? Ideally, an active, ongoing planning process would have addressed these and other questions, including those raised by the Mayor's wife, as the new houses emerged from the ground in West Poplar.

So, given the critical need for ongoing planning, why wasn't such a process under way during the 1990s? The answer is that, although Home in North Philadelphia was a major Rendell Administration housing priority during that time, its priority status did not extend beyond housing. The City Planning Commission was more than busy enough with assignments involving other areas of the city. The highest North Philadelphia priorities of the Commerce Department, the agency with which OHCD could have collaborated on a Girard Avenue revitalization plan, lay elsewhere. Every agency regarded itself as underfunded, understaffed, and unable to take on new challenges without more resources. Mayor Rendell was not a vigorous advocate of planning, which he seemed to feel was unnecessarily time-consuming, while his need for decision-making was immediate. Although, as described in the Introduction, the management approach adopted by the Rendell Administration reduced infighting among municipal departments, it did not necessarily foster forward-thinking interagency collaboration.

The prospects for successful commercial development on Girard Avenue to complement the residential land uses north and south of the corridor were severely limited by the fact that an organization headed by a political ally of Street's had staked out a claim to several key development parcels along the avenue. A successful collaboration with the organization's leader seemed highly unlikely. During the 1990s, one redevelopment site obtained by the organization was developed as a discount drug store, built in the middle of a surface parking lot and lacking display windows that could have visually linked the store interior with Girard Avenue auto and pedestrian traffic. Another redevelopment site secured by the organization was to be developed as a retail shopping center, but the project was halted by construction-period litigation and remained unfinished years after groundbreaking; by 2009, it was still unbuilt. Plans for a supermarket on another Girard Avenue-area site never materialized but made the site unavailable to other prospective developers. These issues were important, but not important enough to warrant an attempt by Mayor Rendell to try to persuade Council President Street to strengthen the city administration's hand in determining how these sites would be developed.

The criticisms of West Poplar did not rise to the level of a major controversy and were soon overshadowed by the attention being devoted to the Neighborhood Transformation Initiative, a comprehensive neighborhood reinvestment policy that had been a key element of John Street's 1999 mayoral campaign and that was launched in 2001, a year after his inauguration as mayor. During these years and afterward, the Center City residential market expanded north of Vine Street, with ambitiously-priced condominiums, lofts, and new townhouses developed in formerly vacant buildings and lots between Vine and Spring Garden Streets, extending up to the southern boundary of the Home in North Philadelphia target area.

A few blocks north of Spring Garden Street, the final stages of the West Poplar townhouse development were completed after the turn of the century, and the last new residents moved in. Homeowners installed landscaping and garden plots, and furnished and decorated their porches. The street trees grew fuller, and the developed area began to take on the appearance of a settled community.

What You Have To Do

Bill Clinton took office in 1993, a year after the start of Mayor Rendell's first term, and Clinton appointed Henry Cisneros, the former mayor of San Antonio, as HUD Secretary. Later that year, Cisneros contacted Mayor Rendell and asked to meet with him and City Council President John Street privately, not at City Hall. A conference room was reserved at Rendell's former law firm, located in one of the generation of modern office towers that had been built on Market Street West during the previous decade. From the conference room, you could look down on the first of the ribbon-windowed Penn Center office buildings that had been constructed across from City Hall. Looking north of City Hall, you could see past the central business district—past the convention center, the old and new office buildings, the Vine Street Expressway—to Lower North Philadelphia. You could see the entire Home in North Philadelphia area. Even at that distance, the vacant acreage was visible.

I was notified of the meeting by Rendell's staff and told to attend. We knew the topic that Cisneros wanted to discuss: the Philadelphia Housing Authority (PHA) and the state of public housing in Philadelphia. The state of public housing in Philadelphia was disastrous. All of the descriptive terms employed in late twentieth-century urban-studies literature to depict the failed housing projects of the time[19]—crime-infested, drug-ridden, poorly-maintained, centers of poverty, unemployment, and social disorder—applied to the worst of Philadelphia's public housing inventory. Frustrated by PHA's persistently poor performance, HUD had taken over administrative control of the agency during George H.W. Bush's presidency, but no discernible progress in reforming the agency or improving the condition of PHA-owned housing had been achieved.

Cisneros was the most engaging federal appointed official you could ever hope to meet, and he and Rendell had maintained a friendly personal relationship from the start. Cisneros' background as a mayor who understood the challenges of managing an older city distinguished him from many other inhabitants of the federal-government infrastructure and made him a particularly valuable ally

After a few minutes of friendly conversation, Cisneros described the purpose of the meeting: to propose the creation of a new partnership between HUD and the City of Philadelphia in support of the improvement of the city's public housing system. Cisneros wanted Philadelphia's city government to get directly involved in the governance of the Philadelphia Housing Authority which, like other housing and redevelopment authorities, was not a municipal agency but a state-chartered entity, led by an appointed board. He wanted Mayor Rendell to become chair of the PHA board and City Council President Street to become vice chair. Through their leadership of PHA, they would demonstrate their commitment to public housing reform and would give a reform agenda credibility. For his part, Cisneros would end the HUD takeover of PHA and would make additional commitments of HUD resources to Philadelphia. As one example, he would find ways to help out with the redevelopment of one of the city's worst public housing sites: Southwark Plaza, a deteriorated tower complex in South Philadelphia.

For a few months that year, I had filled in as acting director of the Housing Authority to help manage the agency during a leadership transition while continuing to serve as OHCD director. I saw the interim appointment as an opportunity to pursue a personal goal: to dismantle key components of the dysfunctional housing authority and integrate them into the structure of municipal government. Cisneros was proposing collaboration; my goal had been to shrink the agency and eventually make it disappear. I had explored privatization strategies with housing policy and public finance experts. I had scheduled a daylong charette at HUD headquarters in pursuit of a plan to convey a thousand PHA-owned vacant houses and lots to private and nonprofit development organizations. Because PHA's maintenance and repair system was highly unreliable, I had arranged for the City's code enforcement agency to inspect substandard PHA-owned row houses, issue code-violation notices, and contract with a City-controlled agency, the Philadelphia Housing Development Corporation, to complete the repairs and bill PHA for the expense. Underlying these actions was my conviction that PHA should ultimately be taken apart. The Housing Authority had failed to uphold its responsibility to develop and maintain quality housing; in my view, PHA didn't deserve to exist.

These interventions might have produced constructive results over a period of years, but they had little impact during my brief tenure as PHA's interim director. The structure of the public housing system, particularly as it had existed in 1993, made substantive reform extremely difficult to achieve. The following obstacles to reform in Philadelphia had their equivalents in many large cities:

- The Mayor did not control the housing authority's governing board. Based on the authority's charter, two PHA board appointments were made by the Mayor, another two by the City Controller, and the fifth by the other four members. The board members' terms were staggered, with one member's term expiring each year, making a complete overhaul of the board unlikely or impossible in the short term. An incoming mayor might not even have control of the two mayoral appointees; if one or both of them chose not to offer their resignations, the new mayor would have to wait out their terms. A case in point: during his administration as Mayor, John Street held the position of PHA board chair, as Rendell had done previously, based on the commitment made to Cisneros. However, when Michael Nutter, a political adversary of Street's, succeeded him as Mayor in 2008, Street remained in place, with no indication that he would be leaving anytime soon.
- As a state-chartered agency, PHA's annual budget and plan was not subject to review and approval by the Mayor and City Council, the elected representatives of local government. Notwithstanding PHA's state charter, no state government agency provided oversight of the authority either.
- The federal regulatory structure that supported housing authorities across the country was archaic and resistant to change. In past decades, legislative and regulatory mandates had led to the construction of high-density public housing in high-poverty neighborhoods and had made it difficult or impossible for local housing authorities to screen out bad tenants. Regulations governing housing authority procurement, contracting, and financial management often made big-city housing authorities slower and less reliable than their counterparts in municipal government.

This situation was made even worse by the fact that, from a purely political perspective, public housing was a treasure chest. Those who controlled the housing authority could give someone a house, a contract, or a job. Those who controlled the housing authority had access to a large annual budget and the ability to spend money in a manner that was not subject to city or state approval, that would probably not be reviewed in detail by the authority's board members, and that would probably not be subject to HUD monitoring or auditing until years after expenditures had been made. From a political perspective, the best approach to housing authority management would be to place political operatives in key leadership positions while employing administrative staff with sufficient brainpower and technical expertise to manage the agency and stay a step ahead of HUD's inspector general.

Rendell and Street agreed to support Cisneros' partnership proposal and joined the PHA board (two board seats were available at the time). A new PHA Executive Director was hired; John F. White, Jr. had headed the Pennsylvania Department of Public Welfare after serving as a respected Philadelphia City Council member and state legislator. The competence and professionalism of the agency was significantly upgraded, working relationships with tenant council organizations improved, and more construction and repair projects were launched and completed. However, Philadelphia's public housing system did not change fundamentally until the appointment of Carl R. Greene as PHA Executive Director in 1998. During Greene's tenure, public housing development ventures also fundamentally changed the character of Philadelphia neighborhoods, including those in Lower North Philadelphia.

I had been too inexperienced to understand the need to clearly articulate goals and manage expectations. I had assumed that the West Poplar development would speak for itself: vacant tracts had been filled with high-quality housing; the houses had attracted buyers who were pleased with their new homes; the development plan had been favorably reviewed in the local and national media. What else was there to say? As described in the previous section, I later learned how important it was to be clear about the limitations of a venture such as the West Poplar townhouse development and about the additional work that needed to be done, on Girard Avenue and elsewhere in Lower North Philadelphia, during and after the construction of these homes. Carl Greene was more experienced than I, and he was candid about what to expect and not to expect of the Housing Authority under his leadership. A month after his appointment, he told a *Philadelphia Inquirer* reporter:

> "Ultimately, we're judged by the quality of living conditions we provide for residents . . . Our basic goal is to focus on our core business. And our core business is maintenance and management of property . . .

> "The Colonel makes chicken," Greene said. "He does a lot of other things in his restaurant, but if the chicken's not good, we're not going there for the macaroni and cheese."

> He said he would like to link with other government agencies that are skilled in health care, job training and law enforcement . . .

> Greene said that in many cities, housing agencies came to take on so many different roles because they were historically isolated from the rest of government . . .

> "I think we were going it alone when we didn't have to," he said.[20]

Greene reiterated his position in meetings with city agency directors: PHA's priority would be the improvement and maintenance of public housing. He was well equipped to lead PHA in addressing this priority. Through his experience as a housing authority administrator in Atlanta and Detroit, he had learned how to navigate an agency through the complex and potentially treacherous regulatory environment. He was sufficiently well acquainted with the minutiae of the HUD rulebook that he didn't need to depend on anyone else to tell him how to manage the federal funding available to PHA. He knew what he wanted to do and how to direct his staff to get it done. He knew how to handle the political dimension of PHA as well. He was not opposed to patronage, he told elected officials and political power brokers, as long as an employee carries out the responsibilities of the job. But an employee that doesn't perform the work satisfactorily won't be transferred to another part of the agency; he'll be fired.

Carl Greene also articulated two principles about those residents who were in need of human services, from drug and alcohol rehabilitation to job training. Most of the services required by current public housing residents, he said, should be provided by municipal government and by government-affiliated service organizations, not by the housing authority. And in the future, PHA would not be as available as it had been to serve as a resource for people with high service needs, such as individuals with drug and alcohol problems and ex-offenders recently released from prison. Priority would be given to working families and to individuals who were completing education and training leading to employment. Public housing would no longer be the housing of last resort, available to anyone.

Greene toured Cambridge Plaza and Richard Allen Homes, the two public housing sites located in the West Poplar neighborhood. He expressed agreement with a recently-completed internal report that recommended demolition of the two fourteen-story Cambridge Plaza high-rise towers, described as "filthy, stained with graffiti and neglected." Fifteen percent of the Cambridge Plaza units were vacant, according to the report, as were half of the apartments at the Richard Allen complex. At the time of Greene's arrival, PHA had not established a comprehensive plan for the redesign and reconstruction of either site.[21]

The plan that Carl Greene advanced for both Cambridge Plaza and Richard Allen was the demolition of the existing housing and its replacement with new housing similar to the West Poplar townhouses: detached and attached homes built on large lots with yards, driveways, and porch and gable features that resembled those that could be found in many suburban tracts. He showed me a site plan for Richard Allen, the development that extended east of 12th Street across from the West Poplar townhouses. In the drawing, both sides of 12th Street looked similar to one another in terms of density, lot size, and house size. The west side of 12th Street already consisted entirely of owner-occupied housing built as part of the West Poplar townhouse venture. When PHA's plan was implemented, the east side of the street would consist entirely of rental housing, but the houses would have an appearance similar to the homeowner housing. To an outsider, they might appear to be a subsequent phase of the West Poplar homeownership development.

I liked the concept. Implementing this plan would transform the unsightly and dangerous Richard Allen complex into a neighborhood with attractive houses fronting on major streets. Greene and I had one significant difference, however. I wanted to see the Richard Allen site privatized, to have the new homes developed and managed by a private developer. This approach was not consistent with Greene's view. He liked real estate development, and he wanted PHA to be a real estate developer, both in West Poplar and elsewhere in the city. Under his leadership during the next ten years, PHA became Philadelphia's biggest real estate developer.

New federal legislation, new HUD regulations, and HUD budgeting decisions facilitated Carl Greene's plans for the Cambridge Plaza and Richard Allen sites as well as his ambition to make PHA a highly active real estate developer.[22]

- Section 202 of the Omnibus Consolidated Rescissions and Appropriations Act of 1996 (OCRA) called for all public housing sites of 300 units or more (later revised to 250 units or more) to be evaluated for financial feasibility. If the evaluation produced a finding that a site could not be operated cost-effectively (that is, for an amount less than or equal to the cost of providing Section 8 rental assistance subsidies) and "reasonably revitalized," the site was to be "removed from the public housing inventory."[23]
  An assessment of the two sites by the consulting firm of Abt Associates produced a recommendation that the Cambridge Plaza towers and the Richard Allen development be demolished.

- The process through which housing authorities were to obtain HUD approval to demolish public housing units was streamlined, and more HUD funding was made available for the demolition of obsolete public housing sites.
  PHA obtained $2.6 million in HUD funding to support the demolition of the Cambridge Plaza high-rises, as well as the 124 low-rise units on the site.

- The long-standing federal "one for one" replacement-housing requirement, that had mandated the development of a new unit of public housing to replace every public housing unit proposed for demolition, was repealed.
  The density of the Cambridge Plaza site was reduced from 372 to 227 units. Richard Allen was reduced from 1,324 units to 328 new rental townhouses for families and 80 apartments for seniors.

- Section 202 of OCRA enabled a housing authority to satisfy its obligation to make replacement housing available to residents who had to leave an obsolete public housing site by providing the displaced residents with Section 8 rental assistance certificates.

"Most who lived in the Cambridge high-rises . . . won't be coming back," the Philadelphia Daily News *reported in its coverage of the Cambridge Plaza demolition plan.*[24]

- The Quality Housing and Work Responsibility Act (QHWRA) of 1998 granted discretion to housing authorities to use Public Housing Capital Fund resources to leverage Low Income Housing Tax Credit (LIHTC) investment equity and other private financing.

  $8.4 million of the $91.2 million development budget for Richard Allen was provided by LIHTC funding obtained by PHA.

- The federal Moving to Work (MTW) initiative gave selected housing authorities the discretion to reallocate funds from one budget line item to another. PHA used this discretion to accumulate more funding for housing construction.

  One source of financing for the new Cambridge Plaza housing was $4.9 million in PHA funding reallocated from other line items based on MTW.

Several federal actions had the effect of compelling housing authorities to generate more income by producing rental units that could be marketed to higher-income households. QHWRA required that no more than 40 percent of new public housing residents be extremely low income households.[25] Funding made available to housing authorities through the HOPE VI program supported the replacement of older, high-density public housing sites with new mixed income communities consisting of a much smaller number of new public housing units blended with new homeowner and rental units, including some that could be priced at market levels. HUD's 2007 budget submission to Congress requested funding for housing authorities at only 78 percent of the amount that HUD itself had determined was necessary to support the "costs of services and materials needed by a well-run [housing authority]," with no provision to fill the resulting 22 percent gap with government funding; increased operating revenues would have to be generated by housing authorities on their own.[26]

What you had to do as a housing authority director to overcome the risks and manage the opportunities that had emerged in this radically changed environment was clear. You had to reduce the size of the public housing inventory and get rid of the poorest performing older sites. You had to use Section 8 certificates as a relocation resource in order to move a lot of public housing residents out of older sites and into privately owned and managed rental housing. You had to build new housing that could attract higher-income tenants who could pay higher rents. You had to get your housing authority selected as an MTW site, and you had to use the flexibility granted under MTW to create a consolidated pool of funding for new housing construction. And because MTW funding would not be sufficient to finance all the new development that needed to be completed, you had to compete with private developers and community development corporations for funding that had rarely or never been available to housing authorities, including city-administered Community Development Block Grant funds and state-administered Low Income Housing Tax Credit funds, in order to assemble enough layers of subsidy to finance property acquisition, demolition, and new construction activities necessary to produce attractive, marketable new assets.

To make substantial inroads in obtaining city and state funds that previously had been denied to your housing authority, you had to cultivate strong working relationships with elected officials and representatives of important political constituencies. To elected officials who had been advocating for affordable housing and for better living conditions for public housing tenants, you had to promise to substantially improve the quality of assisted housing for low-income residents. To elected officials who had been angered over past housing authority mismanagement and the poor quality of older public housing sites, you had to promise to demolish the older sites and replace them with new housing that would be equal to or better in quality than the best housing in the surrounding area. To the building trades unions, you had to promise to create years of construction work opportunities for union members. To public housing tenant councils, you had to promise construction jobs and union apprenticeships for housing authority residents, a goal you had to achieve by funding resident training programs from the MTW dollar pool and by leveraging apprenticeship commitments from the building trades in exchange for the jobs you were generating for union members. You had to make all of these commitments in order to enable your housing authority to survive as a viable agency in this changed environment; and, because of the nature of the changes that had occurred in this environment in recent years, you could make good on all of your commitments if you were a leader and manager as capable as Carl Greene was.

The development of the Cambridge Plaza and Richard Allen sites substantially extended the acreage of low-density, subdivision-style housing south of Girard Avenue. With the completion of the West Poplar sales housing and the PHA rental housing, a new residential zone had been created south of Girard Avenue from 9th Street to within half a block of Broad. The West Poplar homeowner development west of 12th Street and the PHA rental development east of 12th Street were similar in appearance, but the two development plans had been motivated by entirely different considerations. I had supported the construction of the West Poplar townhouses as a City priority because I wanted to execute an area-wide development strategy that would produce a significant impact: many new houses and many new residents on a collection of previously vacant blocks. Carl Greene had implemented the build-out of the Cambridge Plaza and Richard Allen sites because he wanted to replace old PHA assets with better-designed, more marketable new ones, to demonstrate PHA's capability to be a real estate

Figure 3.3 Richard Allen/Cambridge Plaza Townhouses

developer, and to generate a higher level of PHA rental revenue in order to offset severe HUD funding cuts and reduce PHA's dependence on HUD.

Carl Greene achieved comparable successes in other areas of the city, as the Housing Authority demolished many obsolete older buildings and replaced them with new housing laid out on a traditional residential block grid. Between 2000 and 2007, PHA developed nearly 6,500 new units, through new construction or the rehabilitation of vacant houses and funded this development with more than $1 billion in public and private financing, including $290 million in Low Income Housing Tax Credit funds. The PHA ventures had a transformative impact on neighborhood real estate markets. For example, between 1999 and 2004, average residential sales prices in the vicinity of Cambridge Plaza and Richard Allen increased from $50,000 to nearly $125,000.[27]

By early 2009, much of this southern margin of Lower North Philadelphia had been built out as a result of my Home in North Philadelphia initiative and Carl Greene's reconstruction of the two public housing sites. Stimulated by the expansion of the City's ten-year tax abatement and the influence of the high-energy real estate market that prevailed during the early years of the new century, market-rate residential development had pushed north, up from Center City. More former factory buildings had been converted to lofts and condos, and more vacant lots had been infilled with sales townhouses and apartments designed in townhouse style. Walking north across Spring Garden Street, the northern edge of this Center City-influenced development, you entered the Home in North Philadelphia target area and encountered blocks of affordable homeowner and rental housing, extending all the way to the Temple University main campus.

What was left to do? Small-scale private investment and development—older storefronts being refurbished as restaurants, shops, and cafés—was taking place further east on Girard Avenue, in the vicinity of the higher-priced Northern Liberties and Fishtown neighborhoods, but the segment of Girard Avenue west of 9th was still in need of redefinition. Absentee buyers had begun purchasing some of the formerly owner-occupied Yorktown houses and renting them to Temple University students; complaints about overcrowding and bad behavior were accompanied by concerns about the future identity of this previously all-homeowner community.

The changes that I had tried to institute during my brief tenure as head of PHA had not been pursued by anyone else since then. Other organizational issues remained unresolved. Working relationships between PHA and government-funded human-service providers had improved, but the respective roles of PHA and city agencies in responding to the problems of individuals and families with both housing and supportive service needs had still not been clearly delineated. Nowhere was this lack of definition more evident than with respect to Philadelphia's approach to homelessness. PHA administered the Section 8 rental assistance program, a resource that could enable formerly homeless people to move out of emergency shelters into rental housing in neighborhoods. However, during most of the first ten years of Carl Greene's tenure, the City and PHA were not able to agree on an annual commitment of a specified number of Section 8 certificates that could be used to address this pressing problem in a systematic way.

In addition, the housing authority, now acting as a real estate developer, was actively competing with private and nonprofit developers for a shrinking pool of federal and state subsidy funds. Because PHA could leverage more funds from other sources than other developers and because PHA had established strong working relationships with the people who had the most influence over development funding decisions, the housing authority was able to obtain a substantial amount of subsidy funding that, in the decade before Greene had taken over the agency, would have been awarded to others. However, for many people who had been concerned about the condition of public housing in Philadelphia, this expanded PHA presence as a developer was a benefit, not a problem. The quality of PHA housing was at least as good as that produced by many other developers. Through his creative use of MTW and other funding resources, Carl Greene had brought more development financing to Philadelphia than would have been possible if PHA housing development activities had been privatized, as I had wished in 1993. I still believe that big city housing authorities should be merged with municipal governments in order to consolidate resources and facilitate a unified approach to challenges such as homelessness. My argument may be more logical, but the results that Carl Greene produced were ultimately more convincing to most people in a position to influence PHA's future; no changes in the relationship between PHA and city government were seriously considered after my interim assignment to PHA ended in 1994.

One critical issue that had not been studied carefully by either OHCD or PHA in executing their respective activities in Lower North Philadelphia was the impact of these activities on residents who were displaced from the development sites. The West Poplar venture involved the relocation of about a dozen households. These households received federally-mandated relocation payments as well as assistance in locating new places to live. No rules were broken; but the effectiveness of the relocation process and the outcomes of relocation for the affected households were never studied in depth. One West Poplar homeowner had used his relocation funding to purchase a home in East Germantown, in a neighborhood that he subsequently found to be unsafe. He tried to get help from the city in finding another, more suitable home. He wrote letters and expressed his dissatisfaction at public hearings, but no action was taken; he had received the required funding and services; he had chosen the house; the case was closed. No one within city government was responsible for doing more than ensuring that mandated relocation procedures had been complied with.

The issue of PHA resident relocation was more critical because far more PHA households were displaced during this period in order to make way for the many new development ventures being undertaken by the housing authority. Many of these residents were issued Section 8 rental assistance certificates and given help in finding suitable private rental housing. However, the outcomes associated with PHA displacement and relocation were apparently not evaluated in depth. Two studies of resident families that had been displaced in connection with HOPE VI development ventures in several cities (not including Philadelphia) found that while:

> most of those who have been relocated have experienced real benefits and are living in better housing in safer neighborhoods . . . these new neighborhoods are still extremely poor and racially segregated, and residents continue to report significant problems with crime and drug trafficking.[28]

This research also included the finding that a substantial number of prospective relocatees were residents characterized as "hard to house" because they had:

> physical and mental health problems and other serious personal challenges that make them unappealing to landlords. Others live in households whose composition—large numbers of children, elderly or disabled heads of household with young children—makes it nearly impossible for

them to find suitable units in . . . the newly transformed public housing or the private market. Without concerted effort to address their housing needs, these families will be at risk for homelessness.[29]

If the impacts of these "hard to house" residents on the neighborhoods to which they were relocated or on the homeless housing system in Philadelphia had ever been studied in depth, the results of these studies were never made known publicly. Without such research, it is not possible to determine whether the substantial improvements that took place at the Cambridge Plaza and Richard Allen sites were offset by the social problems that "hard to house" families from these sites brought to the neighborhoods to which they were relocated.

The Palette

As the south-of-Girard development ventures were being completed, a community development corporation organized by the nonprofit Asociación Puertorriqueños en Marcha (Association of Puerto Ricans on the March, known as APM) was pursuing development opportunities in the section of Lower North Philadelphia that had been designated as the "Temple Area" in the Philadelphia City Planning Commission publications. APM's section of the Temple Area had no distinctive landmarks or highly visible assets; it was defined in part by two substantially deserted corridors. One corridor consisted of the blocks facing either side of a northbound railroad viaduct on which commuter trains traveled from Center City to Chestnut Hill in Northwest Philadelphia, ending near the city's border with suburban Montgomery County. The other corridor was Germantown Avenue, a diagonal two-way street that cut through the area, from southeast to northwest, continuing through the city and into the northwestern suburbs.

Puerto Ricans had moved into this part of Lower North Philadelphia to work in manufacturing jobs that, for a time, were everywhere: at the multistory Quaker Lace factory near 5th and Lehigh; at the Hardwick and McGee rug plant at 7th and Lehigh; at the manufacturing firms that lined the nearby North American Street corridor, a two dozen block-long industrial boulevard. The Puerto Ricans wanted to make money and eventually return to the island or make a life in North Philadelphia.

By the last quarter of the twentieth century, however, the Temple Area had been drained of manufacturing activity. The Quaker Lace building had been vacated, then torched. The Hardwick and McGee plant had burned to the ground. The colossal manufacturing complexes that had employed thousands of workers—such as Stetson Hats at 4th and Montgomery or Baldwin Locomotive at Broad and Spring Garden—were long gone. The number of occupied factory buildings on the American Street corridor had dwindled, and the remaining factories were separated by the tracts of vacant land that remained following the demolition of abandoned manufacturing plants. Opportunities for Puerto Ricans to make a living in North Philadelphia shrank or disappeared altogether.

In 1970, Dr. Jesus Sierra and a group of community members organized APM as an organization that would focus on addressing the need for mental health and mental retardation services in the Latino community. That year, the organization brought suit against the Commonwealth of Pennsylvania over the treatment of Spanish-speaking residents of the Pennhurst State School and Hospital, with the intent of obtaining a state commitment to provide community-based group living arrangements for these individuals. According to a history posted on APM's website, "Up until that point, little care had been offered. People were often ignored, and with no Spanish speakers on staff, meaningful communication was de-prioritized."[30] The litigation was settled through a consent decree which included a commitment of state funds to enable APM to establish its first program of mental health and mental retardation services. APM's mental health orientation was a relevant one; depression was a chronic, area-wide problem.

Under Dr. Sierra's leadership as APM's Executive Director over a period of more than thirty years, the organization obtained many more contacts and grant awards. By the turn of the century, APM had developed the capacity to administer primary health, behavioral health, substance abuse treatment, Head Start, and day care programs, as well as a variety of activities benefitting children and families. Following Dr. Sierra's retirement, Nilda Ruiz took over as the organization's CEO and stabilized and professionalized APM's operations. By this time, the organization was operating its programs from twenty-three neighborhood sites, maintained by nearly 200 employees who served an estimated 40,000 people annually.[31]

APM's role as a housing producer was established midway through this period of growth. During the late 1980s, Dr. Sierra and the APM board had concluded that the organization would have to involve itself in producing affordable housing. The blocks surrounding APM's headquarters on Germantown Avenue were devastated. The private real estate market was nonexistent, and conditions were bound to worsen if no one took action. As important, many APM clients were in need of safe and affordable places to live.

After a few less-than-satisfactory attempts to launch small-scale housing development ventures with the assistance of consultants, the board became convinced of the need for APM to develop the capacity to produce housing on its own. A new APM-controlled community development corporation was formed. After a shaky startup period, during which the first generation of CDC management proved to be too inexperienced to take on the challenges of development in the area, the APM board hired Rose Gray as CDC director. Gray was not a Latina and had no prior connection with APM's service area, but she had a solid background in the construction industry and had managed development ventures in and around residential neighborhoods and on commercial corridors. She had never worked in a place like the Temple Area; but she had worked in many areas that resembled the future community that APM's leadership wanted to create within the Temple Area's nearly-deserted blocks.

In 1991, Gray and the APM board designed a strategic plan that would guide development in the area for the next two decades. The plan was straightforward: Germantown Avenue would be the backbone of the reinvestment strategy. Investment and development activity would initially begin on parcels located on or near Germantown Avenue, then expand outward as the avenue was built out.

APM's opportunity to build from strength in the Temple Area did not involve adjacency to a major institution, similar to Yorktown's adjacency to the Temple University main campus, or proximity to a stable neighborhood, similar to the West Poplar townhouses' proximity to Yorktown. APM's center of strength was its base of human-service resources, located in the organization's Germantown Avenue service facilities. Housing built by APM and located near APM's headquarters would have the best prospects of success because the residents of this housing would have the most direct access to APM services.

The high-vacancy surroundings were viewed as an asset, not a dis-advantage. "The beauty of the area," Rose Gray said later, "was that there was nothing there." Guided by a strategic plan, you could create a mixed-development palette with apartments, stores, townhouses, and green space. Gray viewed the vacant land as particularly attractive because low property values made site assemblage for future development much less expensive than in most other sections of the city. Inexpensive land could be more readily acquired, then used to leverage development financing to rebuild the area. Although not adjacent to big centers of investment, the community had important locational advantages. Center City was a ten-minute drive away. Temple University's campus lay a few blocks to the west, on the other side of the railroad viaduct. Buses ran regularly across and down the neighborhood street grid.

The development of APM's disinvested target area proceeded in the his-torical urban expansion pattern: a movement outward from a transportation corridor, Germantown Avenue. Clusters of new residential construction emerged along Germantown Avenue: transitional housing for people with AIDS, service-supported housing for people with chronic mental illness, and rental apartments for families with children. By the turn of the century, APM owned and managed 210 new rental units.

APM's housing production activity generated other benefits for the community. In a nearby public school that might have been shut down due to the previously declining population of school-age children, classrooms began to fill up again as new families moved in. Based on the new residents' grocery-shopping needs and food-purchase buying power, APM was able to obtain financing for the development of a new supermarket that employed twenty residents and operated profitably every year.

New sales housing had not been built in the area for nearly a century. The single-family homeowner market had been anemic for decades. Could sales housing be marketed successfully in this changing but still disadvantaged environment? APM's board decided to test the market by building eight townhouses on a vacant lot near the avenue. The location appeared to be a tough sell, next to an abandoned factory and facing a mostly vacant block. But the houses sold in less than a month.

Encouraged by these results, APM's leadership decided to pursue a more ambitious homeowner housing goal. The organization's staff surveyed the surrounding area and identified six adjacent blocks that were 85 percent vacant; among the remaining occupied buildings were some of the area's worst drug houses. The blocks formed a rectangular shape that lay parallel to the railroad viaduct. Dozens of new houses could be built there, and the housing construction, north to south, would create a residential bridge linking APM's target area to the Ludlow community, where townhouse development had been under way for several years as part of the Home in North Philadelphia strategy.

This large-scale sales housing venture was named Pradera, the Meadows. OHCD provided funding for a fifty-house first phase of construction, and APM obtained an additional award of development financing through the new state-administered Homeownership Choice program, which the Pennsylvania Housing Finance Agency (PHFA) had created to promote sales housing construction ventures similar in scale and scope to Pradera.

By the late 1990s, for the first time in recent memory, two developers were vying to acquire the same Lower North Philadelphia blocks, tracts of real estate that had been shunned by developers for decades. Rose Gray wanted enough land to build a hundred new houses in the APM-Ludlow zone. Carl Greene wanted to develop some of the same land as part of a PHA development venture for which he was seeking financing through the federal HOPE VI program: a plan for infill new construction, combined with the rehabilitation of PHA-owned row houses in and near the Ludlow community. After some sparring, Gray and Greene reached an agreement: PHA could include APM's supermarket and Pradera ventures within its proposed HOPE VI target area, so that APM's investment could be counted as leveraged financing, thereby earning PHA's proposal a higher score in the HUD-administered nationwide competition for HOPE VI funding. In turn, Greene would support APM development on the Pradera blocks and would convey scattered PHA-owned houses and lots on these blocks to APM. Some of the PHA houses were occupied, and PHA handled relocation based on the authority's established routine, by offering the residents rental units at other public housing sites or by issuing them Section 8 rental assistance certificates for use in obtaining private rental housing.

After 2001, the availability of funding through Mayor John Street's Neighborhood Transformation Initiative enabled APM to assemble enough land to support the construction of a total of 135 homes. NTI bond financing produced far more funding than had been available in prior years, enabling APM to implement a more ambitious acquisition plan. If APM had been dependent on the scarce HUD grant awards that had served as Philadelphia's primary property acquisition resource prior to NTI, the Pradera sites would probably have taken most of a decade to assemble.

Much of the Pradera site acquisition was accomplished through the use of eminent domain. All of the associated relocation, other than the relocation of PHA tenants, was managed by APM, working in coordination with the city's Redevelopment Authority. A total of thirteen families were relocated by APM, and, as Gray put it, "They all left happy." Every resident received federally-mandated relocation payments. Each homeowner was offered a new house in the Pradera development or an apartment at one of APM's nearby rental sites. A few households took their relocation funds and left the area, but most of them moved into the APM housing that had been offered to them. The homes they left were isolated and in need of serious repair. One elderly couple, the owners of a big old three-story house, had been living on the third floor for years after abandoning the lower floors due to lack of heat. Other families had been living in similar circumstances. Because APM had been a presence in the neighborhood for nearly two decades, these families were more inclined to work with the organization's staff in finding new housing than would have been the case if Redevelopment Authority or Housing Authority staff had been managing the relocation caseload. In addition, the fact that APM could offer each family a nearby, high-quality house or apartment improved the prospects for a successful outcome.

The first-phase Pradera townhouses sold for $55,000 to $60,000, the second phase homes for $83,000 to $90,000, and the third-phase homes for $125,000 to $150,000. Based on a City Council ordinance dating back to the 1970s that mandated all City-financed housing to be priced at levels affordable to lower-than-median income buyers, the prices of the second- and third-phase Pradera homes had to be marked down lower than APM had wished. By the turn of the century, the homes were drawing the interest of prospective buyers with incomes substantially higher than median.

During the years in which Pradera was being built, institutional development by Temple University expanded the campus eastward, and a private developer built apartments for students on blocks adjacent to the viaduct. This activity and the success of Pradera helped APM to convince a national developer to enter into a joint adaptive-reuse venture: the construction of retail stores and market-rate apartments at a former railroad station, a development that would straddle the viaduct and establish the first link between APM housing and the Temple University campus.

APM's interest in Lower North Philadelphia differed significantly from that of OHCD and PHA. APM wanted to supplement a human-services program and build out an area with housing that, in its initial phases, would be developed primarily for APM clients. APM development was diverse and mixed, including special-needs housing, rental housing for families, and

Figure 3.4 Pradera Townhouses

a supermarket, in addition to the cookie-cutter detached and semi-detached homes that resembled those produced by OHCD and PHA. Because APM was concerned about producing favorable outcomes for all community members, APM created an approach to relocation that, unlike that of OHCD and PHA, was an unqualified success.

By 2009, much of the East-of-Broad transition zone had been redefined, although many deteriorated, disorganized, high-vacancy blocks remained. A municipal budget crisis, influenced by the global economic upheaval that began in 2008, made the prospect of substantial public sector investment in the area very unlikely in the short term. What was needed to complete the revitalization of the area—the remaking of Girard Avenue, the retail development, the services and amenities, the development of the still-neglected blocks—would have to be supported largely by private investment, if these activities were to happen at all in the foreseeable future.

The experience of building out large sections of Eastern North Philadelphia provided insights that are relevant to other transition zones and other high-vacancy areas. Development should be guided by planning. The plan should be focused and discrete; it should provide clarity about what is to be accomplished in the initial phase of activity and what will remain to be accomplished later. Development strategies based on the plan should be organized through a collaborative process involving city planners, housing and economic development agency staff, and community constituencies. Finally, a primary focus of the plan and associated strategies should be the people who still live on the area's largely depopulated blocks. The questions of how development will affect their lives and how their moves to other homes, within their neighborhoods or elsewhere, will affect the future of the community or of other city neighborhoods must be addressed.

The design of the new Eastern North Philadelphia housing could be criticized from a smart growth, new urbanist, or transit-oriented development standpoint. The plans that produced this housing could have been more creative and inspired. But the new housing had two virtues, which should also be taken into account by future transition zone planners and implementers: they didn't resemble the government-subsidized projects of prior decades; they looked like products of the present-day real estate market. And because they looked like private market housing, they brought thousands of new residents into Philadelphia's most depopulated area.

4 A Citywide Revitalization Policy, I

Neighborhood Transformation Initiative Organization and Planning

Despite the fact that the problems affecting distressed urban neighborhoods are severe and highly visible, elected officials do not usually make public commitments to solve these problems, or even to make them a top priority, for two reasons.

From a political perspective, a neighborhood reinvestment policy—even the best-designed policy that is most responsive to community concerns—will not have a decisive influence on the outcome of an election. Instead, the policy issues that contribute most to the outcome of municipal elections are crime, taxes, jobs, schools, and public services. To a limited degree, attention has to be paid to neighborhood concerns during the course of any local political campaign. A candidate must make presentations at neighborhood meetings, propose new housing policies and programs or promise to manage the existing ones more efficiently and cost effectively, join community leaders in touring drug-house blocks, and pose for photo opportunities in front of buildings rehabilitated by nonprofit groups. However, a candidacy will not stand or fall based on an incumbent's neighborhood revitalization record or on a challenger's neighborhoods platform. Although neighborhood issues cannot be ignored altogether, they are too low on the list of voter priorities to decisively influence an election.

The other reason why elected officials do not ordinarily make commitments to fix the problems of distressed neighborhoods is because some of the most important of these problems are not fixable in the short term—very likely, not before a newly-elected mayor or city council member has to run for re-election. A dramatic improvement in neighborhood conditions —clearing a blighted area and redeveloping it as an attractive community of town homes, apartments, and stores, for example—would take years to complete and would need to be supported by an eight-figure development budget. And even if the necessary resources could be assembled for such a project, on what grounds would the candidate or elected official justify a massive financial commitment to one section of the city in the absence of comparable commitments to other areas in need of reinvestment? The Lower North Philadelphia strategy described in Chapter Three was criticized by neighborhood advocates from other areas of the city on just these grounds.

Given these constraints, it is noteworthy when an elected official makes an ambitious commitment to improve conditions in older-city neighborhoods. It is even more noteworthy when such a commitment is made the central focus of a city administration and is elevated to such a level that it is bound to influence a mayor's political future.

Philadelphia's Neighborhood Transformation Initiative (NTI), a high-profile policy launched during Mayor John F. Street's administration (2000–2007), was the largest and most ambitious neighborhood revitalization initiative to be undertaken by a mayor during the first decade of the twenty-first century.* Street's predecessor, Mayor Rendell, had made downtown revitalization a high priority during his eight years in office, committing what some viewed as a disproportionate amount of government resources to Center City development projects. With an awareness of this criticism, Street, like his political opponents in the 1999 primary and general elections, promised to devote more attention to improving conditions in the city's neighborhoods. However, NTI amounted to far more than political promise-keeping. The broad scope of the policy and the depth of the city administration's commitment to it was reflective of Street's background as a housing activist and of his longstanding interest in fundamentally improving economically distressed communities similar to those that he had previously represented as a member of City Council.

Because NTI was a multi-faceted policy that took shape over most of the decade, a thorough evaluation of the entire policy is beyond the scope of this book.[1] Instead, this chapter focuses on the initial organization of the policy and on the relationship between NTI goals and city-supported planning activities in neighborhoods most affected by NTI. The next chapter describes how the Street Administration managed real estate transactions and pursued the goal of housing agency reorganization during the years in which NTI was implemented. The discussion of these topics is intended to provide insights into the strengths and weaknesses of NTI and the challenges that the designers of any similar citywide neighborhood revitalization initiative must confront and overcome.

Two Previews

The Abandoned Car Campaign

How many abandoned cars were sitting on the streets of Philadelphia in 1999? You could find them in every section of the city, especially in neighborhoods where unemployment, poverty, and crime were most pervasive. In those communities, the virus of abandonment had spread from vacant houses, storefronts, and factories onto the public spaces, the streets and sidewalks

---

*   Runner-up status must be granted to Project 5000, a commitment by Baltimore Mayor Martin O'Malley to acquire 5,000 vacant and abandoned properties for redevelopment.

where trashed, stripped, torched, and vermin-infested vehicles were parked, never to restart. In 1998, two years before John Street took office as Mayor, a municipal agency had collected more than 23,000 abandoned vehicles from the city streets. In 1999, the city removed 27,000 vehicles during the first nine months of the year; but an estimated 40,000 remained, and new wrecks appeared on a daily basis.[2]

Much of the abandoned vehicle inventory was scattered through neighborhoods in former industrial zones that extended along the Delaware River north and east of Philadelphia's downtown. Empty factories, overgrown railyards, trash-filled alleys, and half-occupied rowhouse blocks were common sights in the sections of North and lower-Northeast Philadelphia known as Port Richmond, Kensington, Fairhill, and Frankford. Many of these dead-zone blocks were places where truckloads of debris could be dumped and remain indefinitely.

Municipal elections would take place in November 1999. A new Mayor would be chosen, as would all seventeen members of City Council. A local group decided to elevate the abandoned-vehicle problem to a higher-profile status during the election year. Members of Eastern Philadelphia Organizing Project (EPOP), a faith-based coalition of religious congregations, civic groups, and neighborhood organizations, deposited flyers on thousands of abandoned cars. The flyers displayed photos of the two mayoral candidates— Street was the Democratic nominee, Sam Katz his Republican opponent —with the following message:

VIOLATION of our neighborhood

The next mayor will decide how long this car sits on your street

But you will decide who the next mayor is![3]

The flyers, combined with EPOP-sponsored organizing and advocacy, made an impact. Both mayoral candidates announced plans for getting rid of the abandoned-vehicle backlog and for instituting an accelerated wreck-removal process. Because neither plan could be tested until a new administration took office in 2000, no one knew whether or how either plan might work. Furthermore, abandoned cars would not be the decisive issue in the 1999 general election; as usual, taxes, crime, schools, and other topics would take center stage. However, as a result of EPOP's activism, there was no question that the next mayor was going to be expected to solve the problem.

Election Day came and went, and winter passed. Then, early on the morning of April 3, 2000, Mayor John Street climbed up onto a blue flatbed truck parked outside City Hall. A crowd of people and vehicles surrounded him. "Rock and roll, everybody!" the Mayor shouted. Then he climbed into the cab of the truck and drove up North Broad Street, leading a fleet of 127 trucks—lights flashing, diesel engines roaring—operated by towing firms from around the region. The first stop: a block in the Francisville neighborhood, where Street himself hooked the first two wrecks of the day. The fleet of trucks spread out across the city. Within forty days, nearly 33,000 abandoned vehicles had been removed from the streets, more than the number of vehicles collected during all of calendar year 1999.[4]

This success was achieved through a combination of coordinated decisions and actions. The city opened an abandoned car hotline and staffed the initial wreck-removal campaign with forty police officers and five clerks. The Managing Director's office and the Police Department enlisted the participation of twenty-five salvage companies, creating a capability to remove about 825 cars a day. A state regulation was changed, enabling the city to designate junk cars valued at less than $500 as "trash to be removed" and taken to the crusher immediately (the previous immediate action threshold had been $250). Other vehicles would be tagged with a "notice to remove" and towed after eleven days; although an effort would be made to contact each owner, the tagging of the vehicle would serve as sufficient legal notice for any owner who could not be found. The state assigned an abandoned-car specialist to work with Philadelphia police in expediting paperwork so that cars could be towed sooner and tow companies paid faster. And then, as word of the wreck-removal campaign spread, some junk-car owners took their vehicles off the street on their own, realizing that the city would remove the wrecks and make them pay fines if they failed to act quickly.

What had begun as a campaign in April was subsequently operationalized and made a routine process. The hotline stayed open. The assigned staff remained in place. The accelerated processing of paperwork and payments continued. A challenge that had been regarded as overwhelming had been cut down to size and was now being managed as a routine. Rev. Carlos Santos of Christ and St. Ambrose Episcopal Church in Kensington told *The Philadelphia Inquirer*:

> We are very happy here in the neighborhood . . . Before, you'd see abandoned cars everywhere. You are not seeing many anymore. Now you see the street more clean and you see the people taking care of it . . . People are more conscious of how clean their neighborhood is.[6]

Rousseau on the Boulevard

A thousand wooden folding chairs in the big Catholic church hall were all occupied, and dozens of people, still in their winter overcoats, stood in back and along the side aisles. The audience was more than 99 percent white. How many of these people had voted for Republican Sam Katz in the November 1999 mayoral election two months earlier? Probably most of them—possibly all of them. On this winter night, as the temperature outside on Roosevelt Boulevard dropped well below freezing, many of these people were seeing

John Street in person for the first time. The mood of the assembled crowd did not feel hostile; it was not what you would call cordial, but it was civil. The mood of the gathering felt like, So now what?

On the stage, directors and commissioners of municipal agencies sat on folding chairs that had been set up in a row behind the podium with the City of Philadelphia seal. Some of the agency heads were new faces, appointed shortly after the Street Administration took office that month. Others were incumbents who had served in the Rendell Administration and were being retained. A few were like me, Rendell-Administration holdovers who had been neither dismissed nor reappointed. At the first of these meetings, which had been held in a church in Germantown, I had slipped into a front-row seat, next to a development agency official who did a double-take. "What's your status?" he hissed in a stage whisper. The answer: my status was undecided. Some people who were politically close to John Street wanted me gone. Other people who were politically close to John Street were lobbying him to retain me. I was in transition-period limbo (I resigned from OHCD in June, 2001, a month after NTI was launched).

In big cities, most of the gatherings that are termed "town meetings" do not have much resemblance to traditional New England-style town meetings, those models of civic engagement and collective decision-making. Instead, big-city mayors most often convene town meetings to try to show that they are in touch with ordinary people and responsive to their concerns. A typical urban-style town meeting begins with an opening presentation by the mayor, followed by introductions of other officials, some of whom may deliver briefer presentations. Then the question-and-answer period starts, and city-service requests soon predominate. A man in jeans and a sweatshirt stands up and complains about a pothole on the 3100 block of Dickinson Street. The Mayor turns to the Streets Commissioner. The Streets Commissioner stands up and says that a work crew will have the pothole filled by Thursday afternoon. Next question? The performance is designed to make city government look well-managed, reliable, and caring—and, to a degree, the performance is effective. The pothole gets filled as promised, and people take note, talk about it, and remember. The city may not reliably fill all the other potholes, the ones that were not identified that night; but the participants in the town meeting, and the people they talk with afterwards, experience a demonstration of the mayor's power to get things done.

The back-office staff of Mayor Frank L. Rizzo, who had served two terms during the 1970s, were masters of town-meeting choreography. Prior to a typical meeting, someone from the mayor's office would scour lists of the most pressing city-service requests that had been received from the neighborhood where the meeting was to be held, then got on the phone. As a result, many of the neighborhood's city-service problems would get solved during the days preceding the event: the street light would get replaced, the playground equipment would get fixed, the trash-filled lot would get cleaned. On some occasions, a veteran employee of the city's code enforcement agency told me, a work crew would be sweeping up the remaining debris from a just-demolished abandoned building at the very moment that Rizzo's car was pulling up to the curb in front of the recreation center on a nearby block where the town meeting was about to begin.

John Street had seen his share of traditional town meetings, and it was clear that he was not interested in following traditional protocol. Staff from the departments of Recreation, Licenses and Inspections, Public Health, Public Welfare, and others sat at tables near the entrance to the hall, handing out information and taking city-service requests and complaints. If you need information or have a specific problem that requires our attention, the audience was told prior to the introduction of Mayor Street, the people at the tables in the back are available to assist you.

A few moments later the mayor was introduced and received a round of polite applause. Tonight, he said, I want to hear from you about the ways that we can improve the city of Philadelphia, and I want to share some of my thoughts with you. We can't succeed in improving the quality of life in our communities unless city government does a better job of working with neighborhood residents to deal with the issues that are important to all of us. So tonight I want to have a discussion with you about how we can work together to improve our neighborhoods and our city.

The dialogue began. Audience members were called upon and offered opinions, comments, recommendations, and proposals about jobs, taxes, crime, schools, kids, housing, drugs, grocery shopping, and other issues. The mayor responded to each speaker with information and personal insights. His tone was informal and down-to-earth, but he was concise, and he didn't ramble. He described the perspective he had gained on some of these issues through experiences as a neighborhood resident and as a parent of public-school children. He did not hesitate to express a difference of opinion when he disagreed with something that was said, but he was not argumentative. When he wanted to provide more detailed information about a particular policy, regulation, or program, he asked one of the city agency directors and commissioners to speak. He voiced some strongly-held beliefs: Every block should be organized! Every block should have a block captain! But he did not lecture the audience or try to impress them with demonstrations of the power of the mayor's office. He showed that he was listening and paying attention.

At this meeting and at similar meetings held in locations around the city that winter, Mayor Street described his views about the ideal working relationship between municipal government and neighborhoods. Our expectations about what city government can and should do need to change, he said. City government needs to do a better job of delivering the basic services that only government can perform: collecting trash, preventing crime, and demolishing dangerous buildings, for example. At the same time, neighborhoods need to be better organized, so that they can resolve smaller, quality-of-life problems on their own. If a resident leaves trash out at the curb two days before trash-collection day, the trash spills out onto the sidewalk and streets, and neighbors call the city to clean up the mess. But if the neighbors would get together, speak with one another, and get everyone to put the trash out on trash-collection day or the night before, the problem is solved without the need for city involvement. Then the city's trash pick-up crews will have more time to devote to doing their jobs more efficiently. By the same token, if parents and neighbors get together and disperse a group of kids who are causing a disturbance on the corner rather than calling 911 to ask the police to do it, the Police Department will be able to use its resources more effectively to arrest hard-core wrongdoers and improve public safety. The neighborhood takes more responsibility for managing itself, and the City devotes more attention to the performance of basic services, to the benefit of everyone.

We have to create a new kind of social contract, Mayor Street told the participants in these meetings. City government has to do a better job of governing and delivering services. Communities have to become better organized to deal with problems that should be resolved at the neighborhood level. When you call 911 to ask the police to break up the group of disruptive kids—your kids—you're asking us, the city, to protect you from you, to get involved in dealing with a problem that an organized neighborhood could resolve on its own.

Street held the attention of the crowd in the Northeast Philadelphia hall. He received no standing ovations, but people didn't start trooping out during the middle of the session either. Street may not have won the support of most of the participants; they might all vote against him at the next opportunity. But, watching the people in the crowd from my position on the stage, one thing seemed clear: the level of respect with which Street was regarded had risen.

The Mayor's Story

Before he became Mayor, before his fellow City Council peers voted him Council President, before he won his first election as Fifth District Councilperson, before he served as a housing-activist lawyer, before he completed Temple University Law School and passed the bar exam, John Street was a hot dog vendor with an undergraduate degree in English from Oakwood College in Huntsville, Alabama.

Street was a highly disciplined person. He had spent his early life on a farm that had no electricity or running water. After college, when he was making ends meet through teaching jobs supplemented by cab driving, he became a fat man, weighing nearly 260 pounds at one point. Then, according to Street, "I looked up one day and saw a 260-pound man and no good reason for it." Through diet and exercise, he shed nearly eighty pounds and kept it off.

At Temple Law School, he was known for the long hours he devoted to study.[7] Later, in City Council, his fellow elected officials came to respect his in-depth understanding of the dynamics of city government. "Anyone who's going to debate John Street on city government had better do his homework, because you'd better believe he's done his," said a former Council colleague.[8]

As a legal services attorney during the 1970s, Street became best known as the brother of Milton Street, a housing activist who had led a high-profile squatters' movement in which John Street played a supporting role. Milton Street was subsequently elected state representative, then state senator, representing North Philadelphia legislative districts.

In 1979, John Street was elected Councilperson for the Fifth District, which included much of North Philadelphia and part of Center City (Philadelphia is divided into ten Council districts, from which residents elect district Councilpersons; in addition, seven Councilpersons at-Large are elected by citywide vote). During Street's first month in office, news of the Abscam scandal broke. Abscam, an FBI sting operation that had been designed to catch bribe-taking officials, resulted in indictments that dislodged long-term Council members who had held key leadership positions. As a result, Street had an opportunity to become head of the Appropriations Committee shortly after his re-election in 1983, far earlier than would otherwise have been expected. An advocate for more funding for teachers and social services earlier in his Council career, by the end of the 1980s, Street had gained a reputation as a fiscal conservative.[9]

Street was elected Council President in January 1992, the same month in which Rendell took office as Mayor. Departing from the past practice of many previous mayors, Rendell formed a close working relationship with Street and attempted to accommodate the Council President wherever possible. In return, Street, who exercised tight control over Council operations—rewarding allies and punishing dissidents—shepherded Rendell's policy initiatives through the local legislative process.

When he took office as Mayor in 2000, Street did not have a comparable opportunity to forge a similar partnership with newly-elected Council President Anna Verna because Street, unlike Rendell, had already established close working relationships with most Council members during the years he had spent as a Councilperson. More important, Verna did not have the ability to deliver Council majorities with the same consistency as Street had for Rendell. From a political perspective, it would make little sense for Street to be as accommodating to Verna as Rendell had been to him when, based on the ties he had formed with most of the other Council members, he could do as well as or better than she in producing favorable votes when needed.

Street's relationship with Council President Verna, and with Council in general, had an important influence on his neighborhoods policy. During his campaign for Mayor, Street had proposed a plan to finance an anti-blight initiative with $250 million in bonds.[11] After Street took office, the plan became known as the Neighborhood Transformation Initiative and was budgeted at $295 million. Although NTI was formally launched in April, 2001, implementation was delayed until March, 2002, while the Street Administration and City Council worked to reconcile differing views about the role that Council would play in determining how the bond financing would be allocated.

Street was re-elected Mayor in November, 2003, and NTI continued during his second term of office, which ended in 2007. Documentation for the Street Administration's Fiscal 2008 budget presentation showed a total NTI budget of $306.7 million, with $141.6 million allocated for demolition, $72 million for real estate acquisition, $40.7 million for basic systems repair and home modifications to accommodate disabled and elderly people, and the remainder to a variety of property development and preservation programs.

Coordinated and Competing Plans

Financial Plan

The NTI financing approach was not the first use of bond debt to support blight removal and development projects. During the years after World War Two, several major cities had made use of bond financing to support demolition and construction activities, most associated with downtown projects. Between 1945 and 1958, for example, local government commitments to blight removal and new development contributed substantially to a 92.7 percent increase in Philadelphia's net long-term municipal debt.[12] NTI differed from these previous financing commitments in two important respects. First, NTI bond financing was designed exclusively for investment in neighborhoods, not in the central business district. Second, NTI was the brainchild of the city's mayor, linked to Mayor Street's view of the opportunity to substantially improve Philadelphia's economic prospects. Unlike NTI, many of the earlier bond-financing transactions had been associated with more limited projects—sewer reconstruction, for example—endorsed by municipal government in concert with business interests.

The narrative accompanying the NTI budget presentation in the City's Fiscal 2002–2006 Five-Year Financial Plan identified six major NTI activity categories: community planning; blight removal; code enforcement; real estate acquisition and conveyance; strategic investment in neighborhoods; and the leveraging of additional resources to support NTI goals. These six activity categories contained a total of twenty-five proposed actions, some specific ("Safely eliminate the backlog of imminently dangerous buildings" through the demolition of 11,000 to 13,000 structures over a four-year period), others more general ("Combat littering and increase public awareness regarding proper trash disposal and recycling").[13]

"A Strategy for Investment and Growth," published by the City in April 2001, described nine actions that were identified as "specific goals" of NTI.

Four of these actions were measurable: develop 16,000 new housing units, complete 14,000 demolitions, encapsulate (that is, clean and seal to prevent weather damage and vandalism) 2,500 properties for future rehabilitation; and clean and maintain 31,000 vacant lots. Two of the actions involved organizational changes: the creation of a Philadelphia Land Bank (an entity that would serve as a clearinghouse to facilitate property acquisition and conveyance) and the "reform of Philadelphia's delivery systems" (that is, the reorganization of city housing agencies to increase efficiency and lower administrative costs). Two of the actions were broader in scope: "Restore citizen faith and sense of optimism for the future of the City," and "Facilitate neighborhood planning in a citywide context."[14]

The City's "Strategy for Investment and Growth" described NTI as "a bold agenda to enhance Philadelphia's position as an economically competitive city supported by thriving neighborhoods." Implementation of NTI was anticipated to stimulate a 5 percent increase in Philadelphia's population by 2010, "the first time in fifty years that the City's population will have risen." NTI was described as the first in a series of "comprehensive neighborhood growth strategies" that would be complemented by initiatives to address commercial development, public education, children and youth, job creation, and workforce development.[15]

During each year between fiscal 2003 and fiscal 2008, an annual NTI program description and budget was presented to City Council for review and approval as part of the City's budget process. These budget submissions did not (and were not designed to) include a description of how the proposed NTI funding allocations would fundamentally change neighborhoods—of how NTI would amount to more than the sum of its parts.

Market Value Analysis

In the darkened conference room at The Reinvestment Fund (TRF), some of the city staff gasped when they saw the series of PowerPoint slides that one private-sector planner later called "the invasion of the black dots." The slides displayed identical outline maps of Philadelphia with dots indicating the locations of vacant properties. The first two slides illustrated the results of vacancy surveys that had been completed in prior years. In the first slide, dots were clustered in North and West Philadelphia, more dispersed in South Philadelphia and some other neighborhoods, and non-existent in much of Northeast Philadelphia and other sections of the city. The second slide showed that the North and West Philadelphia clusters had grown, that concentrations of dots were emerging in some other sections of the city, and that new dots were appearing in areas that previously had none. The third slide displayed a hypothetical picture of future property vacancy, based on an assumption that the first two slides revealed a trend that could be projected into the future. The third slide was frightening. The proliferation of black dots made the map of Philadelphia look like an anthill, or like the

Martian landscape overrun by black beetles in the sci-fi movie "Starship Troopers."

TRF's President and CEO, Jeremy Nowak, was previewing the Power-Point presentation for a group of staff from Mayor Street's office and the city's development agencies prior to public release in conjunction with the roll-out of NTI. Should the black-dot sequence be included in the final version, he asked? The vacancy projection was not really accurate; the dots were disproportionately large. But the sequence conveyed a powerful message about the need for intervention to address a growing problem. The audience members agreed that the black-dot series should stay.

TRF, a nonprofit organization founded as the Delaware Valley Community Reinvestment Fund in 1985, started out as a financial intermediary —an organization that provided loans and working capital to nonprofit organizations for community projects that would ordinarily have difficulty qualifying for conventional financing. By the start of the Street Administration in 2000, TRF had grown to the point where its portfolio was far larger than those of the local program branches of national organizations such as the Local Initiatives Support Corporation and the Enterprise Foundation. TRF had earned national recognition for its success in packaging debt and equity transactions for a variety of development ventures, from rental housing to charter schools. TRF had also completed several high-quality policy research projects supported by a sophisticated in-house data analysis and GIS capability. Based on these qualifications, the Street Administration had asked TRF to assist the City in completing early-stage development planning for NTI.

The core of TRF's presentation was a typology of neighborhood real estate markets. TRF had organized a data base that combined a variety of census tract-specific, census block-specific, and, in some cases, address-specific variables. Some of the variables were census data, such as age of housing and poverty level. Other variables were associated with the real estate market, such as credit scores and incidence of subprime lending. The variables were weighted, aggregated (initially by census tract; then, in subsequent versions of this analysis, by census block), then mapped and color-coded, using GIS software. The color-coding produced a citywide map that displayed six different market clusters.

- *Regional Choice* markets contained older housing in good condition and a mix of residential and commercial uses. These neighborhood real estate markets, most of them in or near the downtown area or in well-off neighborhoods bordering the suburbs, were populated by people with high credit scores and the financial means to buy or rent anywhere in the metropolitan area.
- *High Value/Appreciating* markets were similar to Regional Choice markets, with generally high credit scores and high average housing values, although the latter were not the highest in the city.

Figure 4.1 TRF Market Cluster Map

- *Steady* markets had relatively high housing values as well, but had not experienced strong price appreciation during the 1990s. Much of the housing in these areas was built after 1950, and credit scores were not as consistently high as in the other two clusters.
- *Transitional* markets had high homeownership rates and values that exceeded the citywide average; but vacant and deteriorated housing, some of it in hazardous condition, was becoming a significant problem in these places. Lower credit scores gave these markets greater susceptibility to subprime lending.
- *Distressed* markets had older, more deteriorated housing, lower housing values and credit scores, and a higher concentration of vacant and hazardous buildings.
- *Reclamation* markets had the oldest, lowest-value housing and the highest levels of vacancy and deterioration in the city.[16]

TRF's data-crunching and computer-mapping produced a view of Philadelphia as a multi-colored mosaic. The map provided a more nuanced picture of the city and its neighborhoods than had ever been shown in map form. Maps produced by government agencies or the private sector in the recent past had displayed individual variables such as income, poverty, crime, unemployment, and housing vacancy. They all looked like the same map: conditions in North Philadelphia were worst; conditions in Center City, the far Northwest, and the far Northeast were best; everything else was somewhere in between. Unlike these conventional maps, the market cluster analysis showed many variations within and among neighborhoods. A single neighborhood, Mount Airy in northwest Philadelphia, for example, could contain High Value/Appreciating, Steady, and Transitional clusters—three distinct sets of housing-market strengths and weaknesses. As your eye traveled from a city boundary toward Philadelphia's geographic center, neighborhood market patterns changed incrementally. Predominantly Regional Choice census blocks would became interspersed with High Value/Appreciating blocks, which then became predominant, then merged into Steady and Transitional blocks, which then became Distressed and Reclamation blocks.

The market cluster map conveyed a message that was better-grounded than the message conveyed by the black-dots map but just as unnerving: blight, deterioration, and disinvestment are no longer confined within relatively concentrated areas; these problems are spreading into previously stable areas and have now become a citywide crisis. The core of Center City was a Regional Choice zone surrounded by a variety of different lower-value market clusters. Distressed and Reclamation blocks could be seen within a half-mile of some of the highest-value Regional Choice blocks.

Although the TRF presentation was not a funding formula, the map did provide a frame of reference for considering the manner in which public funds should be invested in neighborhoods. For example, most demolition funding was likely to be allocated to Reclamation areas. In Transitional areas, NTI funding could support housing counseling aimed at preventing mortgage delinquency and default.

During most years prior to the advent of NTI, the City of Philadelphia had depended on HUD funding, made available through the annual Community Development Block Grant and other programs, as its primary source of support for neighborhood reinvestment activities. Little or no money from the City's operating or capital budgets was allocated to affordable housing. In light of a federal requirement that low- and moderate-income households receive most of the direct benefit associated with the expenditure of HUD funding, the map that city housing administrators knew best was the Philadelphia census-tract map in which lower-than-median-income census tracts were shaded to indicate eligibility for the federal funding. Such a map had no relevance to resource allocation decisions associated with NTI, because the "keystone" of NTI was municipal bond financing that was not constrained by federal income restrictions; any area of the city was potentially eligible to receive funding. As the "Strategy for Investment and Growth" put it, "All neighborhoods in the City are customers of NTI's programs and policies."[17]

From the perspective of Mark Alan Hughes, senior fellow at the University of Pennsylvania's Fox Leadership Program and, at that time, the author of a weekly column in the *Philadelphia Daily News*, the Mayor's endorsement of an all-neighborhoods-are-customers approach that "has something for every neighborhood," was a serious strategic error. "By changing this from a blight plan [as had been proposed in Street's mayoral campaign] to a citywide transformation," Hughes wrote in April 2001, "the mayor has diluted the message." Hughes criticized the Mayor for the absence of a housing agency reorganization plan, which had been identified a year earlier as an administration priority, and for counting as "leveraged" funds more than a billion dollars that had already been committed for other activities.[18]

In Hughes' view, the TRF map was illustrative of this flawed approach:

> The mayor's blight plan is full of [maps] . . . In fact, it's really less a blight plan than a blight analysis . . . After 15 months and many, many colorful maps, we still have nothing but a bullet to a Powerpoint presentation calling for someone to "reorganize housing agencies."[19]

In my view, the TRF presentation was more limited as an analytical tool than Hughes had suggested and may have been more useful as a guide to implementation than Hughes had indicated. Although the neighborhood typology was, as its proponents described it, "data-driven" and comprehensive, the map was not so much an analysis as a snapshot of existing conditions that provided no indication of current or future market potential. Almost any area of the city could be said to have potential as a site for the investment of NTI funds. Distressed, Transitional, and Steady census tracts that were located near Center City, it could be argued, were excellent prospects for investment because of their proximity to the higher-value downtown area. But a similar argument could be made for neighborhoods that were located near academic and health care institutions, near the Delaware and Schuylkill River waterfronts, or near city/suburb borders. Nearly every area of the city could be said to have some potential for investment, and the TRF map could be used to prove the point.

A description of the NTI experience posted on TRF's website suggests that the map was also intended to guide decision-making about investment:

> By developing a taxonomy of market types and linking the taxonomy to prioritization of public action (i.e., code enforcement, land assembly), TRF created a new kind of policy conversation regarding how government can best stimulate market forces in distressed neighborhoods. The Philadelphia MVA [Market Value Analysis] was designed to discover

whether there were indeed areas of the city that share common housing market and population characteristics. The picture that emerged of the City served as a framework for its plan of action.[20]

Patricia Smith, who served as the Street Administration's Secretary for Neighborhood Transformation during the initial years of NTI planning and implementation, found the TRF presentation particularly helpful with respect to setting priorities and identifying associated program actions. For example, marketing the City's expanded home improvement loan program became a priority activity in neighborhoods that had been shown to contain older housing with signs of deterioration.[21]

Hughes was right in suggesting that the TRF analysis, by itself, did not resolve tough decisions about the allocation of limited funding. Should more money be invested in Reclamation areas because they represented the greatest blight-removal challenge? Or should a triage approach be adopted, in which priority would given to stabilizing neighborhoods in relatively good condition? How should the NTI funds be allocated among the ten City Council districts into which the City was divided? If NTI was to be a citywide strategy, why not treat all areas of the city equally and just divide the budget by ten (Smith told me that the Street Administration was continually resisting pressure to do just that)?[22] In light of the limited impact that NTI funding would have in addressing all of the issues brought forth in the TRF analysis, city officials would have to determine how to make the link between the map and the plan of action.

Blight Free Philadelphia

During 2001, a year in which the Street Administration and City Council struggled to resolve their disagreements over Council's role in the allocation of NTI funds, EPOP reappeared, this time as co-author, with Temple University's Center for Public Policy, of a report entitled "Blight Free Philadelphia: A Public-Private Strategy to Create and Enhance Neighborhood Value." Published in July, 2001, the report identified attracting and retaining population as the primary goal of the strategy and stated that:

> Urban renewal strategies focused primarily on demolition and land assembly have not proven effective in addressing the underlying deterioration of neighborhoods in other cities or in Philadelphia. Demolition and land assembly do not necessarily stabilize neighborhoods or lead to new development.[23]

The centerpiece of "Blight Free Philadelphia" was a proposal that the City create "blight free zones" in each Council district. The zones would be selected through a competitive proposal submission, in which proposals from business/community partnerships would be solicited and evaluated.

To qualify for consideration, a proposal would have to include a commitment of private-sector funding from the business entity or entities participating in the partnership. Through this advance commitment of financial support for each proposed zone, the authors of the report maintained, leveraging opportunities could be identified before the City made any commitment of public funds, not afterwards. In addition, pursuing this approach would ensure that demolition (other than tearing down buildings in danger of collapse) and land assembly would take place only when these activities would be followed by development.[24]

The blight free zone approach was based on several related assumptions. The first was that economic anchors that offer good opportunities for investment can be found in many neighborhoods across the city. These anchors could include academic and health care institutions, private businesses, or even locations such as a commercial corridor with a high level of retail activity. The authors of the report contended that local institutions or businesses in a neighborhood could be persuaded to invest in the zones based on self-interest; their investment would leverage city funds and upgrade their surroundings, increasing the value of their assets and strengthening their competitive position:

> This is not a new idea. The Tastykake Baking Company and the University of Pennsylvania have already developed various sophisticated programs to achieve the stabilization of the blocks surrounding their real estate. Their work has already proven that neighborhoods that are facing challenges can turn-around if public and private partners collaborate thoughtfully to build upon existing strengths.[25]

"Blight Free Philadelphia" was well thought out, well-documented, and creative. The proposal to create blight free zones in each Council district would have political appeal, but the proposal was not a carve-up of public funding based on political considerations. City funding was conditioned on commitments of private investment in the zones.

Had it been adopted, the blight free zone approach would not necessarily have been an unqualified success. In a section of the report that identified proposed blight free zone locations, the authors suggested that Mantua, a West Philadelphia community with Reclamation characteristics, might be a location in which the City could leverage private funding commitments from area institutions such as the University of Pennsylvania. But because Mantua was blocks away from Penn and other West Philadelphia institutions, institutional self-interest would seem to dictate against making a commitment to this area. If Penn and other West Philadelphia institutions were to respond to a proposal solicitation, the neighborhoods that would be likely to benefit would be better-off locations adjacent to or near their campuses. Mantua might not receive any funding if the zone-designation plan were to be adopted as proposed.

EPOP and Temple representatives presented the Blight Free Philadelphia plan to City Council at a public hearing on October 30, 2001. Council President Verna "praised the logic of getting private investment commitments before spending on massive demolition work" and suggested that each Council district might need more than one Blight Free Zone.[26] NTI staff was not receptive to the EPOP/Temple proposal; the administration had its own ideas about how to allocate NTI funding.

The blight free zone proposal was not adopted, and the Street Administration and Council resolved their differences several months after the October 30 presentation. The EPOP/Temple team was able to claim credit for some revisions in the overall NTI plan that had been proposed in the Blight Free Philadelphia report, such as an expanded focus on housing rehabilitation and home repair. But any collaboration between the EPOP/Temple team and the Street Administration was out of the question. The administration resented EPOP's attempt to get in the middle of its efforts to resolve its differences with Council. This was unfortunate because, at that time, the approach that EPOP and Temple were proposing was more comprehensive than the Street Administration's NTI presentations, and Blight Free Philadelphia provided a well-reasoned implementation methodology that, at that time, NTI lacked.

Community Planning

Midway through the first year of the Street Administration, Maxine Griffith was appointed head of the City Planning Commission. Griffith was a New Yorker who had managed her own planning practice years earlier, had served on the New York City Planning Commission, and had been a board member of the American Planning Association. During the late 1990s, she had been Regional Representative for New York and New Jersey for the U.S. Department of Housing and Urban Development, after which she worked in Washington as a HUD Assistant Deputy Secretary.

In 2000, Griffith had learned about the successful execution of Mayor Street's abandoned car initiative and about the opportunity to direct the Planning Commission. The prospect of working with a mayor who had served in City Council but was also skilled in policy development and policy implementation appealed to her, as did the prospect of participating in an initiative to rejuvenate neighborhoods.

Mayor Street had made it clear that community planning was to be an important part of his administration. After recruiting Griffith to lead the Planning Commission, the Mayor also appointed her to the Cabinet-level position of Secretary of Strategic Planning. Participation in weekly Cabinet meetings provided Griffith with an excellent opportunity to interact with the directors of the city agencies that were responsible for implementing projects and plans.

Griffith found the Planning Commission to be substantially understaffed for a city the size of Philadelphia. At her request, Mayor Street authorized the hiring of more community planning staff. Griffith recruited a cadre of young city planners, whom she described as "energetic, excited about their work, and tech-savvy."

The status and influence of the Planning Commission had declined during the Rendell Administration years. Rendell had often seemed to regard city planning as an impediment to timely decision-making, particularly with respect to the review and approval of development projects that he felt were critical to Philadelphia's future. Some veteran Planning Commission staff, after feeling marginalized during this period, had adopted the view that, in Griffith's words, "We're the good guys, but no one's going to listen to us," and had maintained a low-profile existence. They needed to be energized, and Griffith made sure that the younger incoming staff members were assigned to work in partnership with them. The new staff had to adapt as well and learn from the veterans. As a group, the latter had substantial institutional memory and in-depth knowledge of Philadelphia neighborhoods. Some had a high level of expertise in using the Planning Commission's GIS computer-mapping resources, and this capability was superior to that which could be found in many other cities at the time.

The challenge Griffith faced was determining how to operationalize community planning on a neighborhood level. The initial charge to the Planning Commission had been to complete community plans for seven neighborhoods in which NTI investment was anticipated to take place. A high level of disinvestment had occurred in several of these places. For example, the population of North Philadelphia's Strawberry Mansion community, the first neighborhood in which NTI-related community planning began, had declined by 15 percent between 1990 and 2000. Neighborhood median income was half the citywide median, and 41 percent of the residents had incomes below poverty level.[27] In addition, the community had no neighborhood organization or business association. Churches were a potential resource for civic engagement, but because the congregations were small, with many members who no longer lived in the neighborhood, the churches could not be counted on to take the lead in a community planning process.

New York City's community board system, mandated by the city's charter since 1963, makes it much easier for city agencies and neighborhood residents to work together to address community planning issues; the community board serves as a structure for civic engagement. Board members, who are appointed by borough presidents in consultation with City Council, review and vote on land use applications, special permits, urban renewal area designations, the acquisition and disposition of city-owned property, and the siting of major community facilities. Although the status of community boards is advisory, community board actions can influence subsequent Planning Commission and City Council decisions.[28]

According to Griffith, the community board structure also gave community members and city officials a shared understanding of neighborhood identity—the boundaries, defining characteristics, and even the community outlook on various issues. In some Philadelphia neighborhoods, there was far less cohesion. Griffith even encountered disagreements over neighborhood boundaries —on where the neighborhood geography began and ended. During one community meeting in which Griffith participated, a City Council member ordered some of the attendees to leave because they lived across the street from the neighborhood boundaries as the Councilperson defined them and therefore, from the Councilperson's point of view, should not be allowed to participate.

Under Griffith's direction, Planning Commission staff strived to avoid creating the impression that they were setting out to remake neighborhoods wholesale. In coordination with community members, they assessed existing conditions and community needs, identified overall goals, drafted plans, discussed and debated alternatives, and revised the plans for final approval.

Griffith devoted particular attention to ensuring that community planning was conducted "in the realm of reality." In Strawberry Mansion, Planning Commission staff created a development pro forma illustrating the cost factors associated with NTI investment in the community. The pro forma helped illustrate, for example, why the City would not be able to build 500 units of new housing in the community at a subsidy of $100,000 each. The community members appreciated this presentation—they applauded at the end of the meeting. "You shouldn't try to truncate people's aspirations," Griffith said, " but you should be honest with people about what realistically can be paid for."

Areas such as the Southwest Center City neighborhood, located just south of the downtown area, provided some of the best community planning opportunities, due to the influence of a growing real estate market nearby. These kinds of neighborhoods were places where private-sector resources could be leveraged to support the implementation of community plans. From Griffith's perspective, leveraging was critical; without a high degree of leveraging, NTI would not succeed.

Griffith did not think that "Neighborhood Transformation Initiative" was the best name for the City's neighborhoods policy, and she said so in a City Hall discussion about the naming of the policy. Her view was reinforced by an experience she had upon returning to her office just after the NTI launch event in April, 2001. On her desk she found a message left by a neighborhood resident who identified his address and added, "Please note: This neighborhood should not be transformed. Thank you very much."

The data that had been generated by TRF in connection with its citywide market analysis helped inform community planning activities; but, for Griffith, the way in which the data was presented, through the colored map illustrating TRF's neighborhood typology, became a problem. The presentation was similar to an academic product—it had a scientific appearance—

but, because it had no connection to existing studies, plans, or codes, its utility as a planning tool was limited.

Griffith also found that the TRF analysis created communication problems between city agency staff and neighborhood residents. Some community members, she said, "freaked out" over the way in which their neighborhoods had been characterized, particularly community members from areas that had been identified as "reclamation" zones suitable for substantial demolition, relocation, and new development. In other instances, neighborhood leaders told Griffith that conditions in their communities were worse than had been suggested by the TRF typology and expressed fear that not enough resources would be allocated to these places as a result. "Colors on a map have a powerful impact," she said.

For his part, Jeremy Nowak of TRF was not an ardent supporter of public sector planning. In a 2007 presentation to a meeting of the Design Advocacy Group which I attended, he characterized public sector planning as an out-moded industrial-age, command-and-control model that was out of place in today's economic environment.

Mayor Street's designation of staff to work exclusively on NTI—to manage decision-making associated with the NTI financial plan—was not in itself a problem from Griffith's perspective. The problem was that planning was not being viewed as integral to NTI, and NTI program decisions were being made in the absence of planning. NTI staff was too compartmentalized, and NTI implementation was moving forward in too linear a fashion. During the years of NTI implementation, opportunities did emerge for community planning and NTI decision-making to interface with each other, and these opportunities were pursued whenever they became apparent. However, a more integrated approach would have been beneficial to both the adminis-tration and the community.

As community planning got under way in the seven neighborhoods initially designated for this activity, City Council members submitted requests for more neighborhood plans. The list of neighborhoods in the community planning pipeline grew from seven to thirty-four. This broadening of the commitment to community planning at an early stage of NTI implementation far exceeded Planning Commission staff capacity. As late as 2008, a Planning Commission representative estimated that only about half of the thirty-four plans could be completed within the foreseeable future.

From Griffith's perspective, the City should have begun working with a smaller number of neighborhoods, as had originally been anticipated, but should also have let everyone else know where they stood in the neighborhood-planning sequence. Her experience was that "people will not mind waiting if they know their position in the queue and feel that the process is being conducted in an orderly way." In Griffith's view:

> NTI should have started with the identification of a few communities in which planning would be undertaken first, on a pilot basis. The

development community and elected officials should have been brought into the process systematically, then everyone could have moved forward together.[29]

But the larger shortcoming of NTI was the lack of coordination. "Planning is really about coordination," Griffith said, "and if you recognize that NTI involved actions that required the participation of many departments—Housing, Recreation, Streets, and others—not a whole lot of coordination was going on. You have to coordinate to make sure you're not digging the same hole twice."[30] The compartmentalization of NTI as a separate program unnecessarily separated NTI resource allocation decisions from community planning. As a result, Planning Commission staff had to be entrepreneurial and pursue opportunities to link with NTI on a case-by-case basis.

What the administration lacked was a strong relationship between planning and the investment of NTI funds. The TRF presentation had limited value, both as an analysis and as an investment tool; the market-cluster map could be used to justify commitments of NTI funding almost anywhere in the city. A linkage between planning and NTI investment was not achieved through the community planning process either. After an initial focus on planning within a small number of neighborhoods, community planning became, in effect, citywide, reducing the Planning Commission's effectiveness. As suggested by Maxine Griffith's comment, an interdepartmental process was lacking as well. During one of the middle years of NTI implementation, I heard a senior Philadelphia Housing Authority administrator tell an audience that "PHA isn't part of NTI." I later heard similar comments from Planning Commission managers.

The town meetings at which Mayor Street spoke in early 2000 could have served as the launch pad for a community planning phase that would have been citywide in scope, that would have engaged all of the constituencies that had an interest in NTI, and that would have been the primary NTI activity during the first eighteen months of Street's administration. Street could have identified a citywide community planning dialogue as the best way to determine, on a neighborhood-by-neighborhood basis, how to combine the two related themes that he had emphasized in his town-meeting presentations: government self-improvement and neighborhood self-help. If Mayor Street had identified community planning as the first step in redefining the working relationship between municipal government and neighborhoods, then every municipal agency would have been involved in the citywide dialogue, and the separation between NTI staff, the Planning Commission, and other departments would have been minimized. Other city agencies would have provided staff support, and this support, combined with the outsourcing of some community plans to private planning firms, would have prevented Planning Commission staff from being overwhelmed by the volume of requests for community plans. Launching and executing an ambitious citywide endeavor of this kind would have been a major challenge;

but it would not have been more challenging than towing 33,000 abandoned vehicles in forty days. The potential political liabilities associated with such an approach would have been formidable; but they might not have been greater than the political problems that Street encountered and finally resolved, at considerable political cost, during the second year of his administration.

5 A Citywide Revitalization Policy, II

NTI Real Estate Transactions and Housing Agency Reorganization

The Control of Land

The ability to acquire and convey vacant real estate to developers, when managed efficiently, can give older cities such as Philadelphia a competitive advantage over built-out suburban areas. However, in Philadelphia and many other older cities, most of the vacant properties are small, with many less than half an acre in size. Few postindustrial cities resemble Detroit and St. Louis, where large parcels of cleared land can be found, in some cases extending over several blocks. In addition, cities like Philadelphia have many largely vacant blocks that contain single or clustered occupied houses; assembling such blocks for development will necessitate decision-making about relocation and replacement housing for displaced residents.

Real estate acquisition was identified as a key element of NTI from the start. One of the "NTI Framework Goals" was to "improve the City's ability to assemble land for development," and this goal quickly assumed high-priority status. The five-year budget for NTI-related Land Assembly grew from $50 million to $74 million, then was further increased through the addition of $15 million in non-NTI funding. During the first years of NTI, City Council authorized the acquisition of more than 6,000 vacant buildings and lots.[1]

Under the Street Administration, eminent domain continued to be used as the primary method for assembling property for development. In a city such as Philadelphia, where legal titles to many vacant properties are in the names of deceased persons or corporations and partnerships that no longer exist, acquisition through direct purchase is frequently not an option. Bidding on properties at tax and mortgage foreclosure sales, used as the primary acquisition approach by government agencies in a number of cities, limits the scope of acquisition opportunities; some vacant properties may be blighted but not tax- or mortgage-delinquent. In addition, the city may be outbid at a tax or mortgage foreclosure auction, or the owner may appear and exercise the option to repay the debt, plus any additional charges, during a "right of redemption" period following the sale.

Eminent domain acquisition costs more money and requires a higher level of administrative support, but this approach gives the government clear title, in most cases, within a predictable period. From a Philadelphia perspective, the cost and administrative burden associated with eminent domain is more than outweighed by the ability to acquire property and convey it for development in a reliable and timely manner.

After an extended period in which the use of eminent domain was restricted to land assembly for major economic development ventures such as the Pennsylvania Convention Center and was rarely used in neighborhoods, the Rendell Administration reinstated this approach on a large scale to support acquisition for neighborhood development during the 1990s.

During 2002 and 2003, a series of actions took place that set the stage for NTI-related acquisition activities through 2007, Mayor Street's final year in office:

- In March 2002, the Street Administration and City Council resolved their disagreement over the extent to which Council would have oversight and influence over the expenditure of NTI bond funds. The compromise agreed to by both parties called for the City to submit a detailed plan and budget for City Council review and approval on an annual basis. Once the plan was approved, the Administration could not make a line-item transfer within the NTI budget without returning to Council for review and approval of the proposed change.
- The Administration allocated NTI funding for property acquisition requests submitted by the ten district Councilpersons. The amount assigned to each district Council member was based on a vacancy analysis completed by the Administration. High-vacancy districts would each receive an allocation of $7.025 million in NTI funds, each moderate-vacancy district would receive $3,475 million, and each low-vacancy district would receive $1.450 million. A total of $37 million had initially been budgeted for this purpose; this amount later increased to $52 million.
- The Administration also budgeted NTI funding to support its own acquisition priorities: land assembly for large-scale development and land acquisition within Acquisition Zones. The Acquisition Zones were, in effect, landbank districts, largely vacant areas not yet proposed for development, "within which and subject to the availability of funds, all vacant lots will be acquired for aggregation and future redevelopment."[2] A total of $37 million in NTI funding was allocated for these two activities.
- In order to authorize eminent domain acquisition of properties identified by district Councilpersons and the Administration, redevelopment plans were drafted by city agency staff and submitted for approval by the City Planning Commission and City Council. During 2002 alone, redevelopment plan proposals involving the acquisition of as many as 3,000 properties were brought forward for City Council approval.

- Administration officials anticipated that, barring unforeseen circumstances, the acquisition process would take six months and that NTI-funded demolition and NTI-funded acquisition would take place at about the same time, creating many cleared parcels for subsequent development.[3]

This approach differed from past housing and redevelopment practice in two significant ways. In previous years, Council approval was not required for budget line-item changes. Once the annual CDBG budget had been approved, for example, line-item changes could be made administratively during the course of the program year, without legislative review and approval. More important, the commitment to grant district Council members control over allocations of funding that they could view as, in effect, theirs, was a major departure from past practice. For ongoing programs such as CDBG, past Philadelphia city administrations had avoided allocating funds by Council district and had instead created generic line items (such as "Acquisition") in order to provide agency staff with maximum flexibility in determining where and in what amounts the funding should be allocated.

Although the expenditure of the acquisition funds that had been allocated to Council districts would be preceded by consultation between city agency staff and Council members, the approach that the Street Administration had agreed to amounted to a ceding of the Administration's control over resources that were originally intended to support high-priority strategic investment. The compromise with Council increased the possibility that resource allocation decisions would be politically motivated rather than based on strategic planning considerations. Land assembly to support a developer favored by a district Councilperson would be likely to receive funding, unless the Administration could convince the Councilperson that the developer's proposal was infeasible. And once an acquisition funding commitment had been made and site control achieved, that developer's prospects for also receiving NTI or CDBG construction subsidy funding would be greatly enhanced, because site control is such an important factor in leveraging financing.

City Council approval of a redevelopment plan is not all that is needed in order to enable local government to gain ownership of properties that are identified for acquisition in the plan. Two other actions must follow: the Redevelopment Authority board's issuance of a Declaration of Taking (through which the Authority assumes legal title to the property) and the RDA board's selection of a redeveloper (at which point a contract can be executed with the designated developer and the property can be conveyed for development).

The Fels Institute of Government reviewed RDA board meeting minutes during the last three years of the Rendell Administration and the first seven years of the eight-year Street Administration in order to record annual performance in terms of these two metrics. The results were as shown in Table 5.1.

Table 5.1 Redevelopment Authority Board Actions: Declarations of Taking and Redeveloper Selections, Calendar Years 1997–2006

Calendar Year	Number of Properties Approved for Acquisition and Disposition	
	Declarations of Taking	*Redeveloper Selections*
Rendell Administration		
1997	277	261
1998	291	247
1999	251	287
Street Administration		
2000	334	508
2001	102	182
2002	105	62
2003	175	51
2004	443	318
2005	432	186
2006	192	156

Source: Redevelopment Authority Board Meeting Minutes, 1997–2006. Data compiled by author.

During the final three years of the Rendell Administration, declarations of taking were issued for an annual average of 273 properties, and redeveloper selection actions authorized for the conveyance of an annual average of 265 properties. During the first seven years of the Street Administration, the comparable averages were 255 and 209, respectively.

The RDA's relatively low level of performance during the NTI years can be attributed to several factors. By 2002, the year in which the compromise with City Council over NTI implementation issues was achieved, property values in many Philadelphia neighborhoods were reaching unprecedented levels, consistent with the price escalation that was occurring in many areas of the country during the "housing bubble" period. During this period, it also became increasingly difficult for the RDA to obtain appraisals for properties designated for acquisition, as required by statute. Appraisers who had previously been available to contract with the RDA were now busy handling transactions in Center City and the better-off neighborhoods that were now experiencing a surge of development activity (strongly influenced by the ten-year tax abatement). Appraisers were far more likely to choose one of the increasing number of opportunities to work for a private developer or lending institution in appraising properties downtown or in the stronger neighborhood real estate markets in preference to working for the RDA to appraise vacant properties in lesser-known neighborhoods with weaker markets.

Citywide increases in property values limited the number of properties that could be acquired with available NTI resources; the per-property cost of acquiring vacant houses and lots more than doubled during the NTI years. In addition, real estate speculators were able to move ahead of the City in acquiring properties located in Acquisition Zones and at sites designated as priorities for large-scale construction, further increasing acquisition cost.

In January 2008, NTI officials were reported as stating that, of more than 6,200 properties originally anticipated for acquisition, about 5,000 were likely to be acquired, due to the problems already described. However, the data presented in Table 4.1 suggests that this estimate was far too high. Between 2000 and 2006, the RDA had acquired (through the issuance of declarations of taking) only about 1,800 properties. Without a major increase in acquisition activity, it seems unlikely that more than twice that number could be acquired within a reasonable period. As of January 2009, there was no evidence of such an increase.

Between 2000 and 2006, the developers that received the most properties (and are included in the "Redeveloper Selection" totals above) were three developers associated with the Cecil B. Moore Homeownership Zone in North Philadelphia (a total of 329 properties), the Philadelphia Housing Authority (288 properties), and Neighborhood Restorations, a private rental property developer that worked in close coordination with Councilwoman Jannie Blackwell (107 properties). The properties conveyed to these three developer groups, totaling 724 in all, account for nearly half of the 1,463 Redeveloper Selection actions completed between 2000 and 2006.

The Best Organization

The three City-affiliated housing agencies needed to be reorganized. Consolidation would increase efficiency and save money. In Fiscal 2001, housing agency administrative expense amounted to $11.5 million of the $79.2 million housing and community development budget. "Program delivery" expenses (the salaries of housing inspectors, for example) consumed another $18.2 million. Reducing these costs would provide more funding for bricks-and-mortar housing production, for housing repair and improvement, and for supportive services such as homeownership counseling. These were the arguments that were presented in favor of housing agency reorganization at the start of the Street Administration. The transition-team task force on blight elimination recommended this measure in its report to the newly-inaugurated mayor.[4] "There are just some painfully obvious inefficiencies," Mayor Street's Chief of Staff, Joyce Wilkerson, told City Council. "There are three personnel departments, three legal departments, and three procurement offices."[5] Although not specifically identified as an NTI goal, reorganization was felt to be essential to the successful execution of the policy.

The three housing agencies had emerged during three different post-World War Two decades. The Redevelopment Authority (RDA), a state-authorized agency governed by a five-member, mayorally-appointed board, had administered federally-funded revitalization programs in urban renewal areas during the 1950s and 1960s. The Authority had acquired land and provided financing to support the development of Society Hill and Yorktown. During the mid-century decades when the federal Title I program was in effect, the Authority employed architects, engineers, property maintenance crews, relocation caseworkers, real estate acquisition and real estate marketing specialists, housing program analysts, and an array of administrative and management personnel. At the direction of one City administration after another, the Authority had used eminent domain powers to acquire real estate and had issued bonds to finance development ventures in every decade of its existence, up to and after the turn of the century.

The Philadelphia Housing Development Corporation (PHDC) was created during the 1960s as a city-controlled nonprofit organization. Most of its board members were mayoral appointees, and other board positions were designated for the City's Managing Director, Finance Director, and other city officials. PHDC was formed to acquire property and develop housing, including both single-family homes and, in some instances, apartment buildings.

After the federal Housing and Community Development Act of 1974 replaced a series of longstanding federal programs, including Title I, with a single Community Development Block Grant, OHCD was created to serve as the City of Philadelphia's policy center and coordinating agency responsible for managing CDBG-funded activities and overseeing the activities of the RDA and PHDC. OHCD had maintained a lead-agency role throughout the tenure of its first Director, John Andrew Gallery. Gallery reported to the Mayor and gave directives to the RDA and PHDC (some of which were met with bureaucratic and political resistance). However, OHCD's standing eroded during the 1980s, after Gallery's departure; by 1991, the year before Rendell took office, the directors of OHCD and the RDA were openly quarreling over the level of CDBG funding that should be allocated for RDA overhead expenses.

OHCD's relationship with the RDA improved during the Rendell Administration, based on a clear delineation of roles. OHCD would draft the annual CDBG plan, set goals and priorities, organize the budget, apply for and receive the funding, and, through service contracts (primarily with public and nonprofit agencies), would allocate funds and monitor performance. The RDA would acquire and convey real estate, solicit, review and rank development proposals, and make financing available to selected developers. The two agencies frequently engaged in discussion and debate, but the underlying understanding was that OHCD would have the final word with respect to policymaking and the RDA would have the final word with respect to development proposal underwriting.

During my tenure at OHCD, from 1992 to mid-2001, the three agencies maintained a collegial relationship. I determined the broad goals and priorities that would guide RDA and PHDC implementation activities, but I didn't issue directives to anyone. The other two agency directors and I communicated frequently—Noel Eisenstat of the RDA and I spent time on the phone nearly every night of the week for eight years in order to keep in touch about current goings-on—and most OHCD policies reflected an interagency consensus. The Street Administration proposed to change these interagency relationships. The consolidation approach that the administration supported would position one agency, which might or might not be OHCD, to absorb or direct the other two in a manner more consistent with the premier role that had been OHCD's during the Gallery years.

A consolidation of the three agencies—which together employed about three hundred staff at the start of the Street Administration—could take place in one of two ways: two agencies could be eliminated altogether and their responsibilities assigned to the remaining one; or one agency could be designated as the alpha agency, which would lead the City's housing programs and direct the activities of the other two.

Which of the three housing agencies would be given the lead role? Each one had different characteristics that presented their own advantages and disadvantages:

- OHCD was the agency that, at the start of the Street Administration, most resembled a lead housing agency. However, unlike the other two agencies, OHCD was a city department, and its ability to undertake actions such as issuing a check or entering into a contract was constrained by the City Charter and city administrative process. For example, every payment issued by OHCD and other city departments had to be reviewed and approved by the City Controller. Every contract had to be prepared, reviewed, and approved by the City's Law Department, the staff of which worked for the City Solicitor, not for the OHCD Director. These limitations restricted the ability of OHCD to act quickly. Some of the investors and developers that the City needed to attract would not tolerate weeks-long delays in contract administration or construction-period payouts of project financing.
- The RDA was the agency that possessed two important state-authorized capabilities that the other two did not have: the power to use eminent domain to acquire real estate, and the ability to issue bonds. Eminent domain was already being employed as the City's primary means of property acquisition, and RDA bonds were being issued every year to support activities such as the City's home improvement loan program. However, thanks to collective bargaining agreements that had been negotiated during the 1980s and extended since that time, the RDA was expensive to operate. RDA staff, by contract, worked fewer hours than other city agency staff, and some RDA staff positions were paid at substantially higher wages than equivalent positions in city government. If the RDA were to be built up as the other two agencies were downsized, some administrative costs would increase.
- As a nonprofit organization, PHDC had the ability to enter into contracts and issue payments without the constraints of the City Charter or city

administrative processes. This ability was particularly valuable with respect to a PHDC-administered emergency repair program, which required timely processing of a large caseload of housing emergency cases, followed by expedited payouts to home repair contractors, most of which were small firms with little working capital. However, PHDC staff did not have a significant degree of capability in either real estate acquisition and disposition or development project financing, and the organizational capacity-building needed to achieve this capability would be substantial and time-consuming.

At the time when NTI was launched, the RDA was best positioned to take on the lead role. The five-member RDA board consisted of Street appointees. They had taken their seats in November 2000 and had elected John Dougherty, head of the electricians union and a Street ally, as chair. Herbert Wetzel, appointed as RDA Executive Director toward the end of the Rendell Administration, had strong community development credentials and had maintained a good working relationship with both City Council and key Street Administration officials. OHCD under my direction was not being seriously considered for this leadership position, nor was PHDC.

The Street Administration had planned to make the RDA the center of a consolidation plan, but these plans came to an end in June, 2001, when the Republican-controlled Pennsylvania House of Representatives passed legislation that placed the Philadelphia Parking Authority, like the RDA, a state-chartered agency, under state control. The measure took from the mayor and gave to the state the power to appoint Parking Authority board members, who in turn would control staff appointments and the agency budget. The legislation mandated that the Authority's annual net profits be transferred to the School District of Philadelphia, rather than to the City's general fund and aviation fund, as had previously been the practice. However, the extent to which this measure would benefit the School District could not be determined; the Authority had traditionally been populated by beneficiaries of political patronage, and the amount of net profit remaining after the funding of generous payroll and overhead expenses was unclear. What was clear was the fact that the agency was under the control of Republican elected officials in state government, most of whom were not friends of the Street Administration. The legislation had been crafted in stealth by House Majority Leader John Perzel, had been approved by the Republican-controlled Senate shortly after the House had acted, and was signed by Republican Governor Tom Ridge, who had clashed with Street over the control of the Philadelphia public schools.[6]

The City took legal action to block the change. The litigation failed. The conclusion to be drawn from this experience was obvious: why build up the power and resources of the RDA if it all could be taken away by your political adversaries virtually overnight?

Mayor Street made one early-stage decision about overall municipal governance that had an impact on the housing agencies. He created a small number of Cabinet-level positions associated with key issues, each with the title of Secretary: for example, the head of NTI was Secretary of Neighborhood Transformation, and the head of the City Planning Commission was Secretary of Strategic Planning. A Secretary of Housing and Neighborhood Preservation, Kevin R. Hanna, was appointed in November 2002, near the end of the third year of the Street Administration. Following the abandonment of the plan to create a central role for the RDA in housing reorganization, it was decided that Hanna would head a new office, the Office of Housing and Neighborhood Preservation, created by mayoral executive order in 2002, and that OHNP would be the new housing leadership entity.

Hanna had more housing industry experience than most of the then-current Philadelphia development administrators and many of their predecessors, and it was anticipated that he would play an important role in strengthening relationships with local builders and in leveraging private-sector investment in Philadelphia neighborhoods.[7] However, Hanna had no significant experience in managing municipal housing agencies that had been supported largely by federal funding programs during most of their existence, as Philadelphia's had been.

During Hanna's tenure, the next major step taken by the Street Administration was a consulting project: a study of what and how to reorganize. Following the solicitation of competitive proposals, a team led by Public Financial Management, Inc. and The Reinvestment Fund was selected for the job. PFM had substantial expertise in crafting public financing strategies; the firm had helped the Rendell Administration stabilize the City's finances in the early 1990s.

Phase I of the consulting project consisted of an "organizational assessment" involving a review of documentation, interviews with management staff, and a survey of agency employees. Phase II consisted of a series of discussions by "business process groups," made up of volunteers from the three housing agencies, to assess current processes and identify ways to improve them. In Phase III, the consultant team identified three reorganization options: total consolidation under OHNP, and two different restructurings of OHNP, RDA, and PHDC.[8] A fourth option—no reorganization—was not part of the consultant team's assignment.

The business process teams produced over a hundred recommendations for improvements, and the recommendations were documented in the consultants' final report. The volunteers who participated in the teams were primarily management-level employees; for the most part, unionized employees did not participate.

The consultant team's report was published in Fall 2005, nearly midway through Street's second four-year mayoral term of office. At the time, having occupied a position outside city government for more than four years, I could not see the need for the consulting project. If you had already decided in

Year One that the City's housing agencies are going to be reorganized, why would you devote time in Year Six to asking employees how they felt about process issues?

The Street Administration had not previously demonstrated a great deal of interest in the housing agency employee perspective. In addition, the early identification of housing agency reorganization as a priority at the start of the administration strongly suggested that there was something wrong with current agency employees or with the manner in which they were working together. The cumbersome nature of the real estate acquisition and disposition process had been singled out as a major problem early on; the March, 2000 report by Street's blight elimination task force indicated that as many as fifteen different agencies had one role or another in addressing vacant property issues.[9] But was the problem an issue of structure—requiring major organizational changes—or one of process? By the end of the Rendell Administration, the RDA had developed the capability to acquire a property through the eminent domain process within six months, and the RDA had maintained this capability during the Street Administration. There was no evidence that reorganization could improve this process.

Other flaws in the reorganization concept could be readily identified. Mayor Street's Chief of Staff had been correct in pointing out that, under existing organizational structure, each agency had its own legal counsel. But agency consolidation would not reduce the number of lawyers paid with city funding. If all agency operations were consolidated under the RDA, for example, the City's Law Department would still have to assign legal staff to handle issues related to the administration of city dollars; as a state-chartered agency that did not report directly to the Mayor, the RDA could not staff this responsibility in-house. If another city agency were to become the consolidated entity, the RDA would still need to retain its own legal counsel to advise the RDA Board on eminent domain and bond financing transactions. A lawyer employed by the City's Law Department, which reported to the Mayor (through the City Solicitor), could not simultaneously be responsible for representing the RDA board's interests with respect to these issues. The number of lawyers supported with city funding would remain unchanged.

The delay in implementing reorganization was not good for agency morale at all levels. Prior to the Street Administration, the City's housing agencies had not been corrupt or incompetent. Agency operations and staffing structure were not problem-free, but compelling evidence of severe structural flaws that could not be corrected through process improvements (such as the one hundred-plus recommendations published in the consultant team's report) was lacking. Without difficulty, you could learn of horror stories involving housing agency mishandling of certain issues—inexcusable delays in processing a contract, for example—but horror stories about the Department of Licenses and Inspections (L&I), the City's code enforcement agency, were far more prevalent. However, L&I was not being reorganized, despite the critical relationship between code enforcement and housing preservation, and the emphasis given to the latter as a key strategy for neighborhoods in need of stabilization. In addition, for reasons that, to my knowledge, were not made clear, the Philadelphia Housing Authority was never considered as part of the housing agency reorganization plan.

As the end of the Street Administration neared, labor issues came to the forefront of the housing reorganization process. Union members in the three housing agencies, represented by AFSCME Local 1971, knew that they had the least to gain from a reorganization. The housing agencies had been reorganized at least once in each of the past three decades, and it was certain that layoffs of union members would be an integral part of any plan that the City Administration adopted. The reorganization dialogue had always included some discussion of interagency transfers that could be undertaken as part of a consolidation process—so that, for example, an RDA employee who was laid off on a Friday afternoon would be hired by OHNP on the following Monday morning—and of placing laid-off employees in other city departments. However, specific employee placement plans could not be worked out in advance because the identity of the laid-off employees could not be determined beforehand. Based on seniority, a union member who received a layoff notice could "bump" down to a lower level union-represented job in his or her agency, displacing a person with lower seniority who held that job; that person, in turn, could bump to another lower level position occupied by a person with less seniority than the "bumper." Because the effects of multiple "bumping" actions could not be known ahead of time, the definitive list of employees who would ultimately be displaced could not be compiled until after the layoff notices had been issued and the bumping process completed.

Even if such plans could have been developed in advance, some individual staff members would be disadvantaged by reorganization. For example, for an RDA staff person transferred to OHNP who had not been employed long enough to be vested for pension benefits, the time spent at the RDA would not be counted by OHNP for vesting purposes; the staff person's pension eligibility timetable would have to be restarted, and the employee would have to wait ten years before being vested.

In addition, the staff members likely to be most vulnerable in a layoff were secretaries, clerks, and other lower-level staff. Executive-level staff would probably be laid off as well, but it was impossible to imagine a reorganization that would not threaten the individuals in these lower-paid, lower-status positions in a major way.

Labor relations problems were important to the senior administrators who reported to the Mayor and his Chief of Staff, regardless of whether or not reorganization was to be implemented. Bargaining-agreement language that had been agreed to in the 1980s and carried over into successive labor contracts included provisions that imposed heavy burdens on management. The OHCD contract, for example, included a requirement that the union review and approve any changes in the job specifications for a particular position before they were instituted. No other city department was bound by a comparable requirement; in all other municipal agencies, management's only obligation was to notify the union in advance, with no union sign-off needed.

Another provision in the OHCD contract required management to make "all possible efforts" to place laid-off employees in new positions. I learned about the power of this seemingly innocuous phrase when labor grievances were filed following an early-1990s reorganization which became the subject of an arbitration proceeding. Local 1971's attorney was ready with questions for me: Did you write to the Governor to ask the state to hire laid-off employees? Did you contact the Secretary of HUD and ask for more federal funding? Did you ask the Mayor to create new jobs for laid-off workers? Any responses in the negative could be counted as evidence that the "all possible efforts" provisions had not been honored.

When the City's four-year bargaining agreement with Local 1971 expired in 2004, six months into Street's second term, a new agreement was not signed due, in large part, to unresolved disagreements over these and other contract language issues. As is required under such circumstances, the existing contract language was carried over and remained in place. However, the lack of a new contract meant that Local 1971 members would not receive periodic cost-of-living raises that were granted to management staff and to all other City employees (who were covered under separate labor agreements that had been successfully negotiated and executed). This situation did not improve staff morale, but no one could offer a reasonable plan for overcoming the stalemate. For the administration, the existing contract language was an unacceptable burden; the language needed to be changed in order to improve housing agency performance. For the union, the existing contract language was union-represented employees' only defense against the threat of job loss. What sense would it make to agree to a giveback of these provisions?

During the early months of 2006, it became clear that the Street Administration planned to adopt the first reorganization option described in the consultant team's Fall 2005 report and consolidate as much staffing as possible under OHNP. By this time, the next-to-final year of the Street Administration, the political calculus had changed. RDA board chair John Dougherty, the powerful construction trades leader whose political alliance with Mayor Street had been an important factor in Street's election and re-election, made it clear that he would not be willing under any circumstances to preside over a reorganization involving layoffs of union members. Dougherty would run for state senator in 2008 (unsuccessfully, as it turned out); he had nothing to gain by accommodating Street, whose support would be more of a disadvantage than an advantage in the senatorial district which he wished to represent. The disagreement between Street and Dougherty escalated into a bitter public feud, with Street expressing his determination to move ahead and Dougherty vowing to resist.

City Council Majority Leader Jannie Blackwell, one of Street's strongest political allies, also opposed the proposed layoffs. She threatened to hold up City Council authorization of Philadelphia's annual application for federal CDBG funds, and the issue dominated the annual housing budget hearing. A partial compromise was reached in early June: the administration softened the language initially used to describe the overall reorganization without cancelling layoff plans; the identification of OHNP as the lead housing agency was deleted from the plan; it was agreed that OHNP would disappear and that the lead role would now be assumed by OHCD, under Kevin Hanna's direction.[10]

Layoffs began in 2006, and some staff transfers were made as planned. A fund-transfer that needed to be approved in order to enable OHCD to hire laid-off workers from other agencies was held up by Councilwoman Blackwell until February 2007.[11] Some of the laid-off employees were left in limbo, without a job until the funding was approved by Council. During the remainder of the Street Administration and the end of the first year of the mayoral administration of Michael A. Nutter, no significant cost savings or increases in productivity could be documented as a result of the reorganization actions. Labor grievances were filed, citing unfair labor practices in connection with the City's handling of the layoffs. People conversant with housing agency labor relations issues anticipated that these grievances and subsequent arbitrations would result in a series of rulings against the City, accompanied by directives to compensate and/or rehire laid-off employees.

The Transformational Experience

The topics described in this chapter and the preceding one are evaluated below, in reverse order. To the extent that NTI fell short of expectations, the shortcomings in each case were associated with the same core problem: a transformation of neighborhoods could not be undertaken successfully unless preceded by a transformation of government.

Who's in Charge?

State-chartered housing and redevelopment authorities governed by boards will continue to be a part of the urban development landscape for the foreseeable future. For this reason, a mayor must make an accurate assessment of the prospects for creating and sustaining a strong working relationship with both state elected officials and authority board members. The former may not be contemplating takeover legislation similar to that which House Majority Leader John Perzel crafted to bring the Philadelphia Parking Authority under state control; but, to the extent possible in the existing political environment, they need to be brought on board at the same time as major neighborhood revitalization initiatives are planned. State government can play a strong role in financing development activity, and state lawmakers can approve legislation that will facilitate the acquisition of vacant or neg-lected property (in fact, the Pennsylvania General Assembly had approved several such measures during the Street Administration).

Authority board members should be respected for their contributions to dialogue and debate over program development and project financing issues; but when the discussion ends and the time comes to vote, the board needs to understand the mayor's position on a particular issue (as articulated by a representative of the mayor who participates in every board meeting) and to consistently support it. During the Rendell years, RDA board members were not always pleased with Rendell's policies or with the manner in which he expected the RDA to implement them; but a public feud comparable to that carried on by Mayor Street and RDA Board chair Dougherty would have been unthinkable during that time.

The call for consolidation of Philadelphia's housing agencies was based on a misperception. Consolidation per se does not ensure improved performance. Some highly successful for-profit and nonprofit real estate development organizations have very small staffs, and these organizations outsource planning, design, financial packaging, and construction management services. Other such organizations staff some or all of these functions just as effectively in-house. A multi-agency approach can be as efficient and cost-effective as a consolidated-agency approach.

The most important organizational development issues during the NTI period were the need for leadership and the need for process improvements, and neither of these issues were substantively addressed. Administrative leadership was dispersed. The Mayor was not in control of the RDA board. The Secretary of Neighborhood Transformation was not responsible for supervising the housing agency reorganization that had been deemed critical to the success of NTI. This responsibility was instead assigned to a Secretary of Housing who had no significant experience in administering the federally-financed housing programs that had been the three agencies' resource base for decades. Furthermore, the Secretary of Housing had no control over the biggest local housing agency, the Philadelphia Housing Authority; the housing authority was not even included in the reorganization plan.

The need for process improvements was not addressed with respect to the process for which the need for improvement was greatest: the acquisition and conveyance of real estate. As already shown, the Street Administration's performance in completing land transactions was not an improvement over the Rendell Administration's record, despite the larger infusion of funding made available through NTI.

Both leadership and process issues should be addressed in the following way. The mayor should appoint and consistently support a person who is given the authority to make policies and implement programs based on goals articulated by the mayor. That mayoral appointee—the administration's development policy leader—should be given the power to hire and fire development agency directors, and should make the hiring and firing decisions during the first six months of the administration. The agency directors who are recruited or retained should have two characteristics: they should be consistently responsive to the mayor's policy directives and, with respect to their areas of expertise, they should know more than the development policy leader who hired them. Because they are smarter than the administration's development policy leader in these respects, they should be given a high degree of responsibility for implementing activities within their respective areas of expertise. Up to a point, they should be allowed to compete with each other and argue with each other; but the policy leader should keep them on track by mediating their dialogue when needed and by making decisions when the time for action has come.

Acquisition

In a postindustrial city, the control of land is even more important than access to financing; site control leverages financing commitments far more frequently than the reverse. When the Street Administration agreed to give district Council members control over more than half the NTI acquisition budget, opportunities for strategic investment were greatly weakened.

The Street Administration appropriately made acquisition for large-scale development a priority. However, a government-wide transformation initiative would also have included a fundamental change in the business model for the taking and conveyance of tax-delinquent properties (some of which may not be blighted or abandoned). In Philadelphia, as in many other cities, many tax delinquent buildings and lots are sold at public auction, with the proceeds of sale used to pay the taxes owed. In most instances, this process, supervised by the county sheriff or a court-appointed official, has no relationship to neighborhood plans or strategies. Bidders at the public auction are not screened or pre-qualified with respect to their experience as developers or their ability to improve and maintain the properties they acquire; in many cities, the highest bid is about all that matters.

In 2005, a total of 186 properties were conveyed by the RDA as a result of the eminent domain process, with each property conveyance documented by a redevelopment agreement that described in detail the manner in which each property would be developed for constructive reuse. During the same year, a total of 614 Philadelphia properties—twice as many—were conveyed as a result of tax foreclosure, with no comparable documentation and no oversight by any planning or development agency.

During the same years in which NTI was taking place, an alternative approach to property conveyance via tax foreclosure, designed for the highly disinvested city of Flint, Michigan, had been gaining national attention. Based on state enabling legislation, a landbank authority headed by the Treasurer of Genesee County (the county in which Flint is located) was empowered to take control of all properties eligible for tax foreclosure. Daniel Kildee was the Genesee County Treasurer who designed and managed the authority's operating plan. At the start of the fiscal year, he would issue a bond and use the proceeds to pay off all the tax obligations associated with the properties designated for foreclosure. Then he and his staff would make decisions, working in coordination with neighborhood constituencies, about the conveyance of the properties that the authority now controlled. Some of the properties were houses in marketable condition; they would be assigned to real estate brokers who would sell them and turn over the proceeds to the land bank authority. Some of the properties were houses that were poorly located or infeasible to rehabilitate; they would be demolished. Some of the properties were vacant lots; they would be sold to adjacent owners for development as side yards or parking, or combined with adjacent lots to produce larger sites for future development.

The prospects for enacting comparable state legislation to support the creation of a Philadelphia landbank (one of the priorities highlighted in the initial NTI presentations) may or may not have been good during the early years of NTI. However, state legislative leaders of both parties had expressed interest in the Michigan model, and some of them had met with Kildee to discuss it. At a minimum, the City could have pursued an agreement with the Philadelphia Sheriff to give the RDA right of first refusal on foreclosure-eligible properties before they went to public auction. Failing that, RDA staff could have been assigned to participate in tax foreclosure auctions and to bid on properties located within areas that had been designated as strategic priorities. By 2005, the landbank model managed by Kildee was generating profits as well as producing sensible property-disposition outcomes. Philadelphia could have done the same.

The Plan

NTI was implemented during a period in which Philadelphia real estate values increased dramatically, due, in varying degrees, to the influence of national trends, to the successful management of the downtown area, and to the availability of the ten-year tax abatement. Most of the development that occurred in Philadelphia during Street's eight-year tenure was not NTI-financed; the extent to which NTI investment decisively influenced this development could not be determined. Joyce Wilkerson, Street's Chief of Staff, said, "I don't buy this idea that if our dollars didn't actually fund the demolition, acquisition or subsidize the development that we can't take credit for it." Another point of view was expressed by Kevin Gillen of Penn's Wharton School, who said, "The mayor is correct that the boom happened on his watch, but the idea that it is attributable to NTI is laughable." Gillen credited the Street Administration with strengthening some neighborhood real estate markets, but commented that: "The idea that you could drive an entire market that large just by concentrating your efforts in a few locales is stretching your faith in public policy."[12]

Studies of HOPE VI ventures had shown that the demolition of obsolete public housing and the development of mixed income communities that followed have the effect of substantially increasing property values in surrounding neighborhoods.[13] Although most Philadelphia Housing Authority development had not been supported with NTI funding, NTI paid for much of the PHA-related acquisition described earlier in this chapter.

Many vacant buildings in dangerous condition had been demolished, and other demolition had created sites for new development as proposed in initial presentations of NTI. But the expenditure of a large amount of NTI funding on demolition did not reduce the need to budget City operating funds for demolition in post-NTI years. In Fiscal 2008, for example, the City was paying debt service on the NTI bonds at the same time as it was budgeting $8 million in operating funds for demolition that had not been addressed by NTI or for demolition needs that had emerged after NTI. In January, 2009, an administrator at the City's Department of Licenses and Inspections told me that L&I inspectors were finding about thirty buildings each month to add to the list of "imminently dangerous" properties requiring demolition—an average of one a day.

Compromises with City Council over the allocation of NTI funding and the decision to give district Council members their own acquisition budgets reduced the impact of NTI in large measure. Just after the end of the Street Administration, Wilkerson said:

> If left to our own devices, we would have made investments and development decisions based on what we knew was happening in neighborhoods. In many instances, it was different from what City Council wanted to do . . .
>
> The whole data-driven approach ended up being diluted. It was in no way fatal to the program, but decisions weren't always based on hard data.[14]

The pessimistic characterization of NTI was that, after all was said and done, the policy amounted to the expenditure of $306 million in public funding to pay for a hodgepodge of development ventures, public improvements, and public services that had relatively little impact. Despite the shortcomings of the policy as implemented, this characterization of NTI would be unfair. NTI financing brought market-rate housing construction to neighborhoods such as Brewerytown and East Poplar, which were located near strong real estate markets but had not previously benefitted from this proximity. NTI subsidies enabled PHA to extend the geographic scope of the Mill Creek HOPE VI venture in West Philadelphia to build out an area much larger than the site of the demolished public housing. NTI-financed land acquisition enabled APM to assemble sites for the Pradera venture, which brought neighborhood investment closer to the Temple University campus. These and other accomplishments required commitments of public funding at a level that would not have been available had NTI not been launched.

The most positive characterization of NTI would be one that placed the policy in a broader context, on three levels:

- During his first year in office, Mayor Street authorized a major expansion of the ten-year tax abatement, and this incentive helped stimulate large-scale housing development downtown and in higher-priced neighborhoods, financed largely through private debt and equity.
- In order to broaden the impact of this private market activity, NTI financing was used to produce a combination of market-rate and subsidized housing in areas that were marginal but close enough to higher-value downtown and neighborhood real estate markets to attract higher-than-median income buyers and renters.
- For neighborhoods with less market potential, the biggest barriers to investment were vacant structures and deteriorated older public housing. With NTI funding support, the worst of the vacant-structure inventory was removed and development activity following the demolition of the obsolete public housing was enhanced by NTI investment on adjacent blocks.

Given the opportunity, many elected officials could find strategic ways to spend $306 million. The more important question to be addressed in an assessment of NTI is determining whether this policy had, in any respect, a genuinely transformative impact, in terms of the three ways in which "transformation" is characterized in the Introduction. The abandoned-car campaign was genuinely transformative. Blight had been removed, and the competitive position and wealth-building prospects for neighborhoods that had suffered from this problem were substantially improved.

The single activity that had a transformative impact on neighborhoods and that can be linked directly to NTI investment is a program for the interim maintenance of vacant lots, many of which were the by-product of NTI-financed demolition, others of which had been longstanding neighborhood eyesores. The Street Administration entered into a $4 million contract with the nonprofit Pennsylvania Horticultural Society (PHS) to maintain a large number of vacant lots in locations around the city. PHS established partnerships with neighborhood-based organizations and businesses who removed the trash, cut the weeds, and landscaped the lots. The landscaping treatment was minimal: grass was planted; a double rail wooden fence was erected around the perimeter of some lots, a row of saplings planted around others.

The improved condition of the PHS-maintained lots influenced higher property appraisals and increased property values on the blocks where they were located.[15] As important was a new insight gained through the

Figure 5.1a Vacant Lot Before Interim Greening

Figure 5.1b Vacant Lot After Interim Greening

implementation of this program: on most of the lots where fencing and tree-planting had been completed, these innocuous perimeter markers were respected. Even in some of the city's most distressed neighborhoods, the fences and trees were not broken, and the lots did not become short-dumping sites where tires or construction debris piled up. The modest perimeter improvements conveyed the message that someone was looking after the property, and, in many instances, that subtle message was enough.

This experience radically differed from what, prior to 2000, had been the common wisdom about how to maintain vacant lots in the worst-off areas: install a chain-link fence, six feet high or higher—and then worry about whether vandals will rip off the fence.

The vacant lot maintenance experience and the abandoned-car initiative are the positive learning experiences that should inform NTI-like initiatives in other cities. An elected official who launches an initiative of this kind has to talk big, but many of the people who do the work of implementation have to think small and focus on completing incremental improvements. Ambitious goal-setting and campaign-style promotion are essential prior to and at the launching of a major revitalization initiative; but what will count most at the end of each year of implementation is the aggregate value created through a larger number of small- and medium-sized investments. Through his leadership of the Genesee County landbank authority's activities in Flint, Daniel Kildee was able to generate substantial aggregate value by managing a large portfolio of properties, most of which he characterized as "dogs," but which, altogether, generated enough value to make the authority profitable each year.

Local elected officials know how to talk big, and the best of them know how to think small when it matters. On election nights, they pore over the vote tallies as they are reported from individual precincts or divisions, each of which may consist of not more than a few hundred registered voters, in order to assess the manner in which the results from each of these areas, in combination, will affect the political fortunes of the candidates in that day's elections and in elections to come. Elected officials know that their political future depends in large part on their ability to think, plan, and execute their political campaigns on a micro level. I heard John Street describe how, as a first-time candidate for a district Council seat, he had, in effect, grid-mapped the entire district—one-tenth of the city—in order to determine, block by block, how he could use the resources available to his campaign to market his candidacy to the voters most likely to consider supporting him. Development opportunities need to be assessed and pursued throughout the city in the same manner, on an individualized, block-by-block basis at the same time as larger-scale ventures are being organized in the highest-priority target areas.

Andres Duany, one of the cofounders of the New Urbanism movement, articulated this perspective in a presentation to the 1999 "21st Century Neighborhoods" conference cosponsored by OHCD and the Foundation for Architecture:

Now don't make this mistake when you bring developers. The increment of investment [should] be small. [A] great mistake left over from the 70s and 80s is actually putting together vast tracts of ownership so that somehow it's easier. You know, "Let's get the whole block together." Well, you know, when . . . the increment of economic activity is the whole block, there are very few corporations that have the wherewithal to do the . . . project. So what they do is they come in and say, "We need subsidies from A to Z . . ."

But if you keep the city in its natural, small plotting instead of having a dinosaur that needs to be fed two tons of fodder a day—you have a magnificent beast but two tons a day or it's dead—why not get the same biomass with a hundred chipmunks or a thousand chipmunks that only need two acorns a day? And they get their own little loans . . . They can simply activate the system that is now available . . .[16]

Elected officials considering the adoption of a major neighborhood revitalization initiative should be prepared to plan and monitor progress based on annual plans and performance reports that set forth goals and report on accomplishments at a small, property-level scale. A big opening campaign, the financing of large-scale development ventures, and the strategic targeting of public improvements and public services will not be enough to ensure success. Unless comparable attention is devoted to property-by-property development opportunities, the most ambitious revitalization initiative will fail to realize its full potential value.

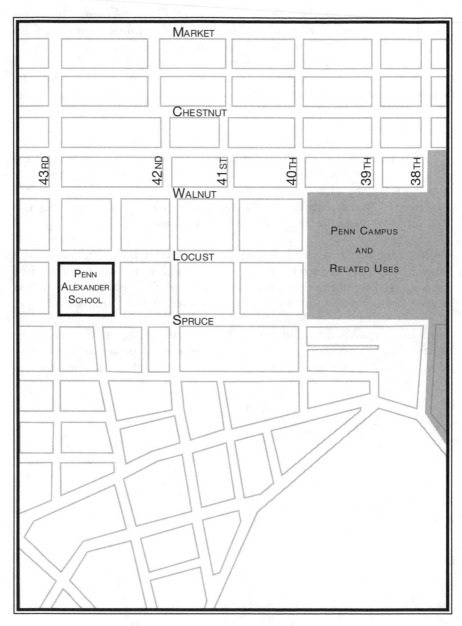

Figure 6.1 Penn Alexander School and Penn Campus

6   Broadening Public Education Options

The Penn Alexander School

A World Still Round

Academic and health care institutions are contrarian players in the twenty-first-century urban economy. While the new economy is borderless and global, they remain place-based.*

In the new economy, a typical corporation can be located at any one of a variety of sites. Consider, for example, two Fortune 500 corporations: Comcast and Campbell's Soup. These corporations could be headquartered in many locations other than Philadelphia and Camden; like many other corporations before them, they could have chosen to move out rather than invest in expansion projects within their home cities. Institutions such as the University of Pennsylvania and Cooper University Hospital have fewer options, however. Their continued presence in Philadelphia and Camden, where they were founded and grew up, is a necessity because, for them, location matters. In his bestselling book, Thomas L. Friedman described the ways in which globalization has leveled the economic playing field; in terms of economic competition, he wrote, the twenty-first-century world is "flat."[1] This conclusion, however, does not apply to city-based institutions, because some of their most significant competitive strengths and weaknesses are place-related. In many respects, their world remains round.

Enhancing the value of their fixed capital—the real estate, machinery, and equipment they own—in an era of high capital mobility is a major challenge for urban academic and health care institutions. Many of these institutions cannot move to new sites; they have to succeed in place. Viewed in terms of their locations, they are similar to the old-economy factories that had thrived in cities during the industrial age. Like older manufacturing firms, they originated in or moved into the fast-growing population centers of the eighteenth and nineteenth centuries, places where workers and managers

* My recounting of the University of Pennsylvania's involvement in the planning and implementation of the Penn Alexander School project is based largely on information and comments provided by Lucy Kerman. However, the opinions expressed in this chapter are mine alone, as is the responsibility for the manner in which I have used the information and her insights.

lived already or could readily move to, and places that consumers—students and patients—could readily travel to. In some instances, their early twentieth-century architecture, the multi-story brick, masonry, and metal buildings that these institutions developed and occupied, resembles that of the manufacturing plants that rose up in these cities. The institutions were production industries too. They produced information, knowledge, and graduates; they produced repaired and enhanced human bodies.

Special challenges confronted academic and health care institutions as the urban demographic changed during the mid- and late twentieth century. For neighborhood-based hospitals, population decline and an increasing number of lower-income households meant a smaller customer base with a larger proportion of uninsured patients. Many small community hospitals closed, and many of those that survived merged with regional and national health care chains.

The residency of middle- and upper-income employees of hospitals, colleges, and universities became more regionalized, as members of the institutional workforce moved out of urban neighborhoods. At the same time, an increasing number of newly-hired employees were people who did not live in the city, including many who had never lived there. Due to the declining quality of urban public schools and the growing number of urban neighborhood residents lacking basic work-readiness skills, more lower-paying job openings at these institutions began to be filled by better-qualified individuals who did not live nearby either.

Urban institutions could not leave the central city as readily as some commercial and industrial businesses had done. They had made substantial investments in fixed assets which could not be moved and which were not likely to attract buyers who might pay a price approaching replacement cost. The weak real estate market that prevailed in postindustrial cities made a successful sale or adaptive reuse of an institutional campus unlikely. Abandoning their urban campuses and starting over in a suburban or exurban location was just as infeasible for most such institutions.

Under these circumstances, urban academic and health care institutions had to work harder to convince customers to travel to a place that was increasingly being regarded as distressed: a deteriorating city with a disintegrating social structure. For some health care institutions, this disadvantage was partially offset through affiliation with regional or national hospital chains and through the establishment of specialized services of sufficiently high quality to draw patients from around the region and nation. In addition to its medical complex in Camden, for example, Cooper University Hospital has created a regional network of facilities based in the New Jersey suburbs, as well as in Pennsylvania and Delaware. The hospital's website promotes high-quality services provided by six "Centers of Excellence," each of which "offers the best medical technology and clinical expertise to provide world-class care."[2]

As central city economies weakened, urban institutions began making facilities-design decisions based on the perceived risks associated with the

Figure 6.2 Penn Library Frontage

surrounding environment. For health care institutions, secure structured parking came to be regarded as essential. For many, the most desirable parking facility was a multistory garage attached to the main hospital building, enabling visitors to drive in, park, and enter the hospital without setting foot on a city sidewalk. In some institutional complexes, visitors and employees travel from one building to another by means of pedestrian bridges that span city streets. Urban institutions have been walled, gated, and guarded in varying degrees to discourage or limit entry by unauthorized outsiders, which may include members of the adjacent residential community.

Other mid-twentieth-century facilities-design decisions addressed this concern in a more subtle way. University of Pennsylvania buildings constructed along Walnut Street, a major east–west artery that runs adjacent to the campus, were built with entrances facing inward, opening onto interior-block pedestrian walkways or landscaped quadrangles. Much of the Walnut Street frontage of these buildings consists of stone or masonry walls with no windows at ground level. The Walnut Street frontage of the Van Pelt Library (built in 1962) consists of a service driveway and loading area. The Walnut Street frontage of the adjacent Lippincott Library consists of narrow windows, resembling those of Camden's Riverfront Penitentiary, many of which are positioned higher than the top of a pedestrian's head.

The physical condition of neighborhoods adjacent to urban academic and health care institutions can vary widely. Pennsylvania Hospital is located in

Philadelphia's Society Hill neighborhood, which remained one of the metropolitan region's strongest and most stable real estate markets following the completion of urban renewal activities in the 1960s and 1970s. Temple University Hospital, on the other hand, is located in one of the most devastated sections of North Central Philadelphia, near a deteriorated neighborhood commercial corridor and surrounded by residential blocks with high levels of abandonment.

In many neighborhoods, the most stable residential areas are those adjacent to an institution, and some neighborhood housing development ventures are deliberately positioned on sites next to or near an institutional campus. As described in Chapter Three, Yorktown in Eastern North Philadelphia was intentionally developed on blocks immediately south of the Temple University main campus, based on an awareness of the institution's potential value as an anchor for development. The value of this proximity to campus was confirmed years later by Yorktown residents who responded to survey questions about the positive characteristics of the neighborhood with comments such as "convenient to Temple University" and "double protection with Temple and City Police."[3]

As time goes on, institutions in disinvested neighborhoods characterized by declining housing values, rising crime rates, and lower-quality public education experience a workforce-related problem that is twofold. As already described, fewer of the residents who remain in the neighborhood are qualified for jobs available at the institution, because the neighborhood has a smaller proportion of individuals with high school degrees and appropriate skills. The status of the Cooper Plaza/Lanning Square neighborhood where Cooper University Hospital is located is illustrative of this situation. In this neighborhood, more than 40 percent of the population had incomes below poverty level in 2000, and more than half the adults over twenty-five did not have a high school diploma.[4]

At the same time, housing options were not available for workers who were already employed at these institutions, despite the fact that, in some institutions, a significant number of employees would likely be interested in moving into the city if housing were available. One illustration of this employee interest could be found in a 2006 survey of academic and health care institution staff, medical professionals, and graduate students conducted by the Camden Higher Education and Healthcare Task Force. Most of the 837 respondents (679 of whom were associated with Cooper University Hospital) were living in suburban areas not immediately adjacent to the city and were paying an average of $1,335 a month for housing.[5] Forty-four percent of the respondents answered "yes" to the question, "If new housing were built in the city of Camden and cost was not a factor, would you consider living there?" At the time when the survey was taken, no major new housing development was under way within the census tracts where Cooper is located.

Despite the challenges they face, academic and health care institutions remain a strong presence in postindustrial cities because they are centrally located and accessible to a regional customer base. As central cities lost the large manufacturing firms that had made them prominent in the industrial age, many of these institutions became, for their cities, the largest private employer, largest service provider, and most powerful magnet for attracting wealth from outside. The University of Pennsylvania, for example, is Philadelphia's top employer, with a workforce of more than 20,000. The Hospital of the University of Pennsylvania had nearly 15,000 employees as of late 2007.[6] Customers from around the world purchase knowledge, health care, and professional services from Penn, just as buyers from around the world used to buy Stetson hats manufactured in Philadelphia's Kensington area or razor blades manufactured in the city's Tacony neighborhood. By the end of the twentieth century, "knowledge industries" occupied the lead role in the urban and regional economy where the manufacturing sector had been predominant a century earlier. In December 2007, the percentage of workers employed in education and health care within the Philadelphia metropolitan area was more than double that of workers employed in manufacturing (18.6 percent, as opposed to 7.8 percent).[7]

From the perspective of neighborhood residents, an institution may be recognized as an economic asset, but also viewed as a problem. The authors of the Spruce Hill Civic Association's "Community Renewal Plan" for the neighborhood immediately west of Penn state that:

> Undergraduate students attending the University of Pennsylvania are generally poor neighbors in Spruce Hill. They tend to stay out late on weekends, their automobiles invite crime to the neighborhood, and the outsides of their residences are often trash-filled.[8]

For some, the institution is regarded as a hostile political power, as expressed in a submission to the Defenestrator website:

> [Although Penn] claims to be a private institution, the fact that every governor of the Commonwealth of Pennsylvania is also a *de facto* trustee of the University of Pennsylvania provides a key to unlocking a chest of concentric networks of political power at both the municipal and state government levels, as well as influence in the bureaucratic forces at the federal level of government . . .
>
> [Penn's] destructive policy culminates in the seizure and purchase of real estate, the deliberate extermination of indigenous family-owned businesses and the unrelenting harassment of black males by the Penn police (who serve as vanguard of this corporate invasion of our community).[9]

The self-interest of community members differs fundamentally in important respects from that of the institution with which they share a neighborhood.

Student residency in the neighborhood can be a nuisance for community members but a benefit for an academic institution with a limited supply of on-campus housing and no desire or ability to expand the campus in order to build additional dorm rooms. For academic and health care institutions, the key to survival, and potential success, in the postindustrial environment is identifying and addressing those issues in which the self-interest of institution and community is shared or identical.

Between Two Halloweens

On October 31, 1996, a Penn biochemist, Vladimir Sled, and his fiancée were accosted on a neighborhood street in West Philadelphia a few blocks from the Penn campus. During a struggle with the assailants, Sled was stabbed to death. A few weeks later, at a forum on public safety issues held during Penn's Family Weekend, Penn President Judith Rodin and Mayor Rendell were confronted by angry parents. According to Dr. Rodin's account:

> The parents did not want to hear us talk about what we planned to do [about incidents of violence on and near the campus]. They wanted to see immediate results, or else they would pull their children out of Penn. And to make sure we got the point, they . . . booed us off the stage. The time for further study was over. Penn's future was at stake. We needed to act.[10]

At the time when these events occurred, planning for a major commitment of Penn resources in support of reinvestment activity in West Philadelphia (with improved public safety as a top priority) was already well under way. However, the face-off with the angry parents underscored the need for both action and results. Penn's location in an urban neighborhood where the crime rate had grown by ten percent in ten years, where litter and graffiti was evident on streets and public spaces, and where vacant and deteriorated buildings could be found on many residential blocks, had become not just a disadvantage, but a threat.[11]

By Halloween, 2002, six years after Sled's death, Penn had successfully completed a series of interrelated investments designed to improve the surrounding environment and strengthen the West Philadelphia neighborhood economy. In partnership with community constituencies and private-sector supporters, Penn spearheaded the creation of the University City District (UCD), a special services district (similar in some important respects to the Center City District); launched an ambitious employer-assisted housing program to stimulate homeownership; acquired and upgraded deteriorated apartment buildings and vacant single-family houses; supported the development of a bookstore, a hotel, a supermarket, a movie theatre complex, and other retail ventures; and cosponsored the development of the Penn

Alexander School, an outstanding new neighborhood school. Results achieved during the period from 1996 to 2002 included a 40 percent overall decline in crime reports requiring a response from the University's Division of Public Safety, with a 56 percent decrease in robberies, a 28 percent decline in assaults, a 31 percent decline in burglaries, and a 76 percent drop in auto thefts. Respondents to a resident survey conducted by the UCD characterized the area as "cleaner" or "much cleaner" (95 percent of respondents), "safe," (71 percent of respondents), with an atmosphere that was "better" or "much better" (95 percent of respondents).[12]

The centerpiece of the Penn investment program was the new Penn Alexander elementary school:

> The . . . $19 million, 83,000 square-foot school building includes 28 classrooms grouped around a three-story atrium, as well as a gymnasium/ auditorium, a cafeteria, specialized art, music, and science facilities, and an instructional media center that combines a library, computer facility, and broadcast studio. The landscaped school grounds provide students with a play field, rain garden, and an outdoor science classroom.[13]

In undertaking this ambitious program, Penn had three advantages that many other institutions confronting similar challenges do not possess: a

Figure 6.3 Penn Alexander School

relatively stable community environment, access to substantial investment capital, and a well-designed, community-supported neighborhood strategy published by the civic association representing the residential area most affected by the University's plans.

Although the West Philadelphia neighborhoods in the vicinity of the Penn campus were experiencing serious signs of distress, these neighborhoods needed stabilization and improvement rather than full-scale rebuilding. The neighborhoods near the campus had many strengths. During the last half of the twentieth century, they had retained a stable base of moderate- and middle-income residents, with a significant number of longtime homeowners and a relatively high degree of racial integration. Most residential blocks consisted of twin and row houses in good condition, with little housing abandonment. The problem, viewed from the perspective of Penn administrators, was that these positive characteristics were being negated by a growing crime rate, a weakening sales housing market, the deterioration of older apartment buildings, the decline of neighborhood retail areas, and the proliferation of litter and graffiti. In the aggregate, these factors represented a serious threat to the University's ability to market itself successfully to students, faculty, and staff, and to maintain a safe and presentable campus.

To address these problems, Penn's trustees approved the expenditure of University funds in support of a broad portfolio of neighborhood reinvestment activities, including a financial incentive to encourage employees to buy homes in West Philadelphia neighborhoods, major operating support for the University City District, a per-pupil subsidy for students at the new University-assisted school; and development financing for vacant house rehabilitation, the acquisition and upgrading of apartment buildings, and the construction of retail ventures. Some of the latter were high-risk/high-opportunity undertakings. For example, Penn, in partnership with Sundance Cinemas, invested University money in the construction of a movie theatre, a project that had been partially completed when Sundance's parent company declared bankruptcy two years later. Concluding that mothballing a half-completed building would harm Penn's other investments in the area, the University searched for a new partner, then committed $2 million in additional funding for the project. Fortunately for the University, this strategy proved successful. A new partner was found, the project was reconfigured based on the new partnership's goals, construction was restarted and completed, and the finished venture proved successful.[14]

Penn also had the opportunity to develop projects that were consistent with a comprehensive, well-organized neighborhood strategy, the "Spruce Hill Community Renewal Plan," completed by the Spruce Hill Civic Association with the assistance of Penn's Center for Community Partnerships. Approved by the Association's Board in late 1995, the plan includes a neighborhood analysis, an overall "community renewal strategy," more detailed individual strategies for five planning areas within the community, and an implementation approach.

An introductory section of the plan states that poor public schools and expensive private schools are among the "specific reasons why middle-income families and individuals choose to not reside in Spruce Hill." One of the neighborhood goals set forth in the plan is to "radically improve public and private education in and around Spruce Hill."[15]

In the Neighborhood Analysis section, the plan's authors note that:

> Only 11% of Spruce Hill's population is under 17 years old. This is in stark contrast to both the city and Mt. Airy [a Northwest Philadelphia neighborhood with some characteristics similar to those of Spruce Hill, included in the analysis for comparison purposes], where the under-17 population is approximately 23%. This indicates that families are leaving Spruce Hill as children reach school age . . .
>
> Of all households in Spruce Hill, only 34% are families. Of these households, over 60% have heads of household between the ages of 25 and 44 years . . . In Spruce Hill, as the age of the heads of household increases, the percentage of families declines significantly. This loss of family households reflects the poor quality of neighborhood public schools. Spruce Hill parents with school-age children often opt to leave the area to avoid paying for private school. [16]

In the Community Renewal Strategy section, the authors emphasize that:

> The local public schools must be dramatically improved in order to serve the neighborhood and to create educational options that are more attractive to families with school-age children. The neighborhood must have public schools that promote high academic achievement, maintain smaller class size, support a diversity of teaching and learning styles, provide a safe and secure environment for learning, and encourage the enrollment of a population with diverse backgrounds. [17]

The plan notes that, out of the 171 public elementary schools in Philadelphia, the four elementary schools located in Spruce Hill placed 107th, 112th, 130th, and 160th among city schools in national standardized tests, with a very low percentage of students in each school testing in the highest quartile in national reading and mathematics.[18]

Years before the negotiation of an agreement between the University, the School District of Philadelphia, and the Philadelphia Federation of Teachers (PFT) that led to the creation of the Penn Alexander School, the Spruce Hill plan called for "the development of a new public school alternative for Spruce Hill residents":

> through the creation of a public school . . . This may include a partnership with the University of Pennsylvania. Any arrangement must avoid

the diversion of resources from the existing public schools and must result in a school that reflects the racial and ethnic diversity of Spruce Hill. SHCA must maintain an active role in the ongoing discussions about the development of this new school. [19]

The plan called for the University, in partnership with the School District and PFT, to develop a new "charter public school" and stressed that the development venture "should be a full partnership between the School District and the University and integrate a range of Penn resources."[20]

Penn also benefited from the proposals set forth in "Priorities for Neighborhood Revitalization: Goals for the Year 2000," a "call for action" published in 1993 by Penn Faculty and Staff for Neighborhood Issues (PFSNI), an organization of Penn employees residing in Penn-area neighborhoods. PFSNI called for "the creation of desirable local public schools for Penn faculty and staff who reside in University City and neighboring areas," stating that: "Without this, the stability of our neighborhood is jeopardized as families flee the area in pursuit of better schools located in the suburbs."[21] The publication contained several proposals for the improvement of existing schools and the enhancement of education options for West Philadelphia residents.

In an essay published by *The Philadelphia Inquirer*, West Philadelphia resident Joanne Barnes Jackson urged Penn to get directly involved in the development of a high-quality education alternative, writing that the University should:

> re-evaluate the idea of creating a university-affiliated elementary and secondary school in the area . . . The truth is that, despite much effort, two of the three local elementary schools are not very good . . . Having a high-quality local school would encourage faculty and staff members to live in University City . . .[22]

The eventual success of Penn's West Philadelphia initiatives was due in large part to the University's adherence to several key principles:

Leadership begins at the top. A reinvestment strategy will have limited strength and credibility if it is led by anyone other than the governing board and President of the institution. A Vice President for Community Affairs or an Office of Community Relations will not be able to exercise the authority or earn the recognition needed to overcome bureaucratic and political challenges and produce constructive results. At Penn, President Judith Rodin asked the University's Board of Trustees to create a standing Committee on Neighborhood Initiatives, equal in status to other board committees, to which a steering committee of senior administrators would report three times a year. The President's Office provided overall leadership and direction, with the

President and her chief of staff directing and monitoring key administrative responsibilities.[23]

Everyone's job description changes. The responsibilities of senior administrators and many other staff were augmented to include new tasks associated with the West Philadelphia initiatives, and some job titles were changed with this consideration in mind. The University's Executive Vice President supervised most implementation activities, with real estate development as a high priority, and other vice presidents with implementation responsibilities reported to him. The Division of Public Safety worked in coordination with University City District "safety ambassadors" to develop plans for security patrol coverage of the area and established a stronger working relationship with the City's Police Department (the division's office is co-located with the local police district). The Vice President for Business Services set ambitious goals for University procurement through minority and neighborhood-based businesses, and procurement staff under his supervision designed training and mentoring programs to assist small businesses in developing the capacity to submit competitive proposals. Penn's Office of Real Estate and Office of Facilities Administration were merged into a single entity in order to consolidate all real estate acquisition, development, and maintenance responsibilities within a single operational center, positioning the University more effectively for participation in private real estate development ventures. These and other changes elevated the status of neighborhood reinvestment as a University priority and ensured that more University staff would be working to address this issue on a daily basis.

Do everything together. Penn's homeownership incentive (through which, at the outset, the University offered $15,000 to each employee household that purchased a home within a designated target area of West Philadelphia) was motivated by security concerns rather than purely by an interest in promoting homeownership for its own sake. Residential blocks populated by homeowner-occupants are safer than blocks in which rental housing is interspersed with vacant single-family homes posted with numerous "for sale" signs. A high-quality neighborhood-based school is essential for attracting younger middle-class families and persuading them to buy the for-sale housing. Better-quality retail facilities with a "crossover" appeal that attracts both the campus population as well as community members who may have no connection to the University will influence residents to remain in the community and will generate a higher level of pedestrian traffic, making the streets safer and more interesting (the bookstore, supermarket, movie theatre, and other retail ventures were designed with this consideration in mind). By themselves, neither an ambitious homeownership incentive, nor a campaign to improve public-education options, nor institutional investment in new retail ventures will be sufficient to generate the critical mass of activity needed to reverse decades of economic decline; nothing other than a multi-faceted approach, consisting of a series of integrated, interrelated activities, will work.

Don't wait for foundation and government funding. Like other large institutions, the University of Pennsylvania receives many millions of dollars annually in foundation and government funding to support academic research, university programs and events, facilities development, and other activities. However, Penn did not pursue foundation or government funding as a first step in advancing the West Philadelphia initiatives; the money would not be available soon enough, and Penn had no time to lose. Instead, Penn began self-funding its investment in West Philadelphia, leveraging financing from other sources as opportunities emerged. Developing a series of proposals for foundation funding or working to establish a collaboration with an individual foundation or a consortium of grantmakers would have taken too long and might not have produced the desired results.

In some other cities, a charitable foundation commitment in support of institutional investment in neighborhoods is established at an early stage. For example, The Cleveland Foundation has a long-standing commitment to support revitalization activities in the Greater University Circle district where Case Western University and a cluster of academic and health care institutions are located. In the absence of a comparable commitment, however, Penn's view was that it would not pay to wait.

Waiting for government funding is likely to be unproductive as well. During my tenure as Philadelphia's housing director, I met with Penn's Executive Vice President and others at the time when the West Philadelphia initiatives were getting under way. The meeting was cordial but did not produce any worthwhile results. During those pre-NTI years, nearly all of the housing and community development funding available to the City of Philadelphia was income-restricted federal funding provided by the U.S. Department of Housing and Urban Development. HUD required that most beneficiaries of its housing programs be low- and moderate-income residents, meaning residents with incomes at or below 80 percent of area median income. In 1995, the 80-percent threshold amounted to $26,400 for a single-person household, $37,700 for a household of four. Although none of the census tracts adjacent to the Penn campus would be characterized as wealthy, many of the residents who lived there or whom Penn wanted to attract there had incomes that exceeded the HUD-mandated income threshold. Even if NTI funding or other unrestricted funding had been available, it is not likely that a substantial commitment would have been made to support Penn's initiatives. Other, more distressed West Philadelphia neighborhoods were regarded as a higher priority, both by key members of the mayor's administration as well as by City Council. Mayor Rendell would have been sympathetic to an appeal from Penn's President and trustees and would have been able to find some amount of unrestricted funding to invest in Penn-area neighborhoods. However, Penn's leadership concluded correctly that University energy and resources should be focused on getting started as quickly as possible rather than in launching a major lobbying and advocacy effort that would likely fall short of expectations.

Don't wait for "the market" either. Established supermarket operators studied Penn's proposal to build a new supermarket at 40th and Walnut Streets, at the western edge of the campus. Their conclusion: the project isn't feasible; the market isn't strong enough; the numbers don't work. Subsequently, after much time and effort, Penn identified an operator who was willing to commit to the project, and the supermarket was built. Within a short time, the store became a successful twenty-four-hour/seven-day operation, drawing customers from both campus and community, including students, weekly grocery shoppers, and hospital workers coming off shifts in the middle of the night. The experts' analysis of "the market" had been far off the mark.

As an employee of the Fels Institute of Government in 2002, I participated in a meeting between a well-known suburban housing developer and a Penn Vice President. The developer had past ties to Penn and he told the Vice President that he wanted to give something back to the University and the West Philadelphia community. If the University could identify a few city blocks of cleared land, his firm would be willing to work with Penn in producing a large-scale sales housing venture. This meeting was also cordial but unproductive, primarily due to the developer's lack of understanding of the realities of the West Philadelphia housing market. No blocks of cleared land existed anywhere near the campus. More to the point, by the time of the meeting, the neighborhood real estate market had been stabilized and was growing stronger by the year, thanks to nearly a decade's worth of investment by the University during years in which established players in the regional real estate market had not been ready to take on the challenge of revitalizing West Philadelphia. By the time the developer had contacted Penn to schedule the meeting, there was no opportunity for a suburban developer to play any constructive role. Some opportunity might have existed eight to ten years previously; but risk-averse conventional developers would not have come forward at that time. Penn had moved ahead without them.

After initial commitments of self-financing, Penn's ability to leverage outside funding increased as the positive results of the University's investment became evident and attracted outside interest. By the turn of the century, Penn's role as development financing source had ended; everything was being financed through the resurgent private real estate market.

What, if anything, can be done by an institution that has none of the three advantages that Penn had and that has little or no access to investment capital to support the development of supermarkets and movie theatres, the opening of new schools, or the upgrading and retenanting of older apartment buildings? A great deal, according to Lucy Kerman, who played a central role in managing the West Philadelphia initiatives as a senior administrator in the Penn President's Office. Her advice: for any institution, the first step is to change the institutional business model. Don't start out by trying to create new projects and programs; start by realigning current business practices in order to maximize the potential for community benefit.

Kerman and I had lunch with administrators at Camden County College one afternoon at a college building in Camden's downtown area. "Where did our sandwiches come from?" I asked. The answer: from a caterer located outside the city. In the downtown blocks surrounding us, there were a lot of people who knew how to make sandwiches, but local businesses did not have the capability to compete for catering service contracting opportunities advertised by the College.

To stimulate local and minority business participation in University procurement, Penn realigned its procurement approach in several ways: by offering training to business operators in Internet-facilitated procurement and other business practices; by creating mentoring relationships to support neighborhood-based business capacity-building; and by encouraging established out-of-town suppliers to subcontract with local businesses or to open branches in West Philadelphia. The result: in fiscal 2003, Penn purchased $61.6 million in goods and services from West Philadelphia suppliers, compared with $20.1 million in fiscal 1996. Of this total, $54.2 million consisted of purchases from minority suppliers, compared with $31.8 million in fiscal 1996. None of these expenditures were based on the establishment of set-asides, quotas, or mandates to buy from or contract with community businesses.

Kerman has encouraged other institutions to examine the volume and type of procurement that they are currently conducting and to consider the best opportunities to realign some of this procurement in order to increase opportunities for neighborhood business development and community jobs. For example, a relatively small institution may procure a total of $50 million worth of products and services annually. If such an institution were to change its procurement practices in a manner similar to Penn's and, in this way, to spend 10 percent of its procurement within the community, then $5 million in community economic benefit would be achieved without the need for a set-aside from the institution's budget or for fundraising to obtain a government or foundation grant.

Based on Kerman's advice, a group of academic and health care institutions in Cleveland's Greater University Circle conducted a survey of existing procurement in 2007. The institutions found that laundry services—the pickup, cleaning, and delivery of towels, sheets, and uniforms—were a major expense for all of them, but that none of these services were being provided by businesses based in Cleveland. If the institutions together were to express interest in contracting with a Cleveland-based supplier and were to work with city business leaders and economic development agencies to promote the development of a city-based institutional laundry service or to encourage an existing out-of-town business to move to or near Greater University Circle, the benefits to the community and city would be substantial.

Kerman's advice applies to other aspects of the institutional business model as well. An institution that wants to support the economy of the neighborhood in which it is located should re-orient its approach to purchasing, to hiring, to facilities development, to master-planning its own campus. Thoughtful planning and design decisions, the opposite of those described earlier in this chapter, can produce economic benefits and increase the level of positive interaction between campus and community. The university bookstore that Penn operated prior to the 1990s faced onto a pedestrian walkway and had no prominent signage or window displays that might attract prospective off-campus customers. In fact, based on the appearance of the store, it was not clear that outsiders would even be permitted to enter. By contrast, the university's current bookstore is operated by Barnes & Noble, occupies a prominent position on a busy street corner with a block of other retail stores on each side, and presents itself not simply as a Penn textbook provider but as a private retailer that, based on its location, has a strong Penn orientation. To reach the Penn textbook area at the Barnes & Noble store, you travel past the hardback and soft-cover bestseller displays, past the well-stocked magazine and periodical section, up an escalator to the second floor, past the art books and the entrance to the CD and DVD section, past the stationery and supplies section, and past another series of special interest book displays before entering the textbook section, which occupies a side area on the second floor. On your way there, some of the people whom you see shopping and browsing are individuals who have no connection to the university and may have no awareness that the store is a textbook supplier.

Test–Tube School

If you were designing a school in vitro, with no consideration in mind other than producing students with high test scores and positive traits that would maximize their prospects for successful advancement to the next level of education (middle school, high school, college), your school would probably have the following characteristics:

- Secure, appealing, campus-like grounds, with generous amounts of open space developed as lawns, fields, and recreation areas.
- Large endowment, or a consistently high level of funding from state and local government or charitable foundations.
- State-of-the-art built space, with attractive, well-designed classrooms and activity areas suitable for community programming during off-hours.

Figure 6.4 New Penn Book Store

- Up-to-date, well-equipped facilities, including a library, computer lab, music room, and an auditorium.
- Private-school, charter-school, or magnet-school business plan, with admission-by-application requirement in order to maximize control over curriculum and ability to select students with best potential for success.
- Lower-school student body, rather than middle- or upper-school (the younger the child, the better the potential for success).
- Principal and faculty with outstanding professional qualifications and high degree of commitment to the school's formula for academic excellence.
- Teacher and principal selection based on merit rather than seniority; teacher accountability to principal and parents.
- Small class size.
- High degree of parent involvement. Higher-income parent population with no social needs that might interfere with students' educational advancement.

In the education universe, a relatively small number of schools possess all of these characteristics, and only a fraction of that small number consists of public schools. However, no school that does not possess some of these characteristics is successful.

Penn wanted to make its neighborhood surroundings safer and more appealing by attracting and keeping a diverse population with more middle-income families and more homeowners. In order to achieve this goal, Penn needed a neighborhood-based school that could compete successfully with suburban schools in some of the ways that matter most. However, it would not be possible or desirable for the University to pursue a school concept with academic success as the only goal; a Penn-supported school had to succeed as a community resource as well.

In order to succeed on these terms, the school needed to be a part of the neighborhood environment; it could not be located on the Penn campus or in a walled or gated enclave. To be accepted as part of the neighborhood, the school also had to be inclusive. Penn's neighborhood reinvestment goals would not be fulfilled if the school were a charter school or a magnet school that brought in students from all over the city, nor could it succeed as a Penn-owned private school. The school could not screen prospective students in order to select those most likely to succeed and filter out those with less success potential. The school had to be recognized as a location for evening and weekend activities for parents and other community members. These standards, established after much discussion within Penn and between Penn and community members, were viewed as necessary in order to make the school relevant to neighborhood interests, not just Penn's interests, and to increase the prospects for community buy-in. As Judith Rodin wrote:

> We wanted a neighborhood school in the fullest sense, one that would express the shared value of community that Penn was trying to embody.

A school enrolling a relatively small and select group of students would not meet that standard. We had the same reservations about a private school . . . [and a magnet school would have] clashed with the goal of creating a school that was in and for the neighborhood.[24]

Partnering with Adversaries

David W. Hornbeck, who became Superintendent of the School District of Philadelphia School District in 1994, was a believer in the do-everything-together principle as it related to his efforts to reform the city's public education system. Point number ten in the ten-point "action design" for his Children Achieving policy was simply an admonition to implement all of the other nine points:

> The agenda is not a pick-and-choose menu. We must approach the challenge of education reform in a comprehensive and integrated way. If one or more features of the whole agenda is not implemented, its power to yield high performance by all students will be significantly diminished.[25]

Hornbeck resigned in 2000, after having reached a political impasse with the state government over the funding of programs that he felt were essential for education reform.[26] During his six-year tenure, he had not been successful in implementing his transformative policy, which had called for, among other things, performance and accountability standards and incentives, decentralized decision-making, more support for staff development, greater emphasis on early childhood education, additional funding for adequate facilities, supplies, technology, and services, and a high level of public engagement.

Children Achieving was described as a "calculated risk by [School] District leaders who believed that they could effect sufficient gains in student achievement to convince the public and political leaders to increase the dollar investment in the city's schools."[27] The calculated risk did not pay off as hoped. Key constituencies opposed Children Achieving outright or failed to provide the level of support that had been viewed as essential to the success of Hornbeck's approach.

The teachers union charged that its members had not participated in the initial planning for Children Achieving. Calling the policy a "fraud," Philadelphia Federation of Teachers President Ted Kirsch said: "We were not part of the planning of the program, and [the exclusion of the union from planning activity] was not unintentional."[28] Kirsch strongly opposed Hornbeck's proposal to change the seniority system (through which first preference in school and classroom assignments was given to teachers with highest seniority), as well as Hornbeck's plan to financially reward teachers in successful schools and deny raises to teachers in schools that consistently failed to meet performance standards. Kirsch argued that the seniority system protects teachers from arbitrary or politically-motivated decisions by administrators. He contended that pay-for-performance programs had not demonstrated their worth in other cities where they had been attempted. "Nobody has come up with an answer to these problems," he said.

The state government, under the leadership of Republican Governor Tom Ridge during most of Hornbeck's tenure, was not a strong supporter of either Children Achieving or of increased funding for Philadelphia public schools. On a per-pupil basis adjusted for inflation, state aid to Philadelphia public schools fell by 5.9 percent between 1993 and 1998.[29] Teachers in the Philadelphia school district, who had been among the highest-paid public school teachers in the region during the early 1980s, had become among the region's lowest-paid teachers by the mid-1990s.[30] During the latter period, one elementary school principal reported having as many as eighteen vacancies among fifty-one staff positions at her school.[31] Ridge was a proponent of school vouchers, for which he tried to obtain legislative approval three times. Although these attempts proved unsuccessful, the state legislature was not strongly supportive of Hornbeck's policy. In 1998, the legislature approved Act 46, which provided for a state takeover of the school district if the district "failed to provide an adequate educational program."[32]

Greater Philadelphia First, the region's business leadership organization, had agreed to oversee the expenditure of a $50 million Annenberg Foundation grant in support of Children Achieving.[33] Not all business leaders supported Hornbeck's policy, however, and some "diluted their support of Children Achieving by jumping on Ridge's ill-starred voucher bandwagon."[34] As one person knowledgeable about the business community's perspective commented, business leaders tend to like policies that are straightforward, clearly articulated, and easy to grasp; the complex, multi-faceted nature of Children Achieving was not overly appealing to them. "When you use complex terms to explain an issue to an audience of businesspeople," she said, "you end up excluding them without even knowing it."

As Mayor, Edward Rendell had enthusiastically supported Hornbeck's appointment, and he and his chief of staff David L. Cohen, helped mediate differences between the School District and the PFT. Rendell and then-Council President Street had also conspired with Hornbeck to orchestrate a showdown with the Ridge Administration in 1996: the city and school district filed a lawsuit against the state, charging that Pennsylvania's system of financing public education was unfair to public schools and demanding more funding, starting with an initial commitment of $52.8 million to address what Hornbeck termed "a history of underfunding." At the same time, the school district adopted a budget that could only be balanced if the $52.8 million were obtained. "We know it's a gamble," Hornbeck said. "We're counting on the state living up to its moral and constitutional responsibilities."[35] Although the Rendell Administration had joined with the School District in bringing the lawsuit, the risk was all Hornbeck's. "Ed Rendell and John Street crafted a train-wreck strategy," according to one insider, "And David was in the front car."

Hornbeck had many adversaries, and the Philadelphia Federation of Teachers was chief among them. However, the union was not viewed in a particularly favorable light by many who were concerned about public education in Philadelphia, regardless of how they felt about Hornbeck's performance. "As the public runs out of patience with public education, the city's 12,000 teachers are often seen more as part of the problem than the solution," *The Philadelphia Inquirer* reported in 1997. The level of teacher absenteeism was second highest in the nation. "On any given day, one-third are not there."[36] The state legislature was running out of patience as well, with potentially adverse consequences for the union. In 1997, State Representative Dwight Evans, a Philadelphia Democrat, introduced the School District Reform and Accountability Act which, among other things, would have eliminated the seniority system and prohibited the union from negotiating issues such as teacher assignments and class preparation time.[37] Evans' proposal did not receive legislative approval, but Evans subsequently helped secure the passage of Act 46, the 1998 legislation that authorized a state takeover of the school district. A PFT-orchestrated effort to deny Evans re-election by mobilizing support for his opponent in the 1998 spring primary election proved ineffectual.

For both the School District and the PFT, the Penn Alexander School proposal represented a welcome opportunity to advance their respective self-interests without making concessions to the other. For both, the proposal offered an opportunity to participate in the creation of a valuable new public-education asset during a time when their relationship was at its most adversarial and when many were criticizing them for the slow progress of education reform.

Choices

As an administrator who was conscious of how his leadership would be viewed after his tenure had ended, it is likely that Hornbeck welcomed the opportunity to participate in this project. According to another School District administrator with whom I spoke years later, the Penn Alexander School proposal began as a "handshake deal" between Judith Rodin and David Hornbeck. After satisfying himself that the school would be a public resource serving the community as a whole (rather than a lab school or magnet school), Hornbeck approved the School District's participation in the project and assigned his senior aide to represent him in the planning sessions that led to the execution of a memorandum of understanding with Penn and the union.[38]

For its part, the PFT wanted to identify itself with education reform, but not at the cost of jeopardizing its membership through the creation of a precedent that would weaken its position in future contract negotiations. Penn's proposal was appealing to union leaders because the University-supported school would not be a charter school or privatized public school and because the school would maintain reduced class sizes and offer amenities for which the union had advocated for years. The PFT's participation in implementing the Penn proposal would demonstrate the union's support for meaningful education reform and would illustrate the kinds of improvements in the public-school classroom environment that the union had consistently maintained were essential for success.

Jerry Jordan, who succeeded Kirsch as head of the PFT, called the Penn Alexander School "one of the greatest achievements that the union has been involved in." Jordan and other PFT leaders had felt frustrated by what they viewed as Hornbeck's unwillingness to work collaboratively with the union. The planning process for the Penn Alexander School was a refreshing change, with union leaders working together at the same table with senior administrators from the School District and their counterparts from the Penn President's Office and Graduate School of Education.[39]

University representatives engaged in an extended period of coordinated planning with the School District and PFT before presenting a specific proposal to community members. A number of important choices had to be made during this planning phase.

One choice that had preceded the "handshake deal" was Penn's decision to support the development of a new school rather than to invest money in substantially improving an existing neighborhood-based public school. Penn had assessed the prospects for major investment in the Lea Elementary School, located seven blocks from the western edge of the University campus. Penn representatives had visited classrooms, inspected the school building, and conducted discussions with teachers and administrators. The conclusion reached as a result of this assessment was negative. Lea's physical infrastructure was in need of major repair and replacement. The building was poorly designed; for example, the cafeteria was on the third floor rather than at ground level where it would provide best access for young children. Teachers had been selected based on seniority, per the PFT's contract with the School District, and their buy-in (as well as that of the principal) to a Penn-sponsored school improvement plan was not assured.[40]

The Penn administrators concluded that an attempt to remake Lea or another existing public school would fail. Instead, the University decided to develop a new school that, through the design and quality of its facilities, the scope of its curriculum, and the commitment of its principal and teachers would create, as one administrator termed it, "a new culture of learning."

To demonstrate support for existing public schools at the same time as the new school was being developed, Penn financed the development of a library and the employment of a librarian at Lea. Penn also paid a subsidy to the School District that would ensure that class size in kindergarten through third grade at Lea would remain as low as that at Penn Alexander. Penn also entered into "partnership schools" agreements with the School District, through which the University provided technical assistance, professional development support, student assessments, performance monitoring services, and parent workshops at Lea and two other public elementary schools in the area.

Notwithstanding these commitments, the issue of equitable treatment was raised by critics of Penn's initiative during the years leading to and following the opening of the Penn Alexander School. The issue of equity could be framed in terms of a question: Is it right that some West Philadelphia children should benefit from access to education in an outstanding new public school while all the others must attend public schools of substantially lower quality? The question could be framed in the opposite way: For the sake of equitability, should all children be required to attend a group of existing public schools that are ranked below the citywide median, rather than enabling some children to benefit from a high-quality education opportunity? Penn's self-interest dictated that the University support the development of a new school. Even if the University committed all available resources to existing public schools in the area and launched a major advocacy campaign in support of systemic reform of public schools in Philadelphia, the University would not be successful in achieving its goal of attracting and keeping middle-class families. Parents with the ability to move out of the neighborhood or send their children to private schools would not be satisfied with this approach; they would continue to leave the neighborhood and abandon the public education system.

In exchange for an unprecedented commitment of its resources in support of the proposal, the University wanted to control everything. Penn wanted to design and build the school, to sign off on the curriculum and programming, to manage professional development and technical support for teachers, to obtain a commitment in support of "site selection" of teachers (the hiring and placement of teachers by school leadership rather than by reference to the seniority system), and to define the boundaries of the catchment area from which students would be drawn. Penn wanted the school to be a lower school—kindergarten to eighth grade—because a lower school would present the best opportunity for success and would be most appealing to the families that the University wanted to attract to the neighborhood and keep there: younger families with young children.

Penn did not get everything it wanted. The School District retained control over catchment area boundary decision-making. The catchment area decision was a critical one, because catchment area boundaries would be the sole determinant of eligibility to attend. If you lived within the catchment area, your child would be eligible; if your home was across the street or a block away from the catchment area boundary, your child couldn't attend. The issue was loaded with political, racial, and economic implications.

In exchange for the control of most key issues, Penn would provide a development site: the one-block campus of a former Episcopal divinity school three blocks from the University campus. Penn would contribute operating funds—$1,000 per student per year for seven years—that would pay for significant advantages: small class sizes, a library, a music program, and more. Through its Graduate School of Education, Penn would provide classroom assistance, teacher training, and in-kind support in a variety of forms.

Penn's approach had a strong economic development emphasis as well as a strong human capital development emphasis. The University was proposing to use economic development resources (capital and operating funds, as well as administrative staff, professional staff, and faculty) in order to make a major contribution to human capital building in the community (through the creation of a high-quality public education option for community residents) in order to promote economic development (in the form of a stronger real estate market with more homeowners) within that community.

From the School District perspective, the proposed plan was a highly attractive opportunity. Penn was offering to build a suburban-quality, magnet-school-quality neighborhood school on land that it owned. At a time when the School District was battling the state over per-pupil funding for children in the Philadelphia system, Penn was offering a $1,000 per pupil funding supplement. The additional funding would make possible the kinds of curriculum enhancements and supportive services that the School District had maintained were critical to student success. As important, Penn was offering to bring into existence the kind of small learning community that Hornbeck viewed as the heart of Children Achieving, along with other key elements of Hornbeck's approach: ongoing staff development programs, a strong emphasis on early childhood education, high-quality facilities and technology, and a high level of community involvement.

The School District did not get everything it wanted either. The School District's highest priority for the area in the vicinity of Penn had been the relocation of the George Washington Carver High School for Engineering and Science from North Philadelphia to a site near the University. Penn had agreed to assist the School District in achieving this goal. However, the relocation of the school did not take place as planned. A site recommended by Penn was rejected by the School District, and an alternative site that both parties subsequently agreed to involved the acquisition of property that the University did not own; site acquisition was never completed.[41] The School District was displeased with this outcome; from the School District perspective, Penn had reneged on a commitment.

As the three parties were preparing to finalize the memorandum of understanding, news of the deal was leaked to the press, and, ready or not, the public phase of planning for the new school began.

In the Living Rooms

A Penn administrator had a conversation with Barry Grossbach, a longtime member of Spruce Hill Civic Association, the neighborhood organization that represented the area immediately west of the Penn campus. The University is planning some activities in West Philadelphia, the administrator said. Before we get started, I was thinking about meeting with civic groups in the area to ask what kinds of projects they would support. Grossbach's response was unequivocal. "If you do that," he said, "It'll be the worst mistake you ever made." His advice: figure out what you want to do and can do, and then make your plans known. If you start an open-ended community dialogue, you'll never get anything resolved.[42]

The Spruce Hill Community Renewal Plan provided guidance that made it easy for Penn to follow Grossbach's advice. The plan was wide-ranging; it addressed not only the issue of public education but many other topics, including public safety, housing, retail development, and parks. Grossbach characterized the plan as a road map that illustrated the kinds of activities that the community would be willing to support. Of particular benefit to Penn was the fact that the plan was not simply a community wishlist; it was a well-documented series of specific proposals for improvement.

As word of the Penn proposal spread through the neighborhoods near the campus, rumors and conjectures abounded. Penn wanted to create a private school. Penn wanted to create a school that would primarily benefit Penn employees. Penn wanted to create a school that would exclusively benefit Penn employees. Penn was abandoning existing public schools in the area. Penn was seeking to remake the neighborhood adjacent to its campus as a middle- and upper-income enclave. Penn had a longer-term agenda with respect to the nature of the school and the composition of the student body, which Penn was not disclosing.

These concerns needed to be addressed; but, as important, many substantive decisions about the school needed to be made, and the school plan would not be implemented successfully if these decisions were reached without meaningful community involvement. The latter meant engagement in a process that gave community members the ability to influence key decisions about how the school would be developed and operated. The community would not become a partner in the school project and would not be a signer of the memorandum of understanding. The community would not have the ability to veto fundamental provisions of the memorandum of understanding. But, because decisions about the school's design, curriculum, operating plan, and role as a neighborhood facility had not been made or, in some instances, even studied in detail, the opportunity for community members to guide the development of the school plan was significant.

A framework was created to air these issues and conduct a dialogue. Three committees would be organized: Education, Community Programming, and Site and Facilities. The membership of the committees would include representatives of Penn, the School District, and the PFT who were playing the lead roles in organizing the project, along with representatives of the Spruce Hill Civic Association and other community members. The Community Programming Committee, for example, was co-chaired by a Penn health educator (who was also a community resident), along with the staff director of the nonprofit West Philadelphia Partnership, a coalition of area neighborhood organizations and institutions. The Site and Facilities Committee was co-chaired by an administrator from the School District's Design and Construction unit, along with Penn's managing director for real estate. Ten months of planning followed, involving the participation of more than seventy individuals, and concluding with the publication of detailed "Final Recommendations for Vision and Framework" in October 1999, two years before the opening of the school.

Referral to a committee or task force has proven to be the death of many worthwhile ideas. In this instance, however, the committee process made sense and succeeded, primarily for three reasons. All the key participants in the plan were committed to the process and stayed involved. Community participation was taken seriously, and it became clear at an early stage that community members had an opportunity to influence the plan in ways that mattered. As important, the idea of a new school in Spruce Hill was not an issue that divided the community; community members wanted an outstanding new school. The Civic Association and PFSNI documents had identified a new school as a priority, and the Civic Association plan had specifically called for Penn to pursue an alliance with the School District and PFT. University and community self-interest converged on the need for a new school as a top priority, as vital to the future of both Penn and the neighborhood.

Ongoing community access to senior administrators at Penn also helped bring the planning process to a successful conclusion. Stephen Schutt, a Penn vice president and Rodin's chief of staff (who had played the key role in bringing the School District and PFT together to get the dialogue started) would attend any meeting, however large or small, and would show up in anyone's living room for a discussion. Carol Scheman, Penn's Vice President for Government, Public and Community Affairs, and Glenn Bryan, Director of City and Community Relations, were in constant communication with City Councilwoman Jannie Blackwell and other elected officials. Not every issue would be resolved to the satisfaction of all parties, but no detail would be left out of the dialogue.

Describing his experience as a member of the Site and Facilities Committee, Barry Grossbach characterized the meetings as "constructive and totally noncompetitive." The meetings took place in the early evening and lasted a couple of hours. No one who wanted to participate was excluded. Sometimes food was served; it "made people mellow," Grossbach said. "A feeling was created that we're all in this together, that this is something positive that we're working toward." In his view, the outcome of the school project would decisively influence all the rest of Penn's West Philadelphia initiatives; the school was, by far, the most important of the initiatives. If the school succeeded, then the other elements of Penn's approach would be strengthened and regarded in a positive light. If the project failed, the entire Penn enterprise in West Philadelphia would be viewed as a failure.[43]

According to a summary memorandum prepared by the co-chairs of the Site and Facilities Committee, the planning and design process for which the committee was responsible began with several months of general meetings to discuss "the site, its physical development, community impact, educational objectives, and historic preservation." These meetings were followed by a presentation and discussion of school design options in June 1999 and a final meeting in July to review the preferred plan. The memorandum described the strengths of the recommended plan:

> Educationally, the plan separates the school into age-based learning communities and activity areas. Strong, clear circulation patterns link these areas in ways that provide an appropriate but not overwhelming level of interaction among different student age groups. Additional strengths of the plan include sufficient, flexible classroom space; generous natural lighting in classrooms and common areas; accessible green and landscaped play areas located throughout the site; easily accessed community and public spaces; and retention of existing trees and other natural resources.[44]

As the committee meetings progressed, the issue of a catchment-area approach to student eligibility became a source of conflict among community constituencies. A substantial number of community members supported a lottery system as the basis for determining who would attend. A catchment-area approach, they contended, would create a new division within the community at large, a boundary separating the haves from the have-nots. The housing market in Spruce Hill was already stronger than that in neighboring communities, in part because of Spruce Hill's proximity to the Penn campus. A catchment-area delineation would increase the gap between housing values in Spruce Hill and housing values elsewhere. Some lottery proponents also viewed this approach as more equitable to the West Philadelphia community as a whole. How could you justify telling a family living in a house outside the catchment area that they had absolutely no opportunity to send their children to the best school in West Philadelphia? A lottery wouldn't guarantee enrollment in the school; but a lottery at least wouldn't deny the potential opportunity outright.

Proponents of the catchment area approach agreed with Penn that the school could not be a genuine neighborhood school if (as a result of the adoption of a lottery or magnet-school approach) some residents of the immediate neighborhood were not eligible to attend. As a more practical consideration, the School District had never indicated that it would entertain the idea of instituting a lottery.

Disagreement over the catchment area approach became a high-profile neighborhood controversy. The disagreement was intense; it destroyed longtime friendships and longstanding relationships between neighbors who previously had worked together for years to support community improvement activities. The disagreement resulted in the withdrawal of Spruce Hill Civic Association from the University City Community Council, a leadership coalition in which representatives of all Penn-area neighborhood organizations had participated. The Civic Association was pro-catchment area, while other members of the UCCC were anti-. The School District moved ahead with a designation of catchment area boundaries, but the Civic Association and the rest of the UCCC coalition never reunited.

An only-in-Philadelphia-could-this-happen kind of controversy also emerged during the planning period. Dog owners who had been permitted by Penn to walk their pets on the grounds of the then-underused former divinity school would not be allowed to do so after the Penn Alexander School development had been completed. The prohibition was based on health concerns: dogs should not be walked in an area where small children would be playing. Dog-owner expressions of concern, as well as outright opposition to the school plan, became ongoing and persistent. A school can be built anywhere, some of the dog advocates argued.

The controversy continued in public and over the Internet. Participants in chat-room dialogues, apparently desiring to show their fair-mindedness, prefaced their postings with self-identifications of the number of dogs and children in their households: two dogs, two children, would be the heading on one message; one dog, no children on another; one dog, three children on another. Some dog walkers took stronger action, engaging in protests at the school site. On several occasions, bags of dog droppings were deposited on the outside steps leading to the office of a Penn staffer. As the dialogue continued, an alternative site for the development of a dog park was proposed, but the plan never went anywhere. When the school construction was completed, the dog-walking prohibition took effect and remained in force.

Penn was sensitive to community concerns and disagreements, and University staff tried to be responsive and conciliatory. Some residents of St. Mark's Square, a single-block street of attractive older homes that ran perpendicular to the school grounds, complained about the visual impact of the air conditioning equipment on top of the school building. The sight of the air conditioning equipment would adversely affect the block, argued some residents, including a distinguished member of the Penn faculty. An extended dialogue ensued, but the issue was not resolved. There was nowhere else to put the air conditioning equipment, and none of the houses on this tree-lined block faced directly toward the building where it was to be installed. The opponents were not satisfied with this outcome. The school opened with the rooftop air conditioning equipment in place. No significant adverse impacts could be documented in the years that followed.

Lucy Kerman played a central role in coordinating the community planning process and in keeping the dialogue moving to a conclusion—to a consensus whenever possible. Already a perceptive listener and observer, the experience had fine-tuned her sensitivity to potential problems, large and small. She passed by the school site one day shortly after the start of construction. Some tall trees had been cut down in order to create room for the new school building, and thick sections of tree trunk were scattered everywhere. Kerman, who had been a history scholar before becoming a university administrator, imagined the scene as resembling a corpse-strewn Civil War battlefield. She phoned Facilities and Real Estate Services: Could someone come and move away the tree sections as quickly as possible? A work crew followed up, and the battlefield was cleared.

Planning for Diversity

"I've gone here so many years I don't really want to leave," said one seventh grader. "I love the building and the teachers are really cool," said another. The Penn Alexander School had been open for six years. According to state test scores, the proportion of Penn Alexander students who were proficient or advanced in math and reading was roughly double that of students in the Philadelphia school district as a whole. These results were achieved at a school that was drawing its students from a racially, ethnically, socially, and economically diverse catchment area.

"The expectations are high and the curriculum is rigorous," said school principal Sheila Snydor, a West Philadelphia native with thirty-two years of service in public education. Snydor had been selected for the position following a review of the credentials of sixty applicants. "I don't think we teach just enough. We go beyond just enough and that's made a difference." The beyond-just-enough approach was facilitated by a site-selection policy for teacher recruitment in place of the old seniority system and by amenities such as instrumental music instruction for every student, a well-equipped media lab, and computers in every classroom.[45]

Nearly three-quarters of the homeowners who responded to a 2005 survey of catchment-area residents conducted by the Spruce Hill Civic Association reported that the school had been a factor in their decision to purchase, and roughly the same proportion indicated that Penn's continued support of the school was a factor in their decision to stay.[46]

The real estate market in the area surrounding Penn's campus had grown much stronger. Within the service area of the University City District (the special services district that Penn had helped create during the 1990s), the number of single-family home sales increased from 73 in 1995 to 132 in 2006. The median single-family house price increased from $72,700 in 1995 to $312,000 in 2006. The early twenty-first-century surge in the housing market nationwide had a significant effect on Penn-area property values, but the influence of the Penn Alexander School was undeniable. A house located within the catchment area would sell for $50,000 more than a comparable house located outside the catchment area. Nearby neighborhood housing markets grew stronger as well. As Barry Grossbach of the Spruce Hill Civic Association had suggested, the success of the school positively influenced community perceptions of all of Penn's other initiatives and created a positive view of the area as a whole.

School demographics reflected the diversity of the catchment area that the School District had delineated. In 2006–2007, the student population was 50 percent low-income and 72 percent minority, with a student body that was 48 percent African-American, 28 percent white, 13 percent Asian, 6 percent Hispanic, and 5 percent other ethnicities.[47]

As property values increased, concerns about housing affordability and its relationship to student diversity grew. As the school's reputation became more widely known, the proportion of white students increased by 10 percent between 2002 and 2007.

No plan is ever complete, and all planning must be viewed as an ongoing process that never really ends. In conducting its planning, Penn had not anticipated the extent to which the opening of the school would cause an escalation of property values in the neighborhood real estate market. If Penn had been able to do so, then the University might have considered two strategies to support affordable housing preservation in the area.

Providing a household with rental assistance—funding to make up the difference between the "fair market" cost of a rental apartment and the amount that a household can afford (that is, not more than 30 percent of gross income)—costs much less than developing rental housing through new construction or vacant property rehabilitation. Table 6.1 shows the cost to the city of providing rental assistance payments for ten households in ten different Philadelphia zip codes during 2008. Although the rents in this sample (from a City program that serves formerly homeless people, people disabled by AIDS-related illness, and other very low-income households) are entirely or almost entirely City-subsidized, the total annual cost of supporting the housing needs of these families is less than $80,000, far lower than the cost of developing a single subsidized rental unit. If Penn and other West Philadelphia institutions were to raise $100,000 annually and use it to leverage matching-fund commitments in equal amounts from city and state government, rental assistance in the catchment area could have been provided to thirty families with school-age children. Organizing a rental assistance fund would have been a challenging task, and convincing the city and the state to make an annual commitment of matching funds would have been particularly difficult; but Penn would have been offering a lot in return.

Penn might also have explored the possibility of investing in apartment buildings located within the catchment area and in taking steps to ensure that

Table 6.1 Rental Assistance Payments in Ten Philadelphia Zip Codes

ZIP Code	No. Bedrooms	Monthly Rent Amount* ($)	Monthly Rental Assistance Amount* ($)
19145	1	575	575
19124	1	650	650
19141	1	600	600
19124	2	625	542
19104	2	725	725
19144	2	650	598
19139	3	775	509
19138	3	850	850
19132	3	800	800
19140	4	850	802

* Does not include utility reimbursement.

Source: City of Philadelphia, Office of Housing and Community Development.

some of the units in these buildings were available to families with below-median incomes. As part of the West Philadelphia Initiatives, the University had organized an equity fund, known as the Neighborhood Preservation and Development Fund, in 1999. The Fund financed the rehabilitation and upgrading of a $5 million portfolio of properties that Penn acquired. Over 200 rental units in an area extending nine blocks west of the University campus were upgraded with funding provided through this resource.

Some apartments in the Fund portfolio were rented to students, while others were rented to community members who may or may not have been affiliated with the University. If the Fund organizers had made the Penn Alexander catchment area a priority for acquisition and had rented some of the units it acquired at slightly reduced rents, the housing affordability problem in the catchment area would have been alleviated.

According to Spruce Hill residents, there was no question that the success of the school brought more children into the community. You couldn't take a short walk in the community without encountering young parents with infants and toddlers, I was told in 2008. At the end of the school day, parents converged on the schoolyard, and children burst out of the doors.

The change in the neighborhood was especially evident on Halloween. During the early evening, the sidewalks filled up with children. If you lived in the vicinity of the school, you would inevitably run out of candy by mid-evening. Kids and parents gathered at Halloween parties in homes around the neighborhood. A late-afternoon Halloween parade took place every year, with a noisy procession of children marching down the tree-shaded sidewalks to Clark Park. The line of children went on forever.

7 Commercial Corridor Redefinition

The West Philadelphia Fire House

The Economy of the Avenue

The most successful national retailers dictate their own site-selection standards, and everyone in the industry knows them. Expressed in terms of variables such as building footprint size, parking availability, and volume of existing traffic flow, these standards influence a company's decisions about whether and when to open a store in a new location. After a site-selection decision is made, pre-development activity follows in a more or less linear progression: property is acquired or optioned; zoning, infrastructure, and permitting issues are addressed through interaction with one or more units of government; planning and design work is completed; construction financing is obtained; permits are approved; agreements are executed; and construction begins.

Traditional storefront-lined neighborhood commercial corridors in older cities generally have few or no prospective development sites that are consistent with the site-selection standards of national retailers. When investment and development occurs in these corridors, the process preceding it is often organic rather than linear; the completion of every action is connected to and often complicated by, one or more other issues. The property to be acquired or optioned is encumbered with tax liens, asbestos, or lead paint. An older sewer line connected to the site has to be replaced, and financing to support this infrastructure investment is not readily available. The zoning board opposes the proposed size, use, or design of the development; and so on.

The West Philadelphia Fire House venture is a case study in contradictions and unintended consequences. This venture, in which an ambitious development concept succeeded, failed, then succeeded again in another form, illustrates the special challenges associated with the pursuit of investment and development in an older neighborhood commercial corridor.

Baltimore Avenue begins west of 38th Street, just beyond the edge of the University of Pennsylvania campus, and runs at a southwest diagonal, cutting through a square-block street grid pattern all the way to the city border twenty blocks away. A pair of trolley tracks emerges from underground at

Figure 7.1 West Philadelphia Fire House

40th Street, and a two-way trolley line, linking Baltimore Avenue with Philadelphia's downtown, extends along most of the avenue's length, with a stop at each street corner. The surrounding neighborhoods were developed as "streetcar suburbs": Victorian-era row and semi-detached masonry homes, with porches, bay windows, slate roofs, and distinctive features such as wrought-iron hairpin fences, ornamental wooden porch columns, and stone and masonry arches and lintels. From 40th to 45th Street, the properties lining Baltimore Avenue are primarily three-story homes. A mix of residential and retail uses begins at 45th Street, and this pattern continues, with some variations, to the city border just past 61st Street.

Although Baltimore Avenue has a distinct retail identity, the avenue was never as prominent a retail center as the nearby 52nd Street corridor. Other neighborhood commercial districts were even larger; during the peak years of the Germantown Avenue/Chelten Avenue district in Northwest Philadelphia, the district's retail square footage exceeded that of the downtowns in many Pennsylvania cities. Although less prominent than these areas, Baltimore Avenue had a strong retail presence, strong enough to support assets such as a movie theatre on the 4700 block and a stone-columned bank on the 4900 block.

During the last half of the twentieth century, as Philadelphia population declined and large shopping centers strategically located in heavily trafficked areas became increasingly accessible to both car owners and users of public transit, many of the city's neighborhood commercial corridors lost their vitality, and many retailers moved or went out of business. Between 1975 and 2000, for example, the segment of Baltimore Avenue between 45th and 50th Streets lost a pharmacy, a bank, a real estate agency, a funeral home, a furrier, a butcher shop, and a family restaurant and was about to lose a hardware store (which closed in the early years of the twenty-first century). During this time, active retail establishments were replaced by vacant space and storefront churches. "Stop and go" takeout food establishments—sandwich shops licensed to sell beer and malt liquor—became prominent public nuisances and little centers of drug trafficking.

The late twentieth-century history of this section of Baltimore Avenue was not entirely negative, however. As African immigration into the area increased, African restaurants and grocery stores began to emerge. Dahlak, an Ethiopian restaurant on the 4700 block of Baltimore, was the first, but not the only, African-themed enterprise to succeed in attracting a racially and economically diverse clientele. Fu Wah, a small Vietnamese grocery on 47th Street just below Baltimore, doubled its square footage, broadened its product base, and introduced specialty food items that achieved similar success in attracting a crossover customer base. The Mariposa Food Coop, a wholefoods/health foods venture run by an anarchist collective, maintained its presence a half-block away. The Iron Men, an ornamental iron works, took over a small industrial building on 50th Street just below Baltimore. Hickman Temple A.M.E. Church, located at the intersection of 50th and Baltimore, was re-energized through the leadership of its new pastor, Rev. Joseph D. Patterson.

These positive dynamics did not add up to an economic recovery for Baltimore Avenue. In the area west of 45th Street, the avenue was recognizable as one of many traditional neighborhood commercial corridors with similar histories. They had thrived at a time when population was at its peak and many customers walked to stores from home or corner trolley stops. More recently, each of them had become an overextended collection of scattered retail establishments, many of insufficient quality to compete for customers outside the immediate neighborhood, interspersed with vacant and underused buildings. For the most part, Baltimore Avenue, like its counterparts elsewhere, had lost its identity as a desirable retail destination.

In theory, the appropriate strategy for a disinvested retail corridor such as Baltimore Avenue is straightforward: complete a market analysis to identify retail establishments that have the best prospects for success, given the social and economic demographics of the adjacent neighborhoods; identify the best locations for the development of these retail facilities; organize a merchants association to promote the area; and try to attract investment and development there, with a long-term goal of consolidating more business establishments within a smaller group of blocks in order to eventually generate a critical mass of retail activity.

In practice, this approach would be difficult to implement on a corridor such as Baltimore Avenue. Although a market analysis would show a primary trade area population with a significant level of aggregate buying power, no cleared land suitable for new retail development existed on the corridor east of 51st Street. A plan to consolidate retail development within a small group of blocks would be expensive and could only be financed with public subsidy, which would not be readily available at the level needed to fundamentally change the area. The disintegration of the corridor's retail assets over the years had left behind a collection of merchants in scattered locations, a group with little potential to organize an association and launch corridor promotion campaigns.

Some government funding was available, primarily through the Community Development Block Grant that the City received from the federal government, to support neighborhood commercial corridor improvement programs; in some years, funding could be obtained from the City's capital program as well. When available, the funding could be budgeted for loans and grants to finance small business development and expansion projects; for façade and signage improvements; for the installation of new curbs, sidewalks, street lighting, and trees; for technical assistance provided by city economic development agency staff; and, in rare instances, for operating support to maintain a business association staff and office. However, this limited funding had to be dispersed among more than two dozen potentially eligible neighborhood commercial corridors across the city, and the level of funding available was not sufficient to make a significant impact in most of them. Most corridors only received access to technical assistance and business development loan financing. Relatively few corridors received funding for streetscape improvements; 52nd Street got them, Baltimore Avenue did not. Operating funds for business associations were unattainable for most corridors; the Germantown and Chelten corridor got them, 52nd Street did not.

Public funding was used to test potential opportunities to strengthen neighborhood commercial corridors; some of these tests proved unsuccessful. A major commitment of public capital to develop a block-long pedestrian mall near Germantown and Chelten created one of the deadest public spaces in Northwest Philadelphia. The installation of one-story fiberglass canopies over 52nd Street sidewalks obscured rather than enhanced store frontages, and the canopies were removed years later. A section of Hamilton Street, the city of Allentown's Main Street, underwent a similar sequence of canopy installation and dismantling during the same period.

Like other postindustrial cities, Philadelphia had committed public funding to support economic development policies categorized as "flawed models of inner city development" by Harvard Business School Professor Michael E. Porter. In an early draft of his famous essay on "The Competitive Advantage of the Inner City," Porter criticized government funding for economic development that was "skewed toward social programs" that provide services to individuals "rather than . . . economic programs addressing the requirements of the marketplace and industry."[1] Porter argued that the use of government subsidies to develop real estate in "inner city" areas is expensive and will not make urban locations competitive with the suburbs. Tax credits and tax incentives, he contended, are not sufficient to offset the disadvantages of an urban location, and any businesses attracted by these incentives are likely to move away after the incentive term expires. Appeals to convince firms to locate facilities in or make purchases within urban areas based on charitable or philanthropic considerations will not produce lasting results; if these decisions are not consistent with economic reality, the facilities will be the first to close during an economic downturn, and the purchasing will end. Government mandates designed to compel private firms to support minority business enterprises "create attitudes and resentments that can be self-defeating" and "can dull motivation and slow down cost and quality improvement." Relying on community-based organizations to undertake economic development leading to business and job creation is unrealistic; most community groups do not have the business expertise or resources to do so effectively.[2]

The draft of Porter's essay that included these comments did not appear until the 1990s, but evidence to support his contentions could be found in the vicinity of Baltimore Avenue before then. For example, a church-affiliated group had provided financing as an incentive to persuade a suburban printing company to open a plant in a location near the avenue during the 1980s. Despite the company owner's personal commitment to this endeavor, the venture soon proved unsuccessful.

Baltimore Avenue provided a landscape of examples of what could not or should not be done to stimulate investment and development. But a prospective economic development venture that appeared to represent a new kind of opportunity emerged in 1984, when the fire station at 50th and Baltimore closed.

Three Strategies

The fire house occupied a strategically important location in the neighborhood known as Cedar Park. 50th and Baltimore was a "five points" crossing, where two streets intersected a few yards away from a third, Willows Avenue, which cut away at a diagonal south of Baltimore. The expanded intersection formed by the joining of the three streets created an open plaza-like effect, lending increased visibility to the corner properties. One corner was occupied by Hickman Temple Church; another by a credit union; another by Cedar Park, a half-acre green space with walkways, benches, and a small play area for young children; another by a small storefront; and the fifth by the fire house. If the fire house sat abandoned over an extended period due to City inaction or the failure of a reuse plan, the building would have a powerful adverse effect on corridor development potential. If, however, the right reuse plan could be implemented reliably, the fire house could become an exciting center of energy and activity.

The intersection of 50th and Baltimore was a strategically important location from a racial perspective as well. West Philadelphia's population, from the Schuylkill River to Cobbs Creek thirty blocks away, was primarily African-American. Most of the area's white residents lived in the Spruce Hill and Powelton Village neighborhoods adjacent to Penn and Drexel universities, respectively. Whites also lived in the Garden Court and Cedar Park neighborhoods west of Spruce Hill, but white population dropped substantially west of 50th Street. The best plan for the fire house would be one that appealed to both whites and blacks and brought residents from both sides of the 50th Street divide together in an unforced, spontaneous way.

Not least of all, the fire house was a building that deserved to be saved: a two-story, brick structure with a mansard roof, two arched doorways, and attractive ornamental detailing. The property had been reasonably well maintained and was structurally sound but was too small and too old to be feasible for upgrading and continued use by the City; a new fire station had been built three blocks away.

On an intermittent basis between 1984 and 1988, I had the opportunity to influence the future of the fire house building in three ways.

As a neighborhood resident (I lived on 48th Street, six blocks below Baltimore Avenue), I had participated in discussions about neighborhood development as a member of the Cedar Park Neighbors community organization. CPN was a nonprofit group that sponsored community improvement activities and tackled community problems within an area of West Philadelphia bisected by Baltimore Avenue, between 45th and 52nd Streets. The organization was governed by a board of directors, the members of which were selected in an annual general membership meeting, and the board held monthly meetings at Calvary United Methodist Church at 48th and Baltimore. CPN supported tree planting programs, block cleanups, town watches, and an annual fair, held in the park at 50th and Baltimore. CPN opposed nuisance bars, stop-and-go establishments, negligent rental property owners, and unlicensed personal care boarding homes. CPN's membership was more white than African-American, but in most years the composition of the board was reasonably representative of the community's racial demographic—more so than the leadership of many civic groups in other racially mixed Philadelphia neighborhoods. The group had a minimal program budget, no office, and no staff. CPN's level of activity depended on the ambitions and energy of its leaders and members.

CPN members had learned that the fire house was to be closed and that no reuse plans had been made. The vacated fire house would be designated as city surplus property and sold to the highest bidder at public auction. Some community members, concerned about absentee ownership and speculator activity in the area, were not enthusiastic about the conveyance of the property to a new owner who might not be responsive to community interests and who might not even have any immediate plans to renovate and reopen the building.

With the endorsement of CPN's leadership, I organized a series of meetings to consider possible options for the future of the fire house. With other CPN members, we leafleted nearby blocks and held discussion sessions, both well- and sparsely-attended, over a period of months. Information about these dialogues was published in CPN's monthly newsletter and reported on at monthly board meetings and at the general membership meetings.

The number of reuse options was limited by the small size of the building (with a 4,200 square foot ground-floor interior and upstairs space constrained by low-slanting ceilings), by the unavailability of public capital, and by the weakness of the real estate market. The building was not big enough to accommodate a recreation center, a basketball court, or even a half-court, and no capital funding was available to support uses such as these in any case. The property was not well-suited for conversion to a health care center, human services agency, or office space. The high-ceilinged downstairs with the large garage doors was too roomy to be efficiently converted for residential occupancy, and the adaptation of the cramped upstairs space to create a single apartment unit would be too costly.

As the discussions progressed, I proposed that the fire house be developed as a farmers' market-style retail center, where a group of food retailers would lease counter space and sell their products within an open market hall. The market hall concept was one that had been gaining popularity during the 1980s. The makeover of Faneuil Hall in Boston as a "festival market" had proven successful, and the festival market concept had been proposed as a key element of many older-city revitalization strategies drafted by the then-ubiquitous American Cities Corporation (an affiliate of the Rouse Company, formed in 1968 to provide advice on planning, development, and real estate financing to older cities). In Philadelphia during the 1980s, David O'Neil had succeeded in reviving the nearly moribund Reading Terminal Market, a traditional farmers' market in the heart of the downtown area, in part through the repositioning of the market as a lunchtime destination, where poultry farmers and produce retailers shared space under the same roof as a soul food restaurant and a cheesesteak grill. In the Chestnut Hill area of Philadelphia in 1983, a real estate developer had renovated a 7,200 square foot space within a one-story stone building to create a market hall, also combining fresh meat, fish, and produce sellers with lunch-counter space and prepared-food sales (although none of the retailers were farmers).

At the same time, Libby Goldstein, an energetic representative of Penn State University's Cooperative Extension Service (a program of the University's College of Agricultural Sciences), was working in coordination with neighborhood groups to bring Lancaster County farmers into the city to sell their goods at seasonal tailgate markets on street corners and in parks. A typical tailgate market consisted of a group of small farmers who would drive into the city on Saturday mornings from spring through fall and set out their products on folding tables beside their trucks. The farmers sold lettuce, cabbage, spinach, squash, beans, peas, pumpkins, herbs, honey, jams, and other farm products. These small-scale markets were not comparable to big greenmarkets like the one in Manhattan's Union Square, but the Lancaster County farmers were welcomed in the neighborhoods where they sold their goods, and this small-scale commerce continued over the years.

Penn State helped CPN get a Saturday tailgate market started on the sidewalk outside the vacant fire house building as a temporary measure intended to attract more activity to the 50th and Baltimore intersection. A half-dozen farmers participated during the next four years, while planning for the development of the building was under way. The seasonal market attracted a mixed clientele, more African-American than white, drawing some customers from a dozen blocks or more away.

I had a second opportunity to influence the future of the fire house through my employment at Urban Partners (described in the Introduction). After the market-hall concept for the fire house had been aired at CPN-sponsored meetings, I proposed that Urban Partners complete a study of retail market supply and demand issues in order to investigate the feasibility of developing the building as a farmers' market-style food center. The project was funded by the Local Initiatives Support Corporation (LISC), a national organization that provided financing and other support for development ventures undertaken by neighborhood-based organizations. Because CPN was not staffed to administer a grant award, grant management was handled by the West Philadelphia Partnership, a coalition of University City-area neighborhood organizations and institutions that worked together to facilitate university-community relationships.

The market study, completed in 1985, focused on the four census tracts surrounding the fire house. These tracts contained a 1980 population of 20,201, which was estimated to be spending $17.8 million annually on supermarket and food store purchases. These census tracts were underserved by existing small stores and nearby supermarkets, which captured only about $4 million of the four-tract population's food purchasing dollars. Nearly $14 million in food purchases was being spent outside the area.[3]

Of the thirty-one small stores located within the four census tracts, only fourteen carried items in product lines that might compete with a food market at 50th and Baltimore (such as produce, meat, poultry, and fish), and the quality of these products was generally below average. Based on this analysis, Urban Partners recommended a tenant mix for the fire house market that included retailers of produce, meat, poultry/eggs, and baked goods, as well as retailers of fish, coffee, cheeses, spices, and nuts.[4]

The third opportunity for me to influence the future of the fire house was associated with my role as a Democratic committeeperson in the 46th Ward, where both my home and the fire house were located. Committeepeople are elected in the primary elections (once every two years, at that time) to serve as grassroots representatives of their political parties. Committeepeople represent small geographic areas known as divisions, with two committee-people elected for each division. Division boundaries are drawn to include the home addresses of about 500 registered voters, and groups of about two dozen divisions are organized into wards.

Following their election, the committeepeople in each ward meet and elect a ward leader. The ward leader of the 46th Ward was City Councilman Lucien E. Blackwell, a former longshoreman who was then one of the most powerful elected officials in Philadelphia. He effectively managed a ward with one of the most diverse populations in the city in terms of age, race, income, and gender. During the years in which CPN's planning for the reuse of the fire house was under way, I asked Councilman Blackwell to support a pro-posal to convey the vacant building, at nominal cost, from City ownership to a new entity controlled by CPN. In coordination with CPN board mem-bers, I prepared a proposal and supplied documentation about the market study and development plans. The City's Department of Public Property was opposed to the deal we were seeking; they supported the auctioning of the fire house, which would bring some revenue to the City. With Councilman Blackwell's support, however, CPN eventually prevailed, and City Council approved an ordinance authorizing the sale of the fire house for a dollar.

Constructing a Marriage

Half a decade earlier, Bill Coleman had opened Palmetto Market on the ground floor of an older mid-rise apartment building located at the corner of 46th Street and Chester Avenue, four long diagonal blocks southeast of the fire house and a few blocks south of Baltimore Avenue. With Palmetto Market, Coleman created a little jewel box. He filled a cramped, nondescript space with an appealing variety of high-quality foods: fresh produce, fish, cheese, and baked goods, as well as a selection of packaged and canned goods. He organized the floor plan so that activity in the work area behind the counter—a salmon being filleted, a wedge of Jarlsberg being sliced—could be viewed through the big plate-glass window facing Chester Avenue. He opened the doors and set up displays of flowers and produce on the sidewalk outside. He installed a row of hanging industrial-style lamps to highlight baked goods and fresh foods. He built a staircase and a narrow mezzanine to create more shelf space, flanked by an aisle from which shoppers could look down at the activity below.

One newspaper article praised the selection of fresh-roasted coffee beans and the seafood section that offered cherrystone clams, stewing oysters, mussels, and striped bass.[5] Another article called attention to the yogurt milkshakes, the bread selection (black Russian, French sourdough, pumpkin, and zucchini loaves), the fresh juices, and the home-baked cakes.[6] With

Palmetto Market, Coleman had achieved in West Philadelphia, on a minia-
ture scale, a success comparable to that of David O'Neil at the Reading
Terminal Market and the developer of the Chestnut Hill Farmers' Market:
in a formerly unattractive, under-used space, he had organized an appealing
presentation of an array of high-quality foods.

O'Neil's success at the Reading Terminal Market had drawn on the
strength of Philadelphia's downtown, with a customer base that included
weekly grocery shoppers, lunching office workers, and later, tourists and
visitors to the nearby Pennsylvania Convention Center. The Chestnut Hill
market had drawn on shoppers from the largely affluent surrounding community and the nearby suburbs. Palmetto succeeded because of its location
within a high-density residential area populated with lots of university
students, faculty, and staff. Referring to the fact that five banks had rejected
his application for business loan financing based on doubts that Palmetto
could succeed at this location, Coleman said that "What so many people,
including bankers, don't understand is that this section of University City is
undergoing extensive rehabilitation . . . It's a good neighborhood, and I think
we can make a contribution to it by running the best possible grocery."[7]
However, although Palmetto provided a variety of upscale products, Coleman
was not marketing the store exclusively to middle- and higher-income
people. A lot of people who do not have much money are discriminating
food shoppers, he told me once. When a check arrives and they want to eat
well, they will pay for high quality.

After operating Palmetto Market for three and a half years, Coleman sold
the business to a Korean couple. The market did well for a time, then closed.
After developing grocery markets in two other areas of Philadelphia, Coleman
and a business partner co-founded a business brokerage firm in Northeast
Philadelphia.

The fire house market needed a manager, but no suitable candidates
with previous farmers' market experience could be found. I tracked down
Coleman, described the fire house project to him and, over a series of months,
convinced him to participate. During this time, we met at his brokerage office,
we inspected the vacant fire house building, and we had several breakfast
meetings at diners in West and Northeast Philadelphia. A pre-development
grant awarded to Cedar Park Neighbors enabled us to obtain legal assistance
from Reuben Clark, a capable attorney on the staff of the nonprofit Regional
Housing Legal Services, who facilitated a discussion that led to the formation of a partnership. The partnership structure enabled us to pursue our
respective goals and overcome our respective limitations. CPN wanted a
manager to recruit tenants, lease them stall space in the market, and handle
property management responsibilities. But CPN was a nonprofit, tax-exempt
organization that, based on the mission set forth in its articles of incorpor-
ation, could not participate directly in the operation of a private business.
Coleman wanted a reasonable management fee and a potential opportunity
to provide business-brokerage services for retailers based in the market.

But Coleman's firm was a for-profit entity that could not receive funding from the charitable foundations that we anticipated would support the development of the market.

The organizational structure that resolved these issues was multi-layered. The fire house property would be owned by a newly-formed private partnership called West Philadelphia Fire House Associates. Associates would consist of two partners, each partner a corporation that would possess half the ownership of the property:

- One corporation, West Philadelphia Fire House, Inc. (WPFH) would be controlled by a single shareholder, the Cedar Park Neighbors organization. CPN would appoint members of the corporation's governing board. WPFH would serve as managing general partner, empowered to make decisions about the operation of the building.
- The other corporation, Fire House Management Services (FHMS), would be wholly owned by Coleman. Through a management agreement executed with WPFH, this corporation would populate the building with retailers, operate the market, and maintain the property.

This structure was designed to address the interests and priorities of both Cedar Park Neighbors and Coleman. The future operation of the building would be determined by a community-controlled entity (WPFH) in its capacity as managing general partner. The leadership of this organization was selected by the board of CPN, and the board members of CPN were chosen by community members in an annual election. The management of the farmers' market would be controlled by Coleman, through his wholly-owned corporation. Coleman would receive a management fee for his services and, if the market proved successful, the value of his ownership share in the property would increase.

Project financing was multi-layered as well. The total project budget was about $485,000, approximately $270,000 of which was allocated to the rehabilitation of the vacant building. The CIGNA insurance company provided a $310,000 mortgage through its Community Investment Program. Each of the two parties in the Associates partnership contributed $25,000 in equity. WPFH's equity contribution and other costs were financed primarily through city and state grants. FHMS' equity came from Coleman's own funds. Construction financing was provided by Provident National Bank.[8] CIGNA's commitment of permanent financing had been made contingent on a requirement that the management agreement with Coleman remain in effect for five years.

A neighborhood contractor was selected to manage the building rehabilitation project. About three-quarters of the construction funding was awarded to minority subcontractors, most of them based in West Philadelphia. The building rehabilitation employed thirty minority construction workers, most of them West Philadelphia residents.[9]

When the market opened in September 1988, leases had been signed with retailers of meats, poultry, produce, fish, baked goods, flowers, and coffee. One of the three anchor tenants in the market (the butcher) was a minority-owned business, and at least one-quarter of the leaseable counter space in the market was proposed to be designated for minority-owned retailers. As a provision of the standard lease for space in the market, each retailer agreed to give preference to jobseekers from West Philadelphia in hiring to fill job openings.

Cedar Park Neighbors appointed the first WPFH board members in 1988 as well. The board drafted and approved by-laws and began holding meetings. The board members, eight in all, were residents or businesspersons in the Cedar Park neighborhood. Six were African-Americans, and four were women.

At an intermediate stage during the months of discussions that led to financing settlement and construction start, Coleman had sent me a letter. I'm beginning to believe that this project will really happen, he wrote. I had the letter framed and presented it to Coleman after the construction loan documents had been signed in May 1988. When the rehabilitation of the fire house had been completed and the farmers' market opened, Coleman hung the framed letter on the wall of his office.

What Went Wrong

The Lancaster County farmers were angry. They were furious. Under CPN's sponsorship, the farmers had been selling fresh goods at the seasonal tailgate market in front of the vacant fire house. Now that project financing had been obtained and the building was about to be rehabilitated, the farmers were left with no further opportunity at 50th and Baltimore; they would neither be able to move inside the renovated building nor remain in place on the sidewalk outside.

"They used us to help get [government funding]," said one farmer. "They used us to help get their people to lease, and now they don't want us anywhere nearby." An official of the Pennsylvania Bureau of Agricultural Development, an agency that had provided a grant to support the rehabilitation project, agreed. "You just don't simply cut off the little guys like this," he said.[10]

The future of the tailgate market had been under discussion for several months. The fire house market that was to operate under Bill Coleman's management would need rent-paying retailers in order to support its mortgage debt and operating costs; the Lancaster County farmers couldn't afford any rent expense. The fire house market needed retailers who would operate year-round; the Lancaster County farmers operated on a seasonal basis. The market hall was too small and the operating budget was too tight to make it possible to offer free or discounted indoor space to the farmers. And how could the market attract a produce retailer—an essential anchor tenant—if a competing tailgate market were allowed to operate on the sidewalk outside?

Meetings between Bill Coleman and the farmers proved unsuccessful in resolving the problem. Later, Coleman told a newspaper reporter that, to be successful, the market management must "defend the people who are going to pay the rent."[11] With the assistance of the Penn State Extension Service, a new location for the tailgate farmers was found, at the edge of a public park a few blocks away. The new location was nearby, but not nearly as accessible for shoppers who had frequented the tailgate market in previous years. No one was satisfied with these outcomes.

The disagreement with the tailgate farmers was not the first controversy associated with the fire house venture. Rev. Patterson of Hickman Temple A.M.E. Church brought forward criticisms of the development proposal midway through the planning process. To respond, I went to the church on numerous occasions to explain the project and answer questions. I addressed the congregation at a Sunday morning service. I engaged in an extensive question-and-answer session with Rev. Patterson and State Representative James Roebuck, within whose district the fire house was located. I met in the church's board room with church representatives who quizzed me about the project; at the start of the meeting, two tape recorders were placed on the table in front of me to record my every remark. I came to another meeting, held in the church's side chapel, expecting a small-group discussion, and was surprised to find fifty parishioners gathered there, with Rev. Patterson's introduction of me delivered in the form of a denunciation of outsiders trespassing in the community.

In fact, Rev. Patterson and the members of the Hickman Temple congregation were of the community, but they were not identical to the community. Rev. Patterson himself did not live in the Cedar Park neighborhood. Many congregation members traveled from homes elsewhere in Philadelphia or in the suburbs to attend church services; others were neighborhood residents. With one exception, no one representing the church had participated in the widely publicized project planning that had taken place in previous years, although the church had been invited to do so.

Community support for the farmers' market venture had been well-documented. CPN's files included meeting announcements and minutes, newsletter and newspaper articles, and petitions signed by residents and businesses endorsing the proposal. The church had been invited to consider renting space in the fire house, and a proposal for renting counter space to sell prepared meals in the market had been presented to Bill Coleman. During subsequent discussion, Hickman Temple representatives objected to the proposed rent amount. Coleman agreed to lower the rent. However, no further action was taken by the church representatives, and phone calls from Coleman were not returned.

CPN chose Rev. Patterson to serve as a member of the WPFHP board during the board's first year. However, Hickman Temple congregation members never became strong supporters of the market and Rev. Patterson continued to voice criticisms of the project.

The most intense opposition to the market, however, came from within CPN and the WPFHP board itself, starting during the first year of the market's operation. The criticisms were numerous. CPN had not done an adequate job of consulting the community to obtain residents' views about the development of the building. The project financing plan had not been satisfactorily explained to community members. The details of the partnership agreement and management agreement had not been sufficiently aired in public. CPN had given over control of the fire house, through approval of the management agreement, for five years without sufficient consultation with the community. Coleman was not devoting priority attention to recruiting minority-owned businesses to rent space in the market. Many of the individuals voicing these expressions of discontent had participated in the planning process that had taken place months earlier. Some of them acknowledged that a level of public disclosure and public dialogue had occurred, but maintained that it had not been enough.

A Firehouse Advisory Committee was formed to address these issues. The Advisory Committee voted on a series of resolutions which its records stated "are to be refined and sharpened by a sub-committee."[12] The committee resolved that WPFHP and FHMS representatives should meet "to attempt to define their roles and responsibilities"; that the WPFHP and CPN boards should "address the causes of alienation in the community and how that alienation can be remedied (perceived issues involved in alienation include lack of minority vendors, response to negative newspaper articles, and perceived belief that the Firehouse Market violated an agreement not to sell dairy products)"; that "we clarify responsibilities in leasing"; that "there be a meeting involving CPN Board, WPFHP Board, and BC, to clarify and summarize the roles of the manager and the managing partner"; that a market survey be conducted "to determine what is needed by the community"; that "WPFHP Board and BC develop a plan to improve market and its image"; and more.[13] All of these activities were to occur during the critical start-up period in which CPN and WPFHP had been expected to assist in promoting the market rather than raising fundamental questions about its right to exist.

It got worse. Disagreements about the farmers' market spilled out beyond the WPFHP board and divided the membership of CPN. The project became a central issue in the 1989 CPN board elections, at which nearly 300 people turned out. The racial mix of the board remained about equal (changing from eleven whites and ten blacks to nine whites and twelve blacks), but a dispute broke out over charges of lost ballots and miscounted results. In an effort to put an end to the controversy, it was agreed that the two candidates for board president would serve as co-presidents.[14] As a result, CPN's leadership consisted of one co-president of the CPN board who was a strong supporter of the fire house project, and another co-president who was a leading critic of the project. The controversy continued. Some of the opponents of the project called for a boycott of the market and refused to shop there.

Coleman felt sandbagged. He felt, with justification, that his business partner was making every possible effort to undermine him and cause the venture to fail. He had never made a binding commitment to guarantee a specified level of minority-retailer participation and felt that he had used all resources available to him to locate minority retailers and promote leasing opportunities. During this time, few community members had done anything to assist him in locating prospective candidates. Coleman also felt that I had deceived him by not being candid about racial divisions in the community during our discussions, in which I had emphasized, based on my experience at the time, CPN's consistent support for the project concept and structure.

The project had become a case study in support of Michael Porter's contentions. Writing in 1994, Porter would state that community-based organizations "are driven by social activism and not a business perspective. Accordingly, they often lack the management expertise, resources, incentives, and priorities necessary to assist in developing significant businesses."[15] Also relevant to this situation was a comment by New Urbanist co-founder Andres Duany about neighborhood plans that had been blocked by community opposition in Miami: "What can you do if basically everything is devolved, if decision-making is devolved to whoever happens to show up in the public meeting? Very little. Very little can be done, and that's a problem beyond planning, let's face it."[16] Our efforts to separate the business expectations and the community expectations associated with the project, by painstakingly crafting partnership and management agreements, had not succeeded.

The disagreement with the Lancaster County farmers had been a preventable mistake. I had had four years to explain the realities of the development venture to the farmers and to help manage a smoother transition. However, even if I had done a better job of transition management, the farmers would not have been any happier with the situation, and the state's Bureau of Agricultural Development might never have made the commitment of grant funding that helped subsidize the cost of rehabilitating the building. On one hand, the farmers were right: I had used them. On the other, we had entered into a business relationship that, for a time, satisfied the self-interest of all concerned. The farmers were apparently profiting from the relationship. If they had not been, it seems unlikely that they would have made the Saturday-morning drive from Lancaster County to West Philadelphia during the growing and harvest season each year.

The opposition within CPN was much harder to understand. The Cedar Park neighborhood had significant racial divisions, but the community was not fundamentally racially divided; it was better integrated and experienced fewer racial tensions than most other Philadelphia neighborhoods with comparable demographics. CPN was not an organization that was unrepresentative of the neighborhood's racial makeup; the organization had been integrated along racial and class lines for years. Neither CPN, the City, nor any significant private real estate developer had any plans to make over the community, acquire blocks of property, or displace longtime residents. Older homeowners were not being priced out of their homes as a result of rising property values, and low-income tenants were not being evicted in order to facilitate the conversion of their apartments into upscale housing.

So what was the basis for the opposition? In 2008, I asked two individuals who were familiar with the project to give me their views.

One response was as follows:

> This project could have been a success; it could have been a win-win situation. The intersection of 50th and Baltimore was a good location for a community-oriented activity. I participated in the recycling program there for years, and the environment was very convivial. Residents in that neighborhood needed good food stores, and that community was one that would support local businesses—so the project had a lot of potential to be successful.
>
> Bill's stewardship of the market was not in touch with what was going on, in terms of the diversity of the community. He was totally unwilling to cooperate. He had an antagonistic attitude toward those who would not share his vision. He refused to let the black butcher sell pickled pigs' feet but thought it was okay to sell gefilte fish. Rather than responding to the racial divisions with some sympathy, he poured grease on the fire.
>
> Because Bill tried to exert so much control over the retailers, he guaranteed that they would fail. He had so isolated himself from the retailer perspective that anyone with business sense would never consider leasing space from him, especially a retailer who was aware that African-American community members were boycotting the market.
>
> Some bad decisions were made at the start of the project, such as demolishing the staircase leading to the upper floors. The stair removal made a large part of the building functionally obsolete—you couldn't rent it because the access had been removed. After a new staircase was constructed along the side of the building, two good tenants moved in.
>
> Community conflicts in University City usually occur along class lines, not racial lines; so when a conflict with racial implications occurs, you take note. Looking back on an experience like that, people don't necessarily remember all the details of what happened, as much as they remember how they felt; and I remember feeling disenfranchised. As black people sometimes say to one another, They would never have let a black person get away with this.[17]

The other individual whom I interviewed responded in this way:

> One person, a person who viewed opposition to the project as a matter of civil rights and social justice, caused the controversy to be far more intense and polarizing than it would otherwise have been. This person disrupted meetings, misrepresented facts, and persuaded other African-American community members to actively work against the project. [Note: this person is not the individual whose remarks are summarized above.]
>
> The individuals who did so were members of the early baby-boom generation who were just beginning to achieve success in their professions. As members of the first generation to experience the benefits of affirmative action, they had been feeling a sense of discomfort that their success was undeserved, and they allowed themselves to be convinced that their participation in the opposition was a form of "giving back to the community."
>
> The opposition group was not a united front—far from it. Longtime, older African-American residents did not join in, and some were dismayed by the actions of those who did. Only one African-American person with any real business experience had participated in the community dialogue—a Baltimore Avenue retailer with a store near the fire house—and he was harassed and ostracized for supporting the market. In a community like Cedar Park, criticisms and fault-finding associated with the fire house development venture and the market concept would have been unavoidable, no matter what; but the hostility would not have reached such a high level had it not been for this misguided activism.
>
> When a proposal for the development of a food market is brought before a community, every community member considers him- or herself to be an expert, because everyone has the experience of food shopping. For this reason, the best approach would have been for CPN members to have agreed on a unified vision of what the market would look like, but this didn't happen. There had been no discussion of related issues, such as the scarcity of independent African-American retailers in the fresh food business. As a result, everyone painted a different picture of the market—and, for some people, that picture was a market in which all the retailers would be African-American. That was all there was to it, and the rest be damned.[18]

These comments, expressed two decades after the occurrence of the events they described, illustrate the fundamental differences in perspective that emerged during that time. Because CPN had neither the resources nor the sophistication and maturity to manage the level of civic engagement that a project as ambitious as this one required, these differences persisted. Under an ideal scenario, the project would have been assigned to a CPN-affiliated community development corporation that possessed years of prior real estate development experience. No such organization existed. I had convinced myself that the necessary resources, sophistication, and maturity could be outsourced to Urban Partners, Bill Coleman and the rest of the development team. I had been mistaken.

No one could have predicted what would have happened if the farmers' market plan had never been advanced; however, a more favorable outcome for the building seemed unlikely to me. The Baltimore Avenue real estate market was weak at best during the 1980s and 1990s. No real estate developer would have restored the building to the level of quality that had been achieved through the expenditure of the development financing that had been assembled for the farmers' market venture. The building might have become another retail-corridor church or another stop-and-go establishment. A speculator might have bought the property. In Philadelphia's downtown, a speculator had taken control of the Reading Terminal Market for a time and, during the market's worst years, had doubled the rents of the retailers who remained there. He was on his way to bleeding the place dry and, if he had not died during this phase of activity, the Reading Terminal Market might have gone out of existence. In a weak neighborhood retail market within a city experiencing financial hardship and within a neighborhood burdened by the crack cocaine epidemic, it was hard for me to imagine an alternative outcome for the building that would have proven favorable.

The farmers' market opened in August 1989. On opening day, the City's Department of Public Property, the same department that had reluctantly turned over ownership of the building to the partnership, assisted us by setting up a platform and public-address equipment on 50th Street next to the building. Gospel singers performed. Councilman Blackwell, State Representative Roebuck, and community members delivered words of congratulation and praise. The rehabilitation project had given the property an attractive new look while preserving the building's noteworthy design features. The bricks had been cleaned and repointed. The door and window trim had been scraped and painted dark green. New heating and air conditioning had been installed. Refrigerated display cases and produce bins were filled with fresh products. The flower stand faced the street directly in front of the Baltimore Avenue entrance, with banks of fragrant, fresh-cut flowers filling the space.

Years of difficult pre-development planning had ended. The building rehabilitation project had been completed on time and on budget. Nearly all the retail space had been leased, and the market had opened. Everything looked fine; but I felt totally defeated.

Performance

In 1996, during my tenure as OHCD director, the New York-based Project for Public Spaces/Public Market Collaborative held its third international conference on public markets in the city of Philadelphia. In anticipation of this event, OHCD and the City's Commerce Department jointly sponsored an evaluation by PPS/PMC of the current status and future prospects for public markets in Philadelphia. David O'Neil, the former manager of the Reading Terminal Market, headed the research team, which produced a report entitled, "The Future of Public Markets in Philadelphia." Bill Coleman was a member of the project advisory committee.

The research team included in the report a comparison of 1993 income and expense figures that had been projected in 1988, at the time of CIGNA's underwriting of the mortgage for the project, with actual 1993 income and expenses. The comparison showed that rental income was 30 percent lower than had been projected ($112,721, compared with a projected $164,101), primarily because the retailers in the market would not have been able to bear the rent increases that had been anticipated at the time of the mortgage underwriting. Although total operating expenses had been held to $90,000, more than 10 percent lower than projected cashflow after debt service amounted to less than $8,000.[19]

The authors of the report stated that "it is a miracle that the Firehouse Farmers' Market is still operating; on a cash basis it hovers around break-even with no reserves for replacement." The report also criticized the organization of the market as a real estate project, stating that "treating it like one did a disservice to the project":

> . . . it was the need to renovate the Firehouse building that generated the large debt burden . . . While the historic preservation of the building was an important goal of the community and clearly adds to the appeal of the market, it also, in this case, increased costs to the project. Leased space or a simple shed structure on a vacant lot would have given the market a better chance to make it economically on its own merits. In developing new markets, it is important to adequately finance the historic preservation component of a project and not to potentially overburden the fragile start-up economics of a market with added costs.[20]

The "miracle" of the market's survival was due primarily to Bill Coleman's expenditure of time and money. Although the management agreement had required Coleman's presence at the market for only three hours of each business day, he constructed a loft space overlooking the market area and moved his brokerage business there. He took over some of the retail spaces on a temporary basis when needed to avoid creating vacancies during tenant turnover periods. He raised money from a charitable foundation to construct a stairway to the second floor, sponsored an event there by a pair of performance artists, and rented the available vacant spaces remaining in the building to a coffee shop and a bike repair shop. In 1999, he helped organize Friday Night Jazz concerts on Baltimore Avenue right outside the front entrance. On a summer evening, a few hundred people might come to listen, gathering on the sidewalk, on the traffic island in front of the building, and in the park across the street.[21]

Some of the community members who had been among the original supporters of the fire house development venture were critical of Coleman's management of the market. He was criticized for not doing more to promote the market to middle-income consumers who lived east of 50th Street, the kinds of shoppers that had made Palmetto Market a big success. He was criticized for being overly defensive about comments by community members who had expressed opposition to the market, some of which amounted to simple rhetoric that did the market no real harm. He was criticized for being stubborn and unresponsive to comments and suggestions, to an extent that he drove away past and prospective supporters. But people who understood the history of the market knew that, notwithstanding any shortcomings that Coleman might have, the fire house venture would never have been completed and the market would never have been opened without him. There was no backup plan; there were no other market managers waiting to step in if he withdrew.

The boycott of the market did not cause the venture to fail, but it did not help either. As years passed, the customer demographic consisted primarily of African-American community residents who lived near enough to the fire house to walk there. This consumer base was not sufficient to produce profitable results, and the market remained a break-even venture at best. Throughout the 1990s, the market never achieved a retail mix and a level of retailer quality equal to that seen on opening day in 1989. During that decade, Coleman acquired CPN's share of the partnership (at an amount based on an independent appraisal, contrary to a rumor that CPN had sold its share for a dollar), CIGNA forgave the outstanding mortgage balance, and Coleman sold the building in 2003 to a neighborhood resident who had some retail management experience and wanted to revive the market. The new owner was unsuccessful, and the market closed in 2005. After sixteen years, the building returned to vacancy.

Love Each Other

"We all work together," said the bright-eyed waitress with the emo hairdo and the tattoo sleeves. "We love each other." She had brought a big mug of Gold Stock Ale (described as "a medium bodied pale ale with layers of character") and a glass of Chadsford Merlot to our table.

The fire house was nearly filled to capacity, with all the tables occupied and the only empty seats, a few of them, at the curved bar that extended along the width of the building, in the space where the butcher's shop had opened in 1989. Gleaming brew kettles could be seen through a glass window in a rear corner. Pizzas were cooking in hardwood-fired ovens in an enclosed kitchen at the rear. Little groups of chairs and tables, both standard size and stool-high, were arrayed around the big room. A sofa sat underneath one of the front windows. A Wilco song could barely be heard in the background, nearly overwhelmed by conversation and laughter.

Dock Street, a Philadelphia-based "craft microbrewery," had moved into the building and opened the brew pub during the summer of 2007. The pub owners applied to the City's Zoning Board to seek approval for this changed use of the building's ground-floor space. Anxious to support the new business, Cedar Park Neighbors mounted a petition drive and collected more than 600 signatures. The pastor of Hickman Temple, Rev. Patterson's successor, expressed reservations about the plan, and several meetings between representatives of the church and CPN, along with other community members, took place. Councilwoman Jannie Blackwell kept track of the dialogue. She had been elected to the City Council seat previously occupied by her husband, following Lucien Blackwell's decision to run for Congress (he served in Congress from 1991 to 1995 and passed away in 2003). When the dialogue was over, with some compromises achieved, the Zoning Board met and unanimously approved Dock Street's application.

In four visits to the fire house during early 2008, I saw a customer demographic that was primarily white and under thirty, with tattoos and piercings in evidence. Although I was twice as old as most of the other patrons and was dressed in a suit and tie, I felt comfortable there. A person of my generation with whom I spoke a few weeks later felt differently. "I walk in there, and I'm the only black man in the room," he said. I had seen African-American customers and African-American wait-staff on each of my visits, but they were in a minority. The fire house customer profile had changed from majority-black during the farmers' market phase to majority-white. However, even with this skewed demographic, Dock Street was more racially diverse than most comparable eating and drinking establishments in West Philadelphia or elsewhere in the city.

A few years earlier, Dock Street owner Rosemarie Certo and her husband had operated a pub downtown, not far from the Four Seasons Hotel. Looking for a new location in 2005, Certo initially had pursued an opportunity to relocate her business to Northwest Philadelphia. Then she saw the fire house building. Her initial reaction had been "It was beautiful. But I said, 50th and Baltimore? No way."[22] By 2006, she had changed her mind about the area. If the Zoning Board denied her application for the fire house site, she said, she intended to look for another location in the vicinity. "We have always been pioneers," she told a reporter. "We plan on being an integral part of this community that calls in change, that harbors change."[23]

Views of Neighborhood Change

Each unhappy development venture is unhappy in its own way, regardless of whether its character is conventional and suburban or edgy and inner city. But development ventures located in urban neighborhoods carry added risk and uncertainty, which is heightened in areas where disinvestment has had a significant impact and racial and economic divisions are in evidence. Personality plays a critical role in these ventures, which are often are rooted in the ambitions of one determined person or a small group of individuals.

A counterpart to the fire house history is the experience of Weavers Way Co-op, a highly successful cooperative food market located in the Mount Airy section of Northwest Philadelphia, which was the brainchild of one such individual, an entrepreneurial community member named Jules Timerman. Timerman began organizing the co-op on his own, leafleting the neighborhood and collecting money from neighborhood residents, He rented a storefront that had previously been occupied by a delicatessen, and the co-op opened for business early in 1973 with Timerman as its first manager. According to a history displayed on Weavers Way's website:

> Jules stocked the store with a good selection of deli products and fresh produce . . . Produce bins lined the right side of the store. Big glass deli cases and a counter for cutting and wrapping lined the left, with one aisle in between . . .
>
> Jules kept it all going by putting in 70 to 80 hours a week, without pay. He had to take each day's income to buy the next day's supplies—no established credit made for limited buying power. But somehow, Jules kept things going, hunting for bargains, making daily trips to the food distribution center. Word got around the neighborhood that produce at the co-op was fresher and cheaper—and the cheese selection was great—so membership kept increasing. By mid 1973, membership was up to 500.[24]

A board was organized that fall, and the co-op purchased a building in early 1974. By this time, however, Timerman's relationship with the co-op board had deteriorated, following a series of disagreements, and Timerman left the co-op before the end of the year.[25] Bad feelings lingered.

Later Timerman opened a food business in a nearby suburb. Based on the concept that he had brought to reality in Mount Airy, the coop's success grew without him. The challenge of achieving long-term success was much easier for the coop than for the fire house. Although both were initially weakened by internal disputes, Weavers Way was located in a wealthier community with a much higher level of economic stability and far less potential for racial and class conflicts. Unlike the fire house market, the coop never became the subject of a broad intra-community conflict.

The Coop's general membership honored Timerman at a thirtieth-anniversary event in October 2004, which he attended. Speaking before a crowd of several hundred people, Timerman, then seventy-eight years old, said, "A lot of water has flowed under the bridge, and not all of it good. But the Coop has surmounted me and all the other problems, and it will go on for another thirty years. You should all feel a part of an enduring tradition."[26]

Nearly twenty years after the opening of the farmers' market, the 50th and Baltimore fire house had also, in some respects, surmounted its past problems, but only by chance. Many viewed the brew-pub incarnation of the building as a success, based on a definition of success that differed significantly from the multiple success criteria that had been established two decades earlier in connection with CPN's proposed development plan. With the opening of the brew pub, the community had gained a valuable economic asset that complemented and strengthened the neighborhood environment as it existed in the early twenty-first century.

For some, the history of the fire house venture, from my initial planning for the project to the brew-pub outcome, might be viewed as reflective of a broader trend of gentrification—the displacement of lower-income nonwhites by higher-income whites—in the residential areas adjacent to Baltimore Avenue. However, this characterization would be inaccurate.

Figure 7.2 shows the boundaries of census block groups adjacent to the Baltimore Avenue corridor, extending from the western boundary of the University of Pennsylvania to 50th and Baltimore. In many instances of gentrification, the changing racial demographic is most in evidence near centers of investment such as a revitalized downtown. This kind of change was not occurring in the Baltimore Avenue census block groups.

In the block group closest to the Penn campus (88/3), black population increased substantially between 1990 and 2000 (by 62 percent), while white population declined (by 18 percent). Black population experienced a net gain in the two census block groups closest to the Penn Alexander School (87/3 and 87/4), while whites experienced population loss in both block groups. Both white and black population declined in the two block groups closest to the fire house (78/3 and 79/3), but black population in these two areas was almost four times as large as white population in 2000.

Table 7.1 Baltimore Avenue Census Block Groups, Population Change by Race, 1990 and 2000

Census Tract/ Block Group	1990		2000		Change (%)	
	White	Black	White	Black	White	Black
77/1	837	308	417	424	−50	38
78/3	148	776	111	709	−25	−9
78/4	633	372	506	246	−20	−34
78/5	568	466	358	739	−37	59
79/2	809	424	609	605	−25	43
79/3	267	888	247	697	−7	−22
87/3	763	172	730	95	−4	−45
87/4	775	177	577	340	−26	92
88/3	713	102	585	165	−18	62

Source: U.S. Census

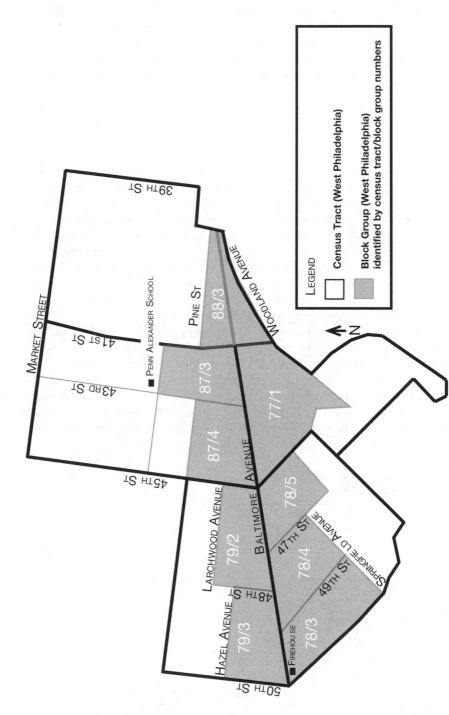

Figure 7.2 Baltimore Avenue Census Block Groups

LEGEND

☐ Census Tract (West Philadelphia)

▨ Block Group (West Philadelphia) identified by census tract/block group numbers

N

Table 7.2 Baltimore Avenue Census Block Groups, Per Capita Income by Race, 1989 and 1999

Census Tract/ Block Group	1989 ($)		1999 ($)		Change (%)	
	White	Black	White	Black	White	Black
77/1	12,146	10,096	11,221	10,294	−8	2
78/3	22,035	9,358	15,715	12,361	−29	32
78/4	15,004	13,118	36,139	14,590	141	11
78/5	16,838	12,308	23,625	15,295	40	24
79/2	20,982	12,475	26,540	25,162	26	102
79/3	19,047	11,141	19,385	17,229	2	55
87/3	17,718	11,002	11,282	17,026	−36	55
87/4	16,505	19,736	24,091	10,211	46	−48
88/3	7,976	11,713	6,855	13,893	−14	19

Source: U.S. Census

The change in per capita income within the white and black populations in the Baltimore Avenue block groups between 1989 and 1999 is also not consistent with gentrification.

As Table 7.2 indicates, black residents experienced a higher increase in per capita income than whites in six of the nine block groups. In the block group adjacent to the Penn campus, black per capita income grew by 19 percent, while white per capita income fell by 14 percent (87/3 and 87/4). In one of the two block groups nearest the Penn Alexander School, the per capita income of blacks grew, while the per capita income of whites declined; in the other block group, the reverse happened. In the block group where the fire house is located (78/3), black per capita income grew 32 percent, while white per capita income declined 29 percent.

The controversy over the fire house was not a symptom of gentrification; it was a disagreement among a relatively small number of middle-class residents, most of whom had not grown up in the community, over the execution of a flawed plan, based on their perceptions—well-founded or unfounded—of what a community should be.

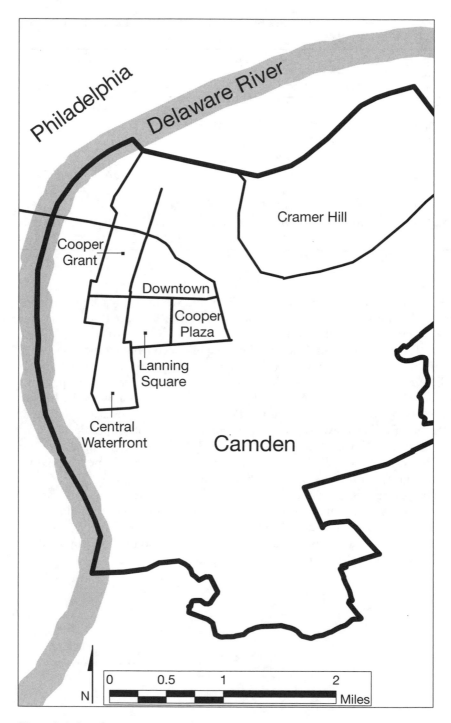

Figure 8.1 Camden

8   The Exercise of State Power
Municipal Reform and Eminent Domain in Camden

During 2007 and the first month of 2008, I spent nearly all of my working days managing the City of Camden, New Jersey's planning and development agencies. Camden has all of the disinvested-city problems described in the preceding chapters—a protracted loss of businesses, jobs, and people, a steadily eroding tax base, a proliferation of vacant and abandoned properties, a depopulated inner-core area, and more. At the same time, Camden may have more competitive advantages—a central location in the metropolitan region, a cluster of academic and health care institutions based in the city's center, and a master-planned waterfront anchored by regional visitor attractions, to name a few of the most evident ones—than any other disinvested city of its size (about nine square miles, about 80,000 people). Many opportunities to take advantage of these competitive advantages have remained unfulfilled over the years, largely due to a combination of corruption, mismanagement, and political interference that produced a disorganized, unreliable, and untrustworthy municipal government. During the thirteen months that I spent in Camden as part of a state-mandated recovery plan, I was in a position to use the authority and resources available to me to help the local public sector get past some of these problems, at least for a time, and—if I succeeded in doing so—to play a constructive role in downtown and neighborhood revitalization.

Camden's early twenty-first century history is particularly deserving of further study for two reasons: the city was the subject of an ambitious state-mandated intervention designed to reform municipal government and reinvigorate the local economy; and, at the same time, controversy over the city's use of eminent domain powers to assemble land for development limited the municipal reform team's ability to achieve key neighborhood reinvestment goals. The question of whether and how state governments should take action to address chronic problems in severely distressed cities and the question of whether and how state-authorized eminent domain powers should be exercised are important issues for many postindustrial cities as well as for the governments of the states where they are located.

The Act

Shortly before Christmas 2006, I was invited to visit Trenton for an interview with several state government officials who occupied senior positions in the administration of New Jersey Governor Jon S. Corzine. That fall, the initial year of Corzine's administration, was the beginning of the fifth year of a state government intervention in Camden, authorized through legislation known as the Municipal Rehabilitation and Economic Recovery Act (MRERA). Corzine had encountered a problem: Melvin R. (Randy) Primas, Jr., who had been appointed supervisor of the Camden recovery plan by then-Governor James McGreevey following legislative approval of MRERA and who had served in this capacity for four years, had resigned. Arijit De, whom Primas had recruited to administer Camden development programs, had submitted his resignation as well. Primas and De had occupied the two central positions in the recovery plan, and these vacancies had to be filled as quickly as possible. The Corzine Administration had recently found an interim replacement for Primas: Theodore Z. Davis, a retired Superior Court Judge and a lifelong resident of Camden, had agreed to a temporary appointment as Camden's Chief Operating Officer. The Corzine team asked me to consider taking over De's position for a few months, during which time permanent appointees for both positions would be found. Following a series of meetings, phone conversations, and email exchanges, an agreement was reached: I would work full-time at Camden City Hall as the person in charge of development policymaking and programming, for what was anticipated to be a three- or four-month period, and I would report to Judge Davis. I would remain an employee of the Fels Institute of Government, and my services to Camden would be supported through a contract between the Camden Redevelopment Agency and the University of Pennsylvania.

MRERA had authorized the state to, in effect, take over the City of Camden, in order to reform municipal government, stabilize the local economy, and stimulate investment and development that was intended to eventually end Camden's chronic dependence on massive infusions of state aid. The first section of the Act summarized the reasons why intervention was needed. The city is in fiscal distress, with high levels of population loss and unemployment. These conditions have eroded the local tax base to a level that is insufficient to support the cost of police and fire services, and tax ratables continue to fall, while ratables in other New Jersey cities are rising. This problem is exacerbated by the under-collection of taxes (at a 70 percent collection rate, according to some sources) from the city's diminished base, due to municipal government inefficiency. For these and other reasons, Camden has experienced significant annual budget deficits, necessitating extraordinary commitments of state support:

> In light of the[se] dire needs . . . and the lack of progress in addressing
> those needs either governmentally or through private sector initiative, and

given the successful interventions on the part of other states in analogous circumstances, it is incumbent upon the State to take exceptional measures, on an interim basis, to rectify certain governance issues faced by such municipalities and to strategically invest those sums of money necessary in order to assure . . . long-term financial viability . . .[1]

This recitation of problems did not include reference to the fact that Camden, to a much greater extent than many other distressed cities, had been plagued by recurrent episodes of government corruption. Mayor Milton Milan, who had become the city's first Hispanic mayor in 1997, was indicted in 2000, the third mayor to be indicted for corruption within the final two decades of the twentieth century.[2]

MRERA called for the Governor to appoint a Chief Operating Officer who would supervise the operation of municipal government and implement reform plans as called for in the Act. The COO would be given the power to reorganize government operations, hire and fire department heads, and enter into contracts and make financial commitments on behalf of the city as well as the power to veto the minutes of any municipal board or authority. In addition, the COO would be charged with supervising the completion of a series of studies and plans designed to create a framework for local government reform and public sector investment to strengthen the city's economy. The latter activity would be supported by a $175 million capital fund. Decision-making about allocations from the fund would be guided by criteria set forth in the Act and by the priorities established in a Strategic Revitalization Plan. An Economic Recovery Board, consisting of representatives of state government, local government, and community constituencies, would review development financing proposals and would approve capital funding allocations at public meetings held at locations around the city.

The Act provided for the dedication of a substantial portion of the $175 million to support downtown development ventures, expansion projects by local academic and health care institutions, and a major addition to the aquarium on the Delaware River waterfront. This investment of capital fund dollars was anticipated to build up these existing centers of employment and to anchor nearby real estate development, business development, and job creation.

Primas, who had been appointed COO shortly after the approval of the Act, appeared to be well qualified for the position. He had been a community activist, a Camden City Council member, the city's mayor during most of the 1980s, head of the state Department of Community Affairs under the administration of Governor James Florio, and, prior to his appointment as COO, an executive with Commerce Bank. He was familiar with Camden city government and the city's neighborhoods, and he had strong working relationships with a number of institutional and business leaders in the city and region. Primas had known State Senator Wayne Bryant, the Camden legislator who had played a central role in drafting and securing approval of

MRERA, since their days as students at Howard University. Bryant, who chaired the Senate Budget and Appropriations Committee, had personally contacted Primas to recruit him as a candidate for the COO job.

During his term as mayor, Primas had brought Arijit De into city government, and De had held several positions in Camden planning and development agencies. Following approval of the act in 2002, De left his position as development director at the Camden Housing Authority to become head of the Camden Redevelopment Agency, which was to serve as the city's center for real estate transactions and development financing.

In this way, by the end of 2002, a recovery plan, supported by a substantial financial commitment, had been approved and Primas and De, two individuals with significant relevant qualifications, had been engaged to lead the initiative.

Camden Rashomon

A senior staff member at the Camden Redevelopment Agency finished reporting to me on the results of a frustrating day that had been spent trying to resolve differences among a group of government and business leaders whose sign-off was needed in order to secure financing for a complex development venture. He shrugged and said, "It is what it is." He added, "You'll hear that a lot around here."

He was right; "it is what it is" was a phrase that recurred in Camden. But, to pose a Zen-like question, reminiscent of an impeachment-period Bill Clinton rejoinder: What is "what it is"? Because Camden was saturated with conflicts and divisions, differing views of "what it is" pervaded the city. No single one could be considered the indisputable truth, but fragments of the truth lay embedded in all of them. The following summary of four perspectives on "what it is" is based on what I observed in Camden during a period that began shortly after the approval of the act in 2002 (when I began the first in a series of foundation- and government-funded consulting projects) and ended in early 2008 (when I completed my thirteen-month tenure as an interim administrator).

Politics

Some people viewed MRERA primarily as a carve-up of state resources by and for the benefit of Camden-area political interests. The largest share of the $175 million in capital funding to be authorized through the act was $47.7 million designated as a "Higher Education and Regional Health Care Development Fund," with allocations to a number of Camden institutions specifically named in the text of the act. The biggest award of dollars from this fund was a commitment of $13.35 million to Cooper Hospital/University Medical Center, part of the regional Cooper Health System. The Chair of the Cooper Health System was George E. Norcross, III, widely regarded as the state's most powerful political figure, whose support had been essential to the election of Governor McGreevey, during whose administration MRERA had been approved. Another major allocation from the fund was a $9 million commitment to the University of Medicine and Dentistry of New Jersey (UMDNJ), which, in the year after MRERA approval, hired Senator Bryant for what was essentially a no-show job (Bryant was convicted on federal corruption charges associated with his UMDNJ dealings in 2008).

Some of those who viewed MRERA from this political perspective held that Norcross and Bryant, recognizing that they would not be able to gain legislative approval of the $175 million without a municipal reform program directed by a COO, had made sure that the COO would be someone who could be taken seriously in this position as well as someone they controlled. From this political perspective, Randy Primas could be viewed as the ideal candidate for the job on both counts. Unlike the mayors who preceded and followed him, Primas had not indulged in criminal activities. He was intelligent, personable, and well-spoken. He had been the beneficiary of Norcross' financial and political support during his mayoral campaigns.[3] At the time when Bryant had contacted him about the COO job, Primas was employed as an executive in the Commerce Bancorp system, where Norcross held the position of Chairman and Chief Executive Officer of Commerce Insurance Services.

From this MRERA-as-politics perspective, the Strategic Revitalization Plan, completed in 2003 by a team led by the firm of Hammer Siler George Associates, was of no substantive value. The MRERA funding that had been specifically designated for neighborhood reinvestment (consisting of a $35 million Residential Neighborhood Improvement Fund and a $43 million Demolition and Redevelopment Financing Fund) was inadequate, and the plan was too broad to be useful in guiding sensible and strategic investment. The plan categorized large portions of the city as "Key Neighborhood Opportunity Areas" and "Key Employment Opportunity Areas," to be given priority consideration in project selection and financing decisions. Before long, the already broad geography of eligibility for this funding became even broader. Following push-back from community constituencies representing a third category of places—so-called "Transition/Future Development Areas" (in which the plan recommended that priority be given to health and safety issues and infrastructure improvements, rather than bricks-and-mortar investment in housing and economic development ventures), the Economic Recovery Board made a commitment to allocate at least $17.5 million to these areas, further weakening the usefulness of the plan as a tool for focused resource allocation. This dilution of the capital funding available for neighborhoods was consistent with the view that MRERA had been deliberately designed to favor the most powerful players in the region with funding set-asides, leaving the remainder for everyone else to fight over.

Institutions

Three institutions—Rutgers University/Camden, Cooper Health System, and Camden County College (the region's community college) had campuses in or adjacent to Camden's downtown core. Other institutions, such as Our Lady of Lourdes Medical Center and Virtua Hospital, occupied central positions in Camden neighborhoods. Although some institutional buildings had been designed in a defensive style similar to that of the Penn libraries described in Chapter Six, none of the institutional campuses were gated or surrounded by high perimeter walls; they were all embedded in their communities.

The senior administrators of these institutions were mindful of the local and regional political dynamic—as any capable administrator anywhere would be—but their perspective on MRERA and Camden's revitalization potential was framed in terms of institutional self-interest rather than party politics. The influence that power brokers like Norcross and Bryant wielded was a blunt instrument. They would make their moves in the political board game; but, for the most part, they would be absent from the day-to-day work that, over the long term, would be the most important determinant of success or failure.

The Camden institutional administrators were more progressive than many of their counterparts in other cities:

- They interacted constructively with community members in the neighborhoods that they occupied. For example, the patrol-area geography of Rutgers' security force included the adjacent Cooper Grant neighborhood; if you lived in Cooper Grant, you knew to call Rutgers security rather than 911 for the most reliable response to an emergency.
- They communicated with each other. They formed a task force and met monthly to consider the best opportunities to collaborate in support of Camden revitalization. By contrast, West Philadelphia institutions had no comparable communications structure during the 1990s, when Penn was implementing its neighborhood investment program.
- They promoted their institutions as key generators of economic benefit for the city, region, and state. In 2004, their task force published an economic impact study that provided information on employment ($360 million in payroll expenditures, with more than half of all employees living in Camden city and county), total spending ($611 million in Fiscal 2001), and tax revenue ($53.8 million in state taxes during Fiscal 2001) associated with the eight institutions participating in the task force.[4]
- They recognized the potentially beneficial relationship between urban institutions and neighborhood revitalization long before the significance of "anchor" institutions became a popular topic in community-development dialogue. They sponsored the housing demand survey,

described in Chapter Six, that had documented the interest of Camden-based institutional employees, medical professionals, and graduate students in considering opportunities to move to housing within the city.[5]

- They were members of the Greater Camden Partnership, a business leadership organization which, among other accomplishments, had produced a well-documented strategy for downtown development and had created a special services district that incorporated some elements of the Center City District model.

The Camden institutional administrators had no interest in seeking to influence all the details of MRERA implementation; but, in the aggregate, their power to use MRERA financing and MRERA-leveraged funding resources to significantly improve the city's economy outweighed the influence of the politicians.

Investors

A "hidden gem just outside Philadelphia"—that was how *The Wall Street Journal* characterized Camden in an article that appeared in May 2007. The city could be viewed as a "gem" for several reasons. Camden was located in the heart of a large metropolitan region. Prices in the South Jersey real estate market to which Camden belonged were significantly lower than in Philadelphia and northern New Jersey. In fourth-quarter 2006, for example, South Jersey office rents were as much as 15 percent lower than Philadelphia's, South Jersey warehouse rents were more than 16 percent below North Jersey's, and South Jersey median house prices ($233,400) were far lower than home prices in North Jersey ($443,400).[6] Camden was a bridge-length away from Philadelphia's hot Center City real estate market. Some South Jersey real estate appeared to be significantly undervalued. The MRERA-authorized public investment in Camden could stimulate broader awareness of the city's potential and generate a rise in property values. Should that happen, private investors who had bought into the market early could make a lot of money. Despite the city's current problems, Camden's longer-term prospects appeared to be favorable.

Camden's city government, like Philadelphia's, had pursued a tax lien sale as a strategy for raising revenues and recycling neglected properties back into the real estate market. Under a contract between the City and Xspand, Inc., a company founded by former New Jersey Governor James Florio, Xspand was organizing a sale of more than 3,000 government liens on tax delinquent properties across the city. Through the sale, prospective buyers were being offered the right to collect and keep the money that had been owed the City and the right to foreclose if payment could not be obtained. An investor who purchased a tax lien would receive a Certificate of Sale and, after recording the certificate at the County Clerk's Office, could seek payment of the lien amount from the property owner and demand an interest charge of up to

18 percent;[7] alternatively, the investor could initiate foreclosure, take title to the property, and develop it, sell it, or hold onto it indefinitely in as-is condition.

Through this process, some investors might acquire title to properties and develop them for housing or business uses that were consistent with city plans and municipal codes. Other investors might follow the example of those who had plagued Allentown and other undervalued urban real estate markets: acquire properties and overcrowd them with substandard rental units. Still other investors might take possession of properties and leave them vacant and unimproved, in the expectation that subsequent development activity in the "hidden gem" would substantially increase the value of the assets they now owned. The worst of these investors would know how to game the city's code-enforcement system and retain ownership of their properties while maintaining them in a deteriorated state.

How many good investors and how many bad investors would participate in Camden tax lien transactions? No one could tell.

Neighborhood Organizations

By 2007, many neighborhood organizations, including community development corporations and civic associations engaged in neighborhood planning, were dissatisfied with MRERA and its implementation. In years prior to MRERA, major commitments of state funding had been made to finance development on the waterfront, with relatively little comparable state investment in neighborhoods, and a continuation of this pattern was reflected in the MRERA financing approach: the aquarium received a $25 million allocation of its own, while all of the city's neighborhoods had to vie for a share of the $78 million available in the two generically designated "neighborhood" funds (some of which would pay for demolition that would not be followed by new development).

By 2007, MRERA investment had produced new waterfront, downtown, and institutional development but only one large-scale neighborhood venture: a HOPE VI remake of the former Westfield Acres public housing site (renamed Baldwin's Run) and the adjacent area that included new home-owner and rental housing as well as the construction of a new public school. St. Joseph's Carpenter Society, one of the Delaware Valley region's top-performing community development corporations, had played the central role in the organization and completion of this venture. In addition to providing a major funding commitment in support of Baldwin's Run, MRERA funding had been awarded to several Low Income Housing Tax Credit-financed rental housing development ventures organized or completed by neighborhood-based organizations; but there was little other evidence of significant development in neighborhoods that would not have taken place without MRERA.

From the perspective of these dissatisfied organizations, Primas and De ignored or were hostile to neighborhood interests, choosing to devote most of their attention to major projects proposed by for-profit developers. De rarely appeared at neighborhood meetings. He wanted the Camden Redevelopment Agency to require nonprofit developers to pay the agency full fair market value for the vacant buildings and lots that CRA conveyed to them, while, in other cities, neighborhood-based groups were not charged anything. He wanted the CRA to become a real estate developer as well as a source of development financing—an apparent conflict of interest—which would establish the agency as a favored competitor for the scarce development funds sought by nonprofit and for-profit developers each year.

Primas and De's signature neighborhood revitalization initiative had been a comprehensive development proposal for the Cramer Hill neighborhood, located on the Delaware River north and east of the city's center. In coordination with community representatives, the CRA had issued a Request for Proposals to select a developer for the entire neighborhood in 2003. The successful proposal was a plan submitted by Cherokee Investment Partners, a North-Carolina-based firm that specialized in the cleanup and redevelopment of contaminated brownfields sites. The $1.2 billion Cherokee proposal, in the version presented to Camden's Planning Board in April, 2004, included the development of 6,000 housing units, most priced at market rates, as well as an industrial park and a big-box retail district. An eighty-five-acre landfill would be redeveloped as a golf course, and a marina would be built on the waterfront. One major downside of the proposal: the relocation of a thousand or more families was called for in order to make way for new construction.

The CRA had tried to respond to growing opposition over the scale of the proposed displacement by drafting a replacement housing plan that included housing options for residents who wanted to stay in the neighborhood. But the opposition hardened. At a community meeting that I attended during this time, one prospective relocatee, a homeowner who had spent years fixing up a house located near the river shoreline, was one of many participants who expressed frustration with the proposed development. He and other owners had invested in the community when no one else would. Why should they be forced to move now? "I'd like to stab Randy Primas," he added.

Anti-Cherokee forces brought suit against the Cramer Hill redevelopment plan that had been drafted in support of the Cherokee proposal. A Superior Court Judge subsequently found fault with the process leading to redevelopment plan approval, based on a technicality: two witnesses had not been sworn in prior to testifying at the Planning Board meeting at which the redevelopment plan had been approved. The Cramer Hill plan was invalidated in 2006, and the CRA subsequently abandoned the Cherokee proposal. From the perspective of many representatives of neighborhood constituencies, the Cramer Hill experience illustrated Primas and De's readiness to side with developers against residents' interests. For some, the issue of whether or not the CRA-proposed replacement housing options were feasible was beside the point; for them, any large-scale displacement was unacceptable.

What They Got Right

"Can't Camden get anything right?" a judge had exclaimed during a court hearing over another contested redevelopment plan. In fact, Primas and De had done several things right during their four-year tenure:

- They resuscitated the Camden Redevelopment Agency, which had been out of business at the time of MRERA approval, and made the CRA a single point of contact for developers interested in doing business in Camden, removing any ambiguity about what government agency was in charge of the economic recovery agenda.
- They restaffed the CRA with development professionals from other municipal governments and from nonprofit housing development organizations. The two dozen staff members of CRA represented a higher degree of professional capability than could be found in many other municipal redevelopment authorities, including, at that time, Philadelphia's.
- They consolidated the leadership of the city's planning and development agencies. Arijit De became both Director of Camden's Department of Development and Planning as well as CRA Executive Director. In an environment where progress had been thwarted by bureaucratic squabbles and turf battles, this consolidation of leadership made sense. De's power under this structure was counterbalanced by that of the City's appointed Planning Board, which had to review and approve all land use and development plans.
- They decided that every Camden neighborhood would be designated a redevelopment area and would have an approved redevelopment plan, so that all community members could be encouraged to participate in the planning process and would feel that they had a stake in the outcome.
- Because City Council was not enthusiastic about the prospect of providing funding for CRA administrative operations (in contrast to other cities, such as Philadelphia, where a significant commitment of Community Development Block Grant funding was made to support Philadelphia Redevelopment Authority operations each year), Primas and De adopted an ambitious approach to CRA revenue-generation: the CRA began charging fees for land acquisition and development proposal underwriting. As a result, CRA dependence on city funding for operations decreased from 100 percent in 2003 to 10 percent in 2006.

The perspective of many planning and development professionals within and outside City Hall differed from the MRERA-as-politics view. Many of them did not accept as a foregone conclusion that the MRERA set-asides of funding for the institutions and the aquarium, funding expenditures managed by Primas and De, were solely politically driven. These places were the city's primary anchors of investment; they would be Camden's best prospects for wealth-building for the foreseeable future.

From this planning and development perspective, the capacity of community-based organizations from which Primas and De received proposals for development financing—with the notable exception of the top-performing St, Joseph's Carpenter Society—was viewed as very weak. Apart from St. Joseph's, no community organization had the capability to develop real estate on a significant scale. And, from the perspective of many in municipal government, some community organization priorities and plans were misguided or flat-out wrong. One group wanted to launch a commercial corridor revitalization plan for a high-vacancy storefront district in which the city had been consistently ineffective in combating a thriving drug trade. Another group wanted to build many new homes on vacant land in an area where environmental problems associated with nearby industries had been well documented (example: a 2002 New Jersey Department of Labor report entitled "Environmental Health Crisis in Camden" listed this area, Waterfront South, as one of the worst census tracts in the country for high risk of cancer from air pollution and stated that the highest rates of particulate pollution in the state come from South Camden[8]). A community coalition lobbied in support of a decades-old plan to develop a supermarket on a CRA-owned parcel that was undersized and poorly located for this use; some of the prospective food market operators to whom the site had been promoted wouldn't even agree to drive by the location.

Primas and De had to deal on a daily basis with two especially difficult challenges. One was the lack of a clear enough definition of the scope of their state-mandated authority—based on Primas' status as an appointee of the Governor—as distinct from the authority of state agencies headed by other appointees of the Governor. The relationship between the COO and the Department of Community Affairs, the state agency that Primas had headed years earlier, was a particular source of conflict. DCA was responsible for monitoring local government operations and was charged with specific Camden-related tasks in the MRERA legislation. During Primas' tenure, DCA was headed by another former elected official, Susan Bass Levin, who had previously served as mayor of Cherry Hill, a Camden suburb.

Primas and Levin, two individuals who were keenly aware of the high-risk political environment in which the Camden recovery plan was being implemented, clashed over a series of issues involving their respective powers. In 2006, for example, the Camden Community Development Association (CCDA), a coalition of community development corporations, proposed to DCA that more than 500 tax-delinquent properties be withheld from the public auction being organized by Xspand, so that these properties could be acquired and developed by CDCs, consistent with their neighborhood strategies (CDC development of these properties would have returned all of them to the tax rolls). The CRA opposed the CCDA request and submitted to DCA an analysis of the development capacity of the CDCs who were seeking to obtain the properties, along with a recommendation that the CCDA set-aside be limited to 126 properties. DCA resolved the issue by agreeing to what the department viewed as a reasonable compromise: an initial commitment of 163 properties to CCDA, which DCA offered to the CCDA member organizations over the CRA's objections.

This relatively small disagreement was illustrative of the larger COO/state dynamic. Despite the powers given to the COO under MRERA, the COO was dependent on state officials—the Treasurer and the heads of state development agencies, in particular—for the funding needed to implement the reform plan and invest in development ventures. State officials, justifiably, were not willing to depart from existing due-diligence practices associated with commitments of their resources. Primas felt, with justification as well, that Camden requests for state assistance were too often being unnecessarily delayed, modified, or subjected to limiting conditions—actions that were not consistent with the spirit of MRERA. In a progress report submitted in November 2006 (which I had helped draft, as a consultant supported by a foundation grant), Primas stated that:

> In approving the act, it was not possible for the Legislature to anticipate and distinguish between those actions which the COO could undertake as an appointee of the Governor without prior review and approval by DCA or any other entity and those actions which would be subject to DCA's oversight of government operations. Because the distinction between actions that could be undertaken unilaterally by the COO and actions that . . . were subject to DCA oversight could not be made in advance, differences of opinion about the respective authority of the COO and DCA caused delays in the implementation of activities mandated by the act.[9]

What this observation left out was the fact that the COO, the DCA Commissioner, and other officials who played key roles in the recovery plan were individuals with their own political agendas, who would use their power as they saw fit to gain advantages over others who got in their way, irrespective, in some cases, of whether or not the consequences would be beneficial to Camden.

The other major challenge to Primas and De's leadership was a ticking clock: the COO's five-year term of office. Given the state of Camden's economy in 2002 when the legislation had been enacted, what could realistically be accomplished in five years? It is unlikely that many people believed that Camden could achieve a high degree of economic success and self-sufficiency within five years—but, that being the case, what measures of success should be considered believable and attainable? Real estate development takes time under the best of circumstances. Property has to be assembled, environmental hazards have to be removed or mitigated, financing has to be underwritten, capable developers have to be selected, and the construction work has to be bid and awarded, after which a building phase, likely to take well over a year at the least, can begin. Given this time-consuming sequence of activity, how many high-impact development ventures could be organized and put into service within five years?

I had completed several consulting projects in Camden during Primas' tenure and had discussed the recovery plan, the Cramer Hill proposal, and other activities with Primas, De, and other city agency staff on numerous occasions. This experience led me to conclude that the ticking clock was a major influence on Primas and De's determination to press ahead with ambitious plans such as the Cherokee proposal. State officials appeared to be driven by a similar determination to move swiftly; Governor McGreevey had hailed the Cherokee proposal at a press conference held in Camden well before sub-stantive community review had begun. Primas and De, however, were the ones who would be held responsible for not devoting sufficient attention to the adverse consequences associated with these plans. By the time the Cherokee proposal had been abandoned, many people shared the view of Judge Theodore Davis, Primas' successor as COO, who later said, "The last thing they were thinking of was the well-being of the people of Camden."

Kelo Conundrums

The 2005 *Kelo v. City of New London* Supreme Court decision could not have come at a worse time for the Camden recovery plan. In *Kelo*, the Court upheld a local government's use of eminent domain powers to seize property in order to implement economic development activities, in this instance, to assemble land for a private venture that included the construction of upscale housing, retail stores, and a marina. The properties to be taken had included occupied homes that no one would have been likely to have character-ized as (to use redevelopment-statute terminology) "blighted" or "in need of redevelopment."

The *Kelo* decision generated a political backlash across the country. The use of eminent domain for private benefit, routinely characterized by public agencies as "economic development" or "community revitalization," had generated controversies in many cities. As a high-profile, well-publicized case, *Kelo* unleashed decades of anger and resentment over what many viewed as an abuse of government authority. In reaction to post-*Kelo* public outrage, legislatures in many states approved new prohibitions or restrictions on the use of eminent domain. The term "eminent domain abuse" became wide-spread.

The basic elements of the eminent domain process, sometimes referred to as condemnation, can be summarized in terms of a few key steps. A place is surveyed and determined to meet state-instituted criteria for designation as a redevelopment area. A redevelopment plan is prepared. The plan documents existing conditions, identifies properties to be acquired, summarizes the development to be completed and the land uses to be changed (for example, changing from "industrial" to "residential" the land-use designation of a vacant lot formerly occupied by a factory and now proposed for new housing construction). The plan identifies, by address, the properties to be acquired in order to complete the activities described. Following review and approval of the proposed redevelopment plan by the local planning board and city council, a redevelopment authority may issue a declaration of taking for any of the properties listed as "to be acquired." At the moment that the redevelopment authority's governing board approves the declaration of taking, legal title to the specified properties passes to the redevelopment authority. An owner may challenge the amount of compensation that the authority proposes to pay, at which point an independent review board will determine whether or not the value assigned to the property by the redevelopment authority is a fair market value and will direct that the amount of compensation be adjusted if appropriate. However, the property taking itself cannot be disputed unless the redevelopment plan or the process leading to plan approval is found to be flawed.

In full detail, the redevelopment process involves many more steps, including the notification of affected residents, the publication of legal notices, the appraisal of properties to be taken, the payment of compensation to property owners, and other actions. However, the principle underlying these actions is the exercise of public authority to take possession of a private property in order to achieve a public benefit.

During the early post-World War Two years when eminent domain was widely used to support public works projects such as the construction of the Interstate highway system, the public-benefit argument was relatively straightforward: property would be taken by a public-agency developer for a project that, when competed, would be owned by the government and that everyone would be able to use. This rationale, though straightforward, was not universally accepted; redevelopment plan approval for some highway projects was denied or stalled indefinitely due to political opposition generated by adversely affected property owners.

The public-benefit logic was less straightforward in cases where the end product of redevelopment would be a private use of the acquired property, as in the taking of property to support the expansion of a university or hospital or the development of housing or a retail center. The rationale for these property takings was that, although the ultimate owner would be a private entity, the public as a whole would benefit from expanded education and health care facilities and that new housing and commercial establishments would generate property taxes and other revenues that would strengthen the local economy, for the benefit of all.

This "economic development" argument for the use of eminent domain in support of private-use projects was often invoked in fast-growing regions of the West and Southwest during the late twentieth century and afterward. In these areas, many of which lacked ruined factories or deteriorating tenement housing that could readily be characterized as "blighting influences," "underutilization" of real estate was often cited as the basis for eminent domain acquisition. In Arvada, Colorado, for example, a redevelopment agency proposed to use eminent domain powers to acquire a lake, which would subsequently be drained, paved, and developed as a delivery-truck lane for a new Wal-Mart Supermarket. As a lake, the property generated $17 in annual property tax revenues. As a delivery-truck lane, the property would help generate $2.5 million in new sales taxes.[10] "With the economy the way it is, cities are looking for more sales-tax revenue because that's what they live on," said the executive director of Arvada's urban renewal authority.[11] In 2004, the Colorado Supreme court ruled against the condemnation of the lake, by which time the Colorado legislature was already approving a series of measures that limited the use of eminent domain statewide and lessened the impact of the subsequent *Kelo* decision. Commenting on the subsequent *Kelo* ruling, the city attorney for one Colorado municipality said: "The fact there's no longer a federal prohibition to condemnation for economic redevelopment doesn't change much here." Nonetheless, *Kelo* angered Coloradans who were concerned about property rights. In the view of one of the opponents of the Arvada lake-taking, the *Kelo* decision "means you no longer own your home. You're only renting it until the next developer comes along and wants to take it."[12] The increasingly frequent use of eminent domain acquisition to support private-end users and the justification of these actions in the name of a broadly defined "economic development" had been met with organized opposition to property taking in many areas prior to *Kelo*, and this opposition coalesced into a strong national movement post-*Kelo*. Decades earlier, urban renewal era eminent domain acquisition had also generated a great deal of opposition; but at that time, many of the people whose well-being was directly threatened by eminent domain actions were nonwhite and lower-income. In the late twentieth century and afterward, many more of the aggrieved property owners were white and economically better-off.

New Jersey differed from other rustbelt states such as Pennsylvania and Ohio in that it contained both large fast-growing regions (such as the northern part of the state, heavily influenced by the New York City real estate market) as well as disinvested cities like Camden where the real estate market was persistently weak. The former locations were places where the most widely publicized violations of state statutes, termed "eminent domain abuses," were discovered and prosecuted; these violations, which included failure to adequately notify affected property owners and insufficient compensation for acquired property, occurred in suburbs and small towns where the greatest profits could be made by developers seeking to benefit from private-use property taking.

Although Camden, as a higher-risk real estate market (notwithstanding the optimistic *Wall Street Journal* article), was not targeted as aggressively by private developers as sites in North Jersey, bad local government practices made the redevelopment process more contentious than it needed to be. For example, under Primas and De's administration, developer proposals were solicited and publicly aired prior to the drafting and presentation of neighborhood redevelopment plans so that, in effect, developer goals influenced the content of the plans. This approach is the reverse of what it should be: the redevelopment plan should reflect an agreement between local government and community constituencies which, after local planning board and city council approval, should serve as a frame of reference for proposals that are subsequently solicited from developers. The developers should not be invited in until after the plan is formulated and approved.

Another bad practice was redevelopment plan designation of certain addresses that "may be acquired" (in addition to the list of "to be acquired" and "not to be acquired" addresses that appeared in every redevelopment plan). The "may be acquired" designation gave local authorities the flexibility to make adjustments in site assemblage plans as redevelopment activity progressed. But this designation also placed "may be acquired" property owners in a state of indefinite uncertainty: their property might—or might not—be taken at any time during the quarter-century in which an approved redevelopment plan remained in effect.

In justifying property takings during past years, governments had used the ambiguous definitions of terms such as "blighted," "blighting influence," or "underutilized" as they appeared in state statutes to their advantage. In more recent years, the tables had been turned: opponents of private-use eminent domain were taking advantage of this ambiguity and the ambiguity of other terms associated with the redevelopment plan approval process to litigate against redevelopment plans on procedural grounds, with increasing success. The outcomes of this litigation did not necessarily resolve the ambiguities; in some instances, the litigation produced more ambiguity. For example, Superior Court Judge Michael Kassel had invalidated the Cramer Hill redevelopment plan, and later, a redevelopment plan for the Bergen Square neighborhood, because witnesses had not been sworn in prior to delivering testimony before the city's planning board. In 2007, however, Superior Court Judge Allan Vogelson upheld a redevelopment plan proposed for a site in nearby Haddon Township, allowing an after-the-fact swearing-in of a witness who had testified before the planning board four years earlier. Camden officials had previously requested an opportunity for a comparable swearing-in to be recognized in the case of Cramer Hill, but Judge Kassel had denied the request.[13]

Other challenges and other judicial rulings based on perceived procedural flaws followed. For example, Superior Court Judge Irvin Snyder nullified the proposed redevelopment plan for Camden's Waterfront South neighborhood because the city's master plan, to which the proposed redevelopment plan made reference, had not been updated. These rulings could have been appealed by Primas' administration with some prospect for success; but the

COO had neither the money nor time to do so. The unsuccessful Cramer Hill litigation alone had cost Primas' administration more than a quarter of a million dollars in legal expenses that had not been budgeted in MRERA.

The rejection of redevelopment plans on procedural grounds and the inconsistent and contradictory nature of some of the court decisions made planning and development agency staff increasingly cautious in starting or restarting the redevelopment planning process in Camden neighborhoods following these court rulings. In consultation with legal counsel, they carefully scrutinized technical issues that they had never felt compelled to deal with in the past. What evidence needs to be documented in order to prove that a proposed redevelopment area unquestionably meets statutory blight criteria? Does the neighborhood survey on which blight-designation is based have to be conducted by licensed planners? Does the redevelopment plan have to be signed and sealed by a licensed planner? What combination of legal notices published in newspapers, letters mailed to residents, flyers placed in mail slots, and posters taped in storefront windows should be instituted in order to satisfy a court that community members have been adequately notified about the redevelopment planning process?

The wave of anti-eminent domain sentiment that followed *Kelo* had fundamentally changed the redevelopment planning process in Camden, and not entirely for the better. As a participant in one of many discussions of these matters at Camden City Hall observed: "We used to be preparing plans to show community members and elected officials why redevelopment was needed and how it would be accomplished; now we're preparing legal evidence to try to convince a judge not to rule against us in response to litigation."

Property-Rights Perspectives

Differing views of the legitimacy of the use of eminent domain came to roost in Camden during and after Primas' tenure as COO. The positions of pro- and anti-private use advocates hardened during this period, without resolution of the issues of whether and how eminent domain should be employed to support the city's economic recovery. One could agree that violations of state law should be prosecuted and that bad practices that created disadvantages for redevelopment-area property owners should be ended. But two key questions remained unaddressed: Under what circumstances, if any, is the use of eminent domain to support a private use justified? And, under what circumstances, if any, is the displacement of residents and businesses justified?

The Washington-based Institute for Justice, which played a leading role in organizing legal challenges to eminent domain actions before and after *Kelo*, produced a report entitled "Public Power, Private Gain" that documents pre-*Kelo* controversies over the private-use issue. Published in 2003, the report provides state-by-state summaries of legislation, government actions, and legal and political challenges to private use condemnations between 1998 and 2002. The report cites the 1954 U.S. Supreme Court decision that approved government taking of private property for a "public purpose" (as opposed to the more restrictive "public use"), as the starting point for a subsequent trend of eminent domain abuses. The Court's action:

> allowed condemnations to accomplish slum clearance, even if the property ended up in the hands of private parties. State and local governments took this as a green light. First, they condemned slums, then blighted areas, then not very blighted areas, and now perfectly fine areas . . .[14]
>
> No one—at least no one besides lawyers and bureaucrats—would think "public use" means a casino, condominiums or a private office building. Yet these days, that's exactly how state and local governments use eminent domain—as part of corporate welfare incentive packages and deals for more politically favored businesses.[15]

The report does not address the use of eminent domain to acquire abandoned buildings and lots or to take dilapidated property from negligent owners, nor does it include descriptions of constructive "private uses" such as the development of affordable housing or neighborhood business enterprises. In older cities such as Camden and Philadelphia, "perfectly fine areas" and properties are not likely to be the focus of eminent domain actions. By way of illustration, during 2003, the year in which the report was published, Philadelphia's Redevelopment Authority approved the conveyance of fifty-one properties, acquired through eminent domain actions. Of these fifty-one properties, forty-four were vacant structures and lots that were to be developed as affordable homeowner and rental housing. The remaining seven properties were vacant lots that were to be conveyed to adjacent property owners for improvement as side yards. No displacement had taken place in connection with the acquisition of any of these properties.[16]

The shortcomings of this report's broad-brush treatment of eminent domain are particularly evident with respect to the coverage of the Neighborhood Transformation Initiative. According to the report, NTI supporters (who are not cited) "hope to create an 'urban prairie,' with vast tracts of open land within Philadelphia's city limits that can be sold to private developers who will be given clear title to the land."[17] The report expresses skepticism about the market potential for additional housing development in Philadelphia, in light of "a large supply of affordable houses close to Center City, many of which are in little demand," apparently unaware that housing demand in and around Center City had been growing rapidly for several years, stimulated in part by the City of Philadelphia's ten-year tax abatement, Between 1999 and 2002, 313 development ventures involving the residential-use conversions of former commercial and industrial properties had been completed, nearly all of them located in and around Center City.[18]

Advocacy associated with the practice of eminent domain in New Jersey did not provide constructive guidance for cities such as Camden with regard to the two fundamental questions posed above. Extreme viewpoints were in abundance. For example, the Stop Eminent Domain Abuse Coalition of New Jersey equated property taking for private use with eminent domain abuse, maintaining that, "It is considered abuse any time property is taken for anything other than a true public use."[19]

In testimony delivered at a March 2006 meeting of the New Jersey State Assembly's Commerce and Economic Development Committee, Olga Pomar, an attorney at South Jersey Legal Services (SJLS), who had represented litigants in the Cramer Hill case and other redevelopment plan challenges, equated economic development and wealth-building with resident displacement:

> . . . I think that there is a fundamental problem in the law that eminent domain and redevelopment is allowed for the purpose of increasing utilization of land, bringing in tax rateables—all those things that by definition allow clearing out poor people and bringing in rich people. And we need a clear statement in the law that it is not an acceptable purpose nor an acceptable outcome, to have a low-income population replaced by a richer population. That is a very fundamental problem.[20]

Pomar also stated that, "in Camden . . . the entire city of 80,000 people is being put in a redevelopment zone," implying that Primas and De's redevelopment planning approach threatened resident property owners citywide.[21] Based on statements of this kind and related actions by South Jersey Legal Services, Primas, De, and their successors assumed that SJLS would litigate against any redevelopment plan that included occupied properties on the "to be acquired" list—and might take action against any other redevelopment plan as well.

New Jersey's state government was not overly helpful in providing guidance that would have been useful to cities such as Camden in resolving key questions about eminent domain practice. In May 2006, the state's Public Advocate released a report entitled "Reforming the Use of Eminent Domain for Private Redevelopment in New Jersey," which stated that: "in New Jersey the current laws governing the use of eminent domain for private redevelopment do not adequately protect the rights of tenants and property owners." One of several findings was that existing state laws "allow for the use of eminent domain in areas that do not meet the constitutional requirement of a blighted area."[22] Although Camden was identified as one of the locations where the Public Advocate's staff had conducted site visits and interviewed government officials, the report does not make a distinction between the exercise of this power in disinvested cities, as opposed to the use of this power in areas of the state where real estate markets are stronger and the prospects for development without the need for eminent domain are greater. The report also proposes that local governments be required to justify eminent domain actions by completing a number of tasks that would be time-consuming and, if legislatively mandated as local-government responsibilities, would facilitate further litigation against redevelopment plans on procedural grounds. For example, the report recommends that redevelopment plans include "an explanation as to why there is no other reasonable alternative to acquiring or condemning each property that is proposed to be acquired,"[23] leaving open the question of what constitutes a "reasonable alternative."

The Public Advocate issued a follow-up report a year later, commenting on a legislative bill that:

> reforms the definition of blight . . . but retains more objective and specific criteria, such as vacancy, environmental contamination, dilapidation, and overcrowding.
>
> Moreover the bill would permit a blight declaration only upon a finding that such conditions were directly detrimental to the safety, health, or welfare of the community.[24]

The report includes a series of case studies that document violations of state law and abusive practices in a number of locations. The circumstances of cities such as Camden, which need to conduct property acquisition in order to stimulate development on a large scale, are not addressed. The 2006 report makes it clear that the Public Advocate is not opposed to all instances of eminent domain in support of private use; however, the remedies proposed for demonstrating that eminent domain is being used only as a last resort, after all other alternatives have been exhausted, would impose new burdens on local governments such as Camden and, if legislatively approved, would make such cities more vulnerable to litigation.

In 2007, with awareness of this problem, Judge Davis, Primas' successor as COO, told me that he intended to write to the state Attorney General asking for guidance regarding the circumstances under which the state would support the use of eminent domain and the displacement of residents and businesses in Camden, with the intent of ensuring that the COO and state government would act in concert with regard to this issue in the future. I did not learn whether Judge Davis had pursued this intention and, if so, whether he had received a response; but if he had, there was no indication that the response provided the guidance he had been seeking.

Primas had expressed a similar concern in the November 2006 COO progress report, stating that:

> In light of widespread opposition to eminent domain that has emerged in many forms since the 2005 *Kelo v. New London* decision, it is not unrealistic to anticipate that objections may be raised to any use of eminent domain powers in Camden and that some of these objections may be conveyed in the form of legal action aimed at blocking redevelopment plans that have undergone community review and have been

approved by the City's Planning Board and City Council. In view of these circumstances, it is essential that the State determine the extent, if any, to which the use of eminent domain in Camden is to be restricted or limited in the future.[25]

This concern remained unaddressed.

Is there a right way to displace people? In cities such as Philadelphia and Camden, there is no question that some displacement is necessary in order to assemble sites for development that will generate broad public benefits. Some developers, including anchor institutions such as those that play a vital role in Camden's economy, cannot build around clusters of scattered occupied properties to construct modern new facilities. Although opportunities to use available vacant property for new development without displacing anyone should be pursued first, some older cities will need to displace some people in order to support reinvestment that will improve the prospects for future economic success. Where possible, it is essential that a city's definition of economic success include, to use Olga Pomar's words, bringing in rich people. But does wealth-building always have to be achieved at the expense of poor people, as Pomar implies?

In assembling the Pradera site in Eastern North Philadelphia, the individuals and families that APM displaced were happy with APM's relocation plan for several reasons: they had been living in housing that was substandard; they were being offered high-quality replacement housing in the same neighborhood; the replacement housing was finished, or would be finished by the time they had to move; and APM was a trusted organization with a history in the community, a known quantity. This combination of reasons to be happy about relocation was almost entirely absent from the relocation approach proposed for Cramer Hill.

Another successful approach to relocation and replacement housing in Philadelphia was implemented by Capital Access, Inc., a private firm working as a fee-for-service project manager for the Jefferson Square Community Development Corporation to build ninety-three new and rehabilitated single-family houses on a group of contiguous blocks in South Philadelphia. After initial acquisition activity had begun, Capital Access encountered a wave of opposition from community residents who did not want to leave the largely abandoned development-site blocks where they lived. Many of them appeared at a City Council hearing that had been scheduled to consider a bill approving the first phase of eminent domain acquisition. "I call it ethnic cleansing," said one property owner. Displacing residents would be "madness," said Councilman-at-Large David Cohen, who had recently toured the area.[26] Before a vote could be taken, District Councilperson Frank DiCicco had the bill tabled in order to buy time to enable the CDC to refocus on gaining community support.

During the course of a subsequent month-long dialogue with residents and housing advocates, Jefferson Square CDC, with the assistance of Capital

Access President Jeremey Newberg, organized a new approach. No residents would be displaced during the first phase of development, which would consist of new housing construction on vacant land, as well as the rehabilitation of some vacant row houses that stood on relatively intact nearby blocks. Residents whose homes were proposed to be taken would be offered first opportunity to buy these developed houses. They would purchase these new homes from Jefferson Square CDC, using as buyer equity the funds they received from the Redevelopment Authority: fair market value compensation for the property they were giving up (each appraised at about $50,000), plus a relocation housing payment ($22,500 in most cases). The difference between the buyer-equity amount paid to Jefferson Square CDC and the cost that Jefferson Square CDC incurred to develop the replacement home would be funded with subsidies.

The approach proved successful. Out of thirty-eight households whose homes were proposed to be taken, twenty-one accepted the CDC's offer, eleven chose to use their relocation payments to finance a move elsewhere, and six moved into subsidized senior apartments that had been developed in a building at the former Mount Sinai hospital complex across the street. Commenting on this outcome, Newberg said, "If everyone were to accept the replacement-house option, this approach would be very expensive; but many people won't choose that option. A lot of them just want to move on." Newberg also made an observation that is consistent with APM's experience: "A big lesson is that when you develop affordable rental housing within walking distance of the development site, you can both make relocation easier as well as reinforce the perception that you're being sensitive to people's needs."[27]

At a subsequent City Council hearing, Dorothy King, a resident leader, stood beside Newberg and asked Council to authorize the taking of her home through eminent domain. This is a fair deal, she said. I don't like moving, but I'm getting a better house, and I'm staying in the neighborhood. Councilman Cohen was enthusiastic. You did this the right way, he told Newberg.

In 2003, the year in which the Cherokee proposal for Cramer Hill was announced, East Baltimore Development, Inc. (EBDI), a nonprofit public/private partnership, was formed to oversee the development of the thirty-one-acre Science + Technology Park at Johns Hopkins, a venture that also includes residential, commercial, and retail construction. EBDI, governed by a board that includes the president of Johns Hopkins, the president of the Baltimore-based Annie E. Casey Foundation, the Lieutenant Governor of the State of Maryland, and other public- and private-sector executives, as well as representatives of community constituencies, is committed to the principle of "Responsible Development." This approach "combines economic, community, and human development strategies in ways that seek to ensure maximum benefit from the revitalization efforts for area residents, businesses, and the surrounding communities."[28]

To implement the Science + Technology Park development plan based on this approach, EBDI's forty-person staff includes Family Advocates who work with each household scheduled for relocation to provide supportive services designed to enable them to improve their economic standing and achieve a better quality of life in a new home within or outside the project area. EBDI manages a Workforce Development Pipeline to provide job training and referrals and to help residents overcome barriers to employment. EBDI also assists residents in gaining access to training programs designed to lead to apprenticeships in the construction trades. For high-school graduates and GED recipients, training that can lead to bioscience-related jobs is available at the Biotech Institute of Maryland.

During Phase I of the project, which started in 2003, homeowners affected by the development plan received an average of $150,000 in relocation benefit packages, and renters received an average of $50,000. According to an independent survey conducted by Abt Associates, approximately 90 percent of the 396 households relocated in Phase I stated that they were very satisfied with the process; approximately 80 percent felt that they were better off after their move.[29]

The level of funding required to support an EBDI replication was not available in Camden. However, the underlying goal of the EBDI approach—to enable relocated families to substantially improve their living situations by providing the right combination of housing options and supportive services—is the goal that should be integral to all relocation plans. The other characteristic of EBDI—executive-level leadership—helps increase the likelihood that this goal will be achieved.

The Way to Intervene

Despite its shortcomings, the $175 million economic development component of MRERA was not fundamentally flawed. This funding could be spent—and, for the most part, was spent—on investment at strategically important sites that had the best potential to generate significant added value for the city.

The flawed element of MRERA was the municipal reform plan. The Act called for the completion of a "municipal management plan,"

> which analyzes the current state of all services provided by each municipal department and the service levels provided in similarly situated municipalities and shall call upon experts or State government officials, as necessary, in order to identify the options available to achieve appropriate levels of service.[30]

However, there was little evidence that the McGreevey Administration was serious about, or knew how to be serious about, the challenge of overhauling Camden's municipal government.

In this instance, being serious would have meant identifying and following through on several actions as priorities:

- Completing a study of the causes of the city's structural deficit and designing a proposal for reducing the deficit during each year of the COO's five-year term.
- Establishing performance measures, annual performance goals, and an annual performance report to support public monitoring of the city's progress in meeting deficit-reduction goals and improving municipal services.
- Identifying a key individual in Trenton who would be personally responsible for managing state actions in support of the Camden reform plan and whose staff would work in coordination with city agency staff on a week-to-week basis to keep the reform plan on track. Although MRERA identified the Department of Community Affairs as the state agency that would have important responsibilities associated with the reform plan, I never saw evidence of an effective management-level working relationship between DCA staff and city departmental staff.

If these actions had been the basis for city–state collaboration, then it would have been easier for Primas and De subsequently to have done the following (which they did attempt to some degree, but with limited success):

- Ask city-based academic and health care institutions to participate in redevelopment planning (including planning for replacement housing and associated supportive services) for the neighborhoods in which they were located, to collaborate with CRA staff on workforce housing and off-campus student housing development plans, and to work with the COO and the county's Workforce Investment Board in designing job training and work-readiness programs that would enable more Camden residents to qualify for entry-level job openings at their facilities.
- Invite the Casey Foundation, the Ford Foundation (which, like Casey, had made several major commitments of funding to activities in Camden during Primas' tenure as COO), and other charitable foundations in the region that had expressed interest in Camden's future to monitor the progress of the reform plan, to provide matching grants for funding supportive service programs (particularly those which would enhance education opportunities for children), and to design a civic leadership development program, similar to those operating in Philadelphia and Newark. Because the city and state were not working closely on municipal reform and because the performance of municipal reform was not being benchmarked annually, foundation administrators with whom I spoke during the first five years of the reform plan were not convinced that the city was heading in the right direction and remained concerned that a commitment of their funds for new activities in Camden might not produce worthwhile outcomes.

As important, the lack of an effective working relationship between city and state made it particularly difficult for the city to determine how to address the issue of eminent domain. No one had anticipated *Kelo* and the impact that the Supreme Court decision would have, coming as it did partway through Primas' COO term. However, had the McGreevey Administration taken joint responsibility, with the COO, for the success of the municipal reform plan and directed state departments to act accordingly, the city and state could have worked together to formalize changes in Camden redevelopment policy based on the impact of *Kelo* and to respond in a more coordinated fashion to the legal challenges that greeted the approval of several Camden redevelopment plans. Lacking this relationship, Primas and, subsequently, Judge Davis, were left to deal with this critical issue alone.

9 An Integrated Strategy
Real Estate Development and Human Capital Planning in Camden

Because a high level of social need could be found throughout Camden, nearly every government-financed plan for real estate development had to be examined not only in terms of how the plan might change the physical environment but also in terms of how the plan might affect the lives of current and future community members. During my thirteen-month assignment in Camden, I had many opportunities to observe this interplay between the evaluation of real estate development ventures and the consideration of related social issues (such as education, public safety, and workforce development), and, with others, to try to advance the former while addressing the latter. During this time, I participated in the organization of a reinvestment strategy for Lanning Square, a downtown-area neighborhood just south of Camden's central business district, that was designed to address both development goals and social needs simultaneously and comprehensively. This strategy is worth examination, both as a reinvestment model that combines place-based development with people-oriented resource building and as an illustration of the obstacles that threaten the prospects for moving such a model to successful implementation.

Thirteenth-Floor View

My first full-time work day in Camden City Hall began very early one morning during the week after New Year's. I drove across the Ben Franklin Bridge, took the downtown exit a hundred yards away from the toll plaza, parked at the MRERA-financed Camden County College garage, and walked two blocks to City Hall, an early twentieth-century building, topped by a clock tower, that housed many city and county offices. The streets were quiet. I had arrived before the beginning of the school-day rush hour and before the start of the government employee work day. A blast of wind from the Delaware River, a few hundred yards away, swept frozen air across the steps that led up to the west entrance of City Hall from a paved parking area.

Just inside the glass entrance door was an airport-style security checkpoint. Metal objects were placed on a conveyor belt for screening, and visitors walked through an electronic threshold with a metal detector. If it beeped, a security guard would approach you and conduct a quick once-over with an electronic wand to ensure that the detected object was a belt buckle or a necklace rather than a weapon. Concern about security was not inappropriate in a place like Camden, where the actions of government officials had drawn anger on many occasions. A City Council member had been shot and killed a few years earlier in New York City; it was not difficult to imagine the possibility of a similar act of violence occurring here, in this building.

Three of the six elevators in the lobby were out of order, and one of the elevators that remained in operation went no higher than the fourth floor. I took one of the two available elevators to the thirteenth-floor offices of the Camden Redevelopment Agency and discovered that I had arrived too early; the entrance door was locked. In the elevator lobby, a big window provided a panoramic eastward view. Looking out to the far left, you could see the Delaware River, bending around the city to the northeast. There was Cramer Hill; there was the Campbell Soup Company headquarters, where more than a thousand administrative and research and development employees worked within a cluster of buildings on a small campus. There was Route 30, the highway that extended eastward, from the toll plaza out to the suburbs, dividing the city on an east–west axis. There was I-676, the highway that branched away from Route 30 and headed southward, dividing the city on a north–south axis. There on the horizon were the smudgy shapes of the modern mid-rise buildings in the office campuses of suburban Cherry Hill.

I supervised about eighty employees of two agencies: the Camden Redevelopment Agency and the City Department of Development and Planning. All of the staff of the CRA, a state-chartered redevelopment authority, had been recruited during Arijit De's tenure; none of them had been employed at the agency for more than four and a half years. None of the CRA staff positions had been integrated into the civil service system (an issue that had been a bone of contention between De and the state's Personnel Department). Many of the CRA staff did not live in Camden. In contrast, many staff of the Department of Development and Planning, a municipal government agency, had worked in City Hall for a much longer time. Most of the Development and Planning job titles were civil service titles, and many of the employees were members of the municipal workers' union. Although Primas and De had consolidated the leadership of CRA and Development and Planning into one directorship—held first by De, then by me—the staffing of the agencies was spatially dispersed. CRA staff occupied the thirteenth floor and part of the fourth floor of City Hall. Development and Planning staff occupied part of the fourth floor, an office on the second floor, and—in the case of the Capital Improvements Division staff responsible for public-works projects—an office in the old armory building, nearly a mile away. As part of a City Hall renovation and space reallocation plan begun during Judge Davis' tenure as COO, I asked that all of the staff be consolidated on the third floor of the building. The renovation project was a long-term endeavor, with courtroom expansion and improvement plans being given highest priority. As a result, the consolidation of planning and development agency staff that I had requested did not begin during my thirteen months in Camden, and, during those months, much time was spent waiting for an elevator to arrive or trudging up and down fire stairs.

Although I did not become well acquainted with every one of the staff members whom I supervised, I got to know many of them through frequent week-to-week interactions. Most of the staff members whom I got to know were not bureaucrats or political deadwood; most of them were responsible and committed to their work. They were mindful of the political dynamic that ran through the affairs of municipal government like an electrical current, and they interacted with elected officials as needed; but most of their activities were completed under the political radar and independent of political influence. Many of the staff had chosen to take on tasks that were not set forth in their job descriptions, without additional compensation, because they felt responsible for doing so—responsible to the city and its residents. Some of the staff worked evenings, weekends, or holidays without additional pay because they wanted to get past a particularly time-consuming assignment and move a project or program closer to implementation. I had already gained a sense of the character of some of these staff during my previous experience in Camden as a consultant, when I had contacted a dozen or more of them at different times seeking information or requesting a meeting to discuss a particular issue in depth. They were responsive and helpful, even though no one had ordered them to cooperate with me; at the time, I was nobody special. They cared about Camden and about the integrity of their work in the city.

The positive qualities that some staff possessed were of great value, but these qualities were not enough to produce a harmonious work environment in which everyone was collaborative, cooperative, and respectful of one another. Development and Planning staff resented CRA staff, feeling that the latter had been given preferential treatment by Primas and De and had, to some extent, been hired to circumvent city process (views for which there was more than a little substantiating evidence). Staff who worked on the fourth floor felt that they had second-class status compared with staff on the thirteenth floor, where the COO and the senior CRA administrators had their desks. The term "thirteenth floor" was used as a synonym for "the people in charge," as in: "We're waiting for the thirteenth floor to make a decision" or: "The thirteenth floor vetoed our suggestion." There were intra-departmental problems as well. One senior administrator had the radio turned up during confidential meetings so that staff in the next room, separated by a hollow-core door, would have difficulty hearing what was going on. In an introductory meeting with me, a city department head prefaced his criticisms of a past policy by saying: "I don't care who hears about this," as though he expected that I would try to make trouble for him by reporting his statements to higher authorities. The tensions that were running high outside City Hall, in neighborhoods such as Cramer Hill, contributed to under-the-surface and outright acrimony among staff and made internal disagreements more difficult to resolve.

I tried to address these problems by using my position to bring staff together more frequently and to institute a more inclusive process for decision-making about redevelopment plans, real estate acquisition, and the financing of development ventures. I scheduled regular joint meetings with the key management staff of both agencies (they had not previously met together on a regular basis), with smaller groups of staff who performed specialized tasks (such as the staff responsible for promoting community participation in redevelopment planning), and with our counterparts in the State of New Jersey housing and economic development agencies whose signoff was needed for all activities proposed for MRERA funding.

These and other efforts on my part to strengthen working relationships within City Hall brought some improvement, but they were not enough. My authority was respected by nearly everyone, but my presence in Camden was not necessarily welcomed by all. The view of those who were less than enthusiastic about me was understandable. I had been recruited by the state, and the state government had made a commitment to engage me without requiring me to be interviewed by the Mayor, the City's Business Administrator, or the CRA board of directors (I had been interviewed by Judge Davis prior to my January start date, but, by that time, it was clear that the Corzine Administration wanted him to support my appointment). Everyone knew that I had agreed to send state officials a memorandum after the completion of my anticipated three- to four-month tenure that would contain an assessment of the two agencies I supervised, along with any recommendations for changes that I felt were appropriate. Viewed from the perspective of the staff who reported to me, I was an agent of the state, who, in a short time, would be delivering judgments that could make their jobs harder to do. These staff members' views were influenced by the experience of the first four MRERA-implementation years, during which disagreements between Primas, De, and the state's Department of Community Affairs increased and intensified. A prevalent City Hall view was that the state was too heavy-handed and controlling; my presence could make it worse. In addition, I reported to Judge Davis, a state appointee with no prior municipal government experience, whose views about CRA and Development and Planning were yet to be learned.

Judge Davis had grown up in foster care. He told me that, as a child, he had gathered driftwood along the Delaware River shore and carried it home for use as firewood. "We were poor as churchmice," he said. He worked as summer help in vacation lodging places at the Jersey shore. He obtained his law degree from Temple Law School and overcame 1960s-era racial barriers to earn the right to practice law in New Jersey. In 1969, he was offered an appointment as Municipal Court judge. "They needed a black," he once said to me, "with the riots and all," without a trace of irony or rancor in his voice (Philadelphia's most serious riot of this period took place in 1964, Camden's in 1971). He was appointed to Superior Court in 1981, where he served for nearly a quarter-century. At the time when the Corzine Administration contacted him regarding the COO appointment, he was working as counsel at the Cherry Hill offices of the Cozen and O'Connor law firm.

Judge Davis described the advice given to him years ago by a mentor, whose voice he imitated in a Churchillian timbre: "Ted, you must be *resolute*." And he was resolute. Meetings began and ended on time. Proposed CRA board actions were scrutinized in detail a week before each board meeting and revised as needed. Not long after his appointment, he issued several directives: no hirings, no promotions, no overtime for any city employee without his written approval. The City budget will be presented to City Council on time (for some years, the budget presentation had taken place months after the start of the fiscal year). All City employees will punch in and out of work on newly-installed time clocks. Every city employee will complete ethics training. The no-overtime order sparked a strong reaction. The Fire Commissioner announced the closing of a fire station; City Council scheduled a special hearing; the Council chamber filled up with city workers. Judge Davis appeared at the session, described the executive order in detail, answered questions, and left. The order remained in place. Then he contacted the Fire Commissioner; the fire station closing was rescinded.

During my first few months at City Hall, Judge Davis and I met almost every day, sometimes to confer together, at other times to meet with people from outside, almost always to discuss one of three subjects: organization, land, or money. The courtroom management style that the Judge brought to City Hall meetings was in many respects a welcome change from that of the less well-organized prior administration. A meeting was convened, and participants were introduced; Judge Davis succinctly described the purpose of the meeting; issues were presented, and the presenters were questioned; decisions were made, and assignments were given; the meeting adjourned.

Outside City Hall, Judge Davis brought a sense of decorum to city government interaction with community residents. He scheduled a town-hall meeting at each of three community centers during the warm weather months. He brought with him all of the city department heads (who were seated in short rows of folding chairs at the front of the room, stage left of the podium at which he stood) and all of the City Council members, as well as the Mayor (seated in a single row, stage right). The sight of all of the responsible elected and appointed officials in city government participating in a public meeting together, and seated on either side of Judge Davis at a meeting over which he presided, conveyed a memorable message about the Judge's authority and the seriousness of his intent to use it.

At the same time, Judge Davis could not be regarded simply as a conservative, old-school stereotype. He could backslap and wisecrack with politicians at a reception or banquet. He could break up the monotony of a CRA board meeting with an unexpected joke. He was a careful observer and listener. He could speak informally with community members and put them at ease.

But anyone who had the experience of working closely with Judge Davis recognized that he possessed an underlying seriousness of purpose that remained present just below the surface, no matter how informal or relaxed the circumstances.

With a few notable exceptions, Judge Davis was consistently supportive of my plans and of the way that I pursued them. Our working relationship was cordial, but it was not a friendship—it was a business relationship with a sole focus: improving Camden through strategies that he authorized and we both worked to implement.

Judge Davis was not uncomfortable with the bricks-and-mortar emphasis of the MRERA legislation (which provided no substantial funding for activities other than real estate development), but his personal priorities were community-building and the improvement of the civic environment. "I'm a human capital guy," he said that he had told Governor Corzine at their first meeting. "I want to achieve some benefit for the people of Camden." Consistent with this orientation, he devoted time to the issues of public safety and public education. He expressed concern about the future prospects for school-age children growing up in Camden. Once, in a van transporting city and state officials on a drive-by tour of neighborhood development sites, he gestured at a crowd of children pouring out of a middle-school building into the afternoon sunlight. "Their moms are all working or on drugs," he said to the state official seated next to him, a person who, like him, had grown up in Camden. "And you can guess where the men are" (in prison).

Judge Davis also expressed dismay about the low level of civic engagement that prevailed in Camden. Because the quality of schools and public services in the city was so poor, he observed, the pool of well-educated, community-minded residents who could be recruited to serve in important appointed positions—to positions on the Planning Board, for example, which played a make-or-break role with respect to the review of redevelopment plans and developer proposals—was meager. As a result, it was more likely that those people who ended up being recruited to serve on public bodies such as the Planning Board would make bad decisions due to ignorance or poor judgment. The number of people who would take the initiative to participate in civic activities such as attending a neighborhood meeting or testifying before City Council was equally meager.

Judge Davis commented on an occurrence that supported his view of the paucity of civic engagement. At meetings of City Council, the CRA Board, the Planning Board, and other Camden governing bodies, the same three individuals would often appear to testify during the time set aside on the agenda for public comment. They were frequently the only ones who showed up for this purpose. All three were men of middle age or older, and each presented comments or raised questions that related to his own area of concern. One of them consistently commented on or brought forward questions about specific development ventures and about the wisdom and legality—or absence thereof—of government actions undertaken in support of certain of these policies (this person had been a plaintiff in a number of legal actions brought in opposition to City-supported development proposals). Another often called attention to government actions that, in his view, evidenced discrimination against nonwhites or lower-income people. The third frequently brought forward criticisms of actions that he viewed as instances of municipal government waste and mismanagement, and he raised questions about the eligibility of certain government-sponsored activities for the public funding they received—or about the appropriateness of funding these activities in the first place. These three men were well-informed and civic-minded; but, to me, they were also strangely reminiscent of Job's three friends, who witness his torment, then chastise him. Judge Davis was not critical of these three men's consistent attendance at public meetings; he praised them on several occasions. His concern was that they were so frequently the only ones who participated.

During the first months of 2007, a number of decisions were made that set our administration apart from that of Primas and De. The CRA would no longer strive to be a real estate developer; the agency would focus on development financing and real estate transactions in support of other developers. Developers would no longer be invited to present proposals prior to the approval of redevelopment plans. The redevelopment planning for Cramer Hill that had been restarted after Primas and De had abandoned the Cherokee proposal would focus on housing preservation; no residential relocation was proposed. And priority attention in redevelopment planning would be devoted to the Lanning Square neighborhood.

New Communication

Lanning Square is a mostly residential neighborhood located just south of the downtown business district, bordered on the west by the Delaware River waterfront and on the east by Broadway, Camden's major north-south artery. Lanning Square is separated from the downtown business district by Martin Luther King Boulevard, a multi-lane street that carries a high volume of traffic to and from Cooper Hospital and nearby highway entrance and exit ramps. As a residential community that is close to the aquarium, City Hall, Cooper Hospital, and a centrally-located light-rail stop, Lanning Square is well positioned for development.

The importance of Cooper Hospital as an anchor for development in Lanning Square would be hard to overestimate. Before the turn of the century, the hospital had been nearing bankruptcy. Now Cooper was well on the way to implementing plans for the development of a $500 million Health Sciences Campus. The centerpiece of the hospital's expansion was the $220 million Pavilion, under construction in 2007 and completed in December 2008. The Pavilion was a ten-story complex with state of the art facilities and "Four Seasons-like amenities and service"[1] designed to attract patients from surrounding suburban areas. A parking garage on the east side of Broadway just south of Martin Luther King Boulevard was already completed, with ground-floor space available for lease. By the end of 2008, 90 percent of the street-level square footage had been leased, to a Veterans Administration clinic and to a physical and occupational therapy center operated by NovaCare Services. Streetscape improvements—the reconstruction of paving, the installation of lighting, and the planting of trees—were under way on the Boulevard and on nearby blocks. Homebuying opportunities in the adjacent neighborhood were being promoted to hospital employees. Hospital administrators were working in coordination with City and CRA staff to ensure that institutional expansion and planned neighborhood improvements complemented each other.

In planning for expansion, Cooper's leadership was mindful of Penn's experience in West Philadelphia, including the attention that the University had devoted to consultation with community members. "I'd be very proud to be in the same sentence as the University of Pennsylvania," George Norcross told a reporter. "They have done an unbelievable job of re-developing a community."[2] Senior administrators held a series of meetings with neighborhood residents. The hospital hired a consultant to manage a civic engagement process designed to present the plans and give community members the opportunity to learn about and influence them before they were finalized. At a well-attended meeting, residents reviewed and commented on building design options, expressed their views about current neighborhood conditions, and about their priorities for development, about what should be changed and what should remain. The community members wanted to see more green space in the area, which had been originally built up as a densely-settled row house community. In response, Cooper made a commitment to finance the makeover of a centrally located small park that was in an extreme state of disrepair and to maintain the completed park for twenty years, after which this responsibility would be turned over to the City (and by which time, it was anticipated, the surrounding blocks would be populated by new residents who would look after the park). The Cooper expansion plan advanced without significant community opposition.

The City's Department of Development and Planning had already drafted and gained approval of a redevelopment plan for Cooper Plaza. Authorized by City Council in 2005, the plan called for the rehabilitation of vacant housing and infill new construction on vacant lots, with no displacement of neighborhood residents. On a single block of Broadway frontage located between the parking garage and the Boulevard, the plan called for the relocation of ten small stores. This block had originally been proposed for the development of a new school. By 2007, however, it was expected that the block would instead be developed for a higher-density mix of retail and residential uses that would draw on the block's proximity to the hospital complex a hundred yards away. In its redeveloped state, the block would include higher-quality stores at street level, with apartments for medical students and interns above. The redevelopment plan, like the hospital expansion plan, did not generate major controversy; no attempt was made to derail the plan through litigation.

Cooper Plaza has many residential blocks that are mostly occupied but broken up by vacant buildings and lots. In contrast, some Lanning Square blocks are almost entirely cleared of buildings. Much of the vacant land that remains is publicly owned and zoned for residential use. The neighborhood also includes some well-maintained row house blocks, a small park, day care facilities, churches, and the Walt Whitman House, a National Historic Landmark, where Whitman spent the final years of his life.

Because Lanning Square was a neighborhood in which miscommunication and confusion about the City's plans had been recurrent problems, the first step in planning for residential development was the organization of a communications strategy.* During Primas and De's tenure, two redevelopment-plan concepts had been drafted, aired in public meetings, then withdrawn without explanation, as goals, priorities, and alliances inexplicably shifted in City Hall.[3] Based on these experiences and in light of the awareness of the City's initial urban renewal-style approach to Cramer Hill redevelopment, concern over the prospect of major property-taking and displacement in Lanning Square was widespread.

In case studies that describe neighborhood-change success stories—those instances in which strategies are successfully adopted to sustain economic, racial, and ethnic diversity and counter the threat of displacement in communities experiencing a rapid rise in property values—a recurring theme is the central importance of communication and information sharing. Attention to communication and information sharing had been a key element of Cooper Hospital's planning in Cooper Plaza, but had not been a highlight of Primas and De's administration of the city's redevelopment programs. Arijit De didn't even show up at City Council meetings, ignoring the established protocol that called for municipal department heads to be seated at tables facing the Council members so that they could be asked to deliver reports or answer questions. Primas and De did not have an ongoing working relationship with Camden's association of community development corporations, and CRA staff was reluctant to participate in dialogue with community members outside the confines of City Hall. During the time when the Cherokee proposal was under review, I attended a big town-hall meeting that a civic coalition had organized to promote dialogue about, among other matters, the issue of relocation and replacement housing. Senior CRA staff members were in attendance, but they were gathered at the back of the room, conversing among themselves and with others while the meeting was going on.

---

* For the sake of brevity, I have used the term "the City" rather than "the City and the CRA" in statements about development-related activity in which both agencies under my supervision were involved.

My influence in Camden was limited, but it was clear that communication and information sharing was one area in which I could make a difference with respect to redevelopment planning in Lanning Square. As plans for this area took shape during 2007, I attended numerous community meetings held in churches and recreation centers. I asked for and received an opportunity to speak at the church with the predominately African-American congregation and at the church with the predominately Latino congregation; at the latter, John Fuentes of CRA delivered rapid-fire translations of my statements. Fuentes also took me to the two local radio stations that reached Camden's Latino population for interviews with talk-show hosts.

Most of the focus of this communication was the future of Lanning Square's residential community, with the possibility of displacement the concern most often raised by residents. During each of the meetings that were held in the early months of the year, at least one person would approach me and ask, "Is my house going to be taken?" In my presentations at these meetings, I tried to address the issue of displacement in the context of a redevelopment planning process:

- The City and CRA will not require that a redevelopment plan be adopted for Lanning Square. Our position is that a redevelopment plan will be beneficial to the Lanning Square community, and we want a plan that makes sense for everyone. If these meetings produce conflicts that cannot be resolved or that divide the community, the plan will not be pursued (City Council, mindful of the Cherokee experience, would not vote to adopt a divisive plan in any case).
- Although the City and CRA will not force the adoption of a redevelopment plan, we support redevelopment planning, and we believe that Lanning Square will be better off with a redevelopment plan than without one. A redevelopment plan will document our agreement on the goals for this area and on strategies to improve this community. Without a redevelopment plan, our ability to acquire property, particularly vacant and abandoned buildings and lots, will be very limited. These properties will remain vacant or will be acquired by others, in some cases, by investor-owners who will be able to develop them as they see fit (within the limitations of the building and zoning codes), with or without the support of the community.
- At this time, the City and CRA have no plans to acquire occupied properties and displace people. The City will not rule out the use of eminent domain powers to acquire occupied properties as part of a redevelopment plan, but we will only do so as a last resort, if we believe that there is no worthwhile alternative. Prior to proposing any use of eminent domain to acquire occupied properties, we will present the case for this action to you, describe the reasons why we recommend it, and describe the options to be offered to residents and businesses that are proposed to

be displaced. If this issue generates a conflict between the community and the City that cannot be resolved, the proposed redevelopment plan will not be presented to the Planning Board and City Council.

These presentations did not produce a dramatic change in the relationship between community members and the City. At best, the message they conveyed was that I was not Arijit De. I would show up at meetings, return phone calls, and meet with civic leaders unaccompanied by an entourage of CRA staff. Like Arijit De, I was not a resident of Camden. Like him, I could leave precipitously, and the person who showed up to take my place might have an entirely different presentation from mine, as mine had differed from De's. The instability and uncertainty that pervaded Camden made it impossible to do more than create this mixed first impression.

People who were preparing to oppose the redevelopment plan—any redevelopment plan that involved any residential displacement—were taking advantage of this instability and uncertainty. "Plaintiff recruitment" was already under way: legal-services staff were encouraging residents to prepare to sign on to future litigation against the redevelopment plan—even though no plan had yet been proposed. At the CRA-sponsored meetings held during this time, some of the individuals who spoke out most strongly against redevelopment planning were not community residents. Some of them were paid organizers who were circulating anti-redevelopment leaflets and flyers. One advocacy group distributed a flyer that included the organization's address at the bottom of the page: a post office box in suburban Cherry Hill. Another flyer with a save-our-community theme was circulated just before the spring primary election in which candidates were running for City Council seats. The flyer featured a blurry photograph of George Norcross at the top of the page, with spider-web-like lines radiating from him to images of Democratic Party-supported incumbent Council members and cartoon drawings of Primas and De in the center of the page, below Norcross (at the time, Primas and De had been gone for weeks; but I was too new and little-known to be a useful addition to such a flyer). Meeting disruption tactics were tested. The activists who attempted to break up the meetings created problems, but they were far less effective than their counterparts in Philadelphia, whose meeting disruption tactics I had painfully experienced during my initial tour of duty as a middle-management employee in the public sector.

In this uncertain environment, a renewed effort to complete a Lanning Square redevelopment plan was launched.

Three Challenges

To make effective use of Lanning Square's locational advantages, a redevelopment plan had to address three key issues: strengthening the community's predominately residential base; creating a an effective linkage between institutional and non–institutional development; and building out a transition zone (consisting of properties on blocks just outside the redevelopment area boundaries) between the community's northern edge and the southern margin of the downtown area.

The Residential Base

As a consultant under contract with CRA in 2005, I had worked with CRA staff to produce a relocation and replacement housing plan for Lanning Square and the adjacent Cooper Plaza neighborhood that was designed to demonstrate how a sufficient number of affordable housing units would be developed within these communities to accommodate households that, at the time, were expected to be displaced from future development sites. The plan anticipated that the first major displacement would involve the relocation of twenty-six households from the southern tier of the redevelopment area, where several blocks were proposed to be cleared to create a site for the construction of seventy-five subsidized rental housing units. Prior to any displacement, up to fifty-nine housing units were to be developed by two nonprofit organizations (St. Joseph's Carpenter Society and Habitat for Humanity), and enough of these homes would be completed in time to be offered as replacement housing for the twenty-six displaced families. A second seventy-five-unit rental development venture (requiring no further displacement) would follow.

The housing plan had been published in concept-paper form in November 2005. When I arrived at City Hall fourteen months later, replacement housing development activity had not proceeded as rapidly as planned, although some SJCS housing development was beginning in Cooper Plaza. Because a Lanning Square redevelopment plan had not been drafted, presented to Planning Board and City Council, and approved, no eminent domain acquisition or residential relocation had taken place, or could take place. This inactivity and the lack of decision-making gave me an opportunity to take a fresh look at Lanning Square.

The two seventy-five-unit rental development ventures were located in a section of Lanning Square where crime and drug sales had been long-standing problems. The other major early-stage development activity that had been contemplated was the construction of twenty-eight market-rate sales townhouses on cleared land in Lanning Square's northern tier, on the same block where the Walt Whitman House was located (known as the "Walt Whitman block"). Building subsidized rental housing in an area known for crime and drug problems did not seem to be the best way to introduce major development activity to Lanning Square—and this activity would displace twenty-six households. In addition, new townhouses on the Walt Whitman block would not be likely to sell unless the mostly-vacant parcels near that block were developed as well. However, the 2005 concept plan did not project construction activity to begin on these blocks until two years after the Whitman-block homes were completed.

I drove through the neighborhood many times. I got out of the car and walked down every street. After a time, I began to look carefully at the northwest quadrant of Lanning Square, the double row of square blocks, eight in all, that extended southward from Martin Luther King Boulevard along the neighborhood's western boundary. The predominant existing condition on these blocks was vacant land, with some scattered vacant houses and clusters of occupied houses. In 2005, CRA staff had anticipated that all of the houses would be demolished in order to assemble large tracts of land for new market-rate housing construction that would take place during later stages of redevelopment activity. However, closer examination of these houses suggested that another alternative might be feasible. The majority of the remaining occupied houses in this section of Lanning Square appeared to be structurally sound, with few or no signs of significant deterioration. In many cases, evidence of exterior improvements such as the installation of new doors and windows and the painting of wood trim, could be found. Many of the houses were owner-occupied, and none of the houses appeared to be linked to community problems such as graffiti, loitering, excessive noise, or trash accumulation.

Based on these observations and subsequent discussions at City Hall and in community meetings, I proposed a new approach to stabilizing and strengthening Lanning Square's residential base. The two previously-proposed seventy-five-unit rental development ventures would be withdrawn from consideration, and the associated displacement would not occur. Instead, the first phase of development would be the build-out of vacant land in the northwest quadrant with new sales and rental housing, both affordable and market-rate. Following redevelopment plan approval, the City would issue a Request for Proposals, inviting prospective developers to submit plans for producing a well-designed, diverse mix of housing types on the available cleared land. To support the selected developer, the City would acquire all the vacant property on the northwest quadrant blocks, demolish vacant buildings that were infeasible for rehabilitation, convey the cleared sites to the developer, and provide grant and loan funding to help current homeowner-occupants repair and improve their properties. No one would be displaced. The City would work with the selected developer to secure the public financing and public-agency approvals needed to support the northwest quadrant build-out, which was anticipated to produce several hundred units of new housing.

The idea of building new construction around existing occupied housing and businesses in order to avoid displacement was not a new concept; the position of some housing advocates was that no other approach should be considered. Most of the for-profit developers who had previously done business exclusively in suburban or exurban areas and were beginning to explore urban development opportunities would not consider such an approach. An executive from one of these firms had told me that the firm's threshold

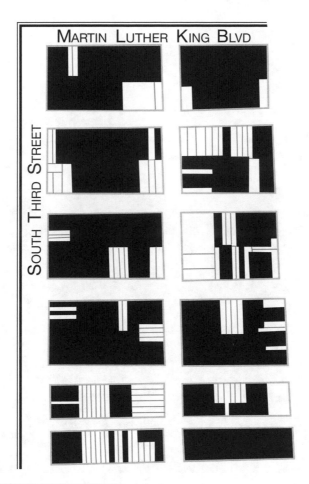

MARTIN LUTHER KING BLVD

SOUTH THIRD STREET

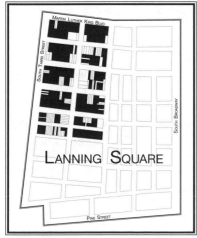

LANNING SQUARE

MARTIN LUTHER KING BLVD

SOUTH THIRD STREET

SOUTH BROADWAY

PINE STREET

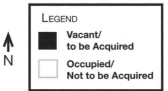

LEGEND

Vacant/
to be Acquired

Occupied/
Not to be Acquired

N

Figure 9.1 Northwest Quadrant

Figure 9.2 Vacant Land on a city block in the Northwest Quadrant

requirement for embarking on a new venture was a cleared site large enough to support the development of at least 300 single-family homes. However, not all developers held steadfastly to this insistence on cleared blocks. Across the Delaware River, the Philadelphia Housing Authority had achieved success in developing the Martin Luther King HOPE VI venture through an approach that integrated new sales and rental housing, including market-rate units, with existing housing in a row house neighborhood. Examples of other housing development ventures that combined new construction with the preservation of existing occupied housing were not hard to find. In Camden, a City commitment to make available most of the acreage on eight contiguous city blocks and to make the northwest quadrant a priority for development funding would, in my view, be more than enough to compensate for the build-around requirement. Some developers would

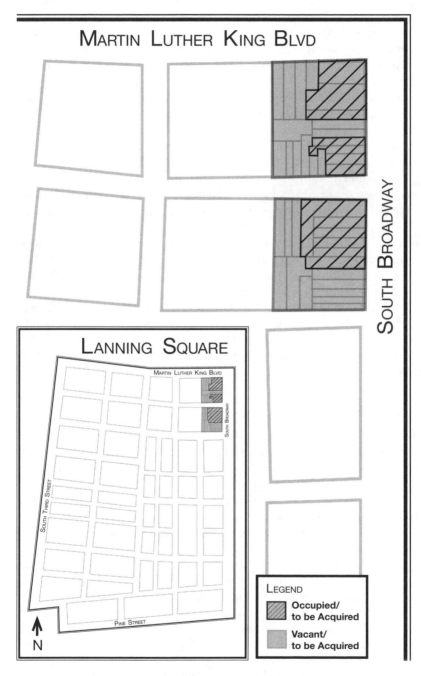

Figure 9.3 Broadway/Boulevard Blocks

be unwilling to accommodate such an approach. But those developers that were most likely to deliver the best performance for Camden would consider it—they told me so. At the time, many urban neighborhood housing markets had been growing stronger, and few other cities in the region were in a position to offer a comparable opportunity for large-scale, mixed housing development.

The northwest quadrant approach was reviewed with Judge Davis, discussed in community meetings, presented in churches and at radio stations, and reviewed with those City Council members who were most interested in Lanning Square. No major objections were raised, and the northwest quadrant was identified as the City's top housing priority in Lanning Square during the continuation of my tenure in Camden.

The northwest quadrant blocks occupied nearly a third of Lanning Square's total acreage. Given the Cramer Hill experience and our recognition of post-*Kelo* realities, the goal of city staff with respect to the remaining area was to avoid or minimize displacement. One element of the redevelopment plan would be the designation of a portion of Lanning Square as a "conservation area" in which no displacement would take place. By the end of 2007, nearly every block in Lanning Square had been proposed for conservation area designation. In order to address the other two challenges associated with redevelopment planning in Lanning Square, the City would propose to displace a small number of residents and businesses on the remaining blocks and to make the case that there was no reasonable alternative to doing so.

Broadway/Boulevard Blocks

The place that provided the greatest opportunity to create a strong connection between institutional and non-institutional development in the core of Lanning Square was a two-block section of Broadway that extended south from the southwest corner of Broadway and Martin Luther King Boulevard. Based on communication with Cooper University Hospital, the CRA supported the acquisition of these blocks as part of an area designated in the plan as a "University and Support Zone." The blocks included a dozen storefronts on Broadway and a small number of apartments on upstairs floors. These properties appeared to be maintained in compliance with health and safety codes, although some were deteriorated and some of the ground-floor retail space in these buildings had been vacant for an extended period.

In 2007–2008, Cooper had a student intern and medical resident population of more than three hundred, anticipated to grow significantly as the new institutional facilities were completed. At the time when redevelopment planning was under way, only about 3 percent of this population, a group with demanding schedules that included long hours of work and frequent overnight shifts, lived in Camden. According to Cooper administrators, no comparable institution anywhere had such a low percentage of medical students and residents living in the city where the institution was based. After the Cooper expansion and the nearby UMDNJ medical school development had been completed, the lack of such housing would be a significant competitive disadvantage that would limit the ability of these institutions to attract medical students and health care professionals.

Proponents of eminent domain acquisition, and the associated displacement of residents and businesses on the west side of Broadway south of the Boulevard, argued that these actions were necessary because Camden needed housing for the institutional workforce. The Broadway/Boulevard blocks were the locations with the best prospects for attracting these desired residents and creating a new identity for the city's core. The centrally located intersection of Broadway and Martin Luther King Boulevard was the most active crossroads in the city, with heavy auto traffic east and west and transit riders entering and departing buses and light rail cars at the Rand Transportation Center on the two northern corners of the intersection. The Broadway/ Boulevard blocks were the sites that had the best potential to attract a private developer capable of producing high-quality housing with attractive ground-floor retail uses. Arguably, you could build rental housing on vacant land elsewhere in Lanning Square that would attract medical students and interns; but such a development would be several blocks away, reducing the benefits of creating a critical mass of activity—hospital, medical school, housing, and stores, in a concentrated area. If the Broadway/Boulevard blocks were left alone, the area would be largely a dead space at night; a fried chicken joint

Figure 9.4 Broadway Streetscape

that was reported to be considering leasing vacant space at the vacant corner property would be the only sign of life after 6pm. Critical mass was essential to economic success, particularly in the fragmented city of Camden. The argument in support of eminent domain and displacement was economic development; but, in this instance, the rationale for eminent domain was strategic investment. It was totally unlike using eminent domain to acquire and pave a lake to please a Wal-Mart in Colorado. Should the opportunity to invest strategically for the benefit of Camden be constrained simply to honor a pre-existing use? Should the past dictate the future?

Opponents of the taking of the Broadway/Boulevard blocks argued that this situation was exactly like the attempted taking of the lake in Arvada. If the synergy between the hospital, the medical school, and housing and retail services for medical students and interns represented such a compelling opportunity for strategic investment, wouldn't private developers respond to this opportunity by acquiring available nearby property through negotiation and developing it for these uses? The very deteriorated Diamond Street corridor in Philadelphia west of Broad Street had become a strong student rental market half a dozen blocks west of the Temple University main campus. The shortage of on-campus housing and a year-by-year increase in student enrollment had stimulated a demand for rental apartments off-campus, and small entrepreneurs had rehabilitated row houses to accommodate this demand. Lanning Square's northwest quadrant, the area that was to be built out for high-quality mixed rental and sales housing, was much closer to Cooper Hospital than most of the student-tenanted West Diamond Street blocks were to the Temple campus. Marketable rental housing could be developed on available space in the mostly vacant northwest quadrant without displacing anyone, and this development would contribute to the diversity of housing types that the City had identified as a goal for this subarea. By the time this housing was developed, owners on the Broadway/Boulevard blocks might realize the wisdom of upgrading their properties in order to attract more profitable Cooper-related housing and retail uses—or of selling their properties to developers who were ready to do so. This sequence of activity was consistent with the dynamics of the private real estate market. Eminent domain acquisition of the Broadway/Boulevard blocks was not a strategic investment—it was an accommodation to Cooper Hospital, just as the attempted Arvada lake-taking had been an accommodation to Wal-Mart. If the pre-existing uses on this block were not to be respected, what other pre-existing uses might also be sacrificed in the future, in the name of economic development and strategic investment?

My experience led me to side with those who supported the use of eminent domain to acquire the Broadway/Boulevard blocks. Unfortunately, the private real estate market did not function as smoothly as described in the preceding paragraph; what is more, the private real estate market in Camden was broken. Nothing less than a kick-start would achieve the level of investment and growth that the city desperately needed. In many instances, in Philadelphia and other cities, owners of deteriorated properties that were adjacent to or across the street from completed development ventures did not see the wisdom of upgrading or selling. Many of them retained ownership indefinitely, with the unrealistic expectation that a future buyer would make them rich. The properties remained unimproved; the blocks they occupied remained dead zones.

My thirteen months in Camden ended before I had the opportunity to pursue a related issue: the possibility of offering business owners and residents on the Broadway/Boulevard blocks replacement retail space and housing at or near their current locations, in places that would have left them better off after relocation, consistent with the practices of organizations such as APM in Eastern North Philadelphia and EBDI in Baltimore. Could subsidized rental housing and subsidized retail space have been lined up for displaced residents and businesses in advance? The subsidy expense would have been substantial, but it would have been lower than the cost of defending against litigation comparable to that which had been brought against the proposed Cramer Hill development plan. I am not aware of whether this approach was attempted after I left, or whether it would have been feasible to do so.

Boulevard Transition Zone

One of the quietest places in the entire city of Camden was a rectangular-shaped area three blocks long and half a block wide that extended along the north side of Martin Luther King Boulevard, just northwest of Lanning Square's Walt Whitman block. The area was maintained as a series of surface parking lots, with most of the spaces occupied by daytime parkers, many of whom worked at the adjacent Waterfront Technology Center. Most of this real estate was publicly-owned. If these parcels could be assembled and developed together, the lifeless transition zone between Lanning Square and downtown could be built out with well-designed retail stores, offices, apartments or condominiums, and structured parking. This site, if aggregated, would be a potentially strong prospect for a new supermarket; the location was easily walkable from Lanning Square and reasonably walkable from the more upscale Cooper Grant neighborhood two and a half blocks to the north.

No one was actively considering plans of this type for this section of the Boulevard. Because the area was located just across the street and to the west of the Lanning Square redevelopment area boundaries, the consideration of development opportunities for these parcels was outside the scope of the planning for Lanning Square. However, if this area were to become a higher priority (and, as a starting point, made the subject of a land-use plan and feasibility study), the resulting development would create a positive identify for this lifeless stretch of the Boulevard and produce a zone of improvement extending from the Whitman block to the waterfront.

My assignment in Camden ended before I had time to advocate forcefully for this concept. The week before I left the CRA, I drove Judge Davis to

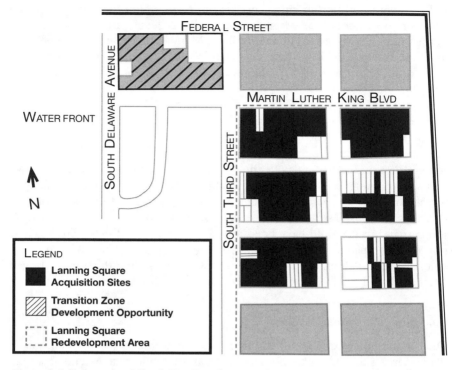

Figure 9.5 Prospective Mixed–Use Development Site

Figure 9.6 Parking Lots on Prospective Mixed–Use Development Site With
Downtown Philadelphia Skyline in Background

this site and four others that I recommended he consider pursuing as future development opportunities. I discussed the idea briefly with state development agency staff, a few of the administrators in nearby institutions, and some of the private developers that had been active in the area; but my time ran out before I could organize, present, and advocate for my position. After decisions are made about the manner in which this area will be developed, the results will illustrate how to build out a transition zone to achieve the greatest potential value—or how to miss out on a potential opportunity.

Social Fabric

In 2001, when I began work at the Fels Institute of Government, Robert D. Putnam's book, *Bowling Alone: The Collapse and Revival of American Community*, was causing a stir among social scientists at Penn and elsewhere.[4] The book stimulated classroom discussions and debates over Putnam's "dominant theme":

> For the first two-thirds of the twentieth century a powerful tide bore Americans into ever deeper engagement in the life of their communities, but a few decades ago—silently, without warning—that tide reversed . . . Without at first noticing, we have been pulled apart from one another and from our communities over the last third of the century.[5]

Despite the attention that *Bowling Alone* generated on campus, I never heard the book mentioned by otherwise well-read people who, in government agencies and community-based organizations, were most active in neighborhood planning and development initiatives in Philadelphia and nearly a dozen other cities that I visited in connection with consulting projects during that time. One possible explanation: *Bowling Alone* had almost nothing to say about the fundamental ways in which the nation's economy had changed during the period with which Putnam is concerned and about the relationship between this economic change—the advances in technology, transportation, and communications that led to the steady erosion of the country's once-robust manufacturing sector—and associated changes in the structure of families and neighborhoods. It was not only that Putnam and his researchers had missed the forest for the trees; they were devoting nearly all their time to the study of one type of tree—say, paper birches—while overlooking or barely recognizing all the others.

One illustration of the relationship between the manufacturing economy and social interaction is provided in this description by the historian Sam Bass Warner, Jr. of Northeast Philadelphia industry during the 1930s:

> Complementary habits characterized the life of the skilled factory workers of the northeast. The mill taught group work and discipline; unions, benefit associations, ethnic clubs, building and loan associations, and

fraternal orders, continued these habits. The abundance of cheap housing in the district, the necessity to cope with the irregular hours of slack and busy seasons, and the job benefits of being close to shop gossip combined to give the social habits of the skilled worker a spatial concentration.[6]

Fifty years later, most of the textile mills and other factories to which this passage makes reference had been closed, dispersed, or downsized because the products they had manufactured were being made at lower cost in other countries and transported quickly and cost-effectively from these places to consumers in the United States. The resulting job loss caused an unprecedented depopulation of the "spatially concentrated" neighborhoods that had grown up around manufacturing industries. The construction of the Interstate highway system and post-World War Two federal mortgage financing programs facilitated spatial deconcentration on a regional basis.

Lanning Square was an extreme example of spatial deconcentration—the neighborhood was half vacant. A residential community in which groups of houses are separated by large tracts of vacant land is, to say the least, not a favorable environment for nurturing social capital, the focus of Putnam's book, which he characterizes as "civic virtue . . . embedded in a dense network of reciprocal social relations." Putnam adds, "A society of many virtuous but isolated individuals is not necessarily rich in social capital."[7]

Lanning Square's dearth of social capital—of a network of mutually supportive relationships—was accompanied by a high level of social need. In Lanning Square and Cooper Plaza, two adjacent redevelopment areas which were combined for the purposes of the human capital planning project that took place in 2007 and 2008, more than half the residents (56 percent) had incomes below poverty level, the unemployment rate was 16 percent, and fewer than half of the residents over twenty-five had received high school degrees. Neighborhood residents who participated in the numerous community meetings that took place during 2007 made it clear that they cared about Lanning Square and wanted to create a future for their families in the community. But the odds were against them in the existing environment. The need to nurture social capital and simultaneously create and expand resources to support the growth of human capital—the economic value that an individual creates for him- or herself through access to education, training, and supportive services—would be too great a barrier for many, if any, community members to overcome.

Judge Davis had recognized the need to address both social capital and human capital issues from the start, and he had emphasized the latter in his initial meeting with Governor Corzine. In Lanning Square, we had an opportunity to try to address both these issues. With funding support provided by the Annie E. Casey Foundation and the Ford Foundation, a nonprofit organization, Urban Strategies, Inc., worked in coordination with the Judge to design a human capital plan that would accompany the Lanning Square redevelopment plan.

Urban Strategies' approach was consistent with Judge Davis' views:

> Healthy communities that nurture healthy families need safe housing, good schools, and a wide range of supportive services. These amenities are tied to a specific geographic area and therefore must be developed as part of a comprehensive, integrated planning and management approach, specific to that geographic area. Central to sustained implementation of a dynamic plan is resident participation and effective resident leadership.[8]

Prior to agreeing to an engagement in Camden, the St. Louis-based Urban Strategies had worked almost exclusively with McCormack Baron Salazar, a real estate development firm (also headquartered in St. Louis) that was nationally recognized for its success in completing well-designed mixed income housing ventures in locations that could be described as socially and economically challenged. Sandra Moore, the President of Urban Strategies, often introduced the organization by describing what Urban Strategies was not: not a developer, not a funding source, not a service provider. Urban Strategies' role was to work closely with community members to create a human capital plan—a framework for identifying and organizing the resources needed to ensure future success—that would subsequently be managed, financed, and implemented by others.

Moore had a law degree and a degree in Urban Planning, along with a wealth of experience in the nonprofit service sector and in government. Among other credentials, she had served as Director of the Missouri Department of Labor and Industrial Relations and had been a member of the Governor's cabinet. Her state-government background was an excellent match for Camden, where state government buy-in was essential, in light of the state's central role in MRERA oversight and implementation.

Judge Davis responded positively to the opportunity to work with Urban Strategies. He and Moore established a good working relationship in no time. The Judge was a conservative member of the South Jersey establishment, but he understood that an activist approach was necessary in order to address the severe social problems that beset Camden. Moore was an activist, but her activism was informed by the conviction that nothing less than a genuine alliance of government, business, and neighborhood interests would produce a successful outcome in a place like Camden.

Urban Strategies' staff reviewed all of the important background information: the census data, the MRERA legislation, the redevelopment plans, the consultants' reports. With Judge Davis, Sandra Moore went to Trenton and met with state officials, joined on some occasions by representatives of the Casey and Ford foundations. Moore met with the leaders whose support was needed in order to make a human capital plan credible. She met with state and local elected officials, with Campbell's Soup executives, with business leaders, and with academic and health care institution administrators. She met with George Norcross—twice, I was told.

Moore also arranged for an Urban Strategies staff member, Tinesar Forrest, to come to Camden from St. Louis, live in an apartment a few blocks away from Lanning Square for six months, and work full-time on organizing the human capital plan. In this instance, "organizing" meant creating a communications structure within a community that was almost entirely lacking in the kinds of social networks described in Putnam's book. This challenge was made somewhat easier to address by the decision to make the combined Lanning Square and Cooper Plaza redevelopment areas the geography of the human capital plan. Many residents did not view these two areas as two separate neighborhoods and felt strongly that they had a stake in the future of Lanning Square, regardless of which side of Broadway they lived on. As a practical matter, this approach would make it possible for Lanning Square to benefit from the civic engagement structure that had taken shape in Cooper Plaza—the relationships between community residents, Cooper Hospital, and city government that had guided the organization and implementation of both institution- and government-sponsored development plans.

In support of the creation of a human capital plan, Urban Strategies completed a neighborhood-wide survey (with a response rate of 13 percent), conducted a total of sixty-eight one-on-one and group meetings with neighborhood residents and other community members; and held focus-group sessions with community members who represented critical areas of interest: senior citizens, male residents, small business owners, young adults, parents, youth, Cooper Hospital employees, and Spanish speakers.[9]

The community meetings, promoted through direct mailings and leafleting, were held in several locations around the neighborhood. Attendance at some heavily-promoted meetings was dismal; I once addressed an audience of six. As the spring and summer months passed, however, participation grew. By that time, it was possible to identify a core group of individuals who might not agree with everything the City proposed, but who wanted a redevelopment plan for the area to be approved and who were opposed to litigation that would block the implementation of redevelopment activities. Typically, the meetings focused on three topics: identifying problems and solutions, assigning a value to each solution relative to the others, and discussing the most practical way to move forward.

Tinesar Forrest of Urban Strategies managed most of the meetings, working in coordination with Donna Helmes of the CRA, who eventually devoted full-time attention to human capital planning. Sandra Moore flew in from St. Louis to participate in key meetings, at which she restated the goals of the planning process, described accomplishments to date, engaged community members in discussion and, when the discussion was over, worked out an agreement on the next steps to be taken.

Urban Strategies' approach was similar in some respects to that employed in community planning sessions in other cities. In one meeting, for example, participants "voted" to identify the most valued existing community facilities and service providers and to rank the most important community improvement priorities to be addressed. However, this approach differed from many others in two important respects. Moore and Forrest emphasized the need for community members to think pragmatically about how the priorities they identified would be funded and implemented. After a point, any agenda time devoted to "visioning" about the ideal future community would end and the discussion of realistic next steps would begin. In addition, while the community process was under way, Moore was communicating with government, business, institution, and foundation executives about the progress of the human capital planning initiative and discussing how available resources might be used to support implementation of the activities that would be named as priorities in the final plan.

Moore's approach was not a shakedown or a plea for charity; in the meetings in which I participated, her approach more closely resembled the presentation of a business proposition. The city and state are preparing to make an unprecedented investment in the revitalization of Lanning Square. This investment, if successful, will improve the physical environment, but will not have a transformative effect unless human capital needs are addressed as well. In seeking commitments of funding or service support, Moore tailored her presentation to focus on the kinds of program activities with which her audience was most familiar. For example, she spoke with Campbell Soup Company executives about the possibility of providing additional funding, through the company-affiliated charitable foundation, to support programs in Lanning Square that were similar to activities that the foundation was already funding. Moore also took care to avoid creating a zero-sum situation, in which a government, corporate, or foundation commitment to the human capital plan would reduce the level of funding or service support available to others. Urban Strategies' mission was to accumulate added value, not to deplete the existing resource base.

The draft human capital plan appended to the proposed Lanning Square redevelopment plan identified four priorities:

1. Rebuild and reopen Lanning Square Elementary School [a school that had been demolished several years earlier, after which plans for a new school had been delayed by state funding shortfalls] and establish an integrated community services center to serve the CPLS [Cooper Plaza Lanning Square] community.
2. Increase employment and educational opportunities for adults in the CPLS neighborhoods.
3. Improve community stability [through measures such as cleaning and greening vacant lots and providing home improvement financing to homeowner-occupants].
4. Increase real and perceived safety and security in the CPLS neighborhood.[10]

The plan included an itemized five-year implementation schedule and budget, with a first-year budget of $2.6 million, to be funded through government, institutional, and foundation sources. If the human capital plan were to be fully implemented, current community residents would begin to benefit from the proposed activities before the first bricks-and-mortar development began. In addition, the publication of the plan represented a successful collaboration between the City and community, mediated by Urban Strategies. At the conclusion of the planning process, Sheila Roberts, a community member who had worked closely with Cooper Hospital in addressing Cooper Plaza redevelopment issues and had subsequently participated in the design of the Cooper Plaza Lanning Square human capital plan, said, "The city has heard the residents' broad and deep concerns . . . I am strongly convinced this has been a true collaboration."[11]

Outcomes

In June, the Planning Board passed a resolution declaring the Lanning Square area to be in need of redevelopment and approving the redevelopment plan that the Department of Development and Planning had drafted, with the draft human capital plan appended to the redevelopment plan document. The redevelopment plan was approved by City Council in July. In its final form, the redevelopment plan called for the taking of twelve properties on the Broadway/Boulevard blocks, as well as five other occupied properties elsewhere in the area.

Opponents of these measures testified at both hearings. Some were opposed to the taking of occupied properties, and others were opposed to the redevelopment-area designation as a whole, arguing that, if the redevelopment plan were to be approved, the City could choose at a later date to expand the list of "to be acquired" addresses as it saw fit, and take any properties located within the area. "We do not live in a blighted neighborhood," the *Courier-Post* reported one resident as saying, "Why do we have to live in fear that we may be asked to move at any time in the next 25 years?"[12] "They can change their mind at any time," a participant in the Planning Board meeting stated. A plan supporter, twenty-five-year old Sean Brown, accused the anti-redevelopment group of using "scare tactics" and said, "By the time I'm 50, I want to see a neighborhood that's not filled with prostitutes, crumbling buildings and people shooting at night."[13]

In July, Governor Corzine signed a school construction bill that provided $42.4 million for the development of a new Lanning Square Elementary School, the top priority item in the human capital plan.

In August, two lawsuits were filed against the Lanning Square redevelopment plan, one by South Jersey Legal Services, on behalf of a group of residents and an organization called Lanning Square West Residents in Action, and the other by a regional retail chain that owned "to be acquired" properties on one of the Broadway/Boulevard blocks. The latter was described by the plaintiff as a "vibrant commercial district."

Judge Davis expressed disappointment to a reporter. "Here we go again," he said. "More litigation which will delay us. I have no idea how long, but litigation is astronomically expensive and it could bankrupt us. Financially, this city is in terrible shape."[14]

The litigation would not delay the development of the UMDNJ medical school on the Broadway site; all of the properties on that block were already publicly owned, and no use of eminent domain was needed. The litigation had no effect on the Cooper Hospital expansion plans either; all Cooper-related development was taking place across the street on the east side of Broadway, in the Cooper Plaza redevelopment area, for which a redevelopment plan had been approved three years earlier.

I have no ability to assess the prospects for a successful defense against this litigation. However, I feel certain that the outcome of these actions will be based not on *Kelo*, but on technicalities—on the question of whether or not the court decides that the plan should be nullified based on perceived procedural flaws such as those that caused the defeat of the Cramer Hill, Bergen Square, and Waterfront South plans. Based on the City's experience with prior litigation, the outcome of the Lanning Square actions could be based on nothing more than the personal perspective of the judge or judges who rule on this litigation. As described in the preceding chapter, the judge presiding over the Cramer Hill case determined that without a swearing-in of expert witnesses prior to their testimony before the Planning Board, the redevelopment plan was fatally flawed and that this flaw could not be remedied by swearing in these individuals after the fact; in a comparable Haddon Township case, however, another judge made the opposite determination. Because the minutiae of redevelopment planning procedure had, for the most part, not been scrutinized by courts pre-*Kelo*, precedents had not been set with regard to determinations about the significance of procedural actions, such as swearings-in, and rulings were being made on a case-by-case basis, sometimes without consistency.

In the meantime, the parties who had brought action against the City would be filing discovery motions seeking documentation that they would maintain was essential to presenting their case. The preparation of this documentation would be an extremely time-consuming activity for City and CRA staff members, who would need to extract material, dating back several years, from files in several departments. The documents would fill a stack of cardboard boxes. Management staff who would otherwise be working to advance revitalization activities in neighborhoods would be devoting a substantial amount of time to this and other litigation-related tasks and would continue to do so until the litigation had been resolved.

What To Make of Camden

In 2006, his first year as Governor, Jon Corzine had inherited a Camden recovery program that his administration had not designed and that he might not have supported had he been given the choice. The risks associated with MRERA had already become apparent and many of the MRERA-financed activities with the biggest political payoff—the high-profile aquarium expansion and the institutional development ventures—had been started or completed during the McGreevey Administration.

Corzine's primary political frame of reference was the North Jersey region, and Camden was a South Jersey city. "He doesn't care about anything south of Montclair," I was told by a person with an insider perspective on New Jersey politics. That characterization may or may not have been accurate with respect to Corzine's personal views; what was more important was the political calculus. Even if Corzine cared passionately about Camden, the recovery plan provided him with meager political capital at best. The city was not going to be demonstrably more self-sufficient and less dependent on state aid by 2007, the end of the COO's five-year "rehabilitation term" (Corzine and the state legislature approved a five-year extension of the rehabilitation term in mid-2007 and made Judge Davis' appointment as COO permanent). The failure of the Cherokee proposal had been widely publicized during the months before he took office, and, with the exception of Baldwin's Run and other HOPE VI projects, no successful large-scale neighborhood ventures had been completed or were in the works. In addition, Corzine's first year in office had been difficult enough. He had raised the sales tax to balance the state budget and was struggling to finance a property tax relief plan for New Jersey, where property taxes were the nation's highest. Little political capital remained available for use in Camden.

Corzine did not ignore Camden. I saw more than a little evidence of his administration's support for Judge Davis, for the Lanning Square proposal, and for other current and proposed revitalization activities. But from a purely political perspective—the perspective that one must employ, apart from personal feelings, if one is to be elected and re-elected—there is little value that Camden could have offered him, and the pitfalls associated with maintaining a strong state presence in the high-risk Camden political environment were potentially career-threatening.

I respected the leadership of Randy Primas and Arijit De to a greater degree than many others who had lived or worked in Camden during their tenure. They had to make their way in a politically charged environment, but their activities amounted to far more than serving as enablers of the political powers that be. Primas had leadership and management credentials that were relevant to Camden. Primas and De had tried in their own ways to make sense of the imperfect MRERA structure, which they did not have a hand in designing; and, to a significant degree, they had been successful. The aquarium and most of the institutional development ventures were completed or under way by the time they left. Most of the city's neighborhoods had City Council-approved redevelopment plans, and most of these plans called for no displacement. In Cramer Hill, it appeared that they had hoped to work out a sensible relocation and replacement housing plan—one that would include an offer of replacement housing within the community for any displaced resident who wanted to stay there—at the same time that the redevelopment plan design, review, and approval process was going on. They had apparently hoped that the participation of community representatives in the Request for Proposal process that had led to the selection of Cherokee, followed by the initial community review that had taken place before the press conference at which Governor McGreevey endorsed the Cherokee plan would serve as a sufficient base for a broader civic engagement process that would follow.

Even if this generous view of Primas and De's record were to be accepted, the reality was that the two of them had violated Rule Number One in the community development playbook: you must communicate with the community before taking action. In a place such as Camden, the interaction that had taken place prior to the Cherokee announcement had been, to say the least, inadequate.

MRERA worked reasonably well as a $175 million, bond-financed investment strategy. MRERA failed as a municipal reform plan, and this failure adversely affected the prospects for successful neighborhood revitalization. The core of this failure was a limitation that former Mayor Primas and Judge Davis had in common. In their own ways, each was well qualified to serve in a role comparable to that of a chairman of the board. Each knew how to deliver a presentation—in a board room or a church basement —how to articulate a policy, mediate a disagreement, and issue directives. But neither was qualified to be an operations manager, a person who could supervise the day-to-day functioning of municipal government, establish and monitor performance goals, recruit capable managers, and dismiss under-achievers. That is to say, neither was qualified to be a chief operating officer in the literal sense of the term: the senior executive in charge of municipal operations.

The state aid that had been made available to Primas and Davis did not include funding for such a person, for an individual who, acting in accord with broad municipal reform goals, would overhaul city government. This person would demand reliable performance on a day-to-day and hour-to-hour basis, and, if performance standards were not met, this person would make heads roll. "You have to build up a body count," of dismissed bureaucratic and political deadweight, I had been told years earlier by a consultant who had managed the reform of a number of failing public housing authorities during the 1980s. No one had been funded, recruited, and appointed to perform this task in Camden.*

Months after leaving Camden City Hall, I was told a revealing anecdote by Alan Mallach, a New Jersey-based educator and consultant. In a conversation with a person he described as a "Trenton insider" in 2002, Mallach

---

* Sean Closkey, then Executive Director of the New Jersey Housing and Mortgage Finance Agency, had commented to me on this deficiency during an early stage of MRERA implementation.

had expressed his hope that approval of the MRERA legislation would be followed by a national search to recruit the best-qualified municipal turnaround expert available. The insider looked at him in surprise, as if to say, "How could you be so hopelessly naïve?" To those in the know, MRERA apparently had nothing to do with municipal reform.

Camden was a political hotbed, but the pervasiveness of politics was not the major impediment to progress in the city. There was no question that, at and after the turn of the century, no one could successfully make their way in the Camden political sphere without the blessing of George Norcross, but Norcross was not the central problem. Norcross was viewed by many as autocratic, heavy-handed, and unethical, with a history of self-dealing and conflicts of interest—but he was not corrupt. Norcross backed candidates for elective office whose qualifications ranged from highly competent to lackluster, and the control he exerted over these politicians, informed by his personal worldview, kept them in check and stabilized a political environment that could otherwise have become chaotic. Under these circumstances, Norcross was a boon to the city; without him, Camden would likely have been in a far worse condition. Was a far worse condition imaginable? I could imagine it; consider the political condition of Detroit in 2008, the year of Mayor Kwame Kilpatrick's decline and fall.

The real barrier to Camden's future success was the absence of a new generation of civic leadership: a critical mass of people who would participate in community affairs, serve on the School Board, the Planning Board, and other government bodies, advocate for sensible and progressive city and county government policies, and support qualified elected officials or run for election themselves. This generation of civic leadership is not going to grow and be nurtured in City Hall, or within most of the city's neighborhood organizations or religious congregations. The places with the greatest potential to contribute to the growth of civic leadership in Camden are the city's academic and health care institutions, based on their special characteristics described previously. These institutions are the city's largest workplaces, employing many Camden residents at all income levels. They are located at strategically important downtown and neighborhood sites, and they are the city's largest service providers. They know how to collaborate with businesses in the city and region and their wellbeing is less dependent on municipal government than is the case with most other businesses in Camden.

Despite the severe problems described in these two chapters about Camden, I feel optimistic about the city's prospects for future success, based in large part on the stronger role that institutional leaders are beginning to play in neighborhood revitalization. In 2007 and 2008, with grant support provided by the Annie E. Casey Foundation, the Greater Camden Partnership, the city's business leadership organization, worked in coordination with institutional administrators to determine the best ways to support the implementation of the Cooper Plaza Lanning Square human capital plan. The administrators' task force formed a closer working relationship with the

Camden School District (for which a new superintendent was recruited from Philadelphia in 2007), and a special focus of planning during this period was the siting of institution-administered service programs at the Lanning Square Elementary School. For example, Camden County College proposed that space in the school be made available as a site for the College's successful Community Gateway program, which provides adults with reading, writing, language, and math skills. A continuing integration of institution-sponsored support programs of this kind into the city's public school system could have a powerful positive impact on the city during the coming years.

To be genuinely successful in influencing positive change in Camden, however, the city's institutional leadership will have to become more assertive in their relationships with city, county, and state government. Because most institutional administrators are reluctant to become actively involved in the political realm on an individual level, they will have to determine how to work together most effectively to pursue their collective self-interest in other ways. Two of the most promising opportunities for doing so—improving public education and supporting the development of housing for students and employees at all income levels—are already being pursued as priorities. Camden's future depends in large part on the extent to which the city's institutions are able to play a stronger role in addressing these and other priorities, to create a healthy civic environment that will produce and sustain competent and reliable municipal governance.

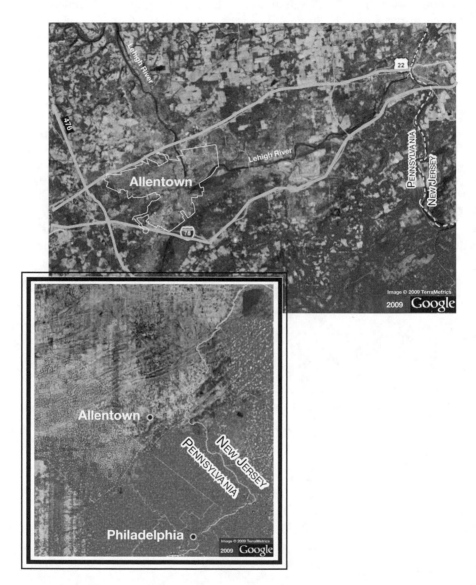

Figure 10.1 Allentown and its Region

10 Rental Housing Asset Management

A Strategy for Allentown, Pennsylvania's Downtown-Area Neighborhoods

Population loss is a defining characteristic of most postindustrial cities. Philadelphia lost half a million residents in the last half of the twentieth century, 27 percent of its 1950 population. Camden lost nearly 45,000 residents during this period, a drop of about 46 percent. But the population of Allentown, Pennsylvania's third largest city, remained relatively stable, varying from as low as 104,000 to as high as 110,000. The difference between Allentown's 1950 and 2000 populations (106,756 and 106,632) was a hundred-plus people.

City populations are often published in rank order like sports-team standings, and a city's ascendancy in the rankings is often greeted with celebration. "Officialdom in Phoenix was ecstatic when the city eclipsed Philadelphia as the fifth-largest in the country," according to an *Arizona Republic* editorial.[1] Population growth is implicitly regarded as a sign of success and wellbeing, and population loss as an indicator of decline, with good reason. During most of the past half-century, a larger population was likely to mean a larger labor force and a growing demand for housing and retail goods, as well as business and personal services that would stimulate new development and generate more jobs. A larger population also qualified a city to receive more funding through state and federal programs that used population as a variable in a fund allocation formula.

However, the link between population growth and economic prosperity is no longer so clear. Through research conducted under the sponsorship of CEOs for Cities, a national leadership organization, Robert Weissbourd and Christopher Berry found that the correlation between population and income growth "broke down for the first time between the late 1980s and the early 1990s, and has not been significant since." In a survey of the hundred largest U.S. cities, Weissbourd and Berry found little overlap between the cities with the greatest population growth and the cities with the most income growth between 1990 and 2000. For example, Las Vegas, Raleigh, and Arlington were among the top ten cities in terms of population growth, but were not among the top ten in income growth. Conversely, San Francisco, Atlanta, and Seattle appeared on the top ten list for income growth but did not appear on the top ten list for population growth. Substantial divergences were found for some cities: Bakersfield was ranked number two in population growth (plus 35 percent), but number ninety-six in income growth (minus 7 percent) during this period. Weissbourd and Berry's conclusion: "*Cities do not need to grow big to grow wealthy, and growing big will not necessarily lead to wealth*" [authors' emphasis].[2]

The dynamic between population growth, income growth, and economic success is more complex within individual cities. The out-of-town residents whose decisions to move to Philadelphia were strongly influenced by the ten-year tax abatement incentive helped repopulate formerly marginal areas of the city, and most of them probably brought with them incomes higher than the citywide median; but, as described in Chapter One, many neighborhood residents clearly did not feel that these economic benefits outweighed the associated disadvantage: a substantial increase in property tax assessments on their fully taxable homes. The mayor of Hazleton, Pennsylvania, who gained national attention for his proposal to impose fines for hiring illegal immigrants, contended that a substantial number of the Latinos who had migrated to the city were responsible for increased crime in the city (no evidence could be supplied as to the actual number of Hazleton residents who were illegal immigrants). At the same time, it was clear that this influx of Latino residents, who, in 2000, amounted to nearly half the city's population of 22,000, had contributed significantly to the revitalization of the city's downtown area.[3] White residency in Camden, once a white-majority city, was less than 17 percent in 2000, but plans for several large-scale, market-rate housing development ventures on and near the waterfront and in the downtown area that began taking shape during the next few years were likely to attract many new white residents when completed. How would the city's predominantly African-American and Latino population react to a large increase in the number of white residents, most of whom were likely to have incomes higher than the citywide median, moving into the area that had been targeted as a priority for public investment in recent decades?

The Allentown reinvestment strategy described in this chapter is different from all the others in several respects. The primary focus of the strategy is rental housing problems. These problems were not citywide but were, for the most part, concentrated within a group of neighborhoods immediately adjacent to the city's downtown business district. In most of these neighborhoods, there is little transition between the downtown and the residential community next to it. Blocks dominated by stores and offices can be found shoulder to shoulder with exclusively residential blocks, consisting primarily of row houses and attached twins. In this section of the city, there are few significant transition-zone areas comparable to the Lower North Philadelphia area described in Chapter Three. Also significant is the fact that Allentown's strategy took shape over the course of more than a decade and that a central role in formulating and advancing this strategy was played by a group of individuals who, at the time, had no significant political power.

Allentown residents' concerns about rental housing were not grounded in antipathy toward renters or investor-owners or in hostility to Latinos or other incoming residents. Instead, these concerns were associated with three related issues: the destabilization of neighborhood blocks, as a result of large-scale conversions of single-family homes to multi-family properties; the neglect of certain rental properties, some of them overcrowded and in violation of health and safety codes; and ongoing instances of disruptive behavior by some tenants. Although the number of criminally negligent rental property owners and extremely disruptive tenants was relatively small, one bad property could undermine an entire block. If a homeowner observes that no action is being taken in response to the sale of drugs, round-the-clock noise, and the accumulation of litter and debris on the porch and in the yard of a house on their block, a logical course of action is to sell out and leave the neighborhood at the earliest possible time—and that is what many Allentown homeowners did during the late decades of the twentieth century. Many of the houses that they moved from were sold to investor-owners and converted into multi-family apartments. Some of these houses, in turn, might become the problem rental properties of the future.

Allentown's Changing Fortunes

The city of Allentown, for which plans were drawn up in 1762, is located on a plateau above the Lehigh River in what was, until the second quarter of the nineteenth century, a primarily agrarian region. The city is well-located in the mid-Atlantic region: about sixty-four miles north of Philadelphia, twenty miles west of New Jersey, and ninety-five miles west—nearly due west—of New York City. During the 1800s, the city established itself as one of the primary manufacturing centers in the Lehigh Valley, due to a combination of luck and circumstance. The completion of the Lehigh Canal in 1829 facilitated the transportation of anthracite coal from the Mauch Chunk Hills, located twenty miles north of Allentown, to Philadelphia and other cities. The development of the Lehigh Valley Railroad, the first segment of which was completed during the 1850s, further enhanced Allentown's position as a transportation node. Serendipitously, limestone deposits were discovered during the construction of the railroad, and by the end of the century Allentown had become a center of the cement industry, with eleven cement mills located within a six-mile radius. The city's iron industry grew rapidly during the mid-nineteenth century as railroads expanded across the country. The Panic of 1873 brought an end to the railroad construction boom, and the iron furnaces closed down; but by the end of the century, other manufacturing industries had moved in and expanded. The truck manufacturer that later became Mack Truck moved from Brooklyn to Allentown in 1906 and became well-known during World War One, when the company sold thousands of trucks to the Army. Between 1890 and 1920, Allentown's population tripled, from 25,228 to 73,502.[4]

Allentown was like other small cities that had initially expanded as manufacturing centers serving a primarily agrarian economy, producing goods such as horseshoes and stoves; but unlike many of these cities, Allentown was able to adapt to the changing market demands associated with urban growth and industrialization. In the early to mid-twentieth century, Mack Truck and nearby Bethlehem Steel took the place of silk mills and furniture factories as major centers of commerce and employment. The dissolution of the canal system was offset, by many orders of magnitude, by the construction of a network of highways and rail lines linking Allentown with the rest of the mid-Atlantic region. The city's population grew from 70,000 to 109,000 between 1920 and 1970.[5]

During the twentieth century, Allentown became a prominent retail center as well. The central downtown corridor, Hamilton Street, had three successful department stores. Hess Brothers, Leh's, and Zollinger-Harned attracted customers from the region and beyond. Hess's became the most renowned of these establishments due in large part to the irrepressible entrepreneurial spirit of Max Hess. "Retailing as theater" is how one Hess executive described the store's approach. "We've taken Fifth Avenue and brought it to Middle America," he told a reporter. The Allentown store had crystal chandeliers, mirrored columns, and, "sprinkled among the suits, dresses, toys, stereos, and other typical department store fare . . . a $27,000 pair of antique porcelain Chinese temple jars, a hot-air balloon for $15,000, and a porcelain figure of Marilyn Monroe, with actual mink fur and diamond necklace, for $5,400." Film and television celebrities made well-publicized visits to the Allentown store. Designer fashions unlikely to be worn by most Lehigh Valley residents made their debut there. In 1959, Rudi Gernreich's topless bathing suit was introduced to the nation at Hess's Allentown store; it sold out within forty-eight hours.[6]

By that time, Hamilton Street had become populated with banks, restaurants, and high-end retail stores: clothing, shoes, jewelry. Each corner of Center Square had a clothing store on it. You could easily buy all your Christmas presents in downtown Allentown, a lifelong resident told me; there was no need to drive outside the city for anything. The 322-foot high Pennsylvania Power and Light (PP&L) Building at 9th and Hamilton, a classic art deco skyscraper built in the 1920s, was a dominant part of the downtown landscape. A new city hall and public safety building were completed by the mid-1960s on the 400 block of Hamilton, where a block acquired by the City's Redevelopment Authority had been cleared of older buildings.[7]

Some of the characteristics that had contributed to Allentown's success during the late nineteenth and early twentieth century created disadvantages for the city during the century's last decades. The Lehigh Valley's value as a central location in the mid-Atlantic region was recognized by transportation planners, and Interstate highway construction decisions were made accordingly. However, the suburban and rural areas surrounding Allentown got most of the benefits associated with highway development and expansion.

The Philadelphia Inquirer reported that, with the 1989 completion of Interstate 78, which ran south of the city, warehouse and distribution center users can "have a nearly direct, two-hour shot to New York . . . or head south to Philadelphia, Baltimore, and beyond."

> Ironically, the spacious warehouses flourishing now are filled with the furniture and housewares, dresses and shoes, computers and hardware and other merchandise once made in Allentown . . . but now made more cheaply in places such as Malaysia, Sri Lanka, Hong Kong and Mexico and brought here for storage until they are shipped to customers on the East Coast. Some of the merchandise is made in factories elsewhere in the United States where production costs are lower.[8]

Industrial parks were developed on formerly agricultural tracts near highway interchanges in order to provide sites for the new warehouse and distribution facilities, as well as for a growing number of high-tech industries and business service companies that were moving into the region. These firms were attracted in part by the relatively low cost of buying or leasing real estate in the Lehigh Valley rather than in the much higher-priced New York and northern New Jersey real estate markets.

The health care industry also expanded. In 1993, Lehigh Valley Hospital and St. Luke's Hospital were among the region's top five employers.[9]

These new industries brought renewed economic strength to the region. Shortly after the turn of the century, the authors of a Brookings Institution report, commenting on the Lehigh Valley's status as the third largest employment center in Pennsylvania, stated that:

> The region's strongest asset may be its commercialization of new products and new technologies, as indicated by its healthy generation of patents per capita, which surpasses the U.S. average, despite the relative lack of federal research dollars and thin layer of research and development workers.[10]

As the new economy took shape, it became clear that household goods and clothing were not the only items that could be manufactured more cheaply in places other than Allentown. In 1986, Mack Truck announced its decision to close down its 5-C factory in Allentown and replace it with an $80 million plant to be built in South Carolina. A total of 1,800 workers who had been earning an average of $23 an hour lost their jobs. The company had made its decision after failing to obtain concessions from the United Auto Workers as a condition for staying in Allentown. At the new South Carolina plant, it was anticipated that the company could produce seventy trucks a week, compared with fifty-two a week in Allentown, with eight hundred fewer employees.[11] For a time, the company kept its corporate headquarters in Allentown, as the Campbell Soup Company had kept its corporate headquarters in Camden following a comparable relocation of production facilities. Then, in 2008, Mack Truck moved its headquarters to South Carolina as well.

The economic transformation of the region also had consequences for the residential real estate market. Interstate 78 and US 22 (an older multi-lane divided highway) made travel between the Lehigh Valley and New Jersey easy. Higher-paid executives, managers, and technicians could commute from upscale suburban New Jersey homes to jobs in the Lehigh Valley without difficulty. Conversely, lower-wage New Jersey workers who were being priced out of the overheated northern New Jersey real estate market could find less expensive housing in the Lehigh Valley and commute to work across the river. Opportunities to buy market-rate housing in the region surrounding Allentown were growing. "All of the new housing is on the west side" of Allentown and the immediate vicinity, a developer told a newspaper reporter in 1999. "That's why Wegman's is where they are."[12]

Residential growth outside the city stimulated commercial development there as well. During the 1980s and 1990s, stores that had once been located exclusively in regional centers such as Allentown were now a major presence in the suburbs. Every kind of retail good that used to be available on the thriving Hamilton Street corridor could now be found in malls and strip shopping centers that were more accessible to most residents of the region and that offered free parking. Downtown Allentown's retail fortunes quickly changed for the worse. After achieving $40 million in sales in 1985,[13] Hess's downtown Allentown store was sold in 1994. The store operated for a little more than a year as The Bon Ton, then closed, leaving 217 employees out of work and 310,000 square feet of empty retail space in the center of the city. Zollinger-Harned had closed long before, in 1978. Leh's Allentown store had closed more recently, in 1994. After sales peaked at $25 million in the late 1980s, the entire Leh's department-store chain was gone by the end of the next decade, after 146 years in the business.[14]

In 1982, singer Billy Joel's "Allentown" (in which the city's name was rhymed with "closing all the factories down") became a Billboard Hot 100 hit, and an accompanying music video was played in heavy rotation on MTV. The city gained international recognition as a place of failure and abandonment.

Interestingly, the physical deterioration associated with economic disinvestment in Allentown was contained within a relatively limited geography. In contrast to Philadelphia and Camden, where blight could be found in many neighborhoods across the city, most neighborhood deterioration was confined to several dozen blocks in the immediate vicinity of the Hamilton Street corridor. Most of the remainder of the city was in relatively good condition, with many stable older residential blocks and, further out from the center, attractive detached and semi-detached houses on larger lots. Allentown was never plagued with widespread housing vacancy, as Philadelphia and Camden had been. The deterioration of existing occupied properties due to poor maintenance and overcrowding proved to be a much greater problem.

The downtown area had been hit hardest by the economic setbacks of the late twentieth century. "We had depended too much on the three department stores," one businessperson told me. No one had designed a contingency plan for downtown. As highway-oriented malls and strip shopping centers expanded, the higher-end Hamilton Street stores moved or went out of business. By the turn of the century, this street, formerly a regional shopping destination, had become a convenience shopping and neighborhood retail corridor.

Neighborhoods in the vicinity of Allentown's business district suffered as well. For people with incomes at or above the median, the prospect of living in or near downtown was not particularly appealing. Many affordable and more attractive housing opportunities were available nearby. Allentown was unlike Philadelphia, where, at the close of a typical business day, traveling from Center City to the suburbs by car is difficult because all the roads are jammed; in contrast, getting out of central Allentown at the end of a work day is easy. A PP&L manager or executive could leave the company's corporate headquarters (which had remained downtown in its 1920s skyscraper), get into a car parked at a nearby lot or garage, and reach many Lehigh Valley or New Jersey suburbs within minutes. For such a person, living near a downtown on the decline would make no sense; and, without appealing dining and entertainment in the business district, there would be no reason to linger in the area after business hours.

A special services district, the Downtown Improvement District Authority (DIDA), was created in 1986, well before the formation of the Center City District in Philadelphia. The Central Philadelphia Development Corporation leaders who organized the CCD during the period between 1985 and 1990 had studied the Allentown district as a model. The creation of the DIDA had been the brainchild of Donald Bernhard, the City's community development director at the time. After learning about the special services district concept and the ways in which it had been operationalized in other cities, Bernhard worked with state legislators to get enabling legislation approved in Pennsylvania, then organized a district plan for Allentown's downtown. In coordination with others, he proposed district boundaries, created a property assessment methodology, and drafted an operating budget. He spent a year selling the plan to the property owners who would be billed for the assessment, starting with the owners who would stand to pay the most.

After DIDA had obtained the required authorizations, formed a governing board, and recruited staff, the organization sponsored a variety of programs: sidewalk cleaning, downtown promotions, the marketing of properties located within the district, the deployment of extra police patrols, and the operation of a free shuttle bus that traveled from one end of the district to the other.[15]

From Bernhard's perspective, there were three keys to downtown success: security, maintenance and marketing.[16] During the early years of DIDA's existence, municipal government maintained a strong commitment to providing services in the downtown area. The City ran a street cleaner through the downtown streets and assigned a five-person foot patrol to cover the downtown area exclusively. At the time of DIDA's founding, Allentown's mayor had promised not to reduce the City's commitment to downtown maintenance and security. Later, however, the City reneged on its pledge; the foot patrol disappeared. Merchants complained about having to pay an assessment to the DIDA for services that the City should have been performing. "I have never been in a city where businesses were assessed extra to pay for things that should be given automatically by the city," the chairman of Hess's said at a 1994 meeting in City Hall. At the time, the department store was paying $900,000 in annual real estate taxes and was being assessed for an additional $38,000 annually by DIDA.[17]

The Center City District had been fortunate in that the organization started and grew during a period in which significant investment in Philadelphia's downtown was beginning to produce noticeable improvements. The opening of the new Pennsylvania Convention Center stimulated a wave of hotel development; the ten-year tax abatement generated large-scale residential development. DIDA's activities were not complemented by comparable signs of revitalization. The city's economic standing was not a source of encouragement either.

Disagreements between downtown property owners and the City over the assignment of responsibility for downtown security and maintenance were never resolved, and DIDA ceased operations in 2003.

The Rental Identity*

During the 1970s and 1980s, a small number of apartments in disrepair could be found in buildings within the residential neighborhoods adjacent to Hamilton Street. At the time, these problems were small-scale and containable. Most rental properties were locally-owned by individuals who were readily identifiable and could be contacted without difficulty. The number of owners who could be termed "slumlords"—owners of thirty to fifty rental units in poor condition—was very small. To respond to the problems as they had existed during the 1970s, the City had designated a three-block area within which city code inspectors visited every property to check for code violations. Housing rehabilitation loans and grants were made available to help finance the cost of code compliance or to encourage owners to upgrade and modernize.

* Most of the information and commentary in this section is based on communications with Eric D. Weiss, an Allentown resident who worked on housing preservation and development issues for the Allentown Redevelopment Authority and the City of Allentown from 1973 to 2007 and served as the Director of the City's Bureau of Building Safety and Standards from 1995 to 2007.

An expanded version of this program operated in the residential zone known as the "collar area" that surrounded the core of the retail district, then known as Hamilton Mall. At that time, rental housing maintenance problems were small enough and the federal funding was substantial enough to enable a city like Allentown to address rental property deterioration through a comprehensive approach of this kind, in which an effort was made to improve every property on a targeted block.

Rental property problems grew by orders of magnitude in the 1980s and 1990s, due to two factors: the conversion of single-family properties to multi-family use and the proliferation of absentee owners.

Single-to-multi-family conversions were nothing new in Allentown; they had been going on for decades. After World War Two, when soldiers returned to Allentown ready to start families, the city did not have enough housing available to accommodate them. Increasing the density of the existing housing stock by converting some single-family houses into two or three units was one way to address this housing shortage. By the 1980s, however, the scale of conversion had reached a critical mass. New housing development in former cornfields was attracting people whose families had lived in the city for years. The houses that they left—houses that had been maintained as single-family homes by successive generations of the same family for decades—were being broken up on a large scale.

During this time, the City routinely approved applications for single-to-multi-family conversions, and a large number of conversions were being completed without City approval. City inspectors visited properties undergoing conversion to review the renovation work, but they used as a guide the housing maintenance code—the code that establishes basic safety and maintenance standards for existing structures—rather than the more demanding building code that establishes standards for construction in a situation in which one type of use is being changed to another.

As a result of this combination of routinely-processed conversion applications and relatively undemanding inspections, a new generation of low-quality rental housing emerged. Conversion-project developers retained single heaters to serve multiple units, making lower-floor units too cold while upper-story apartments were boiling. Apartments were built without their own kitchens; a hot plate was deemed acceptable as a substitute. Bathroom facilities were inadequate for the number of people housed in a building. Firewalls were not constructed, nor were secondary exits, essential in a fire emergency. Overcrowding became a serious problem. Three or four families were living in houses that had been designed for one. Some families were living in basements or in garages that had been converted to apartments. As shown in Figure 10.2, the population of downtown-area census tracts was growing, but not in a way that was favorable to Allentown's economic and social well-being.

The City did not gain an awareness of the consequences of its actions until it was too late. By the late 1990s, rental units represented about 47 percent

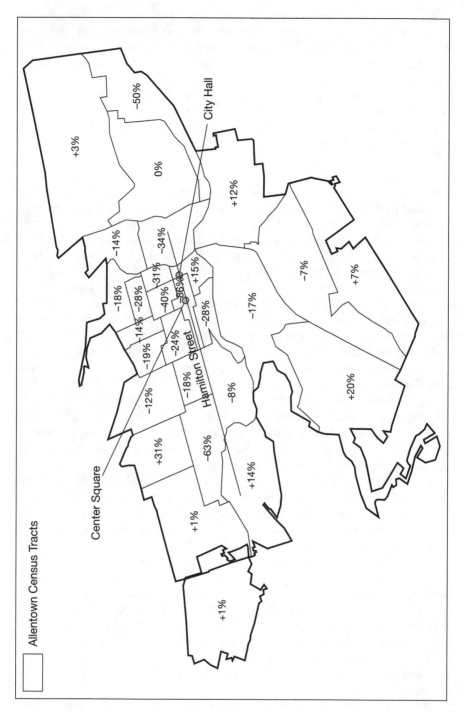

Figure 10.2 Changes in Owner Occupancy in Allentown Census Tracts, 1980–2000

Figure 10.3 Garage Conversion

of all housing units in the city, but these units were generating well over 80 percent of the total number of code-violation complaints received by the city. The vast majority of rental properties in the city were reasonably well-maintained; many of the most serious code violations were associated with fewer than a dozen bad landlords. However, the worst rental property owners had an enormous negative impact on the city, particularly in the downtown-area neighborhoods.

City interventions to address this situation had been proposed and rejected. During the 1980s, Ray Polaski, then head of Allentown's Bureau of Building Safety and Standards, recommended that the City adopt a program through which rental properties would be inspected on a regular basis for compliance with health and safety codes. A hearing to consider the proposal was held in City Council, and a group of investor-owners showed up to express their opposition. They were joined by the Mayor and the head of the Redevelopment Authority, both of whom endorsed the investor-owners' position. Supporters of the proposal were effectively intimidated, and the idea went no further.

The easy approval process for property conversions and the low cost of acquiring real estate in Allentown were two factors that made the city an attractive target for absentee owners. An equally important factor was the scarcity of affordable rental housing in the region. The build-out of suburban areas in the Lehigh Valley and elsewhere consisted primarily of homeowner housing; new construction of rental housing was relatively scarce. According to the Lehigh Valley Planning Commission, between 200 and 300 units of rental housing were built during each year of the 1990s, and much of this housing was restricted to "specialized" populations, such as the elderly. Of the 271 rental units constructed in 1998, for example, 217 were designed as housing for the elderly.[18]

For investors, Allentown represented an opportunity comparable to that offered by Camden, the "hidden gem," as *The Wall Street Journal* had characterized the latter: a city with low-cost real estate situated in the center of a high-cost region. In the years just before and just after the turn of the century, an ambitious investor could easily obtain financing to acquire property in such a city with the expectation of a highly profitable sale years later, as the urban real estate market began to catch up with that of the surrounding region.

These ambitions were fueled by promotions, heavily marketed through direct mail and television commercials, that were designed to encourage people with no previous experience to pursue wealth-building by acquiring real estate at mortgage and tax foreclosure sales, then pursuing investment strategies, the details of which were revealed in seminar sessions held at local hotels and in DVDs that could be purchased by calling a toll-free phone number or visiting a website. Properties could also be purchased, sight unseen, through Internet-facilitated transactions. In communications with Joseph Schilling, co-founder of the National Vacant Properties Campaign, I heard stories about investors who had come to grief as a result of their participation in web-facilitated real estate purchases. An investor in South Africa bought a Buffalo, NY property that had been advertised as "lakefront" but which turned out to be located several miles away from the Lake Erie shoreline. An out-of-town investor bought a house after viewing a photographic image of the front elevation that had been posted on a website. Upon visiting the property following his purchase, he found that the building consisted of little more than a front—the rear wall had collapsed. The purchaser of a property with the address "215A North 15th Street" traveled to North 15th Street but was unable to find a building with the same address as the property which he had bought. He eventually learned that 215A was nothing more than a garage in the rear of a house which he did not own.

As a result of the ease with which inexperienced people could enter into the rental real estate market toward the end of the twentieth century, the relatively small number of traditional local slumlords that could be found in Allentown was augmented by a much larger group of out-of-town investors. Many of the latter had an exclusively bottom-line orientation with little or no real estate asset management experience and little or no concern for the well-being of the residents of the properties they owned or the neighborhoods where these buildings were located. Increasingly, title to properties was passing from local owners and businesses to limited liability corporations with out-of-town post office box addresses. Many of the newer rental property owners were unacquainted with and disconnected from the day-to-day management of the properties they controlled. The practice of designating as "property manager" a tenant who, in exchange for a reduced rent, would take out trash bags on trash collection day or shovel the walk after it snowed but had no real property maintenance qualifications, became increasingly widespread.

The worst of these investor-owners were skilled in gaming the system. A shrewd investor owner will understand how long it will take the city to cite a property for a code violation and to refer a case of noncompliance for court action. A shrewd investor-owner will know how to plead hardship with a judge in order to get a fine reduced or dismissed altogether. A shrewd investor-owner will know how long it is possible to refrain from paying property taxes before the city initiates tax foreclosure sale; for example, if the policy of a particular city is to pursue tax foreclosure following two years of tax delinquency, then a property owner in that city can choose not to pay taxes for at least two years without losing title to the building. The worst instances of gaming the system were horror stories. Within days after his property had been declared unfit for human habitation and vacated, with the tenants moved to safer housing elsewhere, one investor-owner, in violation of an order to cease operations, began renting out the vacant apartments to new tenants, having taken no action to resolve the health and safety code violations.

Commenting on this situation, one city manager said, "We're trying to fix a twenty-first century problem with twentieth century tools." During the period between 1995 and 2007, city government and neighborhood constituencies in Allentown designed and implemented new tools for addressing what had been an increasingly severe problem in the city's downtown-area neighborhoods.

City-Citizen Initiatives

Thomas Burke was a chemical engineer who had moved to Allentown in 1979 to take a new job. He had previously resided exclusively in big cities; Allentown was the first city he had lived in that had no major-league sports team. He found Allentown to be safe and comfortable, with a good downtown and well-maintained neighborhoods that were convenient to work and shopping destinations.

As an Allentown resident who had come to the city from another place, Burke had a fresh perspective on the potential value of Allentown's residential communities. The city had well-established neighborhoods with smaller-sized, modest homes. These homes were conveniently located—you could walk from them to work, to shopping, to the bar, to church—and their value could grow. These homes and their neighborhoods could attract young first-time homebuyers who could not afford homes in the higher-priced suburban real estate market. The Allentown model—appealing, reasonably-priced houses in good neighborhoods—needed to be rejuvenated, not discarded; it wouldn't make sense to start tearing down blocks. Allentown needed to strengthen its position in the market and to prevent its housing from being bastardized.[19]

Burke and other residents had an opportunity to take action against the bastardization of homeowner-occupied housing during the mid-1990s. Earlier in that decade, Muhlenberg College had experienced a growth spurt, primarily influenced by the enrollment of the children of baby boomers. However, the college, which is located in the western section of the city, had not built enough housing on campus to accommodate the additional enrollment. As a result, Muhlenberg students were moving into nearby neighborhoods and causing problems—noise, litter, drunkenness, bad behavior—that disrupted the stability of the blocks where they lived.

In addition to the difficulties that this situation created for community residents, these disruptions generated a wave of complaints to the police, and the Police Department's need to respond to repeated complaints created a distraction from the Department's core responsibilities and generated an additional expense for the City. In March, 1996, for example, police arrested sixteen people (fourteen of them students) who were charged with sixty-one counts of underage drinking, disorderly conduct, and supplying minors with alcohol. According to the police, at least two hundred people were partying at and around the two-story home on North 22nd Street where the arrests were made.[20]

Neighborhood residents petitioned City Council members for help in dealing with the problem; Council members were unresponsive. The residents brainstormed the problem with sympathetic municipal planning and housing agency staff. Michael Hefele, the City's planning director, came up with a solution: amend the City's zoning code to designate a new zone within which occupancy of a single-family house by more than two unrelated persons would be prohibited (at the time, Allentown's unrelated-person maximum was four individuals). Legislation for the zone designation was drafted and presented to Council. Neighborhood residents lobbied resistant Council members to approve the measure. After two years of advocacy, between 1995 and 1997, they succeeded in getting the legislation passed. By that time, Muhlenberg had established limits to future enrollment and had developed additional on-campus dormitory beds. Although students were not entirely absent from neighborhood blocks following the approval of the zone designation, the combination of the cap on future enrollment, the development of on-campus housing, and the restrictions on the density of off-campus housing restored stability to blocks that had previously been overcrowded with students.

Although this experience took place outside of Allentown's downtown-area neighborhoods, it gave Burke and other residents an awareness of the impact that rental property management could have on community well-being, as well as experience in working with municipal agency staff to use public powers to address rental property problems.

During the time in which the Muhlenberg issue was being resolved, the City's Bureau of Building Safety and Standards, in which Allentown's code enforcement division was housed, was regularly writing letters to the City's appointed Zoning Board asking the Board to deny applications for property conversions. The staff appealed to Mayor William Heydt for support, and he got involved during his second term, between 1998 and 2001. Heydt was a Republican who happened to be a rental property owner, and he was not overly enthusiastic about imposing new regulations on private real estate market activity. Like a number of other city officials, Heydt was unaware that absentee ownership and neglect of rental properties had become a critical problem in the city's downtown-area neighborhoods. The bureau staff convinced him to accompany them on a tour of problem rental properties. They showed off examples of their toughest cases. One stop on the tour was a recently-vacated rental property at 10th and Tilghman Streets, a location just a few blocks north of Hamilton Street. The place had been ravaged by recently-departed tenants and was filled with trash. The Mayor's feet stuck to the floor as they walked through the empty rooms. One of the members of the tour group opened a closet door; inside was the skeleton of a cat. By the time the tour was over, the Mayor understood the need for more rigorous code enforcement and oversight.

The city administration organized a Rental Inspection Committee consisting of government, business, and community representatives, which was organized to pursue two goals: tougher code enforcement and deconversion of selected rental properties back to their original single-family status. Ross Marcus, the City's community development director, was at the center of the committee's activity, Marcus was a professional, not a political operative, who made the committee inclusive and kept its planning activities on track. Do you really want to get into this? Marcus had been asked—"this" meaning a revisiting of an initiative similar to the one that Ray Polaski had proposed in 1980—the one that had been met with a dead-on-arrival response in Council chambers. Marcus was undeterred, and the committee went to work.

Some of the community participants in the committee, like Thomas Burke, already had experience in working with those city staff members who were most concerned about rental property issues. Some of the committee members had worked together in an anti-gang task force. Patricia Engler, who referred to herself as the "token woman" on the committee, had been active in the 8th Ward Neighborhood Block Watch (Engler later ran successfully for election as a Magisterial District Justice). The committee agreed that the proposal should address both property conditions and tenant behavior. The committee agreed that its work would be guided by three principles: 1) all rental units should be inspected; 2) the City housing code should include a "disruptive tenant" provision (calling for the eviction of a tenant who is cited for repeated instances of disruptive behavior); and 3) the fee structure associated with rental inspections and permit issuance should generate enough revenue to pay for the cost of administration.

Eric Weiss of the Bureau helped the group calculate the time and cost variables associated with a citywide inspection program. A rental license would be issued to properties that passed inspection. Properties that remained out of compliance with city codes would not be approved for licenses (or their existing licenses would be revoked), and their owners would be forced to vacate the buildings. In this way, the threat of losing rental property income was expected to compel rental property owners to comply.

The committee decided that a five-year inspection cycle, with four thousand dwelling units inspected each year, would be feasible and that this system could be supported with a fee structure that would be viewed as reasonable: they decided to propose a rental property registration fee of ten dollars per unit. The committee members wanted to avoid antagonizing people by creating requirements that would be viewed as too oppressive, and they wanted to make the program simple and clear cut.

A disruptive conduct provision involving a three-strikes-you're-out approach had been successfully enacted in Bloomsburg, Pennsylvania and was subsequently upheld in court following a legal challenge (an incident requiring a visit to the tenant's rental unit by city police or codes staff would constitute a "strike"; three such incidents in a year would result in eviction). The committee reviewed the underlying municipal legislation and decided to replicate it in Allentown, using the precise wording of the Bloomsburg legislation in the hope that the Bloomsburg precedent would help supporters of the Allentown legislation defend it against a possible challenge by investor owners.

Ross Marcus worked on the proposal at home in his spare time and, during 1997, drafted a proposed ordinance in coordination with Thomas Burke. Ross and Burke shared common qualities of thoroughness and attention to detail. Burke's attentiveness to record-keeping and his well-organized newspaper clipping file proved to be especially useful.

The proposal was aired in public meetings and was well received. Different community constituencies responded positively to the proposal for different reasons: negligent property owners would be punished; bad tenants would be evicted; the law would be enforced; neighborhood stability would be achieved and upheld. Good landlords supported the proposal; passing the city inspection would be, in effect, a seal of approval—independent certification that their rental units were of good quality. In their presentations of the proposal, the committee members found it particularly advantageous to be able to say that the fee and penalty revenue generated by the inspection program would fund program costs; not one dollar would need to be spent by taxpayers other than the rental property owners themselves.

Obtaining City Council support was another matter. A provision of the home rule charter adopted by the city's voters in 1996 provided that the approval of six out of seven City Council members was required in connection with the imposition of any new taxes, levies, or other charges. One of the Council members who opposed the proposed ordinance was the owner of two rental properties that had accumulated numerous code violations. One of her properties had been cited for exposed wires, rotted window frames and sills, dormers that leaked rainwater, peeling paint, missing siding, and deteriorated brickwork on the chimney. The other property, which in 1997 was occupied by a family of six adults, had been cited for an unsound ceiling in a stairwell, loose electrical wiring in a ceiling, a front porch in need of repair, a missing smoke detector, and the absence of fire doors on the first floor.[21]

During the fall of 1997, supporters of the legislation worked to get a bill presented to City Council early enough to compel Council to act upon it prior to the November election, so that Council members would have to make known their positions on the measure before Election Day. This expectation was premature. During the course of a two-hour hearing before Council's Community Development Committee on October 13, it became clear that existing language would need to be substantially revised or new language drafted in order to resolve ambiguities and inconsistencies in the text of the bill as originally proposed. The bill was tabled.

Over the next half-year, Ross Marcus worked with a committee of landlords, tenants, community organization representatives, and city officials on a redrafting of the bill. A Community Development Committee hearing on the redrafted bill brought a large number of community members, as well as a small group of landlords who opposed the bill. "You can legislate and legislate and legislate," one of them said, "But the focus is, you have to enforce the laws [against criminal behavior] we have." Another landlord questioned the constitutionality of being required to allow inspectors to enter rental properties without a search warrant.[22]

Additional questions were raised, discussed, and resolved during the spring and summer of 1998; but Council was not ready to act on the redrafted bill. A landlords group, represented by legal counsel, had been organized and had declared its intent to take legal action against the bill if it was approved. The chair of the Community Development Committee reported that each Council member had at least one unresolved problem with the bill and that one district justice had problems with the language of the bill as well (district justices are the local magistrates before whom cases associated with the legislation would be prosecuted). Some key supporters of the bill agreed that it would be preferable to seek a resolution of outstanding issues rather than press for approval of legislation that would immediately be litigated.[23]

Anxious to have a program in place by January, 1999, city officials and other supporters of the legislation began to consider the prospects for a compromise. In September, 1998, a new version of the bill was presented. The provision for citywide rental property inspections was dropped. Instead, the new bill called for a rental unit to be inspected by the city only after being vacated by the tenant. The landlords' group expressed support for this "compromise" legislation, but the measure was still not satisfactory to some Council members, including the Council President, who felt that the proposed inspection requirement and inspection fee would amount to a punishment of good landlords. In a vote on October 21, the bill failed to obtain the required six of seven votes; the Council President and the Council member who owned the unfit properties voted against it.[24]

The organizers of the rental property legislation proposal began pursuit of a strategy that had been discussed during the previous months of delay: end-running Council by bringing the legislation before the city's voters in a referendum. Mayor Heydt, who had consistently supported the rental property inspection legislation in its original form, pledged his support for a referendum initiative.[25]

The enactment of legislation by voter referendum was a provision of the city's new home rule charter, and the rental inspection referendum would be the first referendum initiative to be pursued based on this provision. Thomas Burke spearheaded the referendum campaign, organizing a city-wide effort to obtain two thousand signatures on petitions in support of the referendum within sixty-five days. "We feel we can beat this time line easily," Burke told a reporter. "We think we can do this in half the time." Town watch organizations and civic associations participated in the petition drive. Patricia Engler recruited volunteers. Current and former Council members joined Mayor Heydt in endorsing the campaign.[26]

Sensing that voter-mandated legislation would produce a rental inspection program more stringent than the compromise measure that Council had just rejected, the Council President called for the compromise bill to be reconsidered, and the bill was approved by Council on November 4, 1998. By this time, however, it was too late. Referendum organizers had decided a week earlier to press ahead with the initiative regardless of what action City Council might take. They understood that the compromise measure would not solve the problems that had brought them together to pursue a common goal: effective government intervention against negligent rental property owners and disruptive tenants. Eric Weiss characterized the compromise measure as "toothless":

> City inspectors would have no way of knowing when a unit was going to be vacated, and the worst landlords wouldn't let them know. And, even in cases in which the City was notified that a unit had been vacated, the inspection wouldn't produce a safe living environment because the scope of the inspection would be limited to the vacant unit and common areas such as hallways and stairways—a meth lab could be operating in the unit right across the hall.[27]

The referendum organizers had anticipated that it would be advantageous to conduct the petition drive during a period that included the November

Election Day, so that signatures could be solicited by volunteers in front of polling places. The plan succeeded. After only a week of campaigning, the petition drive organizers had collected almost all of the signatures they needed.

Mayor Heydt had mistakenly thought that the referendum strategy would be dropped once Council passed the compromise legislation, but the referendum supporters were not going to consider doing so. Burke termed the compromise measure "scammable." "The bill provides a lot of loopholes for the bad landlords," he said. "The good landlords are going to abide by the law no matter what passes. The good landlords will be better off under the initiative."[28]

The referendum question supported by the petitioners read as follows:

> Should the city of Allentown amend its property rehabilitation and maintenance code to start a program requiring the systematic inspection of all rental units to assure compliance with city codes and requiring tenants to conduct themselves in a manner that will not disturb the peaceful enjoyment of the premises or neighboring properties by others, to be funded by an annual fee on each unit?

The landlords whose opposition to the earlier bill had led to the compromise legislation suggested that, if the referendum initiative proved successful, they would take legal action to block implementation of the resulting rental property inspection program. One representative of the landlords' group suggested that, as an alternative to the proposed legislation, the City should raise taxes to pay for more code enforcement inspectors.[29]

The referendum supporters submitted petitions with 2,700 signatures in time to meet the deadline. Because the city's home rule charter gave City Council the ability to act in lieu of a referendum by legislatively approving a measure that had been supported by enough petition signatures to qualify for a referendum, Council scheduled a vote on the referendum supporters' measure on January 20, 1999; the measure again failed to receive the required number of votes.

In March, 1999, a landlords' group took legal action to block the referendum, based on a claim that the initiative violated state election laws and the constitutional rights of landlords. A County Court judge ruled against the group. The group appealed to Commonwealth Court. At the end of April, a Commonwealth Court judge upheld the County Court's ruling.[30]

Referendum supporters organized Neighbors for Rental Inspections and funded a $3,868 war chest. Hundreds of red-and-white "Vote Yes" signs appeared in front yards all over the city. The initiative was publicized in neighborhood meetings and promoted in civic group newsletters. On the May 19 primary election day, the measure passed, with more than 80 percent of the voters casting yes votes. "Eighty to twenty! Nobody gets eighty to twenty!" exclaimed Thomas Burke, who said that supporters had been hoping for a 60 to 40 percent result as the best possible outcome. "I was surprised that it was so lopsided," commented one of the landlords who had opposed the referendum.[31]

The City was ready to implement. After the referendum passed, the Bureau of Building Safety and Standards divided Allentown into five inspection districts. Six inspectors were assigned to cover the city; each one could complete about 670 inspections resulting in code compliance each year.

During the first cycle of citywide inspections, several kinds of problems were found to recur in many properties: lack of a second means of exiting the building; inadequate kitchen or bathroom facilities; additional units constructed without obtaining City approvals. The inspectors checked owner documentation as well. They learned that a particular practice had become widespread: an owner would list a post office box or the rental property address as the owner's address, in violation of local regulations that required the listing of a true address. In many instances, tenants had no idea who the owner was; they just mailed a monthly check to a post office box, often at an out-of-state location.

The first citywide inspection cycle was expected to be completed in five years; it took eight years to get done. The number of problems that were uncovered and the time it took to resolve them had been underestimated. The second cycle, begun in 2008, was much easier to manage. Most major health and safety problems had been addressed during the first cycle, and relatively few new problems were emerging.

Fine Tuning

Mayor Ed Pawlowski contacted me in 2006 to ask the Fels Institute to design a housing strategy for Allentown. I visited the city a short time later and participated in a wide-ranging discussion with a roomful of planning and development agency staff people. Several follow-up meetings were scheduled with department heads and smaller groups of staff. At first, I had a hard time understanding what the scope of a housing strategy for the city might be. Allentown had a capable planning division, and its staff had worked with community organizations to complete plans for strategically important neighborhoods. Unlike most of the cities in which I had worked, Allentown had very few vacant properties; there was no need to design a vacant property investment strategy. The city was competing successfully for federal and state funding to support housing development ventures that, when completed, would bring substantial new value to the city. The basic elements of an investment strategy—the kind of strategy that most postindustrial cities need most—seemed to be in place. After several more meetings, however, I gained an appreciation for Allentown's unique situation: what the city needed was a housing asset management strategy that focused on preserving and upgrading the quality of existing occupied housing; and the place where this strategy needed to be implemented first was not a neighborhood area, but City Hall.

When I came to Allentown in 2006, William Heydt, the mayor who had strongly backed the rental housing inspection referendum, had been gone for five years. Roy C. Afflerbach had succeeded Heydt as mayor in 2002. Although Afflerbach had been a well-regarded state legislator during the years prior to his election, he proved to be a disaster as mayor. His administration had prepared a 2004 budget that was later found to have been based on inaccurate data and unwarranted assumptions. As a result, a 2004 budget surplus projection had to be revised; the corrected version of the budget, completed after an audit, revealed a $1.3 million funding shortfall. Quarrels over tax increase and layoff proposals ensued, and disharmony continued through to the end of Afflerbach's first and only term.

Pawlowski had been director of the Alliance for Building Communities, a regional nonprofit housing development corporation that had been successful in financing and developing affordable housing in the Lehigh Valley. In 2002, Afflerbach hired Pawlowski as the City's economic development director, in an expanded role that included supervision of city housing, recreation, and parks agencies. Pawlowski made reinvestment in the downtown area a high priority, and he had worked to bring new development and increased public sector investment into the business district. After three years, Afflerbach and Pawlowski had a falling out over Afflerbach's plans to lay off twenty-eight of Pawlowski's staff in order to balance the city budget, and Pawlowski resigned. A little more than a year later, Pawlowski took office as Mayor.

Pawlowski was a hands-on mayor, like Stephen Reed of Harrisburg; he didn't just make policy; he got directly involved in implementing it. The common wisdom is that mayors should avoid involving themselves in operational issues; however, in small cities, where money is particularly scarce and staff capability is likely to be limited, mayoral intervention can be one way to ensure that priorities are being addressed. A major drawback associated with a hands-on mayor, however, is that the mayor cannot manage every department; as a result, some departments end up waiting longer than they should in order to get the mayor's attention and other departments move slower than they should because the people who manage them get accustomed to having the mayor review and approve decisions they should be making. In a small city strapped for cash, there is no way to achieve an absolutely perfect balance between delegation of authority and hands-on management.

Although Allentown's citywide rental inspection program was being implemented successfully, the city's ability to address rental housing problems was weakening because not enough action was being taken on related fronts.

Even the best citywide rental property inspection program, by itself, will not be sufficient to bring about the preservation and improvement of a city's rental housing assets.

During 2007, I worked with Eric Weiss and Karen Beck Pooley (who would be appointed Executive Director of the Allentown Redevelopment Authority that year) to organize a housing asset management strategy which would both incorporate and complement the housing inspection program.

Local Agent

Many cities require absentee rental property owners to designate a "local agent" or "responsible agent"—in many instances a real estate broker or an attorney with offices in the county where the property is located—who will be, in effect, a local representative of the owner. However, in many instances, the local agent has no responsibility other than to serve as a local address and to accept a judicial summons, if and when one is issued. Allentown's local agent policy is much more stringent: the local agent is defined as equal in status to the owner with respect to responsibility for the condition of the rental property. This legal exposure increases the likelihood that code violations will be corrected before fines and penalties are imposed.

Point of Sale Inspections

Because the number of real estate transactions involving absentee owners was continuing to grow, a more proactive approach to property inspection was needed to reinforce the citywide inspection cycle. The approach adopted in Allentown was a requirement that all residential property transactions (for both sales as well as rental housing) be preceded by a city inspection and, if significant health and safety code violations are identified, by the correction of these violations as a condition of sale. This requirement, authorized through the approval of a City Council ordinance, was intended to stop properties with major code violations from being transferred from one owner to another without improvement. The requirement for a satisfactory inspection imposes pressure on the seller and gives leveraging power to the buyer, who may agree to finance the improvements in exchange for a lowering of the purchase price.

Implementation of the pre-sale inspection policy began in February 2008. As of mid-April, about a hundred homeowner properties and fifty-five rental properties had been inspected. Most of the sellers of the homeowner properties addressed the code violations identified in the city inspection reports and were issued certificates of occupancy. Two homeowner properties were found to be unfit for human habitation. Some of the rental properties were cited for violations that were significant but relatively easy to correct, such as the replacement of missing smoke detectors.

Blighted Property Review Committee

Under Karen Beck Pooley's administration, the Redevelopment Authority revived Allentown's Blighted Property Review Committee (known as the Vacant Property Review Committee in some cities). The Committee's function is to serve as a last resort for addressing the most serious cases of noncompliance with city codes. For buildings in the worst condition, the Committee recommends government intervention (meaning, in Allentown, the use of eminent domain powers by the Redevelopment Authority) to take ownership of the property.

The Committee and the city agencies with which it interacts operate on a yearlong cycle. A city inspector finds serious fire code violations at a rental property, and the inspector issues an order directing the owner to correct the violations immediately. The owner is unresponsive. The City declares the property unfit for human habitation, and the tenants are relocated to other housing. At this point, the City continues to use available leverage to try to compel the owner to fix up the property and return it to occupancy. At the same time, the Committee is listing the property for possible acquisition, and initial steps leading to eminent domain acquisition are being completed. If satisfactory results have not been achieved by the end of the year, a declaration of taking is issued, and the Redevelopment Authority takes ownership of the property. The Authority issues a Request For Proposals, and competitive proposals submitted by nonprofit and for-profit housing developers are reviewed and ranked. A developer is selected for each property. The property is conveyed by the Authority to the developer, then rehabilitated and sold for homeowner-occupancy. In this way, some of the city's worst rental properties are cycled back into the homeowner housing inventory.

In March 2008, Allentown's Blighted Property Review Committee listed twenty-eight properties as possible candidates for acquisition. Within six months, the owners of ten of them had been convinced to complete rehabilitation work themselves, and the rehabilitation was under way or done. Based on communications with the owners during this period, it was clear to Pooley that a number of them were undertaking rehabilitation only because they had realized that the City was getting serious about taking their properties by the end of the year. This experience demonstrates the value of a Blighted Property Review Committee: the Committee's actions get at the core of the property owner's self-interest—the ability to continue to maintain ownership of the real estate.

A city requirement that rental properties be licensed gets at owner self-interest in a similar manner, because the revocation of the rental license puts a stop to the owner's ability to operate a property as income-generating rental housing; if the license is revoked, the property has to be vacated. The City of Allentown had required rental property licensure for many years, but, during the time when I began working on the housing strategy, no one was closely monitoring the extent to which licenses were being renewed and renewal fees were being paid (or not paid). To address this situation, a threatening "30 Day Residential Rental Revocation Notice" was sent to rental property owners whose rental license renewal fees or water and sewer bills had not been paid. Within a few months, the City was $175,000 richer.

With the help of Weiss and Pooley, I packaged the above and other strategy elements in a report with a bluntly-worded introduction:

> This publication describes a framework for the asset-management strategy that Allentown's central city neighborhoods desperately need. If all of the elements of this strategy are adopted and implemented, conditions in the city's downtown-area neighborhoods and the central business district will improve, generating significant economic benefit to the city, county, and region. Without a constructive, wide-ranging asset management approach, conditions in Allentown's core neighborhoods will continue to deteriorate.[32]

The report attracted the Mayor's attention. He directed staff to begin implementing the recommendations before the report was made public. On the official release date in November 2007, he stated that "Establishing a synergy between the business district and the neighborhoods is not an option, it is a necessity. Our housing issues have been a long time in the making. They are not going to be resolved by sitting still."

Allentown's experience provides a good illustration of the need for cities to do everything together with respect to housing asset management—to put multiple strategy elements into play in order to achieve improvements at a higher order of magnitude than is possible by simply reacting to individual housing maintenance problems on a case-by-case basis. Especially noteworthy are the facts that Allentown's approach required no new state legislation and no new funding. The strategy elements were implemented administratively or through the approval of local legislation, and the revenue generated through fees, fines, and penalties supported the cost of the new program initiatives.

Equally important was the interaction that took place between local government agency staff and community members to achieve a major reform: the institution of citywide rental property inspections. This interaction took place at a time when residents of the city were demoralized by the abandonment of Allentown's previously thriving downtown area. The referendum initiative created a foundation for rebuilding and repopulating downtown-area neighborhoods in future years, for achieving the rejuvenation of these areas that Thomas Burke had envisioned. By building on this foundation, Allentown could attract suburbanites as well as former big-city residents like Burke, who could find in Allentown's neighborhoods places to call home.

11 The Future of Reinvestment

The Death of Urban Renewal

Unable to contain himself, Augustine Salvitti sprang from his chair, circled the desk, and tugged Mark Dichter's shirtsleeve. "Come here for a minute—look at this," he said. He swept aside a curtain, revealing a bank of windows, knee- to ceiling-height. Market Street was seven stories below. One hand squeezed Dichter's shoulder, the other gestured at the Gallery complex a few blocks away, its glass skin glistening in the afternoon sun. The Gallery: a newly completed, enclosed mall containing 125 shops linked to parking and two subway stops, the Philadelphia Redevelopment Authority's trophy project of the 1970s.

"You see that?" he said. "What you're looking at is the death of urban renewal!"

It was 1977. Salvitti was Executive Director of the Redevelopment Authority, an appointee of Mayor Frank L. Rizzo. Dichter was board chair of the Washington Square West Project Area Committee (PAC), a nonprofit, neighborhood-based group organized to represent the interests of community members in a twenty-five-square block Center City neighborhood located south of the business district. Earlier in the decade, the RDA had used federal Title I funding and eminent domain powers to acquire a fifth of Washington Square West's land area: empty houses with tinned-up windows, empty lots bordered by waist-high wooden posts planted by the RDA maintenance crew to discourage short-dumping, as well as occupied businesses and residences—the latter mostly apartment buildings and boarding homes.

The PAC supported eminent domain. The PAC wanted the RDA to continue to use eminent domain in order to finish the job of property acquisition and land assembly in Washington Square West during the remainder of the 1970s, just as it had during the 1960s in the adjacent Society Hill neighborhood, also known as the Washington Square East Urban Renewal Area. In Society Hill, a National Register Historic District, the RDA had acquired and demolished buildings, including garages, warehouses, sheds, and some housing—everything that had been deemed unsalvageable or inconsistent with the City-approved urban renewal plan for the area—in order to create a favorable environment for reinvestment.

Then, for every building that remained, the RDA or its affiliates wrote up individual rehabilitation specifications: remove permastone siding, restore cornice, scrape and repaint window and door trim, point all brickwork. Current owners, or the redevelopers that the RDA selected to replace them, could obtain financing to complete the specified work. A cycle of government-driven reinvestment ensued, based on RDA-approved redevelopment goals and land use designations. Some properties were acquired, emptied of their residents and businesses, and demolished for new construction. Other properties —primarily historically noteworthy, brick-fronted townhouses, were restored per the work write-ups. The result: a revitalized neighborhood, with every property newly built or fully rehabilitated based on RDA improvement standards. By 1977, the transformation of Society Hill from flophouse and fleabag district to upper-class community was almost complete.

The representatives of the PAC wanted the RDA to finish the job of acquiring, developing, and revitalizing in Washington Square West as well. A lot of large-scale acquisition had been completed earlier in the decade. More recently, however, acquisition had slowed or stopped, as the RDA refrained from exercising eminent domain powers to take many of the properties originally included on the "To Be Acquired" list in the published urban renewal plan for the area. The un-acquired properties included leading neighborhood nuisances: rundown bars and clubs on the seedy Locust Street Strip, for example; or Meade's Warehouse, a historic nineteenth-century schoolhouse building, now marginally maintained as a furniture-filled fire-trap. The PAC was not in favor of large-scale displacement similar to that which had occurred in Society Hill. In fact, the PAC had successfully lobbied the RDA to develop subsidized housing for residents who were to be forced out of RDA-acquired properties. But the PAC also wanted the RDA to fully implement the urban renewal plan, as it had in Society Hill. The PAC viewed full implementation as an obligation—a moral obligation, some PAC members would say—to the community.

"The death of urban renewal." Translation: the rules have changed; the money is spent; the show is ending. A few years earlier, the Housing and Community Development Act of 1974 had been approved by Congress, superseding the Housing Act of 1949. The Housing and Community Development Act folded Title I and a group of other federal programs into a single annual payment of funding from HUD to cities such as Philadelphia: the Community Development Block Grant (CDBG). Previously, the federal government had required the targeting of Title I funding to designated urban renewal areas, to support reinvestment in an approach that some termed "surgical": cut out the blight and replace it with new development. In contrast, CDBG had citywide applicability. Unlike the Title I funding that it replaced, the new CDBG funding could be spent for eligible activities in many census tracts that met federal income eligibility requirements.

The good news: with CDBG, a municipal government had more flexibility to adopt a broader approach in allocating funds for a variety of activities, from demolition to housing preservation to new development. The bad news: no more explicit or implied federal commitment to finish a designated urban renewal area in the way that Society Hill had been finished. More bad news: less federal funding available overall. No requirement—moral obligation or otherwise—to seize the vacated former Locust Street bar previously known as the Bucket of Blood. No guarantee that public powers would be used to take the old schoolhouse from the curmudgeonly, walrus-mustached Phineas Meade, who at that moment was probably seated at the bar at Dirty Frank's, a block and a half down Pine Street.

"The death of urban renewal." After the completion of the Gallery, in Salvitti's view, the curtain falls. After the Gallery, everything becomes small-scale and piecemeal.

Glued to a brick sitting at the center of Salvitti's desk was a little plaque engraved with a name, Deck Tavern, and a mid-1970s date. On that date, the RDA, victorious after a failed attempt by community members to obtain a court injunction, had demolished the Deck Tavern, along with a row of stores and eateries on the 3400 block of Walnut Street, located within the University City Urban Renewal Area. The RDA planned to replace the old retail properties, popular attractions for Penn students from the campus across the street, with a modern office building.

For Salvitti, the brick symbolized his ability to exercise his will, to use his powers, in the face of public opposition: I took over the block. I tore the buildings down. Salvitti's generation of leadership in urban development was the generation of white-shirted, white men in charge, men like Robert Moses, Edward Logue, and Edmund Bacon. They had been inspired, determined, resolute. Their era was ending. The Housing and Community Development Act of 1974 did not affect their ability to use eminent domain to take land, but their powers were weakening for other reasons: reduced public capital, better organized community opposition, and less ability to control the local government apparatus, as a new crop of elected officials and agency managers began to learn how to bridle their authority.

The white men in charge could be inflexible and arrogant as well as inspired and constructive. As head of the Philadelphia City Planning Commission for two decades after World War Two, Edmund Bacon designed redevelopment plans that were faithful to the formula of that era: acquire, relocate, demolish, rebuild. But Ed Bacon also marshaled public support for an inspired plan to revitalize Center City. He designed the preservation-oriented plan for Society Hill. Ed Bacon was an imaginative, independent-thinking, sometimes arrogant, creative giant. Salvitti, proudly displaying his brick, was a pugnacious munchkin.

Salvitti left the Redevelopment Authority and was replaced by a longtime RDA senior staff member, who was in turn replaced a few years afterward by an administrator from New York. Salvitti was later convicted of having taken a $27,500 kickback in an RDA land transaction and of having extorted $21,000 from an engineering firm that did business with the Authority.[1]

He served time in jail. The desk that occupied the center of his office—a big semicircular slab of wood that resembled half a cross-section of a giant tree trunk—remained for successive RDA executive directors to occupy. But the brick was gone.

A State of Unreadiness

This book describes urban revitalization strategies that were launched during a period of more than three decades that followed the mid-1970s moment that Salvitti had referred to as the death of urban renewal. Within this period, federal aid to cities declined dramatically. During the administrations of Ronald Reagan and George H. W. Bush, for example, the Community Development Block Grant allocation for Philadelphia dropped from $112,000 million to $52,000 million (expressed in 1992 dollars). Government-supported hospitals shut their doors. The Philadelphia General Hospital closed in 1977; the closing of the Philadelphia State Hospital was announced in 1987. As part of the implementation of court-mandated "deinstitution-alization" strategies, many chronically mentally ill people were moved from hospitals into urban neighborhoods, often without sufficient access to supportive services. During this period, homelessness emerged as a significant, highly visible problem in central cities.

Due to federally-imposed moratoriums on subsidized housing construction, little or no large-scale, government-financed affordable housing construction took place in most cities until the last decade of the century. Many development sites that had been acquired and cleared of buildings with Title I financing remained vacant for decades.

An anti–urban renewal backlash reached full strength during the 1960s and early 1970s.[2] In response, many cities stopped using eminent domain to acquire property in neighborhoods. Some cities, like Philadelphia, resumed the use of eminent domain on a more selective basis during the late 1980s and early 1990s, while other cities discontinued its use in neighborhoods altogether.

Welfare reform policies were enacted during the 1990s, and the number of recipients of public assistance declined substantially; however, both the poverty rate and the number of people in poverty rose during the early years of the next decade, from 11.3 percent and 31.6 million in 2000 to 12.7 percent and 37.0 million in 2004.[3]

To accompany changing community development challenges and opportunities, community-development buzzwords changed too. The term "anti-poverty" began to fade during the 1970s, as the Nixon Administration dismantled Great Society program infrastructure. The Philadelphia Anti-Poverty Action Committee, formed by mayoral executive order in 1965, was renamed the Philadelphia Allied Action Commission in 1978. "Low-income housing" was replaced by "affordable housing," then by "workforce housing" wherever possible. The Pennsylvania Low-Income Housing Coalition was renamed the Housing Alliance of Pennsylvania. For housing activists, older terms such as "social justice" made way for newer terms such as "regional equity." Terms such as "holistic plans" and "welfare rights" became archaic. The influence of Michael Porter and others was evident in the increased use of the term "market-driven." As the twentieth century ended, activities that had previously been known as "plans," "projects," or "programs" were now called "investment strategies." As the power of data bases and digital mapping to inform policymaking and strategic planning grew, the use of the adjective "data-driven" grew as well. The word "sustainability," a term for which smart growth, affordable housing, workforce development, and historic preservation advocates could all claim parentage, featured prominently in many dialogues.

City governments have adopted the buzzwords of the post-urban renewal era, but, to a great extent, have not organized themselves effectively to establish a new model for urban reinvestment that will produce big successes during the coming decades. Because there will never be enough public funding to satisfactorily address even the most pressing urban priorities, even the most highly efficient administration of available government funding programs, by itself, will not be sufficient to address fundamental problems affecting urban downtowns and neighborhoods. A government that is honest, well-managed, and transparent will probably do well in performing basic city services such as trash collection and snow removal, but these positive qualities, by themselves, will not be enough to ensure success in revitalization.

Below are ten ways in which many city governments are unprepared to address the challenges and opportunities associated with twenty-first-century reinvestment:

Information

1. *Inventory.* Is the number of vacant houses in the city larger or smaller than it was last year, or five years ago? How many vacant lots that were transferred from a government agency or sold at foreclosure sale have been built on or improved, and how many are still vacant? Most city governments don't know the answers to these questions because they don't have an up-to-date vacant property inventory. In some cities, the vacant properties have never been counted; no one knows whether the number of vacant buildings and lots is increasing, decreasing, or remaining the same. This basic information is essential to assessing the strengths and weaknesses of neighborhood real estate markets and to evaluating the performance of government programs.

2. *Data.* Through their municipal governments, taxpayers own a wealth of information about real estate, and access to this information is an essential resource for downtown and neighborhood strategic planning. Public real estate records include information about property dimensions, zoning, building size and characteristics, owner name, last sale date and price, property tax assessment, annual tax bill, tax delinquency, number and type of code

violations and associated fines, and utility bill delinquency, utility service shutoff history, and the number of children enrolled in public schools who are living at a particular address. However, to my knowledge, there is not a single municipal government that makes all of these public records accessible to citizens through the Internet in an address-specific form. Some cities provide some of this information, but not all; other cities limit access to this information to "authorized users," despite the fact that any citizen is entitled to obtain it.

Organizing a consolidated data base to which public agency records that contain this data are downloaded periodically and making this data base accessible via the Internet is not a complex or costly project; it is a medium-sized administrative challenge. The records identified above are located within different divisions of municipal government, county government, and the public school system; the people responsible for maintaining these records simply have to agree to download them into a secure, accessible data warehouse that is operated by a government agency or an academic institutions.[4]

The value of providing broader access to this information is widespread. Prospective investors and developers as well as administrators, planners, and program managers would benefit from access to it. This information is a key element of asset management, without which local planning and program management will be inadequate.

3. *Outcomes Analysis*. What happened to the houses that were equipped with new heaters five years ago through the city's emergency repair grant program—are they all still occupied? Where did the buyers for the fifty new city-subsidized townhouses come from—did they previously live in deteriorated housing on distressed blocks, or had they lived in good housing on stable blocks? In either case, what happened to the housing that they left? Was it reoccupied or did it remain vacant? In a survey of a sample of buyers of the West Poplar townhouses, 46 percent of the respondents indicated that they would have remained on the blocks where they had previously lived if an opportunity to buy homes there had been available.[5] Based on this finding, should some of the funding that had been committed to West Poplar have been used to reinforce these already stable blocks? Information of this kind is needed to assess the results of past investment decisions, to guide future investment plans, and to assess performance management.

Investment Strategies

4. *Homeownership*. Elected officials, government administrators, and private and nonprofit developers have, in large part, overemphasized the value of homeownership to urban neighborhoods. Homeowners, it is implied, are superior to renters, because they have a stake in the community, in the form of the house that belongs to them. While employing this rhetoric, many advocates for homeownership have been working to do as much as possible

to reduce to an absolute minimum the value that really is at stake for a government-assisted homebuyer. How much of a stake in the community does a homebuyer have if he or she has obtained a no-down-payment mortgage, has received a government grant to pay mortgage closing costs, or is being permitted to use Section 8 funding to make monthly mortgage payments? Few city governments publish guidance on the minimum income necessary for homeownership—the minimum level of household income needed to pay the mortgage, the utility bills, and the inevitable maintenance and repair expenses. Based on an outcomes analysis of the successes and failures associated with city homeownership programs in past years, municipal government agencies should establish and enforce realistic threshold criteria that can be used to determine readiness for homeownership.

5. *Rental Housing.* The federally-authorized Low Income Housing Tax Credit finances well-designed, strategically located, high-quality rental housing at a very high cost per unit. In some cities, the latter can be $150,000 to $200,000 or more. Funding in this amount would be more than adequate to pay for a rental-assistance subsidy for as many as fifteen to twenty years, without the developer fees, legal fees, and syndication fees associated with Tax Credit financing. Cities need to find better ways to make more rental housing available at lower cost. Relatively few cities have organized efficient, cost-effective programs for doing so.

6. *Workforce Housing.* Job training program providers have indicated that, next to child care, housing is the most important issue facing recently-hired graduates of workforce development programs.[6] However, city governments generally do not make a special effort to provide housing assistance for new jobholders who have graduated from workforce development programs. This linkage should become one of a city's highest reinvestment priorities, in light of the need to help more residents move into positions in the regional mainstream economy.

7. *Return on Investment.* Few city government programs have adopted on a house-specific level a mechanism similar to the "clawback" provision included in some tax increment financing deals, which provides for accelerated repayment of indebtedness in the event that a development venture proves to be significantly more financially successful than had been projected. In many cities, the buyer of a house financed with a government subsidy is required to pay back a prorated portion of the subsidy if the house is sold within a certain period (often ten years). However, if the buyer resells after the mandated occupancy period expires (eleven years after purchasing the property, for example), the city usually does not share in the proceeds of sale; in most city housing programs, no subsidy payback is required at all. Given the scarcity of public funding and the likelihood that subsidy funds will continue to be in short supply, it is surprising that local governments have

not done more to recapture and recycle available funding upon the sale of a property or the death of the owner.

Business Practices

8. *Foreclosure Auctions.* As described in Chapter Five, during the period in which the Neighborhood Transformation Initiative was being implemented, Philadelphia's city administration did not make an attempt to influence the tax and mortgage foreclosure process through which a property is sold to the highest bidder with no consideration given to the latter's intent or ability to develop the property in a manner consistent with city and neighborhood strategic planning goals. Many city governments do not bid on tax and foreclosure auction properties located in neighborhoods that have been targeted for revitalization, nor have they secured a right of first refusal that would give them the power to withhold such properties from auction. Because thousands of properties may be conveyed through these auctions during the course of a typical year, the need for a city administration to influence this process in support of the public interest is critical.

9. *Rental Housing Asset Management.* Although more cities are becoming aware of the need to adopt a rental housing asset management strategy similar to Allentown's, many are not doing so quickly enough or well enough. A city that does not have a pre-sale inspection ordinance, a citywide rental property inspection cycle, and a "responsible agent" requirement that exposes the agent to legal liability for problems associated with the rental property is not doing enough to preserve its rental housing resources and defend neighborhoods against negligent investor-owners.

10. *Economic Inclusion.* Cities have done their best to mandate, through the enactment of local legislation and the issuance of executive orders, that recipients of development financing maximize opportunities for contracting for services with and purchasing supplies from minority and neighborhood-based businesses. However, these mandates are often implemented through a government agency that focuses almost exclusively on oversight, performance monitoring and enforcement. Inevitably, this approach produces results that fall far short of expectations, and new legislation, a new executive order, or a reorganization of the implementing agency is called for. The cycle repeats itself, with little benefit to anyone.

The reason why this approach fails is because the government mandate is not linked to a business services program that is designed specifically to help small minority and neighborhood contractors develop the capability to bid competitively on city contracting and vending opportunities. A program of this kind should be designed by employers and service providers, in concert with municipal government, not by municipal government itself. As part of a policy that began at the time of Penn's West Philadelphia Initiatives, staff of the University's Purchasing Services Department was directed to provide training in Internet procurement, to create mentoring relationships between inexperienced businesses and seasoned contractors or suppliers, and to facilitate the creation of joint ventures between larger firms with greater resources and smaller, less well-resourced minority-owned or neighborhood-based businesses. An approach of this kind, designed to produce successes, which is far more productive than a government-driven monitoring/enforcement approach, cannot be found in most cities.[7]

Government unreadiness to focus on establishing a new model for urban reinvestment that will produce big successes during the coming decades is matched by unreadiness among some of the highest-profile supporters of urban communities, who sometimes act in a manner that is contrary to self-interest.

Community advocates often greet major development proposals with demands for construction jobs for neighborhood residents. Seeking the participation of qualified neighborhood-based contractors and suppliers in a proposed development venture or, at a minimum, seeking evidence that a development venture will provide appropriate direct benefits to a community, is essential; but seeking commitments of construction jobs for unemployed neighborhood residents as a high priority makes little sense. In a rustbelt city, construction work is unlikely to produce long-term success for jobseekers. In these cities, construction is not a major growth industry, and construction-work opportunities are spread across the region, requiring extensive travel to the suburban and exurban job sites where most of the construction activity is taking place. In a sunbelt state, a construction project can go on for years. In the rustbelt, the need to move from one job to another is ongoing. In addition, because construction is not a major industry sector, the risk of job loss or extended down time between projects is significant. Rather than construction work, the most promising jobs for urban neighborhood residents are located at city-based academic and health care institutions, particularly the latter. These institutions are likely to be interested in working with neighborhood constituencies, in concert with the local community college and workforce development agency, in designing or improving programs that enable community members to qualify for more of these jobs.

Misguided actions take place in a regional context as well. A case in point is the Habitat for Humanity program. The Habitat model, as described below, has been replicated in many rural and urban regions:

> Through volunteer labor and donations of money and materials, Habitat builds and rehabilitates simple, decent houses with the help of the home-owner (partner) families. Habitat houses are sold to partner families at no profit and financed with affordable loans. The homeowners' monthly mortgage payments are used to build still more Habitat houses.[8]

Habitat has achieved remarkable success worldwide, both in terms of assisting people in need of housing through a self-help approach and in mobilizing people from around the metropolitan region to participate directly in supporting a housing production initiative at the construction-site level, rather than through simply writing a check or attending a fundraising event.

In older cities, the problem with Habitat is that the organization often focuses on building houses in neighborhoods characterized by high levels of poverty and joblessness and by concentrations of racial and/or ethnic minority population. By building in these areas—with volunteer labor provided by work teams from churches and corporations that are based in better-off communities around the region—Habitat is, in effect, reinforcing patterns of economic and racial/ethnic segregation. The last thing that highly distressed urban communities need is more low-income housing—and that is exactly what Habitat is producing in many urban areas.

Habitat should not stop sponsoring housing ventures in urban neighborhoods where the organization's work is linked to broader neighborhood plans that produce a desirable mix of housing types. In Camden, for example, Habitat has played a valuable role in implementing one element of the Cooper Plaza revitalization plan. But in all metropolitan areas, Habitat should be using at least half its economic and organizational resources to help more members of urban communities obtain affordable housing located in the vicinity of suburban job centers. Because relatively little housing is available for service-industry workers such as food service personnel, building and grounds maintenance workers, hotel housekeeping staff and others who work at or just above the minimum wage, many of the people who are employed in these positions need to travel long distances to get to work. An organization such as Habitat could use its considerable powers to locate the best places to produce affordable workforce housing for some of these individuals rather than reinforcing the housing-jobs mismatch by focusing on housing construction in urban neighborhoods.

Realigning for Success

On a policy level, the main reason why urban reinvestment policies are not as successful as they need to be is in large part because leadership and management responsibilities are dispersed among too many parties, and this dispersion leads to an ineffective use of available resources.

In federal government, the most obvious dispersion of responsibility can be found at HUD, where two large housing programs, each headed by its own Assistant Secretary, and each with its own budget and its own rule book, operate within the same headquarters building, largely independent of one another: Community Planning and Development administers the CDBG program and other housing aid to municipalities, while Public and Indian Housing administers funding for public housing development and management. If everyone supports the concept of mixed housing—the concept of below-median income and median-income-and-above households living in the same community in rental and sales housing that is priced at levels affordable to them—then this division of responsibility makes no sense.

Over the years, a number of cities have, on their own initiative, made sensible decisions about the respective roles of municipal housing agencies (such as Philadelphia's OHCD) and housing authorities (such as the RDA and PHA). In some cities, the local housing authority is merged into the municipal government infrastructure; in other cities, the local housing and redevelopment authorities lead and manage all program activities, and the municipal government role is minimized; in still other cities, a city government housing agency and a local housing authority have established strong working relationships that make the best use of their respective resources and capabilities. Some counties with substantial urban populations have made similar decisions with respect to county government and county-level housing authorities.

HUD should encourage more sensible decision-making of this kind by combining the two administrative branches identified above and block-granting to local and county governments the annual funding that is now administered separately. HUD should not abandon its oversight of local performance in administering federal funds and implementing associated programs; in fact, this oversight should be strengthened. City and county governments should be required to demonstrate capability to manage a consolidated block grant effectively and to prove that the organizational approach that they propose for housing program administration will be more productive and cost effective than maintenance of the organizational status quo.

A similar dispersion of leadership and management responsibility can be found in most state governments. In many instances, state funding for urban reinvestment is administered by an agency with an ambiguous name such as the Department of Community Affairs or the Department of Community and Economic Development, and this agency manages a portfolio of many programs of varying degrees of relevance and usefulness. Some of these programs are federally funded and categorical in nature; the funding is available to be used for one purpose only or for a limited number of uses (federally-funded, state-administered weatherization assistance programs are a case in point). However, these agencies also receive program funding every year through the state budget, and this funding can be allocated as the Governor and legislature see fit. For this state funding, the top priority should be financing affordable housing for citizens who are entering the workforce or are completing training that will help them advance in the workforce.

Postindustrial cities and the states where they are located need a qualified, twenty-first-century workforce more than anything else. A capable workforce will attract businesses, and business development and expansion will lead to private investment and generate taxes that will pay for the rebuilding of communities and the improvement or replacement of the public infrastructure on which they depend. State governments administer federally funded job training programs through the Workforce Investment Board structure, and state governments support land grant academic institutions that provide education and training to prepare citizens to compete for good jobs. If more of the funding made available by state governments for housing and community development were directed toward workforce housing as the top priority, and if the ambiguously-named state housing and community development agencies were charged to work in close coordination with the state departments responsible for workforce development, a better combination of jobs and housing would result.

If the approach summarized above were to be adopted, then the following would be readily identifiable as policy centers with responsibility for major issues:

- The organizational consolidation proposed for HUD would create a single source of federal program funding and monitoring for most of the activities described in this book.
- State government's focus would be the development and preservation of housing for current workers and workers in training, at all income levels.
- City government would be responsible for aligning municipal departments and the local housing and redevelopment authorities in the way that produces best results for each city. Given its access to the block grant funding provided by the consolidated HUD program divisions, city governments would have a special responsibility for ensuring that the housing needs of citizens at the lowest income levels are addressed. Although the city government role would not be devoted exclusively to low-income housing, the city would need to determine how to best use resources that had currently been awarded directly to housing authorities in order to provide "housing of last resort" for people without other options, such as formerly homeless people and ex-offenders.

Other participants in urban revitalization need to realign and refocus as well.

- The contrasting experiences of Philadelphia's Center City District and Allentown's Downtown Improvement District Authority illustrate the most important principles on which the formation and operation of a downtown special services district should be based. The district organization should be led by local and regional business leaders. The district organization's core leadership should include some of the property owners who are to pay the most under the assessment plan used to finance the district organization and its activities. City government should make and be held to a commitment not to reduce the level of police coverage and other municipal services within district boundaries. The district organization should be professionally staffed, and the staff should take the lead in designing and implementing programs and services. Basic services that produce a clean and safe environment should be performed satisfactorily before new initiatives are launched. Priority consideration should be given to outsourcing basic services wherever possible. New initiatives should increasingly be supported with funds leveraged from other sources. These initiatives should be undertaken incrementally, with each one mastered before a new one is started.

- For academic and health care institutions seeking to improve conditions in the neighborhoods where they are located, the activity that is easiest to implement is the promotion of financial incentives to encourage employees to buy housing within a designated target area (in the form of small grants or loans that self-amortize over a period of owner-occupancy) or, for employees who already live in the target area, to finance the completion of exterior improvements such as repainting, porch repair, and window and door repair and replacement (through grants that are matched with private debt or equity or with sweat equity).

    The activity that is next easiest to implement is a linkage of institutional procurement of services and supplies with business development services, as described in Chapter Six.

    The activity that is likely to produce greatest added value to the nearby community is an institutional commitment to support one or more public schools with funding, classroom support, teacher training, curriculum development and enhancement, and/or other forms of technical support.

- Charitable foundations that are considering making major commitments of support for urban revitalization would be wise to follow the example of the Annie E. Casey and Ford Foundations in Camden, by evaluating each prospective grantmaking opportunity in terms of the prospects for leveraging other resources and catalyzing positive, measurable change. For example, the two foundations supported the creation of a branch of the STRIVE job readiness program (which originated in East Harlem in 1984 and has since replicated its program model through affiliates in nearly two dozen cities) because of the likelihood that the program would be productive in Camden, as it had been elsewhere. Not long after the approval of the MRERA legislation, Casey and Ford, along with a group of grantmakers based in the region surrounding Camden, had explored the prospects for making major commitments of funding in support of the city's revitalization. However, as of early 2009, this collaborative initiative had not materialized, in large part, I suspect, because the grantmakers were not convinced of the city's ability to deliver on municipal reform goals.

During an early stage of NTI implementation, NTI staffer Lance Rothstein told the Mayor's Chief of Staff that all the components of the municipal-government machinery had to move in the right direction—if only a little—

in order for NTI to work. If the city agencies could work together, if the administration could work with City Council, if city government could work with the community, then NTI would be successful. The same character-ization applies to the elements of the neighborhood-revitalization machinery identified above: if they all could move in the right direction and in coordination with one another—just a little—then great successes could be achieved.

A Program Focus

The housing program area that needs to become the highest priority during the coming years is the creation of more rental housing through strategies that produce or upgrade housing units on a large scale at relatively low cost. The need to address rental housing as a priority is especially great at this time, for several reasons:

- More people are experiencing income loss due to layoffs and downsizing, and many of these people need lower-priced rental housing in order to make ends meet.
- Many families that had been homebuyers at the turn of the century will, as a result of the impact that the foreclosure crisis has had on their lives, need to become renters in the future.
- As a by-product of the economic meltdown that began in 2008, the level of investment equity that can be generated through the state-administered Low Income Housing Tax Credit, for two decades the nation's largest development financing resource for affordable rental housing, has shrunk substantially, significantly reducing the utility of this resource in financing large-scale rental housing production.
- In many older cities, individuals and families who had previously lived in the suburbs are seeking housing in urban downtowns, and many of them want to rent rather than buy.
- More residents of nursing homes or assisted living facilities are seeking opportunities to move out and return to new dwellings in a neighbor-hood environment that has good access to shopping and services. Many of these residents could afford reasonably priced market-rate rental housing in a small-city downtown or a big-city neighborhood.

Late twentieth-century federal policies have influenced this situation adversely in two ways. In light of the demolition of older public housing sites in the absence of a requirement to replace the demolished housing with an equal number of subsidized units, the supply of rental housing afford-able to people at the lowest income levels has shrunk substantially in older cities. This problem is compounded by the fact that the primary resource for financing the development of new affordable housing, the Low Income Housing Tax Credit, is very expensive.

The two best strategies for making more rental housing available to people at a variety of income levels are rental assistance and moderate rehabilitation. As described in Chapter Six, rental assistance is a stream of payments that subsidizes the difference between the amount that is considered a reasonable housing expense (that is, not more than 30 percent of income) and the rent charged for a housing unit in the private rental market. The federal government should give cities the opportunity to use more of the federal funding available to them (including CDBG funding) for rental assistance, based on an annual plan that shows how the rental assistance will be used to address the housing-supply needs described above. Cities should be given more flexibility in determining the extent to which rental assistance will be "tenant-based" (that is, awarded to a household that can then seek available rental housing anywhere) as opposed to "site-based" (awarded to a specific unit of rental housing in order to create a write-down of the rent for any eligible household that moves there). At the same time, the federal government should address the consequences of "portability," through which rental assistance obtained in one city may be used to rent housing in another. Because the "portability" policy has produced disproportionate concentrations of rent-assisted units in certain cities (including small cities such as Allentown), HUD should either impose limits on the use of portability or provide more funding to cities that have become "hosts" for substantial numbers of portability-enabled tenants, in order to support asset-management expenses associated with this growing population.

If municipal and county governments were to adopt as their primary rental housing finance program the award of a modest subsidy to support the rehabilitation of existing rental housing that required the repair or replacement of at least one major system but that was well-located and in reasonably good condition, then developers would find ways to use this resource productively to produce large numbers of rental units where they are needed most: on relatively stable blocks that have one or two vacant houses; in neighborhoods where little or no demolition has taken place but where all of the housing is older and in need of some level of upgrading; and in downtowns and on neighborhood commercial corridors where vacant upstairs space can be found in many buildings occupied by retail businesses at the street level.

Both rental assistance and moderate rehabilitation have to be applied strategically to promote a variety of housing options, not to concentrate lower-income people in weak neighborhood housing markets. The granting of flexibility in the use of these resources should be accompanied by a requirement that cities show how they are being used to address all of the needs and opportunities described above.

Competing for the Middle Ground?

During the decade after the turn of the century, "sustainability" became the newest and most frequently used addition to the vocabulary of urban planners and developers, as well as for environmentalists, smart growth advocates, and others. Sustainability means preserving existing resources for the benefit of future generations, but, in postindustrial cities, the notion of sustainability is paradoxical: the preservation of valued assets cannot succeed unless the assets are changed—unless they are adapted in ways that will make them relevant in a future economic and social environment.

Urban assets are unlike wetlands or wildlife areas; in order to preserve their intrinsic value they need to change; preservation and adaptation need to be linked. In order to retain its historically noteworthy features, the CIGNA building that housed an early twentieth-century corporate headquarters had to be converted into condominiums. In order to renew its reputation as a place of spontaneity and vitality, an older urban downtown needs an operating plan and a professional management structure that, in some respects, resembles that associated with a modern suburban mall. In order to maintain the status of urban institutions as centers of education and health care, some of their administrators need to become experts in neighborhood real estate markets. People who want cities to succeed need to determine how best to respond to the opportunities associated with change, while preserving and renewing those things of value that make a place attractive and give a place an identity of its own.

As the first decade of the twenty-first century nears an end, postindustrial cities face an uncertain future. Older cities may be better positioned for economic recovery during this century's next decade than are many of the suburban and sunbelt areas that had experienced fast growth during the late twentieth century. However, recovery and prosperity are not the same. On a citywide level, economic disinvestment persisted throughout the years in which urban downtowns became enlivened and many urban neighborhoods were revitalized. During the coming years, the threat of increased disinvestment—more population loss, job loss, and business loss—is likely to grow. At worst, some features of the devastated downtown landscape described at the start of Chapter One may re-emerge and have to be confronted again by a new generation of leaders.

Most older cities will always retain certain characteristics to a greater or lesser degree, irrespective of economic circumstances. They will have walkable streets with many attractive older buildings. They will have centers of education, culture, health and human services, employment, and retail activity. They will be the places where the most creative solutions for addressing poverty, unemployment, and social need (conditions that will continue to be concentrated in cities) are designed and tested, in some cases producing extraordinary results. They will be places where people living in poverty will strive to move up into the middle class and where ambitious people can achieve spectacular success in business, politics, entertainment, and the arts. The challenge that postindustrial cities face is that of how to nurture these positive characteristics in order to reduce further disinvestment and offset competitive disadvantages.

Through the CEOS for Cities-sponsored research project described in the preceding chapter, Robert Weissbourd and Christopher Berry found that a traditional pattern of "convergence" among competing cities had taken a different character during the 1990s:

> Historically, economic performance has tended to converge across geographies over time—poorer places have tended to catch up as labor and capital moved to less developed markets . . . Cities that had less developed local economies were able to offer cheaper land, labor, and capital, and consequently attract more investment. As investors and companies flocked to these places, their economies would grow faster and catch up with wealthier cities . . .
>
> This pattern of convergence appears to be . . . giving way to a pattern of divergence; cities like San Jose, San Francisco and New York . . . had high wages in 1990, and also led in wage growth in the ensuing decade . . . Initial advantages may now tend to create further advantages in particular cities, "locking in" paths to success.[9]

Weissbourd and Berry found that, as the most successful cities tend to pull ahead, retaining their leading positions, the others tended to converge toward the middle—toward levels of wages and growth that were comparable to one another, but far lower than those that prevailed in the leading cities:

> . . . the divergent growth effects seem to kick in only past a certain level of economic performance . . .
>
> . . . in an economic landscape where divergence prevails, initial advantages tend to breed further success. In this unforgiving environment, economic development policies can make a huge difference, and *making the right strategic decisions is more important than ever.* [authors' emphasis][10]

In some older cities, inherent disadvantages are likely to be so great that the best that can be hoped for is to try to accelerate the time that it takes to converge with others in the middle group. But government, business, and community leaders in many cities will want to do much better than that; they will desire more than the opportunity to share limited benefits with all the other cities that are competing for the middle ground. For these ambitious people who want more for the cities they care about, the choice of strategies and the manner in which they are designed and executed will determine whether these places will be able to break away, move ahead of the pack, and achieve success surpassing expectations.

Notes

Introduction

1 Much of my experience at OHCD is described in my first book, *Neighborhood Recovery: Reinvestment Policy for the New Hometown* (New Brunswick, New Jersey: Rutgers University Press, 1999).

2 For a detailed history of these efforts, see Jon C. Teaford, *The Rough Road to Renaissance: Urban Revitalization in America, 1940–85*, Baltimore: Johns Hopkins University Press, 1990.

1 Financing Without Cash: The Ten-Year Tax Abatement

1 Joanne Aitken, past President of the Philadelphia Chapter of the American Institute of Architects, called attention to these similarities in several articles and presentations.

2 Delaware Valley Regional Planning Commission, "Regional Planning: Past Efforts/ Housing," www.dvrpc.org/planning/longrange/indicators/past/housing.htm (accessed December 19, 2008).

3 Michael Klein, "Area's Affair with Jen and Ben Ends—After Weeks of Filming in Phila. and N.J., 'Jersey Girl' Is Gone. After 10 Weeks of Filming, Staff and Stars of 'Jersey Girl' Leave," *The Philadelphia Inquirer*, November 1, 2002, Local News section.

4 Dan Baum, "The Lost Year: Behind the Failure to Rebuild," *New Yorker*, August 21, 2006, pp. 44–53.

5 The Century Foundation, *The "Red" States: How Governors Ended Up with Huge Deficits* (New York: The Century Foundation, 2004), pp. 1, 3, 4, 6, 8, 9.

6 Aaron C. Davis, "States' Budget Crises Will Hurt Millions," www.boston.com/ (accessed March 17, 2008).

7 Vernon Loeb, "2 Neighborhoods, 2 Symbols of Housing Policy," *The Philadelphia Inquirer*, October 29, 1987, Local News section.

8 National Association of Counties, Research Division, *Tax Increment Financing: An Alternative Economic Development Financing Technique* (Washington: National Association of Counties, 2000), p. 1.

9 Location within a KOZ does not make a venture ineligible for public-sector loan and grant financing programs.

10 Commonwealth of Pennsylvania, "What is a KOZ?," http://koz.newpa.com/what.html (accessed March 17, 2008).

11 William P. Hankowsky, "Letter to Councilman Michael A. Nutter," November 14, 1997.

12 Jeff Blumenthal, "Cira Center Success Story: Law Firm Moves into City," *Philadelphia Business Journal,* April 14, 2006.

13 Quoted in Andrew Cassel, "Tax Break Favors Few, Costs Many," *The Philadelphia Inquirer*, December 28, 2003, Business section.

14 Andrew Cassel, "Would Comcast Give Themselves a KOZ?," *The Philadelphia Inquirer*, March 10, 2004, Business section.

15 "TIFs: Totally Inappropriate Financing? Why Build the Cow Unless You Can Milk the City for Free?," *The Philadelphia Daily News*, December 7, 2000, Editorial.

16 David Wallace, "Northeast Notebook: Philadelphia: Older Building Goes Begging," *The New York Times*, December 30, 1990, Nation section.

17 Kathleen Fifield, "Will the Bubble Burst?," *Philadelphia Magazine*, March 2005, www.phillymag.com/articles/will_the_bubble_burst (accessed March 18, 2008).

18 John Kromer and Vicky Tam, *Philadelphia's Residential Tax Abatements: Accomplishments and Impacts* (Philadelphia: Fels Institute of Government, December 2005), pp. 32–37.

19 Econsult Corporation, *Building Industry Association: Philadelphia Tax Abatement Analysis* (Philadelphia: Econsult Corporation, June 2006), pp. 8, 9.

20 Marie Reamer, "email message to Donald F. Kettl," February 10, 2006.

21 Earni Young, "Street Mulling End—To Tax Abatements," *Philadelphia Daily News*, April 19, 2005: 5.

22 Kromer and Tam: 49.

23 Advocacy for tax reform is documented in Philadelphia Forward, "No City Limits: The Story of Tax Reform in Philadelphia," www.philadelphiaforward. org/images/stories/the%20story%20of%20tax%20reform%20in%20philadelphia.pdf (accessed March 29, 2008).

24 "Economy at a Glance," Bureau of Labor Statistics, www.bls.gov/eag/eag.pa_ philadelphia_co.htm.(accessed December 19, 2008).

25 U.S. Census Bureau, "Income, Earnings, and Poverty From the 2004 American Community Survey," August 2005: 3, 6.

26 Michael Nutter for Mayor, "The Nutter Plan for Better Housing Now," www.nutter2007.com (accessed December 1, 2008).

27 Alan J. Heavens, "Philadelphia Area Home Sales off 32% for Quarter," *The Philadelphia Inquirer*, May 14, 2008, Real Estate section.

28 Alan J. Heavens, "Incentives for Igniting Sales," *The Philadelphia Inquirer*, August 8, 2008, Real Estate section.

29 Heavens, "Incentives for Igniting Sales."

2 A Managed Downtown: The Center City District

1 For examples of the latter, see David Feehan, MSW and Marvin D. Feit, PhD (Eds.), *Making Business Districts Work: Leadership and Management of Downtown, Main Street, Business District, and Community Development Organizations* (New York: The Haworth Press, 2006); Furman Center for Real Estate and Urban Policy, *The Benefits of Business Improvements Districts: Evidence from New York City* (New York: New York University, 2006); and Lorlene Hoyt, "Do Business Improvement District Organizations Make a Difference? Crime in and around Commercial Areas in Philadelphia," *Journal of Planning Education and Research* 25(2) 2005: 185–199.

2 Eugenie L. Birch, *Who Lives Downtown* (Washington, D.C.: The Brookings Institution, Living Cities Census Series, November 2005), p. 5.

3 Eugenie L. Birch, *Who Lives Downtown*, p. 18, notes 13 and 18.

4 Eugenie L. Birch, *Who Lives Downtown*, p. 13.

5 Carolyn Adams, David Bartelt, David Elesh, Ira Goldstein, Nancy Kleniewski, and William Yancey, *Philadelphia: Neighborhoods, Division, and Conflict in a Postindustrial City* (Philadelphia: Temple University Press, 1991), pp. 16, 17.

6 Jon C. Teaford, *The Rough Road to Renaissance: Urban Revitalization in America, 1940–1985* (Baltimore: The Johns Hopkins University Press, 1990), p. 109.

7 "Penn Center: Site Description and History" at www.edbacon.org/bacon/site.htm.

8 Jane Jacobs, *The Death and Life of Great American Cities* (New York: Vintage Books, 1961), pp. 164–165.

9 Sam Bass Warner, Jr., *The Private City: Philadelphia in Three Periods of its Growth* (Philadelphia: University of Pennsylvania Press, 1968), pp. 188–191.

10 Russell F. Weigley (Ed.), *Philadelphia: A 300-Year History* (New York: W.W. Norton & Company, 1982), p. 712.

11 Carolyn Adams, David Bartelt, David Elesh, Ira Goldstein, Nancy Kleniewski, and William Yancey, *Philadelphia: Neighborhoods, Division, and Conflict in a Postindustrial City* (Philadelphia: Temple University Press, 1991), p. 111.

12 Edmund N. Bacon, *Design of Cities* (New York: Penguin Books, 1976), pp. 293, 294.

13 William H. Whyte, *City: Rediscovering the Center* (New York: Doubleday, 1988), p. 219.

14 Mike Mallowe, "The Life and Death of Chestnut Street," *Philadelphia Magazine* 78 (October 1987): 142; cited in Jon C. Teaford, *The Rough Road to Renaissance: Urban Revitalization in America, 1940–1985* (Baltimore: The Johns Hopkins University Press, 1990), p. 293.

15 "For Future Seasons: Trash and Crime have Reduced the Appeal of Center City, but Change is Coming," *The Philadelphia Inquirer* (editorial), December 23, 1989, p. A8.

16 Jennifer Moulton, FAIA, *Ten Steps to a Living Downtown* (Washington, D.C.: The Brookings Institution Center on Urban and Metropolitan Policy, 1999); and Christopher B. Leinberger, *Turning Around Downtown: Twelve Steps to Revitalization* (Washington, D.C.: The Brookings Institution Center on Urban and Metropolitan Policy, 2005).

17 *Ten Steps to Living Downtown*, p. 14.

18 *Turning Around Downtown: Twelve Steps to Revitalization*, pp. 11, 12.

19 Sam Bass Warner, Jr., *The Private City: Philadelphia in Three Periods of its Growth* (Philadelphia: University of Pennsylvania Press, 1968), pp. 206, 207.

20 Jon C. Teaford, *The Rough Road to Renaissance: Urban Revitalization in America, 1940–1985* (Baltimore: The Johns Hopkins University Press, 1990), p. 211.

21 Paul R. Levy, "Looking Backward, Looking Forward: The Future of Downtown and Business Districts," in David Feehan, MSW and Marvin D. Feit, PhD (Eds.), *Making Business Districts Work: Leadership and Management of Downtown, Main Street, Business District, and Community Development Organizations* (New York: The Haworth Press, 2006), p. 421.

22 Paul R. Levy in interview with author. I have integrated into the narrative that follows a number of observations and comments made by Levy in interviews with me, and much of the "Milestones and Metrics" section is based on his observations.

23 Information and quotations in the preceding three paragraphs are taken from Robin Clark, Steve Stecklow and David Lee Preston, "Center City shops looted in rampage," *The Philadelphia Inquirer*, April 8, 1985, p. 1.

24 Edward Colimore, "Melee drew Attention to Chestnut Street," *The Philadelphia Inquirer*, April 14, 1985, p. A1.

25 Marguerite Del Guidice, Dale Mezzacappa, and Maida Odom, "26 People Charged in Vandalism Acts," *The Philadelphia Inquirer*, April 21, p. A1.

26 Marguerite Del Guidice, Dale Mezzacappa, and Maida Odom, "26 People Charged in Vandalism Acts," p. A1.

27 Linda Loyd and Russell Cooke, "Merchants Fault Lack of City Preparedness for Vandals," *The Philadelphia Inquirer*, April 22, 1987, p. B6.

28 Linda Loyd and Russell Cooke, "Merchants Fault Lack of City Preparedness for Vandals," *The Philadelphia Inquirer*, April 22, 1987, p. B6

29 Information and quotations in the five preceding paragraphs are taken from Linda Loyd and Russell Cooke, "Merchants Fault Lack of City Preparedness for Vandals," *The Philadelphia Inquirer*, April 22, 1987, p. B6; Marguerite Del Giudice, Dale Mezzacappa and Maida Odom, "26 People Charged in Vandalism Acts," *The Philadelphia Inquirer*, April 21, 1987, p. A1; and Joe Clark, Michael Days, Kit Konolige, and Edward Moran, "Melee Spoils Parade: Looting, Fights Erupt," *The Philadelphia Inquirer*, April 20, 1987, p. 3.

30 Central Philadelphia Development Corporation, "Special Services District of Central Philadelphia: Feasibility Report," July 1990.

31 Paul Levy, interview with author.

32 Susan Warner, "The Developer King of Center City: Without Pizzazz, Richard I. Rubin & Co. Has Become the City's Most Visible, Can-Do Developer. Now, It Has Plans for Two Downtown Blocks," *The Philadelphia Inquirer*, February 26, 1990, p. D1.

33 Interview with author.

34 Joseph Grace, "Businesses Willing To Pay Extra: They Offer Plan for Tax Surcharge," *The Philadelphia Inquirer*, February 28, 1990, p. 4.

35 Philadelphia City Planning Commission, "Retail Strategy for Center City" (Philadelphia: Philadelphia City Planning Commission, 1987), p. 15.

36 Interview with author.

37 Joseph Grace, "Businesses Willing To Pay Extra: They Offer Plan for Tax Surcharge."

38 "Crime and Grime: The 'Special Services' Plan is No Panacea, But It Offers Center City a Fighting Chance" (editorial), *The Philadelphia Inquirer*, March 4, 1990, p. D6.

39 "Crime and Grime: The 'Special Services' Plan is No Panacea, But It Offers Center City a Fighting Chance."

40 Joseph Grace, "Businesses Willing To Pay Extra: They Offer Plan for Tax Surcharge."

41 Leslie Scism, "Rubin tells Rotarians to get Involved in City: Merchants are Urged to Help in Crisis," *The Philadelphia Inquirer*, May 3, 1990, p. 33.

42 Leigh Jackson, "Special Services Plan Unsettles Renters," *Philadelphia Daily News*, August 22, 1990, p. 16.

43 Central Philadelphia Development Corporation, undated "Background Information" summary.

44 Larry Fish, "Center City Loved the Party: Wednesday Night's Crowd Warmed Hearts and Cash Registers," *The Philadelphia Inquirer*, September 18, 1992, p. B14.

45 "Center City District" at www.centercityphila.org/about/CCD.php.

46 Central Philadelphia Development Corporation, *Remaking Center City: A History of the Central Philadelphia Development Corporation* (2006), p. 59.

47 Central Philadelphia Development Corporation and Center City District, *Center City Reports: Residential Development 2008*, September 2008, p. 2.

48 Center City District, *State of Center City 2008* (Philadelphia: Center City District, 2008), p. 38.

49 *State of Center City 2008*, p. 40.

50 *State of Center City 2008*, pp. 38, 41.

51 *State of Center City 2008*, p. 42.

52 Available at www.centercityphila.org/about/Publications.php.

53 Available at www.centercityphila.org/about/Publications.php.

54 Interview with author.

55 Center City District, "Center City Reports: Sidewalk Cafes," July 2008, p. 1.

56 Interview with author.

57　Center City District, *State of Center City 2008* (Philadelphia: Center City District, 2008), p. 5.

3　The Transition Zone: Rebuilding Eastern North Philadelphia

1　Depopulation patterns and their relationship to property abandonment were first explained to me by Barbara Kaplan, former Executive Director of the Philadelphia City Planning Commission.

2　Jon C. Teaford, *The Rough Road to Renaissance: Urban Revitalization in America, 1940–1985* (Baltimore: The Johns Hopkins University Press, 1990), pp. 124, 128.

3　Alan Berube and Benjamin Forman, "Living on the Edge: Decentralization Within Cities in the 1990s" (Washington, D.C.: The Brookings Institution Center on Urban and Metropolitan Policy, October 2002), pp. 3, 10.

4　Philadelphia City Planning Commission, *North Philadelphia Plan: A Guide to Revitalization* (Philadelphia: City of Philadelphia, 1987), p. 40.

5　Philadelphia City Planning Commission, *North Philadelphia Plan: A Guide to Revitalization*, p. 40.

6　Carolyn Adams, David Bartelt, David Elesh, Ira Goldstein, Nancy Kleniewski, and William Yancey, *Philadelphia: Neighborhoods, Division, and Conflict in a Postindustrial City* (Philadelphia: Temple University Press, 1991), p. 107.

7　Carolyn Adams, David Bartelt, David Elesh, Ira Goldstein, Nancy Kleniewski, and William Yancey, *Philadelphia: Neighborhoods, Division, and Conflict in a Postindustrial City* (Philadelphia: Temple University Press, 1991), p. 109.

8　Philadelphia City Planning Commission, *The Eastern North Philadelphia Plan and Draft Environmental Impact Statement* (Philadelphia: City of Philadelphia, 1978), pp. 96, 97.

9　Joseph S. Clark, Jr. and Dennis Clark, "Rally and Relapse: 1946–1968," in Russell F. Weigley (Ed.), *Philadelphia: A 300-Year History* (New York: W.W. Norton & Co., 1982), p. 686.

10　Vernon Clark, "Experiment Now Cherished Home," *The Philadelphia Inquirer*, October 21, 2005, p. b01.

11　Philadelphia City Planning Commission, *The Eastern North Philadelphia Plan and Draft Environmental Impact Statement* (Philadelphia: City of Philadelphia, 1978), p. 97.

12　James R. Cohen, "Abandoned Housing: Exploring Lessons from Baltimore," *Housing Policy Debate*, 12 (3): 425.

13　John Kromer, *Home in North Philadelphia* (City of Philadelphia, Office of Housing and Community Development, 1993), p. 5.

14　John Kromer, *Home in North Philadelphia*, p. 7.

15　John Kromer, *Home in North Philadelphia*, pp. 23–29.

16　Thomas Ferrick, Jr., "Hope for the City's Core: In a Once-Dead Area, Houses Are Being Built and Dreams Rebuilt," *The Philadelphia Inquirer* , February 1, 1998, p. A1.

17　Michael Janofsky, "Philadelphia Neighborhood Reborn: Housing and Business Programs Create Stability and Optimism," *The New York Times*, February 24, 1998, p. A12.

18　Nathan Gorenstein, "Rethinking Revitalization," *The Philadelphia Inquirer*, April 11, 2001, p. A1.

19　See, for example: Nicholas Lemann, *The Promised Land: The Great Black Migration and How it Changed America* (New York: Vintage Books, 1992), pp. 226–234; Alexander von Hoffman, "Why They Built Pruitt-Igoe," in John F. Bauman, Roger Biles and Kristin M. Szylvian (Eds.), *From Tenements to the Taylor Homes: In Search of an Urban Housing Policy in Twentieth Century America* (University Park, Pennsylvania: The Pennsylvania State University Press, 2000), pp. 180–205.

20 Peter Nicholas, "PHA Director: Stick to Housing. He Aims to Trim Social-Service Efforts and Zero in on the Basics," *The Philadelphia Inquirer*, April 21, 1998, p. B1.

21 Peter Nicholas, "PHA Director: Stick to Housing. He Aims to Trim Social-Service Efforts and Zero in on the Basics," B1.

22 For a description of these actions and an analysis of their impact, see: Rod Solomon, *Public Housing Reform and Voucher Success: Progress and Challenges* (Washington, D.C.: The Brookings Institution Metropolitan Policy Program, January 2005); Rachel Garshick Kleir and Stephen B. Page, "Public Housing Authorities Under Devolution," *Journal of the American Planning Association*, 74 (1), Winter 2008: 34–44.

23 CFR Ch. IX (4-1-06 Edition), Part 971. Office of the Assistant Secretary, HUD, "Part 917—Assessment of the Reasonable Revitalization Potential of Certain Public Housing Required by Law."

24 Mark McDonald, "A $130M PHA Dream," *Philadelphia Daily News*, May 24, 2000, p. 5.

25 Rachel Garshick Kleir and Stephen B. Page, "Public Housing Authorities Under Devolution," *Journal of the American Planning Association*, 74 (1), Winter 2008: 37.

26 Public Housing Authorities Directors' Association, "Asset Management, Yes—Micromanagement, No" (Washington, D.C., 2006), p. 5.

27 Multiple Listing Service data cited in PHA PowerPoint presentation, "Redefining Public Housing," at www.pha.phila.gov/web_files/Redefining.pdf.

28 Susan J. Popkin, Diane K. Levy, Laura E. Harris, Jennifer Comey, and Marty K. Cunningham, "The HOPE VI Program: What about the Residents?," *Housing Policy Debate*, 15 (2): 387.

29 Susan J. Popkin, Diane K. Levy, Laura E. Harris, Jennifer Comey, and Marty K. Cunningham, "The HOPE VI Program: What about the Residents?": 387.

30 Asocician de Puertorriquenos en March website, www.apmphila.org/about.html.

31 APM website, www.apmphila.org/about.html.

4 A Citywide Revitalization Policy, I: Neighborhood Transformation Initiative Organization and Planning

1 For a broader assessment, see Stephen J. McGovern, "Philadelphia's Neighborhood Transformation Initiative: A Case Study of Mayoral Leadership, Bold Planning, and Conflict," *Housing Policy Debate*, 17 (3): 529–570.

2 Elisa Ung, "Vehicle Eyesores Are Topic of Forum: A Civic Group Wants to Make Abandoned Autos a Campaign Issue, Starting with an Event Sunday," *The Philadelphia Inquirer*, October 7, 1999; Monica Yant, "Abandoned Vehicles Plans Offered: Katz and Street Proposed ways to Speed their Removal," *The Philadelphia Inquirer*, October 14, 1999.

3 Anne B. Shlay and Gordon Whitman, *Research for Democracy: Linking Community Organizing and Research to Leverage Blight Policy* (Philadelphia: Temple University, 2004).

4 Maria Panaritis, "Towing Armada, Led by Street, Fuels Hopes," *The Philadelphia Inquirer*, April 4, 2000; Cynthia Burton, "Steel Away Sweep Cleared 32,852 Vehicles," *The Philadelphia Inquirer*, May 31, 2000.

5 Cynthia Burton and Clea Benson, "Street Plans Sweep of 40,000 Cars: Starting Monday, the Mayor said, Phila. Will Tow 1,000 Abandoned Vehicles per Weekday to Clear a Backlog," *The Philadelphia Inquirer*, March 29, 2000, p. A01.

6 Cynthia Burton, May 31, 2000.

7 Mark McDonald, "After Years on the Fringes of Power, Council President John Street is Second Only to the Mayor in Controlling the City's Future. Some Might

Say He's Become . . . the Ultimate Insider," *Philadelphia Daily News*, November 24, 1992, Local News section.

8 Karen E. Quinones Miller and Cynthia Burton, "The Apparent Heir: John F. Street, Activist Turned Policy Maker," *The Philadelphia Inquirer*, April 18, 1999, Local News section.

9 Quinones Miller and Burton, "The Apparent Heir."

10 The Street-Rendell relationship is well detailed in Buzz Bissinger, *A Prayer for the City* (New York: Vintage Books, 1999).

11 See, for example, Cynthia Burton, "Street Seeks to Fight Blight with $250 Million Proposal," *The Philadelphia Inquirer*, March 26, 1999, Local News section.

12 Jon C. Teaford, *The Rough Road to Renaissance: Urban Revitalization in America, 1940–1985* (Baltimore: The Johns Hopkins University Press, 1990), pp. 67–73.

13 Five-Year Financial Plan, 25, pp. 26–27.

14 City of Philadelphia, *A Strategy for Investment and Growth* (Philadelphia: City of Philadelphia, 2001), p. 2.

15 City of Philadelphia, *A Strategy for Investment and Growth* (Philadelphia: City of Philadelphia, 2001), p. 1.

16 *A Strategy for Investment and Growth*, pp. 2, 3.

17 *A Strategy for Investment and Growth*, p. 1.

18 Mark Alan Hughes, "Blight Plan Caught Mapping," *Philadelphia Daily News*, April 24, 2002, Local News section.

19 Hughes, "Blight Plan Caught Mapping."

20 The Reinvestment Fund, "Market Value Analysis: Philadelphia" at www.trfund.com/planning/market-phila.html (accessed January 5, 2009).

21 Patricia L. Smith, interview with author, December 23, 2008.

22 Smith, interview.

23 "Research for Democracy: A Collaboration Between the Eastern Pennsylvania Organizing Project and the Temple University Center for Public Policy, Blight Free Philadelphia: A Public-Private Strategy to Create and Enhance Neighborhood Value," October, 2001, p. i.

24 "Research for Democracy," p. 44.

25 "Research for Democracy," p. 45.

26 Mark McDonald, "Group Pushes Attack on Blight-EPOP Urges Spending on 'Zones' in City," *Philadelphia Daily News*, October 30, 2002, Local News section.

27 Philadelphia City Planning Commission, Strawberry Mansion Community Plan: Strategies for Neighborhood Revitalization, p. 11.

28 Tom Angotti, "Community Planning in New York City: Neighborhoods Face the Challenges of Globalization and Privatization," *New Village Journal*, www.newvillage.net/Journal/Issue1/1angotti.html (accessed January 5, 2009).

29 Interview with author, December 15, 2008.

30 Griffith interview.

5 A Citywide Revitalization Policy, II: NTI Real Estate Transactions and Housing Agency Reorganization

1 City of Philadelphia Neighborhood Transformation Initiative, Program Statement and Budget FY 06, August 2005, 2, 3.

2 City of Philadelphia Neighborhood Transformation Initiative, Program Statement and Budget FY 06, August 2005, 2.

3 Earni Young, "Blight Plan to Take up to 3,000 Properties," *Philadelphia Daily News*, October 1, 2002, Local News section.

4 Bob Warner, "Blight-Fight Agency Urged: Would Handle Abandoned Properties," *Philadelphia Daily News*, March 8, 2000, Local section.

5　Tina Moore, "Property Plan May Cut RDA Budget—A Plan to Reduce Red Tape in Sales of City Land may hit the Redevelopment Authority Hardest, Officials say," *Philadelphia Daily News*, February 10, 2006, Local section.

6　John Baer, "This Time Perzel's Grab doesn't Exceed Reach," *Philadelphia Daily News*, June 13, 2001, Local section; Ken Dilanian and Thomas Fitzgerald, "Phila. Schools to Get Parking Funds in State Plan—A House Bill Would Give the GOP Control of the City Agency and Transfer its Profits to the District. Ridge Plans to Sign it," *The Philadelphia Inquirer*, June 13, 2001, Local section.

7　Earni Young, "City's New Blight Fighter Gets Taste of the Town—Kevin Hanna Takes in a Sixers Game," *Philadelphia Daily News*, November 7, 2002, Local section; Leonard N. Fleming, "A Tough Task for Leader in Blight Fight—Kevin R. Hanna Called the City's Revitalization Plan 'a Tall Order . . . a Huge Job.' A Tough Task for New Leader Fighting Blight," *The Philadelphia Inquirer*, March 28, 2003, Local section.

8　Public Financial Management and The Reinvestment Fund, *OHNP Reorganization: Final Report*, Fall 2005, pp. 3, 4.

9　Bob Warner, "Blight-Fight Agency Urged: Would Handle Abandoned Properties," *Philadelphia Daily News*, March 8, 2000, Local section.

10　Mark McDonald, "Street, Blackwell Reach Deal on Housing," *Philadelphia Daily News*, June 9, 2006, Local section.

11　Mark McDonald, "Council OKs Funds to Reorganize Housing," *Philadelphia Daily News*, February 2, 2007, Local section.

12　Mark McDonald, "Scrutinizing Street's Neighborhoods Legacy," *Philadelphia Daily News*, January 3, 2008, Local section.

13　"Studies Say PHA Construction boosts Neighborhood Property Values by 142%," Philadelphia Housing Authority, press release, June 20, 2005 (accessed December 28, 2008 at www.pha.phila.gov/press/index.asp?id=22).

14　Mark McDonald, "How the Grand Plan to Fight Blight Meandered," *Philadelphia Daily News*, January 4, 2008, Local section.

15　Susan A Wachter, *The Determinants of Neighborhood Transformation in Philadelphia: Identification and Analysis: The New Kensington Pilot Study* (Philadelphia: The Wharton School, University of Pennsylvania, Fall 2005).

16　Andres Duany, Presentation at "21st Century Neighborhoods Conference," Philadelphia, PA, April 5, 1999. Transcript prepared by Foundation for Architecture.

6　Broadening Public Education Options: The Penn Alexander School

1　Thomas L. Friedman, *The World is Flat: A Brief History of the Twenty-First Century* (New York: Farrar, Straus, and Giroux, 2005).

2　Cooper University Hospital website at www.cooperhealth.org/content/.

3　City of Philadelphia Office of Housing and Community Development, *Learning from Yorktown* (Philadelphia: City of Philadelphia, 1996) p. 6.

4　CAMConnect, "Camden Facts/Lanning Square," at www.camconnect.org/fact/lsquare01.html and CAMConnect, "Camden Facts: Lanning Square, 1990–2000 (accessed January 22, 2009).

5　Camden Higher Education and Healthcare Task Force, *Camden Higher Education and Healthcare Task Force Housing Survey*, December 2006, pp. 2, 3.

6　University of Pennsylvania, "Facts and Figures" at www.upenn.edu/about/facts. php.

7　Bureau of Labor Statistics, in Karl Stark and Stacey Burling, "Nee Heights, but no Troughs—Recession Cushions: Resilience of Health Care and Education; Economic Diversity," *The Philadelphia Inquirer*, March 17, 2008, p. D1.

8 Spruce Hill Community Association, The Spruce Hill Community Renewal Plan, Implementation section, July 1998, at www.sprucehillca.org/development/plan.html.

9 Richard Rodgers, "Penn's Landgrab in West Philadelphia," submitted to the defenestrator website at www.defenestrator.org/node/142, December 11, 2004.

10 Quoted in John Kromer and Lucy Kerman, *West Philadelphia Initiatives: A Case Study in Urban Revitalization* (University of Pennsylvania, 2004), p. 8. This publication is available at www.upenn.edu/campus/westphilly/casestudy.pdf.

11 *West Philadelphia Initiatives*, p. 6.

12 *West Philadelphia Initiatives*, p. 52.

13 *West Philadelphia Initiatives*, p. 46.

14 Judith Rodin, *The University and Urban Revival: Out of the Ivory Tower and Into the Streets* (University of Pennsylvania Press, 2007), pp. 120, 124, 125.

15 Spruce Hill Civic Association, *The Spruce Hill Community Renewal Plan*, 1995, Background section.

16 Spruce Hill Civic Association, *The Spruce Hill Community Renewal Plan*, 1995, Neighborhood Analysis section.

17 Spruce Hill Civic Association, *The Spruce Hill Community Renewal Plan*, 1995, Community Renewal section.

18 Spruce Hill Civic Association, *The Spruce Hill Community Renewal Plan*, 1995, Community Renewal section.

19 Spruce Hill Civic Association, *The Spruce Hill Community Renewal Plan*, 1995, Implementation section.

20 Spruce Hill Civic Association, *The Spruce Hill Community Renewal Plan*, 1995, Implementation section.

21 *Priorities for Neighborhood Revitalization: Goals for the Year 2000, Penn Faculty and Staff for Neighborhood Issues* (PFSNI), 1993.

22 Joanne Barnes Jackson, "Town and Gown: What Penn Needs to do Now," *The Philadelphia Inquirer*, October 19, 1996, Editorial section.

23 John Kromer and Lucy Kerman, *West Philadelphia Initiatives*, pp. 11, 13.

24 Judith Rodin, *The University and Urban Revival: Out of the Ivory Tower and Into the Streets*, p. 148.

25 School District of Philadelphia, "Children Achieving Strategic Action Design," in Jolley Bruce Christman and Amy Rhodes, *Civic Engagement and Urban School Improvement: Hard-to-Learn Lessons from Philadelphia* (Consortium for Policy Research in Education, 2002), p. 18.

26 Jolley Bruce Christman and Amy Rhodes, *Civic Engagement and Urban School Improvement: Hard-to-Learn Lessons from Philadelphia*, p. 44.

27 Jolley Bruce Christman and Amy Rhodes, *Civic Engagement and Urban School Improvement: Hard-to-Learn Lessons from Philadelphia*, p. 2.

28 Yvette Ousley, "Teachers Union Chief Calls 'Children Achieving' a Fraud," *Philadelphia Daily News*, April 15, 1996, p. 5.

29 Jolley Bruce Christman and Amy Rhodes, *Civic Engagement and Urban School Improvement: Hard-to-Learn Lessons from Philadelphia*, p. 12.

30 Dale Mezzacappa, "Kirsch Reelected President of Phila Teachers Union: He Defeated Perennial Challenger Gary Grabar; Now, Contract Negotiations can Proceed in Earnest," *The Philadelphia Inquirer*, February 22, 1996, p. B3.

31 Dale Mezzacappa, "Union Opposition Alters Education Reform Plan in Phila. The Initial Proposal Removed Teachers from Troubled Schools; Now, the PFT Will Run Much of the Project," *The Philadelphia Inquirer*, April 6, 1995, p. B1.

32 Dale Mezzacappa, "Philadelphia Teachers Avert Strike, Affirm Talks; The Union Representing School District Teachers Voted to Authorize a Strike but Its President Urged that Negotiations Continue in Order to Avoid a Walkout," *The Philadelphia Inquirer*, September 6, 2000, p. A1.

33 Jolley Bruce Christman and Amy Rhodes, *Civic Engagement and Urban School Improvement: Hard-to-Learn Lessons from Philadelphia*, p. 34.

34 Dale Mezzacappa, "First Year a Tough Sell, Even for Hornbeck in the City He Saw as Ripe for Change, Phila's Schools Chief Contends with Resistance. Next Year, Observers Say, Is Do or Die," *The Philadelphia Inquirer*, August 27, 1995, p. B1.

35 Richard Jones, "Unity on Schools; Partners in Lawsuit Quell the Feuding," *The Philadelphia Inquirer*, March 9, 1997, p. E3.

36 Richard Jones, "Union President Balances Two Roles: Ted Kirsch is a Defender of Teachers. He also sees the Need for Reform," *The Philadelphia Inquirer*, March 24, 1997, p. B1.

37 Kevin Haney, "Evans Reveals Plan to Overhaul System," *Philadelphia Daily News*, April 18, 1997, p. 7.

38 David Hornbeck, interview with author, January 19, 2009.

39 Jerry Jordan, interview with author, January 21, 2009.

40 Judith Rodin, *The University and Urban Revival: Out of the Ivory Tower and Into the Streets* (Philadelphia: University of Pennsylvania Press, 2007), p. 145.

41 Judith Rodin, pp. 103, 106.

42 Barry Grossback, interview with author, August 11, 2008.

43 Interview with author, April 4, 2008.

44 Tom Lussenhop and Ted Skierski, *Report of Preferred Site Development Plan*, Fall 1999.

45 Mensah M. Dean, "Philly's School of High Marks—500-Student Penn Alexander Excels—and Academics Elsewhere Want to Learn More, *Philadelphia Daily News*, November 9, 2007, p. 3.

46 "Survey of Penn Alexander School Catchment Area," *Spruce Hill Community Association News*, Spring 2006.

47 Jill Khadduri, Heather Schwartz, and Jennifer Turnham, *Reconnecting Schools and Neighborhoods: An Introduction to School-Centered Community Education* (Enterprise Community Partners, Inc., 2007), p. 25.

7 Commercial Corridor Redefinition: The West Philadelphia Fire House

1 Michael E. Porter, "The Competitive Advantage of the Inner City," unpublished draft dated January 11, 1994, p. 3.

2 "The Competitive Advantage of the Inner City," pp. 4–9.

3 Urban Partners, "50th and Baltimore Fire House: Community Food Market/ Neighborhood Facility Proposal: Part I—Review of Supply/Demand Issues," (Philadelphia: Urban Partners, September, 1985), pp. 2–8. The Shuttle January– February 2005.

4 50th and Baltimore Fire House: Community Food Market/Neighborhood Facility Proposal, pp. 4, 14.

5 Edgar Williams, "Starting Small at Palmetto," *The Philadelphia Inquirer*, February 17, 1979, p. B1.

6 Mystery Muncher, *The Philadelphia Inquirer*, February 16, 1979, p. 37.

7 "Starting Small at Palmetto," p. B1.

8 Submission Binder, $300,000 Construction Loan from Provident National Bank ("Bank") to West Philadelphia Fire House Associates ("Associates"), May 2, 1988.

9 "West Philadelphia Fire House: A Partnership in Neighborhood Development," Summary sheet prepared by Urban Partners, 1988.

10 Roy H. Campbell and Thomas Ferrick, Jr., "Abandoned Firehouse to Become a Market," *The Philadelphia Inquirer*, May 28, 1988, p. B03.

11 "Abandoned Firehouse to Become a Market."

12 "Resolutions Voted on by Firehouse Advisory Committee, Sept. 18," Urban Partners files.

13 "Resolutions Voted on by Firehouse Advisory Committee, Sept. 18."
14 Roy H. Campbell, "Disunity Rattles a United Effort," *The Philadelphia Inquirer*, May 18, 1989, p. B01.
15 "The Competitive Advantage of the Inner City," p. 8.
16 Andres Duany, Presentation to 21st Century Neighborhood Conference, from transcript by The Foundation for Architecture, 1998.
17 Interview by author, March 11, 2008.
18 Interview by author, March 8, 2008.
19 Project for Public Spaces, Inc./Public Market Collaborative, *The Future of Public Markets in Philadelphia* (New York: Project for Public Spaces, March 1996), pp. 24, 25.
20 *The Future of Public Markets in Philadelphia*, pp. 26, 27.
21 Al Hunter, Jr., "Firehouse Jazz Program Jams for 5th Birthday," *Philadelphia Daily News*, September 10, 2004, p. 62.
22 Melissa Dribben, "At the Simmering Edge of City Transfiguration," *The Philadelphia Inquirer*, September 28, 2007, p. A17.
23 Susan Snyder, "New Block to Brew On—Dock Street Pub Poised to Return," *The Philadelphia Inquirer*, July 27, 2006, p. B01.
24 "The Store Front Formerly Known as Sid's Delicatessen," at http://weaversway.coop/index.php?page=weavers_way_history.
25 "The Store Front Formerly Known as Sid's Delicatessen."
26 M. Grace Maselli, ". . . Some Co-op Business Snuck In There too," *The Shuttle*, January–February 2005.

8 The Exercise of State Power: Municipal Reform and Eminent Domain in Camden

1 Senate and General Assembly of the State of New Jersey, Municipal Rehabilitation and Economic Recovery Act, Chapter 27BBB, Title 52, Revised Statutes, C.52:27BBB-2.o.
2 Frank Kummer, Renee Winkler, and Kathy Matheson, "Milton Milan Sentenced to 7 Years," *Camden Courier-Post*, June 16, 2001, p. 1.
3 Howard Gillette, Jr., *Camden After the Fall: Decline and Renewal in a Post-Industrial City* (Philadelphia: University of Pennsylvania Press), p. 113.
4 The Roper Group, *Camden City Higher Education and Healthcare Institutions: Economic Impact Report 2003*, June 2004, pp. 2, 3.
5 Camden Higher Education and Healthcare Task Force, *Housing Survey*, December 2006, p. 1.
6 Maura Webber Sadovi, "Hidden Gem Lies Just Outside Philadelphia in New Jersey," *The Wall Street Journal*, May 17, 2007. www.realestatejournal.com/columnists_com/blueprint/20070517-blueprint.html
7 Marshall McKnight, "Read His Lips: More Collected Taxes," njbiz.com, May 29, 2001.
8 Information provided by Camden Redevelopment Agency staff, December 2007).
9 Melvin R. Primas, Jr., *Progress Report: Municipal Rehabilitation and Economic Recovery in Camden*, November 2006, p. 10.
10 Ibid.
11 Alicia Caldwell, " 'Blight' Cases Rise in State—Landowners Crying Foul as Cities Increase Use of Condemnation Laws," *The Denver Post*, November 30, 2003, p. A01.
12 Greg Griffin, "Court Spurs Mixed Reaction—Experts say Colo. Law Restricts Use of Eminent Domain, but Critics still Worry," *The Denver Post*, June 24, 2005, p. C01.
13 Lavinia DeCastro, "Haddon Twp. Can Replace Site of Old Dy-Dee Plant," *Courier-Post*, January 6, 2007, p. 1B.

14 *Public Power, Private Gain*, p. 4.
15 *Public Power, Private Gain*, p. 1.
16 Redevelopment Authority of the City of Philadelphia, Board Minutes, May 13, 2003; July 22, 2003; September 9, 2003; October 14, 2003; October 28, 2003; November 17, 2003; November 25, 2003; December 9, 2003; December 23, 2003.
17 *Public Power, Private Gain*, p. 179.
18 John Kromer and Vicky Tam, *Philadelphia's Residential Tax Abatements: Accomplishments and Impacts*, University of Pennsylvania, December 2005, p. 27.
19 "Stop Eminent Domain Abuse Coalition of New Jersey, What is Eminent Domain Abuse," www.stopeda.org/whatiseda.htm.
20 Testimony by Olga Pomar, South Jersey Legal Services, Committee Meeting of Assembly Commerce and Economic Development Committee, March 13, 2006, p. 24.
21 Testimony by Olga Pomar, South Jersey Legal Services, Committee Meeting of Assembly Commerce and Economic Development Committee, March 13, 2006, p. 23.
22 State of New Jersey, Department of the Public Advocate, "Reforming the Use of Eminent Domain for Private Redevelopment in New Jersey," May 18, 2006, p. 1.
23 State of New Jersey, Department of the Public Advocate, "Reforming the Use of Eminent Domain for Private Redevelopment in New Jersey," May 18, 2006, p. 18.
24 State of New Jersey, Department of the Public Advocate, Division of Public Interest Advocacy, "In Need of Redevelopment: Repairing New Jersey's Eminent Domain Laws; Abuses and Remedies: A Follow-Up Report," May 29, 2007, p. 23.
25 Melvin R. Primas, Jr., "Progress Report: Municipal Rehabilitation and Economic Recovery in Camden," November 2006, p. 6.
26 Rita Giordano, "City Council Delays Vote on Housing/The Jefferson Square Project Created Outrage Among S. Phila Residents Who Fear Being Displaced," *The Philadelphia Inquirer*, June 16, 1999, p. B01.
27 Jeremey Newberg, interview with author, January 21, 2009.
28 East Baltimore Development, Inc., "About EBDI" at www.ebdi.org/about-ebdi.html.
29 East Baltimore Development, Inc., 2005–2006 Annual Report, p. 5.
30 Senate and General Assembly of the State of New Jersey, Municipal Rehabilitation and Economic Recovery Act, Chapter 27BBB, Title 52, Revised Statutes, C.52:27BBB-12.

9 An Integrated Strategy: Real Estate Development and Human Capital Planning in Camden

1 George Norcross, III, "Eds & Meds: How Educational and Medical Institutions are Revitalizing Their Communities," Presentation to Urban Land Institute Philadelphia Region, June 19, 2008.
2 Matt Katz, "What the Doc Ordered for Camden? New Cooper Wing Aims to Turn the City Around," *The Philadelphia Inquirer*, December 11, 2008, National News section.
3 Redevelopment planning in Lanning Square and Cramer Hill during Primas and Dew's tenure is described and assessed in Robert Lake et. al., "Civic Engagement in Camden, New Jersey: A Baseline Portrait" (New York: MDRC, September 2007).
4 Robert D. Putnam, *Bowling Alone: The Collapse and Revival of American Community* (New York: Simon & Schuster, 2000).

5 Robert D. Putnam, *Bowling Alone: The Collapse and Revival of American Community*, p. 27.
6 Sam Bass Warner, Jr., *The Private City: Philadelphia in Three Periods of Its Growth* (Philadelphia: University of Pennsylvania Press, 1968), 180–181.
7 Robert D. Putnam, *Bowling Alone: The Collapse and Revival of American Community*, p. 19.
8 Urban Strategies, Inc., "Our Approach," at www.urbanstrategiesinc.org/approach. html.
9 Urban Strategies, Inc., "Cooper Lanning Human Capital Plan for the Cooper Plaza Lanning Square Neighborhoods, Camden New Jersey," April 28, 2008, p. 4.
10 Urban Strategies, Inc., "Cooper Lanning Human Capital Plan for the Cooper Plaza Lanning Square Neighborhoods, Camden New Jersey," April 28, 2008, p. 4.
11 Jim Walsh, "Lanning Square Residents OK with Renewal," *Courier-Post*, May 29, 2008, p. 1.
12 Deborah Hirsch, "Lanning Square Project OK'd," *Courier-Post*, July 23, 2008, p. 1.
13 Jim Walsh, "Lanning Square Plan Advances," *Courier-Post*, June 13, 2008, p. 1.
14 Eileen Stilwell and Jim Walsh, "Another Camden project Hits Snag," *Courier-Post*, August 23, 2008, p. 1.

10 Rental Housing Asset Management: A Strategy for Allentown, Pennsylvania's Downtown-Area Neighborhoods

1 "Bigger is Not Always Better, and Valley is Proving it" (editorial), *Arizona Republic*, August 16, 2006, Southwest Valley Republic section.
2 Robert Weissbourd and Christopher Berry, *The Changing Dynamics of Urban America* (Chicago: CEOs for Cities, 2004), pp. 17, 20.
3 Matt Birkbeck, "Crowd Shows Hazleton Mayor the Love—Several Hundred People Mass in Support of Barletta and his Illegal Immigration Crackdown," *The Morning Call*, June 4, 2007, National section.
4 Mary Proctor and Bill Matuszeski, *Gritty Cities* (Philadelphia: Temple University Press, 1978), pp. 11, 34–36.
5 Mary Proctor and Bill Matuszeski, *Gritty Cities*, pp. 11, 12, 36.
6 Associated Press, "Philly? No Way! Hess's Thrives by Avoiding the Big Cities," *Philadelphia Daily News*, December 30, 1985, Local News section.
7 City of Allentown, PA, Historical Allentown, at www.allentownpa.gov/Visitors/ HistoricalAllentown/tabid/72/Default.aspx (accessed on January 21, 2009).
8 Julia C. Martinez, "A Revived Allentown Finds Itself Right at the Center of Things —Its Location Brings Warehouses and Distributors into the Lehigh Valley and Carries Plenty of Goods Out," *The Philadelphia Inquirer*, September 20, 1993, National news section.
9 Wendy Warren "'Rust Belt' Revisited—Employers Are Challenging the Notion that the Lehigh Valley is Part of a Region Solely made up of Decaying Plants, 'We Are Not the Same as We Were Twenty Years Ago,' says a Prominent Observer," *The Morning Call*, March 1, 1998, Outlook section.
10 Amy Liu and Bruce Katz, *An Economic Plan for the Commonwealth: Unleashing the Assets of Metropolitan Pennsylvania*, Brookings Institution Metropolitan Policy Program, March 2008, p. 6.
11 Terry Bivens, "Tallying the Cost of Mack's Pullout," *The Philadelphia Inquirer*, January 25, 1986, Business section.
12 Wendy E. Solomon, "Expanding Allentown Malls Encourage Developers—On the West Side, A Commercial Rebirth Brews Following Residential Boom," *The Morning Call*, March 15, 1999, Bethlehem section.
13 Associated Press, "Philly? No Way!"

14 "When Allentown Hits Bottom," Editorial, *The Morning Call*, November 12, 1995, City section; Ron Devlin and Diane Marczely, "Leh's Closes All Its Doors for Last Time—After 146 Years, Family-Owned Chain Could No Longer Keep Up with the Competition," *The Morning Call*, June 30, 1996, Local News section.

15 Bob Wittman, "DIDA Conducts its Final Board Meeting—Authority Ties Up Loose Ends Before Going Out of Business," *The Morning Call*, January 30, 2003, Local News section.

16 Interview with author, January 3, 2009.

17 Dan Fricker, "Merchants Lay It On the Line Discussing City Partnership," *The Morning Call*, March 17, 1994, Local News section.

18 John Leming, "Out of Reach—Apartment Rents in the Lehigh Valley Often Are More Than People Can Pay," *The Morning Call*, September 17, 2000, Local News section.

19 Interview with author, December 15, 2008. This paragraph is my rendering of my understanding of Mr. Burke's views.

20 Dan Hartzell, "Police Arrest 16 at Muhlenberg Students' Party—'We have the Ordinance that will Address the Problem,' Mayor says," *The Morning Call*, March 24, 1996, Local News section.

21 Bob Wittman, "Tropiano Rental Buildings are Declared Unfit—Two Buildings Owned by Allentown Councilwoman have Numerous Code Violations," *The Morning Call*, May 23, 1997, Local News section.

22 Joe McDermott, "Landlord Licensing Discussed—Allentown Hears it Would Rein In Property Owners, Or Is It Just Unnecessary Legislation?" *The Morning Call*, May 27, 1998, Local News section.

23 "Rental Licensing Bill to be Rewritten Again—City Council, Community Activists Will Work Together on New Landlord, Tenant Rules," *The Morning Call*, July 30, 1998, Local News section.

24 Joe McDermott, "Heydt Vows to Support Rental Inspection Question—Mayor Says He'll Help Advocates get Referendum on the Spring Ballot," *The Morning Call*, October 23, 1998, Local News section.

25 McDermott, "Heydt Vows To Support Rental Inspection Question."

26 Bob Wittman, "Residents Start Petition for Landlord Licensing Bill—It Marks First Use of New Charter's Referendum Procedure," *The Morning Call*, October 31, 1998.

27 Interview with author, December 14, 2008.

28 Christine Chiavo, "Smith Hits Ground Running—Allentown City Council Appointee Casts Pivotal Vote on Landlord Bill, Has Questions on Proposed Budget," *The Morning Call*, November 5, 1998, Local News section.

29 Chiavo, "Smith Hits Ground Running."

30 Joe McDermott, "Landlords Referendum Upheld—Commonwealth Court Ruling Means It Will Be on the May 18 Primary Ballot," *The Morning Call*, April 27, 1999, Local News section.

31 Bob Wittman, "Rental Inspections Win in Allentown—Measure's 5-1 Margin Off Voter Approval Amazes Even its Backers," *The Morning Call*, May 19, 1999, Local News section.

32 Fels Institute of Government, "A Housing Strategy for Allentown's Central-City Neighborhoods," October 2007, p. 1.

11 The Future of Reinvestment

1 Tom Infield and H.G. Bissinger, "Rizzo Foes Offer a List of Reminders," *The Philadelphia Inquirer*, September 10, 1987. Local News section.

2 Jon C. Teaford, "Urban Renewal and Its Aftermath," *Housing Policy Debate*, 11 (2): 454.

3 Carmen DeNavas-Walt, Bernadette D. Proctor, and Cheryl Hill Lee, *U.S. Census Bureau, Current Population Reports*, pp. 60–229; *Income, Poverty, and Health Insurance Coverage in the United States, 2004* (Washington, D.C.: U.S. Government Printing Office, 2005), p. 9.

4 Two examples of the latter are the University of Pennsylvania's Neighborhood Information System, through which City of Philadelphia real estate records are downloaded into a Penn-managed data warehouse (www.cml.upenn.edu/nis/), and Northeast Ohio Community and Neighborhood Data for Organizing (NEO CANDO), managed by Case Western University's Center on Urban Poverty and Community Development (http://neocando.case.edu/cando/index.jsp).

5 Todd Baylson, "Homeownership Initiatives and Housing Vacancy: The Status of Properties Vacated by Participants in Selected Philadelphia Homebuyer Opportunities," City of Philadelphia Office of Housing and Community Development, December 1999, p. 1.

6 Ernest Jones, President and CEO of the Philadelphia Workforce Development Program, to name one, cited this need in an interview with the Housing Alliance of Pennsylvania.

7 For more information on Penn's approach, see John Kromer and Lucy Kerman, "West Philadelphia Initiatives: A Case Study in Urban Revitalization," pp. 39–43.

8 "Habitat for Humanity Fact Sheet" at www.habitat.org/how/factsheet.aspx (accessed January 9, 2009).

9 Robert Weissbourd and Christopher Berry, *The Changing Dynamics of Urban America* (Chicago: CEOs for Cities, 2004), p. 22.

10 Robert Weissbourd and Christopher Berry, p. 23.

Index